1 oc

AN INTRODUCTION TO

Color

AN INTRODUCTION TO

Color

RALPH M. EVANS

Color Control Department Head

Eastman Kodak Company

1948

New York · JOHN WILEY & SONS, *Inc.*

London · CHAPMAN & HALL, *Ltd.*

Preface

COLOR is a subject which involves so many people with such different attitudes and intentions that a book useful to all of them is quite difficult to write. There is first the difficulty of a consistent, understandable terminology. This has been met here by the use of words in their common speech meanings with a minimum number of new words defined and used. A second difficulty lies in the exceedingly broad background in the sciences and arts which is required if color is to be grasped in toto. Color sprawls across the three enormous subjects of physics, physiology, and psychology. In the past it has been rare that any intensive worker in color has had the opportunity of understanding all three phases. It is to fill this gap that the book has been written. Each phase of the subject has been developed separately and then the three have been interwoven at the end. It is hoped that this approach, even though it makes some parts less interesting, will make it possible for the student, regardless of his background, to learn the parts of the subject he does not already know.

Almost no knowledge of any part of the subject has been assumed. The aim has been to write in such a way that some grasp of the fundamentals may be obtained by any careful reader. It is for this reason, rather than to simplify the writing, that so many pictures and graphs have been used throughout. Because the writer realizes how frightening graphs can be to the person unaccustomed to their use, they have been explained as though the reader had never seen one before. Except for a few in the late parts of the book they are all simple pictures of the most basic thing in color, the nature of the light with which the text is dealing at the moment. As such they are on a par with all the other illustrations and should be so considered.

A final difficulty, which at times seemed insurmountable, has been that of assuming no knowledge of mathematics beyond that taught in high school. As far as possible the text is completely descriptive and non-mathematical. Although this introduces lack of precision in some of the statements, it is hoped that the appeal to readers outside the realm of the physical sciences will more than justify such a lack.

The subject of color appeals to and affects everyone regardless of his or her particular attitude toward it. Unfortunately the subject cannot be simplified without presenting it in a biased, one-sided fashion. The present book attempts to treat the whole subject without any simplifying omissions. The individual concepts involved are almost all simple and straightforward. In the combinations in which they are found in color some of them are exceedingly difficult. For this the writer makes no apology. This is the subject of color.

For the way in which the concepts are organized and the manner in which they are described the writer must take full responsibility. Written as it is, for the most part, without notes or reference material, the ideas are mostly those of other people inextricably mixed with those of the writer himself. It is thus impossible to lay the blame and give the credit to the proper individuals. The writer hopes only that this writing down of the principles found necessary in twenty years of active work in the fields of color and color photography will be found as useful to others as it would have been to him at the beginning of his work.

The book has been a gradual growth over a period of years, and the author would like to express his indebtedness to the many people with whom he has had the opportunity of discussing different aspects of the subject. Such acknowledgment is impossible within the limitations of a preface; there are some, however, to whom the author feels particularly grateful. First of all my wife, Pauline Evans, has been both helpful and patient. My former colleagues in the Kodak Research Laboratories and particularly my former associate, Dr. W. T. Hanson, Jr., have been both the cause and the means for the completion of the book. The officers and delegates of the Inter-Society Color Council have contributed a breadth of vision and approach to the subject without which little integration of the work could have been accomplished. My thanks are due particularly to Dr. Deane B. Judd and to Miss Dorothy Nickerson.

The author wishes also to express appreciation for assistance given in the work by Mr. F. Richard Holly, Jr., who assembled the data necessary for the various graphs shown; to Miss Jeannete Klute, who took most of the photographs shown, including those in color; to Mr. James W. Watts, who prepared the remaining illustrations including four color drawings; and to Dr. W. L. Brewer, who has been instrumental in editing the manuscript. Use has been made of a considerable amount of data obtained experimentally by others and, wherever possible, credit to these sources has been included.

RALPH M. EVANS

Rochester, N. Y.
March, 1948

Contents

Color Plates

Color and Light

CHAPTER I

COLOR and shape are the chief properties that give objects their own individual characters. Of the two, color is frequently the less important as far as recognition of the object is concerned. Color, however, makes a unique contribution to the appearance of the object, imparting to it qualities that shape alone cannot give. In this sense, color is one of the most important of all visual characteristics. In our civilization, however, it tends to play a supporting role and seldom is seen alone on the stage. It lends its charm, its personality, or its ugliness to the form with which it is seen, but these characteristics are likely to vanish if an attempt is made to view them by themselves. In this sense, and in this sense only, colors are analogous to the individual notes in music. A single sustained note from any musical instrument has little interest or beauty compared to its appeal when heard in a chord, or, more particularly, as part of a whole composition. Color in exactly the same way makes its contribution by the way it differs from the colors and shapes with which it appears, the same color being pleasant or unpleasant, attractive or repulsive, dignified or riotous, depending on the circumstances. Some of the customary meanings of the word "color" reflect this peculiar power that colors have to give quality to an object or scene, and such expressions as a "colorful personality" or a "blue mood" are familiar and truly descriptive.

Any attempt to arrive at a satisfactory definition of the word involves one at once in all the complexities of vision. A list of the different meanings it may have is essentially an outline of a book such as this. It is necessary, however, to start the study of the subject by having clearly in mind this many-sided nature. It is only in recent years that a fairly clear concept has been gained of the various factors involved in the transition of radiant energy to the mental quality "color." It is only natural that in common speech the word has been applied to many individual parts of the long chain, with the result that it now means too many different things for precise use. On the other hand, if an attempt is made to generalize the word to include all the manifestations, it is found to become almost synonymous with the word "light."

In a complex case, for example, the radiant energy from a light source is modified by several substances, enters the eye and is perceived and, perhaps, reinterpreted as properties of the substances by the mind. Under these circumstances we can and do speak of the color of the source, the color of the objects, and the color perceived. It is entirely reasonable in common speech to refer to the light from a "white" source, passing through a "yellow" transparent substance, falling on a "purple" object, and being seen as "red." It is equally reasonable, under other circumstances, to speak of a "yellow" monochromatic light being seen as "green." The words refer to different aspects of the subject and imply vision under different conditions. These apparent anomalies, however, will become clear as the subject develops.

A great deal of thought and labor has been devoted to the establishment of a precise terminology for color. The necessity for such a terminology is apparent. In order to talk precisely about any phase of color, every word used must refer only to the specific part of the subject under discussion. By far the most comprehensive of such attempts is the 1944 Report of the Colorimetry Committee of the Optical Society of America. In this report the subject is divided into three general aspects, and a precise nomenclature is provided for all phases of each. To make it clear why such an extended classification of words is necessary, a complete discussion of the visual process is required.

The eye is one of the receptors of the body. Just as we are sensitive to pressure and so have the sense of touch, to temperature and so have the feelings hot or cold, we also are sensitive to certain types of radiant energy which we call light. Deferring to a later chapter the physical nature of this radiant energy, we may state for present purposes that what is called a light source gives off a certain something which, when it enters the eye, produces effects that give rise to reactions in the brain, and we say that light is perceived. If this light reaches the eye from objects rather than from the source, it will in general be different from that received directly—different in quality and in amount.

Now, unfortunately, no two people are exactly alike in the way this light is perceived; and, furthermore, no person can tell anything about the nature of the images in another person's brain. In a later chapter it will be seen how it is known that vision may differ in the elementary sense; but, even if all people were exactly alike in their sensitivity to light, we still would not know whether any two people perceived exactly the same colors in their minds. There are, then, three sharp divisions of the subject and innumerable subdivisions. In the first place there is the more or less straightforward *physics* of the source of light and of such objects and substances as will modify this light. In the second place there are the sensitivities of the eye itself, measured under known conditions by methods to be considered later. A large number of such measurements on a large number of people permits the formation of an average value for each sensitivity, and all these taken together give rise to the concept of the "average observer." The purely physical light from the source and object can then be evaluated in terms of this average observer by purely mechanical means, and the result is an evaluation of the light in these terms. This is known as the *psychophysical evaluation* of light.* Beyond this, however, come the

* It is to this evaluation (under more explicitly stated conditions) that the OSA Colorimetry Committee has given the word "color," and in that system this is the only meaning that the word may have.

interpreting and perceiving action of the mind and the fact that the same quality of radiant energy does not, by far, always produce the same mental perception even from the same eye. In simple words, the same light is not always seen as of the same color. The third division, therefore, is called *psychology* to indicate that it is determined beyond the elementary psychophysical stage.

It is not the intention in this book to deal systematically with the finer points of the nomenclature involved in color, or to attempt to use any rigidly correct system of words, since to do so and explain them presuppose in large part a knowledge of the field that it is intended to cover. As far as possible, common practice in the use of words will be followed. This does not mean that the author is in any way opposed to the systematization of the words, for that is essential to accurate writing in the advanced phases of any subject. It is rather that he regards this book as an introduction to the concepts underlying that system.

PERCEPTION

A part of the apparent confusion in the meaning of the word color comes from the different manners in which the same object may be seen. The mental process of seeing is a combination of two major factors which may be expressed loosely by the expressions "what you actually see" and "what you think you see." Whatever the scientific explanation of a given case, a careful analysis of any visual situation often shows that it "looks different the second time." Many times two or more ways of seeing are apparent enough, so that it is possible to shift from one to another voluntarily. For example, I am writing on a porch at the seashore. In front of me is one of the windows of the house reflecting a broad expanse of sunlit ocean and beach. Behind the window is a vase containing orange marigolds. A first glance at the window shows nothing but the reflection of the beach and ocean. More careful inspection without moving the head shows the marigolds behind the window. A thorough analysis of what can be seen shows three possibilities: two direct and fairly easy to see, and a third, very difficult but possible. If attention is directed entirely to the landscape or to the plant, the other nearly, but not quite, disappears. Once the flowers have been seen it is no longer possible to see the ocean without some trace of them appearing, but the extent to which one or the other may be seen varies greatly, depending on the amount of attention that is directed toward it. The third way of looking at the window gives a surprising result but is quite difficult. If attention is directed entirely to the surface of the window, and an attempt is made to see it as colored glass, so to speak, for brief moments it can be seen that the orange of the blossom and the bluish green of the sea to a large extent neutralize each other and appear almost, but not quite, gray. The colors seen, therefore, depend on the part of the scene to which the attention is directed and on the intention of the observer with respect to the scene. If an artist were to attempt to portray this particular scene, he would have to decide arbitrarily the extent to which he wished one or the other of the extreme phases to show, and paint them this way. For reasons which are usually different for every scene the painting will look like only one phase of the subject and cannot represent all three. In the present illustration the reason appears to be that the eyes focus for three different distances for the three objects: plant, window, and ocean, seeing clearly the appropriate color for the objects most sharply focused. This whole subject will be discussed in more detail in a later chapter. It is introduced here to clarify the use of the word "perception." The word perception is used in psychology to distinguish between what an observer *does* see, and what, from a knowledge of the nature of the light reaching his eye, he *should* see, in the general rather than in the particular case. That is, perception refers to the actual *mental* image existing at any moment, and not to the image as formed by the eye. "To perceive" is exactly equivalent to the verb "to see" as ordinarily used, but it is not so ambiguous in many of its forms. "Perceiving" and "seeing" are equivalent words, as are "perception" and "sight," but "sight" is seldom used in this sense, except perhaps when we say "what a sight."

In the study of color it is very necessary to distinguish between this mental perception and the physical nature of the light reaching the eye. Failure to do so not only leads to confused thinking but also may cause errors when an attempt is made to reproduce the scene by photography or by painting. Color photography deals with the physical nature of the light from a scene, but the print is perceived, in general, under different conditions. A painting, to the extent that the artist is *trying* to reproduce the scene, deals with the *perceived* scene; and his painting, again, is perceived under different conditions. It is apparent that the subject is exceedingly complex and cannot be simplified greatly, as so many writers have attempted to do. The present approach will be to consider all aspects of the subject systematically from a somewhat elementary point of view, and then, in the concluding chapters, to broaden this point of view by considering the problems of applied color. Previous to these latter chapters, the subject will be discussed under the three broad headings of physics, psychophysics, and psychology.

Since, for proper development of the subject, it is not desirable to keep the various chapters strictly under these headings, it may be well to consider briefly the three divisions and thus have a clear-cut concept of what is meant by each term and just what it does and does not include.

PHYSICS

We see by virtue of the light that enters our eyes. The properties and characteristics of this light can be measured and stated in terms that have nothing whatever to do with the eye. These measurements and specifications fall in the realm of physics, are completely determinable by methods which do not require that the light be seen, and are repeatable. The physicist can state with certainty that two beams of light are identical, or how two beams differ. He cannot, without passing outside the realm of the subject as defined here, state how the two will look. Physics, therefore, deals with the quality of the light *as such* without reference to any observer.

PSYCHOPHYSICS

It is apparent that if we knew enough about the visual mechanism and restricted ourselves to sufficiently simple situations, it should be possible to calculate from the known physical properties of a given light beam the exact appearance that this would have to the observer. This is the realm of psychophysics—the scientific study of the reaction of the visual mechanism under a given, fully specified, set of conditions. Much remains to be learned in this subject, although it has been developed greatly in recent years. Approximate calculations of appearance can be made with relative ease and fair certainty by methods that anyone

4

can use. It is not, however, an affront to the many able and painstaking workers in this field to say that at the present time only one type of calculation can be made with good accuracy. This is the so-called color match for the standard observer. It is possible, and relatively simple, to calculate whether two beams of light will look *alike* to a person with well-defined, "average normal" vision. If they differ, the difference in *appearance* cannot be calculated, although the difference can be evaluated in terms of the known properties of the eye. That is, it is possible to state that two differences are of the same magnitude, although it is not possible to state what that difference *looks* like.

Psychophysics at present, therefore, is limited to the *relative* evaluation of light beams with respect to normal observers under standardized conditions, however much it may be hoped that with increasing knowledge we shall be able to calculate their appearance more and more accurately.

PSYCHOLOGY

Beyond the realm of psychophysics, and embracing all the manifold ways in which light may affect the consciousness, comes the field of psychology. As in most of the other fields of psychology, this one deals largely with tendencies and the conditions under which these tendencies operate. If a definition of the subject matter involved is attempted, it is immediately open to the objection that it is either too narrow or so general that it has little meaning. Perhaps the most general definition that can be given is that psychology is the study of the relationship between the color as calculated for the standard observer and the color actually perceived by the mind. It thus includes all the factors of attention, attitude, feeling,

and so on that must be excluded from the psychophysical calculation. Essentially, it is the study of the effect on the observer *produced by the conditions*, as distinct from predictions based on the eye considered as a standardized mechanism. It is apparent that the dividing line is somewhat vague, and many writers may be found who feel that both subjects are completely included either in psychology or in psychophysics, depending on their own inclination. The line is easily drawn, however, at the point at which calculations must necessarily stop. The point at which the individual's *intentions in looking* become involved is the division the writer will use. When an observer finds that the perception changes with his attitude toward it, psychophysics will no longer predict the result.

PHILOSOPHY

Beyond these considerations of color as produced by the object and perceived by the brain are many considerations of color as a factor in the life of an individual, of theories as to the physiological and philosophical means by which the organism produces the result, and of the nature and cause of the mental perceptions in general. With these this book does not deal except in passing. Some space in the final chapter is devoted to the aesthetics of color and the question of pleasantness-unpleasantness relations, but it is possible to obtain a thorough understanding of the whole subject without reference to theories of color vision or philosophies of life.

Much that is written on the subject of color is of little constructive value, largely because the writers do not see the subject in all its phases and therefore cannot interpret phenomena that may be explained quite readily if considered broadly. This broad approach will be attempted here, but its philosophical implication will not be considered.

OSA NOMENCLATURE

For purposes of later reference and to show the student the interrelation of the variables involved, the table of nomenclature from the report of the Optical Society of America is reprinted in Fig. 1·1. The purpose of the present book is to make it possible for a person coming to the subject for the first time to understand both the necessity for, and the reasoning behind, such a complex organization.

FIGURE 1·1

Physics	*Psychophysics*	*Psychology*	
Visual stimulus	Light	Visual sensation	Visual perception
Radiant energy Spectral composition	Luminous energy Color	Color sensation	
Characteristics of radiant energy:	Characteristics of light = color:	Attributes of color sensation:	Corresponding modes of appearance:

Radiant flux
  a. Radiance
  b. Irradiance
  c. Radiant reflectance
  d. Radiant transmittance
	1. Luminous flux
	  a. Luminance
	  b. Illuminance
	  c. Luminous reflectance
	  d. Luminous transmittance
		1. Brightness	Aperture (1–5)
			Illuminant (1–8)
			Illumination (1–3)
			Object modes:
			  Surface (1–11)
			  Volume (1–9)

Spectral distribution
 	
(Relative spectral composition, quality)
 	
Radiant purity
	Chromaticity
	
	2. Dominant wavelength (or complementary)
	3. Purity
		Chromaticness
		
		2. Hue
		
		3. Saturation
			Attributes of modes of appearance:
			  1. Brightness (or lightness)
			  2. Hue
			  3. Saturation
			  4. Size
			  5. Shape
			  6. Location
			  7. Flicker
			  8. Sparkle
			  9. Transparency
			  10. Glossiness
			  11. Luster

FIG. 1·1   System of nomenclature as given by the Committee on Colorimetry of the Optical Society of America. (*Journal of the Optical Society of America*, Vol. 33, p. 552, 1943.)

The Physical Nature of Light

CHAPTER II

IT is difficult to gain a conception of the nature of light without a rather thorough knowledge of physics. In particular it is necessary to have some idea of the meaning of the word "energy." For practical purposes, however, it is not necessary that the concept be very clear. It is the way in which light acts rather than its true physical nature that is important, and its behavior can be made clear by analogy with other, more familiar phenomena.

There are many forms of energy, all having the property of being able to exert a force of some kind or of being converted into a different kind of energy. A baseball that has been thrown and is in the air possesses kinetic energy due to the force with which it was thrown. This energy is expended when the ball strikes another object, such as the catcher's mitt or a window pane. Electricity is a form of energy. It can be converted to heat, another form, if it is forced through a wire having sufficient resistance to its passage. It can be con-verted into mechanical force when it is used to run a motor, and so on.

RADIATION

Light is a form known as electromagnetic energy. It passes through space without resistance and, like many other forms of energy, cannot be known to exist at all until it is converted into some other form when it strikes an object in its path or is changed in some other way. We see light only because of its effect on our eyes, and we see objects only because of the effect that they have on the light before it reaches us. The eye, however, is not the only instrument by which light energy can be detected or "received"; various other "receptors" such as photoelectric cells (which convert it into electrical energy which can then be measured) are well known.

For light to exist at all, it is necessary first that electromagnetic energy be created and given off into space. The point at

7

which this energy is created is known as the "source" of the energy, and the object emitting the light is known as the "light source." Once created, light travels outward from the light source at constant velocity in all directions until it is modified by striking some object in its path. The process of traveling away from the light source is known as "radiation," and the light itself is often called "radiant energy" since it radiates from its source.

It is important to understand clearly what is meant by the expression "in all directions from the source." If a small light source were giving off light in a large open space, the following facts would be true. There would be no point in that space through which the light did not radiate continuously so far as any ordinary measurements could detect. The light passing through any point would be traveling away from the light source at a constant velocity which would be the same at all points. At all points the direction of this flow of energy would be outward along the straight line which connected the light source with the point. The light source could be seen from all directions, therefore, and any object which intercepted the light would create a region directly behind it in which there would be either no light or the light would have different properties.

It is difficult to find an analogy for this radiation process which is exact enough to use even for ordinary practical purposes, because no material substance expands continuously in all directions after being created at a single point. If one can imagine rubber being created continuously under high compression and then being released continuously so that it expands outwardly as a rubber ball which eventually fills all space, the parallel is fairly exact. This parallel, if it can be imagined at all, makes it easier to understand also the decrease in the intensity

of light as the distance from the source increases. The quantity of rubber at the instant of release is the same as that which at a little later time will find itself spread out over the surface of an expanding sphere having the source as a center. At a later time it will have to cover the surface of a very much larger sphere, and so on. Obviously the rubber must be very compact at the moment it leaves the source to continue to have appreciable thickness when the sphere becomes very large. Eventually, no matter how compressed it may have been originally, the amount of it at any point on an enormously large sphere would become so minute that it would no longer be solid rubber at all. The analogy breaks down at this point, of course, but light does act in exactly this way. Near the light source the density of the radiating energy is high, and if a receptor for the light is placed there a large amount of energy is found, the exact amount depending on the quantity per second that the source is creating. At a greater distance from the source this same amount of energy occupies a very much larger space, and the amount falling on a given receptor is very much smaller. Eventually, at great distances, the amount falling on the receptor will become too little to detect, no matter what the nature or the size of the source may be.

NATURE OF LIGHT

Light, therefore, originates at a source and travels outward in all directions at constant velocity until it encounters some modifying object or some receptor. Each phase of this process will be considered in detail in subsequent chapters. To understand the ways in which light may be modified and how it may be detected and measured, it is necessary to have a somewhat fuller picture of its other characteristics.

Its constant velocity and direction have already been considered, as well as the fact that it is energy traveling through space. What are some of its other properties? In the first place, light may be considered real. It is not a sort of nothingness that spreads out and then suddenly becomes something when it strikes a receptor. Like all moving objects, it strikes an object in its path with a real, even if very small, force, and the pressure of sunlight on an object has been measured. In the second place, it has the property of vibrating at an extremely high rate or frequency.

When an attempt is made to get closer than this to the exact nature of light, we encounter the fact so peculiar to modern physics that it has no parallel in ordinary experience. Many years of research have made one fact abundantly clear. If we are to attempt to visualize the nature of light, we must assume it possible that it acts as though it consisted of two quite different modes of action going on at the same time.

The first of these modes of action is known as the "wave theory" of light and was for many years thought to be a complete explanation of the phenomenon. Under this explanation light was thought of as completely continuous and as being pulsating in nature. The pulsation under this view could be described by saying that sufficiently refined measurements at any point through which the light was traveling would show that the intensity of this light varied periodically at a very high rate (of the order of 600,000 billion times per second). Light such as that from the sun was thought to consist of light of all possible frequencies between an upper and a lower limit. These frequencies covered the range to which the eye is sensitive and existed in definite relative amounts which were necessary in order for it to appear white to the eye (roughly equal amounts of all). This has always been

a difficult concept to visualize, and yet it is the way in which the light acts. Such light can, in fact, be separated into the different frequencies and then proved to consist of a continuous unbroken series of frequencies within any given range.

Somewhat easier to imagine as a phenomenon is the newer "quantum theory" of light emission in which the light is assumed to be given off in separate bundles of energy, each vibrating with a single characteristic frequency and traveling outward with constant velocity, but given off in such terrific numbers that even at great distances from the source there are still no appreciable "gaps" between them. White light, from this point of view, consists of a flow of an enormous number of such quanta of energy, each with its own frequency but with all visible frequencies about equally represented at any point reached by the light.

It is difficult, if not impossible, to reconcile these two views. Recent science indicates that the quantum theory is undoubtedly more adequate. For all practical purposes, however, light may be assumed to be continuous at all points in the space through which it passes and to consist of an infinite variety of periodic fluctuations in intensity, whose frequencies fall between definite limits and whose amounts exist in definite ratio to each other. Both the frequency range and the relative amounts of each frequency present are determined by the nature of the light source. For the rest of this book, therefore, light will be considered in this manner except that occasionally it may become necessary to refer to its quantum nature to explain some of its more unfamiliar effects. Most commonly, such effects occur only when the intensity of the light is so feeble that the actions of individual quanta become appreciable in comparison with the total light received. One such illustration, for example, is photographic film whose action under extremely feeble illumination receives ready explanation on the quantum theory basis.

The possibility of separating light into its component frequencies was first recognized by Newton. A narrow beam of light from the sun was allowed to pass through a glass prism and fall on a white surface. It was apparent immediately that, whereas without the prism there was simply a circle of sun-

obtain this information it is necessary to divide the light into its various frequencies, to measure the intensity of groups of adjacent frequencies, and, for the complete case, to do this for all the directions of approach to the point where the measurements are being made. Instruments for separating the light into its component frequencies are known as spectroscopes and are simply the refinements mentioned earlier of

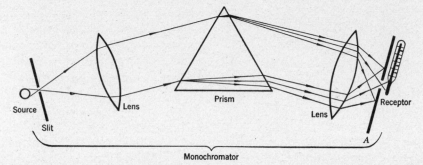

Fig. 2·1 Schematic diagram of the fundamental optical system of a spectroradiometer showing the slit, lenses, and dispersing prism which forms the spectroscope part and a thermometer-type receptor which completes it.

light, with the prism in place, the colors of the rainbow appeared and the circle was elongated into an elliptical type figure. Refinements of this procedure later made it possible to isolate regions of these frequencies and eventually to measure them. The velocity of light also was measured subsequently and found to be constant in free space at a value of 300,000 kilometers per second, independent of the frequency of the light. Since this velocity is always the same in free space (although it is different if it passes through material substances), it is not necessary to specify it if a given beam of light is to be described. A complete description of a beam of light for our purposes would consist of a statement of the direction or directions from which it comes, the frequency or range of frequencies of which it consists, and the actual or relative intensities of the light in each frequency region. To

the method discovered by Newton. The basic optical system is illustrated in Fig. 2·1. Light from the source is allowed to pass through a narrow slit. It then falls on a lens and is made to travel in parallel rays. Close to the lens, with its axis parallel to the slit, is placed a transparent, highly polished prism, usually of glass. The different frequencies of light present in the beam take different paths through this prism and are bent toward the perpendicular to the face of the prism by an amount which depends on the frequency. The lower frequencies are deviated the least, and the higher frequencies the most. On emergence from the prism, the light is picked up by another lens which forms an image of the slit on some surface such as A in the figure. Since the different frequencies have been deviated by different amounts systematically, this image of the slit consists not of a single line but of a whole series of continuously overlapping lines spread out at right angles to the slit. This spread-out series of images reveals that the different frequencies of light vary systematically in color in the same manner as the colors of the rainbow. If the light source is the sun or some similar object which gives off light because of its high temperature, it is found that the low-frequency end of the band or "spectrum," as it is called, appears red and the high-frequency end blue or violet, while in between it varies continuously through orange, yellow, and green.

SPECTROPHOTOMETRY

Definite frequency limits can be assigned to any given range of this spectrum, and the amount of energy in this region can be measured. The general measuring technique consists of placing another slit over the region of the spectrum to be measured and allowing the light which passes through this slit to fall on some measuring receptor. An instrument designed to select a narrow region of the spectrum in this way is called a "monochromator," and an instrument designed to measure the relative or absolute amounts of energy in narrow bands of frequencies through the spectrum is called a "spectrophotometer," or a "spectroradiometer." The addition of a measuring receptor to the optical system of the spectroscope of Fig. 2·1 completes the instrument of that figure which in its entirety is a schematic spectroradiometer.

It is customary in the study of light to distinguish between a measurement of the energy in a light beam and the comparison of this energy with that of another source by means of a particular receptor. The first type of measurement is known as spectroradiometry and the second as spectrophotometry. In ordinary usage the word spectrophotometry is more common because that type of instrument is more common. It is often used incorrectly to refer to an instrument of the spectroradiometry type.

The measurements obtained with spectrophotometers and spectroradiometers are basic to the entire subject of color. It is no exaggeration to say that without some knowledge of such measurements it is impossible to have any clear conception of the ways in which color may be created. On the other hand, if one can learn to think of light in terms of the relative amounts of energy which it contains in the various frequency ranges of its spectrum rather than in terms of its visual color, many phenomena otherwise difficult to understand become apparent. The remainder of this chapter is devoted to an explanation of this way of considering light. Any person who hopes to use color intelligently for any purpose whatever will do well to read it until he is thoroughly familiar with its concepts and its methods of expressing the results. The subject of color is not simple. It consists, as was pointed out in the first chapter, of three almost unrelated phases: physics, psychophysics, and psychology. All three must be understood in order to approach even the simplest problems. The results of spectrophotometry as expressed in the so-called spectrophotometric curves are the heart and soul of the physics phase of color.

The purpose of spectrophotometry or "measurement of the spectrum" is to determine the way in which the total energy in a beam of light is divided among the frequencies which it contains. The beam of light which is being measured may have originated at any source and it may have been modified many times since it left that source. The aim of the measurement is to state its relative energy distribution as it exists at that time. The results of the measurements may then be used either to study how the light has been modified since it left the source or to determine the nature of the source itself.

Direct measurement of the frequency of a beam of monochromatic light is a difficult task requiring highly specialized equipment and, fortunately, does not need to be done for the purposes of spectrophotometry. Once a spectrophotometer has been set up, light of the same frequency is always deviated to the same point in the spectrum; and if the frequency corresponding to each point is known, it does not have to be redetermined. The problem then becomes one of measuring the intensities in the various regions and of expressing the results so that they may be understood.

Measurements of intensity are of two general types as far as the units in which they may be expressed are concerned. The amount of energy reaching the receptor may be measured on an absolute basis (radiometry) and expressed in terms of the actual amount, or, more frequently, it may be measured in relation to some quite arbitrary value (photometry) and expressed as a percentage of this value. For a number of reasons, but chiefly because of the ease with which such measurements may be made, photometry is usually more common. They are the only types of measurements that need be considered here. Absolute energy measurements are necessary for such subjects as photochemistry and for some other types of work but they seldom need to be used for color work. Total energy measurements made without first separating the wavelengths are common and very necessary and will be dealt with later in this chapter and under the general heading of illumination.

RECEPTORS

When light falls on a receptor there is some sort of response. The exact nature of this response depends on the type of recep-tor. In a photoelectric cell the response is a flow of current, and this flow may be measured with a suitable meter. In the receptor known as a "bolometer," advantage is taken of the fact that light absorbed by a blackened platinum wire changes its resistance to the flow of electricity because the absorbed energy raises its temperature. A somewhat similar device is the "thermopile" in which two dissimilar metals in contact cause a current of electricity to flow when light absorbed on the blackened surface raises the temperature.

In the photocell, light is converted directly to electrical energy. In the other two there is first a conversion into heat which produces or controls the electrical energy. Whatever the type of conversion which takes place, the reading obtained indicates only that a certain change has been produced in the receptor. In order to interpret this change, it is necessary to know how much change a known amount of energy should cause. The process of determining this is known as "calibration," and the data obtained in this process completely define the properties of that particular receptor to radiant energy. Absolute calibrations are usually based on receptors which convert light into heat because it is fairly easy to calculate the temperature rise that should be produced by a given quantity of light. The instrument also can be calibrated if readings are taken at different temperatures produced in other ways. Once a standard source of light has been measured by such absolute means, it is then simple to calibrate any other device by means of this light. From this calibration, relative intensity measurements may then be made with great ease. A relative intensity measurement of light in any narrow range of frequencies of light, then, means that the light being received is a certain fraction or percentage of the energy that would be received from some known standard source of light.

This type of measurement is so common and so basic to color that many conventions

FIGURE 2·2

Frequency in Cycles per Second × 10^{12}	Relative Energy
430	97.7
440	99.3
450	99.8
460	99.9
470	100.0
480	100.1
490	100.8
500	101.3
510	100.4
520	99.8
530	99.7
540	100.2
550	99.9
560	99.1
570	99.6
580	100.5
590	101.1
600	102.3
610	101.2
620	100.2
630	98.7
640	96.7
650	92.9
660	89.4
670	85.2
680	79.6
690	74.1
700	69.3
710	67.8
720	64.9
730	61.1
740	55.0
750	44.8

FIG. 2·2 Relative spectral-energy distribution of sunlight.

have become established in the methods of presenting the results. Before considering the receptors further it is necessary to under-

stand these methods and learn to make use of them. It was stated that the two variables of spectrophotometry are the frequency of the light and its intensity. A simple table, in which the central frequencies of the regions of the spectrum that were measured are listed beside the intensity readings obtained, is sufficient; but it is difficult to obtain any good picture of the energy distribution of the light from such a table. It is much more satisfactory to plot a curve of these data which will show the relationship at a glance. Such a table and the curve

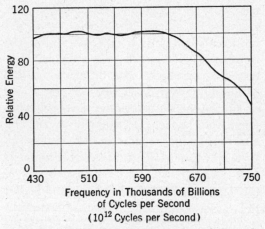
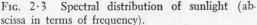

FIG. 2·3 Spectral distribution of sunlight (abscissa in terms of frequency).

plotted from it are shown in Fig. 2·2 and Fig. 2·3.

It is unfortunate that many people who work in the field of color are not familiar with the use of curves to illustrate such measurements. Perhaps it may not be out of place to suggest that any reader who has never done so should take a piece of paper and construct the curve of this figure directly from the table. The lower horizontal line is simply the spectrum itself, represented directly by its frequencies. The total range of frequencies shown has been selected because the eye is not sensitive to light beyond

13

these limits, and they, therefore, are the boundaries of the subject of color. The actual measurements are plotted vertically above the corresponding frequencies, the height above the lower line being directly proportional to the measured value. The scale used for this purpose is shown at the left.*

One other convention used for these curves has become so firmly established that, although it is now known that it should be changed, it is practically impossible to do so. So far the vibrations of the light energy have been referred to in terms of their frequencies; from the standpoint of the newer quantum theory of light, this is the logical and most useful property to consider. From the standpoint of the older wave theory, however, it was thought more desirable to speak of the distance in space between two points of equal intensity in the wave as the wavelength of the light. Radio waves are also electromagnetic energy exactly similar to light except at a much lower frequency. It was customary at first in radio to speak of the wavelength of a particular station, but this is gradually giving way to a statement of the frequency in kilocycles of the wave which is being broadcast. In both cases the two figures are connected by the velocity

with which all electromagnetic waves radiate through space. This velocity is approximately 300 million meters per second. If the frequency of a given monochromatic light is 500 million million per second, then simple division of the velocity by the frequency gives 3/5,000,000 meters for the distance traveled during one cycle or pulse of the wave. This is the wavelength of that light. Because of the awkwardness of the exceedingly minute distance involved, two units have been defined for the purpose. One of these is the millimicron, equal to $1/1,000,000,000$ meters, usually written "mμ," and the other is $\frac{1}{10}$ of this and known as the "angstrom" unit in honor of Anders Jöns Ångström, a Swedish astronomer. It is usually written "A." The visible spectrum extends from approximately 400 to 700 mμ or from 4,000 to 7,000 A. If thought of in terms of these units the fantastically small size of the quantities causes no trouble. Since all visible light falls within these limits, there can be no confusion between the two.

A curve plotted in terms of wavelengths rather than frequencies appears much the same but will be found on close inspection to be quite different. The data of Fig. 2·3 replotted in terms of wavelength are shown in Fig. 2·4. It is well to remember when looking at such curves that the vertical scale indicates *relative* intensities and not absolute. Since the scale actually used is quite arbitrary, this means that it can be enlarged or reduced quite independently of the data it represents. The pair of curves of Fig. 2·5, for example, represents exactly the same data, but the scale used for one is larger than that for the other. It is necessary, therefore, in such curves to compare the heights of the various portions *with each other* in order to understand their significance. If the curves are expressed in percentages of some fixed value, rather than

* While it is realized that most readers are entirely familiar with this procedure, curves of this and similar types will be used very extensively throughout this entire book. The author does not consider it possible to have a clear understanding of the subject of color unless such curves are familiar working tools. If they are thought of as heaps of energy distributed according to the frequency of the light, the height of the pile at any point indicating the amount relative to that at other points, it will be found possible to visualize the "energy distribution." If this curve is then remembered when it is desired to predict the effect of this light on a given object, or in any of the problems which may arise in color, the answer is usually obvious. Without this knowledge, some effects may appear exceedingly mysterious.

on a purely arbitrary scale, the actual heights will then vary with the value to which they are referred, but the same precaution must be taken. The curves of Fig. 2·6, for exam-

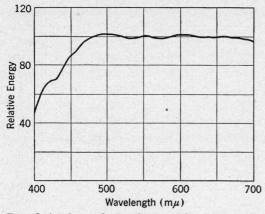

FIG. 2·4 Spectral distribution of sunlight (abscissa in terms of wavelength).

ple, show light of exactly the same quality, except that in one the maximum energy at any wavelength has been assumed 100 percent, whereas in the other an arbitrary figure

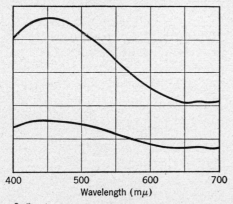

FIG. 2·5 A given set of data on scales whose unit sizes have been arbitrarily set in a ratio of three to one.

five times this value has been taken as reference. They mean the same thing if *relative* amounts are considered but look quite different to casual inspection.

It should be pointed out here that, in order to interpret some curves of this type, it is necessary to state how wide a band of frequencies was included in each measurement on which the curve is based. The reasons for this will become apparent. The

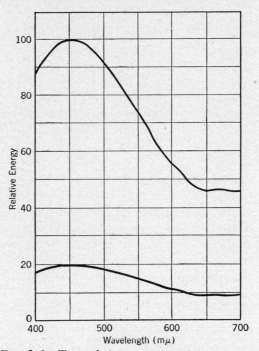

FIG. 2·6 Two relative energy-distribution curves representing light of identical spectrophotometric quality but with one having its maximum arbitrarily set at a value five times as great as the other.

true scale for such a curve can be expressed accurately only as relative or absolute intensity as measured in band widths of so many wavelengths. For a band width of 10 mμ this would be stated as "intensity per 10 mμ wavelength interval."

The purpose of spectrum measurements is to define the physical nature of a beam of light in terms of its relative or absolute energy distribution with frequency or wavelength. By its means, the nature of the light from a source may be described; or, alternatively, if the light from a source is known, the way in which it has been modified by some object may be determined. The nature of the light from various sources will be considered in the next two chapters, and the ways in which it may be modified in Chapter V. First, however, it is important to consider what occurs when light that has not been selected for frequency affects a receptor.

In the previous discussion it was assumed that each measurement was made on a very narrow band of wavelengths taken out of the spectrum. For such selected light the sensitivity of the receptor to different frequencies within this range could be considered constant, and it was necessary to know only how the response varied with intensity to obtain the desired information. If the light to be measured consists of a wider portion of the spectrum, or particularly, if the receptor is simply exposed to the source, it becomes essential to consider how it is affected by light of different frequencies.

As implied earlier, there are very few receptors known which have the same response to all frequencies. The bolometer and thermopile very nearly meet this requirement; but these are almost the only known ones which do, because conversion of light to heat by absorption on a truly black surface is one of the few known light conversions that is independent of wavelength. All types of photocell, the eye, and the photographic emulsion, as well as all photochemical receptors, depend to a large extent on the frequency of the light. Many are sensitive to only narrow regions of the spectrum.

In a manner exactly analogous to the curves that were drawn for relative amounts of the different frequencies in a source, it is also possible to draw curves showing the relative sensitivities to the different frequencies for a receptor. In Fig. 2·7, for example, is shown the "sensitivity curve" for the eye under normal daylight illumination levels.

This and all other curves of this type are to be interpreted as indicating the relative sensitivity directly. In all instances, however, they are obtained by determining the amount of light of a given wavelength required to obtain a given response (in the eye, to match a given light for brightness;

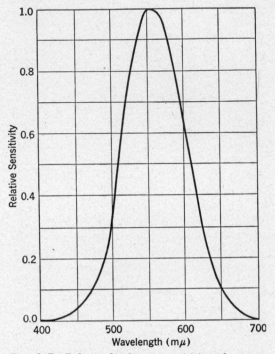

FIG. 2·7 Relative brightness sensitivity of average human eye (ICI standard observer).

in the receptor, to obtain a given output), and the curve is drawn wrong side up, so to speak, so that it indicates the response of the receptor to a given amount of energy. The actual process of obtaining the figures for the final curve is usually to divide an arbitrary value (usually unity) by the measured amount of energy needed. Thus, if it requires five times as much light at one wavelength to get the same response as at another, the receptor is $\frac{1}{5}$ as sensitive to that wavelength, and so on. For the curve shown in Fig. 2·7 the maximum eye sensitivity, that is the wavelength which calls for the least energy for a given brightness, has been taken as unity, and then this unity has

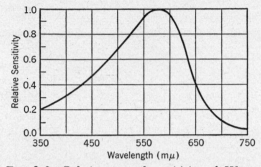

FIG. 2·8 Relative spectral sensitivity of Weston Photronic cell. (W. N. Goodwyn, Jr., *Transactions of the Illuminating Engineering Society*, Vol. 27, p. 832, 1932.)

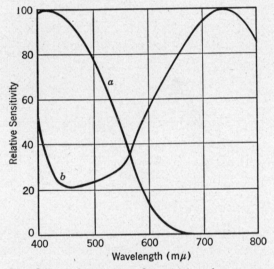

FIG. 2·9 Relative spectral sensitivity of two types of photo tubes (*a*) RCA 1P37 and (*b*) RCA 868. The two curves are not relative to each other (A. M. Glover and A. R. Moore, *Journal of the Society of Motion Picture Engineers*, Vol. 46, p. 380, 1946.)

been divided by the others in turn to obtain their relative values.

The sensitivity curve of a Weston Photronic cell such as is used in the Weston exposure meter is shown in Fig. 2·8. It is

apparent at once that its sensitivity distribution, as it is called, is quite different from that of the eye.

The curve of an RCA 868 cell such as is used frequently in theater sound production systems is shown in Fig. 2·9, as is also that of a recent "blue sensitive" cell (RCA 1P37) manufactured by the Radio Corporation of America for the same purpose and recommended for use with some types of sound track on color films.

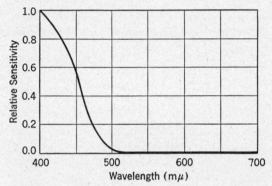

FIG. 2·10 Relative spectral sensitivity of a blue-sensitive photographic film for the visible region of the spectrum.

Figure 2·10 shows the sensitivity for a normal, pure silver bromide photographic emulsion.

TOTAL ACTION OF RECEPTORS

It is apparent on consideration of these curves that, if light which had the same amount of energy at *all* wavelengths were to be allowed to fall on each of these receptors, there would be a different response from each. More important, perhaps, is the fact that they would each evaluate the amount of light in a given spectral region differently *with respect to the whole.*

Light in the region between 550 and 600 mμ, for example, would affect the eye very strongly, as it would the Weston cell; but it would affect the blue sensitive cell very little and would not affect the particular photographic emulsion shown at all.

When light that has not been isolated into narrow frequency regions is measured by a receptor its spectral-sensitivity distribution must be taken into account along with the energy distribution of the source. A measurement of the response of one receptor to a beam of light has no meaning with respect to another unless the sensitivity distribution of both and the energy distribution of the source are all known. If these facts *are* known, however, it is fairly simple to estimate the relative effect of the light on the two.

Suppose, for example, that light of the quality shown in Fig. 2·11 falls on the photographic material shown in Fig. 2·10, and its effective intensity for that film and for the eye is to be calculated in comparison with that of a light source having the same amount of energy at all wavelengths. (This convenient fiction is usually known as an "equal-energy source" and is frequently used as a reference in such calculations because its energy can be considered to be unity at all wavelengths.)

To determine the response of each receptor it is necessary only to consider the effect on that receptor of each wavelength region in turn and then add them all together. Each region is treated alike as follows. The relative intensity of the light in the region from 600 to 620 mμ is 0.681. (It does not matter to what value this is referred, since the same values will be used with respect to the assumed equal-energy source. It is the fractional response for this particular source in comparison with equal energy that is being determined. This fractional response will then be compared with that for the eye.) The response of the film in this region is given as *zero*. This light, therefore, as well as light of all longer wavelengths

does not affect the film. For light with energy in the region 400 to 420 mμ, however, the response is 0.95, but the amount of light available from the source has a relative value of 0.0084. This means that there is 0.0084 of the light available, and so the sensitivity, while high, gives only a small

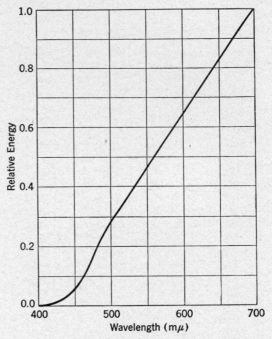

Fig. 2·11 Spectral-distribution curve for filtered tungsten light.

output. In all cases the relative response for each wavelength region is the multiple of the relative energy in the light for that region and the relative sensitivity. The sum of these products will give the total *relative* output. The total relative output from an equal-energy source, since it has a value of unity at all wavelengths, is equal to the sum of the relative sensitivities at each wavelength region calculated. These calculations, which sound difficult but are extremely simple, give two sums, the relative response for the given light and the relative response for an equal-energy source. The ratio of these sums to each other gives the relation of the response of the receptor to this particular light as compared to equal energy. If identical calculations are then carried through for the eye (see Fig. 2·7), a similar relative figure is obtained. Since both responses are calcu-lated as ratios for this light as compared to equal-energy light, the two *ratios* can then be compared directly. Actual calculation of the above cases gives a value of 0.03692 for the film and 0.4965 for the eye. It is seen that for this particular light the film has only

FIGURE 2·12

I	II	III	IV	V	VI	
Wavelength	Relative energy of illuminant	Relative sensitivity of film	Relative sensitivity of eye	Product of Column II and Column III	Product of Column II and Column IV	
400	0.0065	1.0000	0.0004	0.006500	0.000003	$\dfrac{\Sigma V}{\Sigma III} = 0.03692$
410	0.0084	0.9450	0.0012	0.007938	0.000010	
420	0.0129	0.8780	0.0040	0.011326	0.000052	
430	0.0203	0.7890	0.0116	0.016017	0.000235	
440	0.0340	0.6780	0.0230	0.023052	0.000782	$\dfrac{\Sigma VI}{\Sigma IV} = 0.4965$
450	0.0544	0.5500	0.0380	0.029920	0.002067	
460	0.0880	0.3950	0.0600	0.034760	0.005280	
470	0.1290	0.2440	0.0910	0.031476	0.011739	$\dfrac{0.03692}{0.4965} = 0.0744$
480	0.1781	0.1330	0.1390	0.023687	0.024756	
490	0.2336	0.0670	0.2080	0.015651	0.048589	
500	0.2785	0.0260	0.3230	0.007241	0.089956	
510	0.3169	0.0110	0.5030	0.003486	0.159401	
520	0.3535	0.0000	0.7100		0.250985	
530	0.3889		0.8620		0.335232	
540	0.4239		0.9540		0.404401	
550	0.4593		0.9950		0.457004	
560	0.4954		0.9950		0.493023	
570	0.5322		0.9520		0.506750	
580	0.5695		0.8700		0.495465	
590	0.6065		0.7570		0.459121	
600	0.6436		0.6310		0.406112	
610	0.6808		0.5030		0.342442	
620	0.7180		0.3810		0.273558	
630	0.7549		0.2650		0.200048	
640	0.7915		0.1750		0.138512	
650	0.8278		0.1070		0.088575	
660	0.8635		0.0610		0.052674	
670	0.8987		0.0320		0.028758	
680	0.9332		0.0170		0.015864	
690	0.9670		0.0082		0.007929	
700	1.0000		0.0041		0.004100	
Sum Total		5.7160	10.6815	0.211054	5.303423	

Fig. 2·12 Tabulated data used in comparing the reception of the eye and unsensitized film to ordinary incandescent tungsten light.

0.074 of the relative output of the eye as compared with what it would have if both were exposed to an equal-energy source. The actual calculations are shown in Fig. 2·12.

In all these calculations no mathematics has been used except multiplication, division, and addition, and this is characteristic of all applications of spectrophotometric and sensitivity curves. The relative response of a receptor to any light source is simply the sum of the products in each wavelength region of the relative intensity and the relative sensitivity. Those familiar with calculus will recognize that what is being calculated is the integral under the product curve of the light source and receptor.

To aid in visualizing the output of such receptors when exposed to a given light source, curves are sometimes plotted in which the relative amount of light in the source for any region, multiplied by the relative sensitivity of the receptor for that region, is shown for all wavelength regions. Such curves show the relative importances of the various regions in producing the response. Such curves for the two cases above are shown in Fig. 2·13. Note that in this case the two cannot be compared because the outputs are of different types, whereas in the calculation each was expressed as fractions of this response to equal-energy light and so they were placed on the same basis.

The important point to remember in all this discussion, and the point which its introduction is intended to emphasize, is the fact that it is not only the energy distribution of the light or the sensitivity of the receptor which matters in any given case, but also the wavelength-by-wavelength product of the two which matters. When any receptor, whether it is the eye, film, or photocell, is exposed to a beam of light, there is no way

of determining the amount of the response which will be produced other than by breaking both down into their wavelength distributions, multiplying the two together, and adding up the individual effects. In subsequent chapters it will be seen that similar

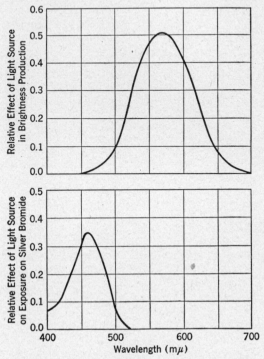

FIG. 2·13 Curves showing the effect of filtered tungsten light on the human eye and on a photographic emulsion.

considerations hold for the way in which colored objects affect a beam of light. It is this process of considering the light and its effect systematically by wavelength regions (and then determining from this the total effect) which is the key to the solution of the majority of the problems which arise in color. Frequent use will be made of this concept in the remainder of the treatment. The serious reader will do well to have the principles clearly in mind before attempting to understand the facts to be considered. It is unfortunate that for many people the concepts are abstruse and difficult to grasp; this is the basis of the whole subject of color, and understanding succeeds or fails at this point.

BIBLIOGRAPHY

Committee on Colorimetry. "Physical Concepts: Radiant Energy and Its Measurement." *Journal of the Optical Society of America*, **34**:183–218 (1944).

Moon, Parry. *The Scientific Basis of Illuminating Engineering*. New York: McGraw-Hill Book Co., Inc. 1936. Chapters I, II, and III.

Parsons, Sir John Herbert. *An Introduction to the Study of Colour Vision*, 2nd ed. Cambridge, England: The University Press. 1924. Chapter I, Section I.

Sears, Francis Weston. *Principles of Physics III —Optics*, 2nd ed. Cambridge, Mass.: Addison-Wesley Press, Inc. 1946. Chapter I.

Walsh, John W. T. *Photometry*. London: Constable and Co., Ltd. 1926. Chapter II.

Wood, Robert W. *Physical Optics*, 3rd ed. New York: The Macmillan Co. 1934. Chapter I.

Wright, W. D. *The Measurement of Colour*. London: Adam Hilger, Ltd. 1944. Chapters I and V.

Zworykin, V. K., and Wilson, E. D. *Photocells and Their Application*, 2nd ed. New York: John Wiley and Sons, Inc. 1932.

Light Sources

CHAPTER III

IN the previous chapter it was shown that the existence of radiation in the form of light necessarily indicates the presence of a source from which the light comes. The present chapter is devoted to a consideration of such sources, the conditions under which they produce radiation, and the nature of the radiation so produced.

LIGHT EMISSION

According to modern theories, light is produced by the release of energy stored in the motions of the electrons composing the outer parts of the atoms. When these electrons absorb energy from sources outside the material, they are placed in a state of more violent motion. They give off electromagnetic radiation when they return usually rather suddenly to their more normal states. This energy absorption and release may take place in a number of different ways, depending on the nature of the energy received. Of all the possible types of energy which can cause the effect, perhaps the most common is heat. If any material which does not decompose at high temperatures is heated it will eventually start to give off visible light and may be seen to glow. The

heat energy is absorbed as mechanical energy by the atoms and these then give off this energy in the form of light. Bodies which are not stable at high temperatures are themselves converted by the absorbed energy to liquids or to gases at a higher state of energy content.

Radiation of light due to high temperatures is the mechanism underlying the greater part of all our known sources. Under this heading come the sun, incandescent lights, burning materials, glowing coals, hot metals and the like, all of which classify as "thermal radiators." The spectral energy distributions of many such sources have been determined. A portion of them classify in a group known as "black-body radiators."

Before considering actual spectra from actual sources, both of this and of other types, it may be well to understand the meaning of the term black-body radiator and gain some idea of the related concept of "color temperature."

BLACK BODIES

If a material which totally encloses a space is heated until its temperature is sufficiently high, it will give off light. Inside the enclosure this light simply passes from one wall to another; it is emitted from the first wall because of its temperature and then re-absorbed by the opposite wall and reconverted to heat. It is apparent that if the walls are maintained at constant temperature, no heat is being gained or lost within the enclosure; furthermore, since the light is radiated in all directions from each point, all parts of the interior are constantly receiving and re-emitting light at equal rates. Now if a very small hole is made in such an enclosing surface, the light which passes out of this hole will be exactly equal to that received by any other similar area of the interior. It is equally true that this is the maximum amount which may leave the hole. If light falls on the opening from outside, it will be absorbed inside, and unless the difference between the two is great enough to change the temperature of the enclosure, there will be no increase in the amount of light leaving.

A body such as that described which absorbs all the radiation that falls on it is called a "black body," and the radiation emitted through a small opening in the enclosure such as described is called black-body radiation. The name is derived from the fact that if the temperature is low enough so that no visible radiation is being produced, any light which falls on the opening is completely absorbed so that no light can leave the aperture at all. Absence of light, as we shall see, is one condition for the production of a black area, in this case a theoretically completely black hole. Such a device as described is represented in Fig. 3·1.

The light which leaves such an aperture has an energy distribution dependent only on the temperature of the surrounding walls of the enclosure. This energy distribution can be calculated from purely theoretical considerations. Theoretical relative energy distribution curves for black bodies over a

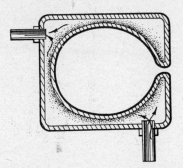

FIG. 3·1 Cross-sectional diagram of a simple black-body radiator consisting of an enclosure surrounded by molten or boiling material. The spectral distribution of the radiation depends solely upon the temperature of the material.

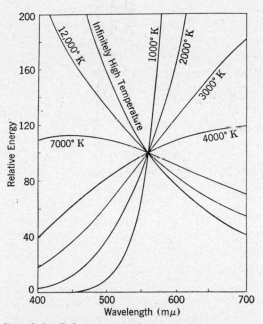

FIG. 3·2 Relative spectral-energy distributions of black-body radiators at various temperatures.

considerable range of actual temperatures are shown in Fig. 3·2. In this figure the relative energies have all been assumed to be equal at a wavelength of 560 mμ, in order to simplify the comparison of the curves.

If the actual energies are plotted, even over a rather narrow range of temperatures, the relative sizes of the curves make comparison difficult. Such curves for a few temperatures are shown in Fig. 3·3. In both of these figures the "absolute" or "Kelvin" temperature scale is used. Temperatures on this scale are obtained by adding 273° to the centigrade temperatures and are designated by the letter "K."

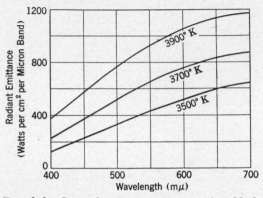

Fig. 3·3 Spectral radiant emittance of a black body at three temperatures.

Just as in the case of the individual wavelength regions of the spectrum, it is found that these different energy distributions appear of different color to the eye. This is a familiar experience for everyone. If a piece of metal is heated until it starts to glow, whether the cause is passage of an electrical current or heating in a flame, the first noticeable glow is red; at a higher temperature this changes to orange and then to yellow. The theoretical black-body curves tell us through calculations to be considered later that at still higher temperatures the color would be white and at the highest temperatures they would be blue. The sun may be considered to be white for this reason; no objects hot enough to be visually blue are known, unless they are some of the stars. The blue of the sky has an entirely different cause, this light originating at the sun.

COLOR TEMPERATURE

Because of the systematic change in color with the temperature of a black body, the concept of color temperature has arisen. If it is known that the light from a glowing body follows the black-body laws, determination of the exact color of the light will act as a measure of the temperature of the material. Conversely for such bodies, specification of the color in terms of the temperature will completely define the energy distribution of the light with wavelength. These considerations, however, are all theoretical. In any given instance it is necessary to know accurately whether this energy distribution law is the one being followed. It is found actually that very few materials do obey these laws accurately, and the application of these ideas to real sources is in the nature of a convenient approximation. Rather than attempting to list those for which it does and does not apply, we will consider the individual sources in some detail, both as to the cause of the radiations and as to their approximation to black-body radiation. Often there is no useful relationship at all, but it is just as important that this fact be recognized as it is to know when it does hold. Radiation due primarily to temperature will be considered first.

SUNLIGHT

Sunlight is produced by the high temperature of the sun. Its energy distribution outside the earth's atmosphere approximates closely that of a black body at 6565° K. This is assumed to be the actual effective temperature of the outer envelope of gases which surround the sun and from which we receive light. In passing through the earth's atmosphere a considerable amount of this light is lost, particularly in the short-wavelength region, and when the light strikes the earth's surface it can no longer be represented by a true black-body radiation curve. Curves for black-body radiation of approximately the same color as the sun in outer space, for the sun at noon in winter and in summer at Washington, D. C., and for the nearest approximation to this radia-

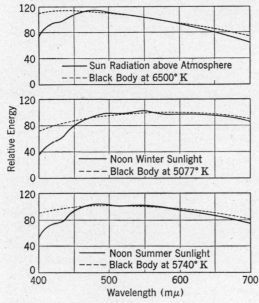

FIG. 3·4 Solar spectral-energy distribution curves as compared with distributions of black bodies of like color. (Solar data: R. Davis and K. S. Gibson, *Bureau of Standards Misc. Publication* No. 114, p. 16, 1931.)

tion if it acted like a black body, are shown in Fig. 3·4. It is seen that the approximation is not good, particularly in the blue region of the spectrum.

At times of day other than noon the sun passes through much more air in reaching the earth, and its energy distribution is still more affected by the losses due to this air. Still other factors such as the direction from which the light comes, atmospheric conditions, and so on may affect the energy distribution markedly, and typical energy distribution curves for five conditions are shown

in Fig. 3·5. It may be pointed out here that changing the amount of atmosphere through which the light of the sun travels causes its color to vary in the same way as does the black-body series, from white through yellow to orange and red, but the energy distributions involved become poorer and poorer approximations to black-body radiation. In passing it may be noted that this fact illustrates a point which will receive much emphasis in subsequent chapters. It is not possible even to guess at the energy distribution of a light source from its visual

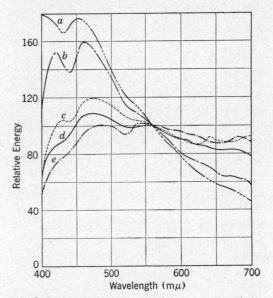

FIG. 3·5 Spectral-energy distribution curves of skylight from different directions and under different conditions at Cleveland, Ohio: (*a*) Zenith skylight, (*b*) North skylight, (*c*) Entire overcast sky, (*d*) Sun plus clear sky, and (*e*) Direct sunlight. (A. H. Taylor and G. P. Kerr, *Journal of the Optical Society of America*, Vol. 31, p. 7, 1941.)

color. It is only when the probable distribution is *known* from actual measurements that the color is significant at all in this respect. Sources such as the modern fluorescent lights, in which the radiation has very little to do with the temperature of the source, can be particularly misleading in this respect.

Aside from sunlight itself, perhaps the most common present-day source of light is the incandescent electric light bulb. As mentioned earlier, these bulbs give off light because of the high temperature of the tungsten wire of which the filament is made. The heat which causes this high temperature comes from the resistance to the passage of electricity through the wire and represents a conversion of electrical into heat energy which, in turn, is converted into light.

The energy distribution of the light from such lamps depends almost entirely on the temperature of the filament. Such a hot filament, inside a glass bulb, does not radiate exactly according to the laws of a theoretical black body; and, accordingly, the energy distribution is not exactly the same as that of a black body at exactly the same temperature. The radiation, however, is due so completely to the fact that the wire is hot that the actual energy distribution is nearly identical with that of a somewhat cooler black body. In other words, as the temperature of the filament of such a bulb is changed, the energy distribution passes through a series nearly identical with a part of those of the true black-body series; but the actual temperature of the filament has to be higher to produce the same result. Radiators which have such a property are sometimes called "gray" bodies to indicate that they are almost, but not quite, "black."

Tungsten melts at a temperature of 3643° K and at this temperature has the radiation characteristics of a black body at about 3600° K. At any lower temperature, down to the point where it gives off too little light to be of importance as a source, it matches closely black-body distributions of lower and lower temperatures. Since the color of the light changes considerably over this range (from yellow through orange to red), the "color temperature," that is, the temperature of the black body whose radiation it matches visually, is a definite description of its energy distribution. Since the temperature of the filament depends primarily on its size and length in relation to the voltage applied across its ends, such

FIGURE 3·6

	Description	Color Temperature
40 w, 120 v	General Purpose Lamp	2775° K
60 w, 120 v	" " "	2805° K
100 w, 120 v	" " "	2870° K
1000 w, 120 v	" " "	3020° K
6.6 amp	Street Lamp	2935° K
20 amp	" "	3050° K
1000 w, 120 v	Flood Light	2975° K
250 w, 115 v	No. 1 Photoflood Lamp	3425° K
1000 w	Regular Color Photography Lamp	3200° K
2000 w	Color Photography Lamp	3380° K
6.15 v	No. 31 Flashlight Lamp	2790° K
115 v	Christmas Tree Lamp	2600° K

FIG. 3·6 Color temperature table of a series of common incandescent lamps. (W. E. Forsythe and E. Q. Adams, *General Electric Review*, Vol. 47, pp. 60–62, October 1944.)

bulbs can be made which give light over an enormous range of color temperatures. Figure 3·6 gives data on a considerable number of such lamps. It must be emphasized, however, that variations of a few percent in the line voltage change these figures by considerable amounts. In any given case, some form of measurement has to be made if the actual energy distribution of the light is important. A line variation of 5 volts in a 110-volt circuit will change high-efficiency lamps by about 50° K in their color temperatures, a change which is clearly visible under proper conditions.

Methods of measuring color temperatures usually involve comparison of the light with the quality of that of a known source. A direct comparison will indicate at once whether or not the unknown is higher or lower in temperature. Higher temperatures will be distinctly bluer and lower ones distinctly yellower than the comparison. Light bulbs are now manufactured which have a color temperature very close to 3200° K when run at the exact voltage marked on the bulb. A convenient comparison instrument can be built with such a bulb and will be quite accurate if combined with a voltmeter and some means of setting the voltage accurately. Ordinary house lights will look decidedly yellow in comparison with such a light, and the familiar photographic photoflood lamp will be slightly bluer. Sunlight will be decidedly blue by comparison; but, unless the sunlight is somehow dimmed below that of the bulb, it is the bulb which will appear yellow, a fact to be considered in some detail in Chapters VII and XI.

CANDLES AND MATCHES

Flames from candles and matches (after they have been burning a few seconds) also have energy distributions approximating those of a black body, the first with a color temperature of about 1800° K and the second at the same or somewhat lower value. These, however, are about the only sources commonly encountered which can be described accurately by the color temperature, *as far as the energy distribution is concerned.* For all other sources the only safe assumption is that when a color temperature is stated in any text or article it refers *only* to the visual *color* of the light and not to the energy distribution. A more detailed consideration of this fact will be given under the general heading Vision, but it is necessary to remember that the fact that two sources have the same color does *not* mean that they have the same energy distributions. They may be completely different in nearly every other respect and yet *look* identical for *color*. It is only for radiation *having a black-body energy distribution* that the distribution can be defined by stating the color temperature.

For convenience, curves of the energy distributions commonly encountered in incandescent lamps are repeated on a somewhat enlarged scale in Fig. 3·7. Again they have

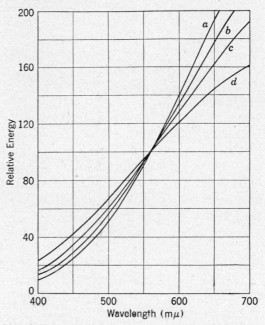

FIG. 3·7 Spectral-distribution curves of some common incandescent lamps. (*a*) 25W, (*b*) 50W, (*c*) 500W, and (*d*) 1000W projection. (A. H. Taylor, *G.E. Review*, Vol. 37, p. 411, 1934.)

all been brought to the same relative energy value at 560 mμ, for convenience in getting them all approximately the same size. Increasing the voltage across any given lamp would raise the relative energy at *all* wavelengths although it would do so proportionately more in the short than in the long-wavelength regions.

A further word of warning about the energy distribution from light sources is necessary, and this, again, will be amplified in a later chapter. What is being said in the present chapter refers *only* to the actual light from the source itself before it strikes *any* other objects. If there is a reflector behind the light or a colored wall near by, or the like, the light reaching a point near the source may be of a distinctly different distribution from that given off by the filament. The same warning applies if the light has to pass through any appreciable thickness of glass other than that of the bulb itself.

FLUORESCENT LAMPS

It is difficult to assign any order of importance to light sources other than the sun and incandescent lights. One very common source now in use, however, is the fluorescent lamp; its importance is likely to increase rather than decrease in the future. Very little, if any, of the visible radiation from these lamps is caused by heat. The light is caused by two different phenomena, one of which is used to produce light by means of the other. The first of these follows from the fact that if mercury vapor fills a tube from which nearly all the air has been removed, an electric current can be made to pass through the tube; the passage of this current causes it to give off light. Unlike the light which is produced by high temperature, the energy of this light is concentrated in a relatively few narrow regions or "lines" in the spectrum. Figure 3·8 shows the position of these lines and their approximate relative intensities. These values for intensity, however, are only approximate since they depend to a considerable extent on the exact construction of the tube and the physical conditions under which it operates. Like other sources, these tubes also give off energy at wavelengths which are both shorter and longer than those visible to the eye. The lines in the region shorter than the visible region (a region known as the ultraviolet) are also shown in Fig. 3·8.

It is seen that a large amount of energy is contained in the line at 253.7 mμ.

The second phenomenon involved in these lamps, and the one from which the lamps get their name, is "fluorescence." There are a considerable number of compounds which have the property of giving off light in the visible range of wavelength when they are placed in the path of a light source which gives off short-wavelength ra-

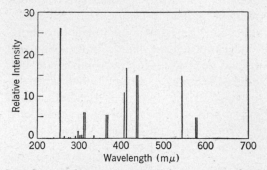

FIG. 3·8 Relative intensity of lines emitted by a low-pressure mercury-vapor lamp. (B. T. Barnes, *Journal of the Optical Society of America*, Vol. 24, p. 147, 1934.)

diation. It is not always necessary that the energy falling on them be in the ultraviolet region, and many compounds are known which fluoresce under the action of visible light. It is generally true, however, that they give off light of longer wavelength than those which cause it.

Fluorescent bulbs have, coated on the inside of the glass of the bulb, mixtures of such compounds, each of which gives off light in a different wavelength region when the ultraviolet radiation from the mercury vapor strikes its surface. The light which reaches the eye from such a bulb, therefore, consists of the light given off by these compounds plus such part of the light from the mercury as gets through them without being absorbed.

A number of such lamps are manufactured at the present time, and more of different types of energy distribution may be expected. The spectra for lamps of several different visual colors are given in Fig. 3·9 from data as published in the professional literature. The black rectangles which project above

It should be noted that the curve for the lamp labeled "daylight" bears little relation to the energy distribution of actual daylight. The name indicates that it matches this source *for color*, not energy distribution.

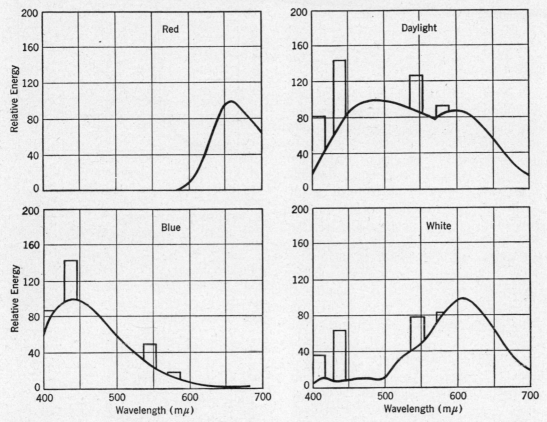

FIG. 3·9 Spectral-distribution curves for several types of fluorescent lamps. The areas under the blocks indicate total energy between the included wavelength limits. (G. E. Inman, *Transactions of the Illuminating Engineering Society*, Vol. 34, pp. 71–72, 1939.)

the smooth curves are to be translated as indications of the total amount of the mercury light energy which is present in that region, the width of the block representing the slit width used in the measurements. Comparison of these with Fig. 3·8 will show the wavelengths of the lines which they represent, the total area under each block representing the relative energy of the lines with respect to the rest of the spectrum.

Because these lamps are cool, inexpensive to operate, and not too bright to look at directly, they represent an important step forward in artificial lighting. The peculiar energy distributions, so different from either daylight or incandescent lighting, however, produce results in the appearance of colors which must be taken into account when these sources are under consideration. This matter is discussed more fully in Chapter

XVI, but it should be pointed out here that two surfaces which appear the same in daylight will not necessarily match under another light source having exactly the same visual color, unless the energy distribution of the light source *matches* that of daylight. The color of objects, therefore, is likely to change under these lights.

CARBON ARCS

Another source of light, used extensively for theater motion-picture projectors, for searchlights, and for a number of other purposes when an intensely bright light of small area is needed, is the electric carbon arc lamp. If two pieces of carbon, preferably in the form of rods, are placed in an electric circuit, the current can be made to flow through the air for a short distance between their tips if they are brought into momentary contact and then separated slightly.

The light which is given off by such an electric arc in air is due to a number of causes. As used in practice, the greater part of the light comes from the extremely high temperature produced at the ends of the carbon rods. This light has essentially a black-body energy distribution. With pure carbon the amount of light from the burning carbon in the "flame" of the arc is relatively small, but there is a fairly large amount of energy given off in the region of wavelength 389 mμ in the form of a single band of light. This is the so-called "cyanogen" band which is thought to be caused by the excitation of this compound, formed by the combination of the carbon with nitrogen from the air at the temperature of the arc. The energy distribution for a 10-ampere pure carbon arc in air is shown in Fig. 3·10.

It is possible to change the energy distribution of such arcs if, instead of pure carbon rods, rods with centers or "cores" of other

materials are used. These materials may be so chosen that the flame produced in the arc has almost any desired color and is many

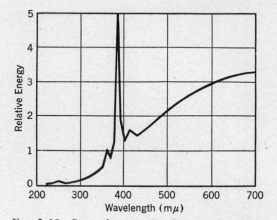

Fig. 3·10 Spectral-energy distribution of radiation emitted from a ¼ inch pure carbon arc operated at approximately ten amperes. (H. G. MacPherson, *Journal of the Optical Society of America*, Vol. 30, p. 191, 1940.)

times as bright as the glowing end of the rod. Proper choice of materials makes it possible to produce arcs which give off essentially white light; thus the "white flame"

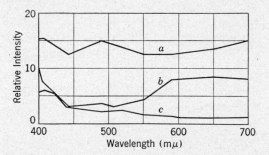

Fig. 3·11 Spectral-distribution curves for three arcs produced from carbons cored with: (*a*) minerals of the rare earths particularly cerium, (*b*) compounds of strontium, and (*c*) compounds of iron, nickel, and aluminum. (W. C. Kalb, *Transactions of the American Institute of Electrical Engineers*, Vol. 53, pp. 1174–75, 1934.)

arcs and the "high-intensity" arcs which are used primarily for motion-picture and searchlight purposes are produced.

The intensity and energy distributions produced by such arcs depend in complex fashion on the size of the rods, the materials of the cores, the separation, the amount of current which flows, and other factors. Energy distributions for a number of typical arcs are given in Fig. 3·11.

It is apparent that these distributions are rather far from those of a black body, and they, again, may affect colored objects in a way quite different from the effect of daylight or incandescent lights of similar colors.

DISCHARGE TUBES

Identical in principle with the mercury vapor tube on which the fluorescent lights are based are a large number of modern light sources, all of which are called "neon" tubes because they were the first to be introduced commercially. Almost any material which is a stable gas at ordinary temperatures will give off light if it is placed in an air-free tube and a current is made to pass through the gas. The light emitted is different for each gas, and the various energy distributions produce a wide range of differing colors. In nearly all instances the energy is in the form of lines at definite wavelengths, and, whereas in some regions of the spectrum there are many lines close together, there is seldom any region where the light has a continuous rather than a line spectrum. Spectra for two such gases, argon and neon, are given in (a) and (b) of Fig. 3·12.

For the most part such sources, often including other inert gases, are used as tubes in the familiar display signs. Two tubes operating on exactly the same principle, however, have become important sources for other purposes. The first of them is in wide use for highway illumination and depends for its action on sodium vapor. Its energy is nearly all in two yellow lines at 589 mμ,

and it contains no appreciable energy at any other wavelengths. Its spectrum is shown in (c) of Fig. 3·12.

The second of these sources is due to mercury vapor under extremely high pres-

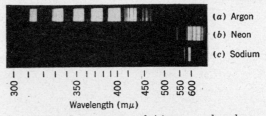
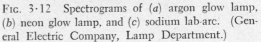

FIG. 3·12 Spectrograms of (a) argon glow lamp, (b) neon glow lamp, and (c) sodium lab-arc. (General Electric Company, Lamp Department.)

sures. The result of having the gas so highly compressed is to produce a tremendous increase in the intensity of the light given off and, at the same time, to add to the mercury-line spectrum a very considerable amount of light whose energy distribution is continuous with wavelength. Photographs of

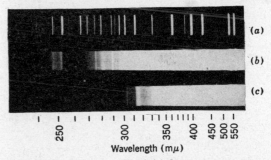

FIG. 3·13 Spectrograms of (a) low-pressure quartz mercury arc, and (b) and (c) Type AH-6 mercury, quartz and glass glow tubes (high-pressure). The difference between (b) and (c) is due to ultraviolet absorption properties of glass and quartz. (General Electric Company, Lamp Department.)

three spectra from such sources are shown in Fig. 3·13. Spectral-energy distributions for high-pressure mercury vapor lamps operating at various pressures are shown in Fig. 3·14. Because of their high brightness, such

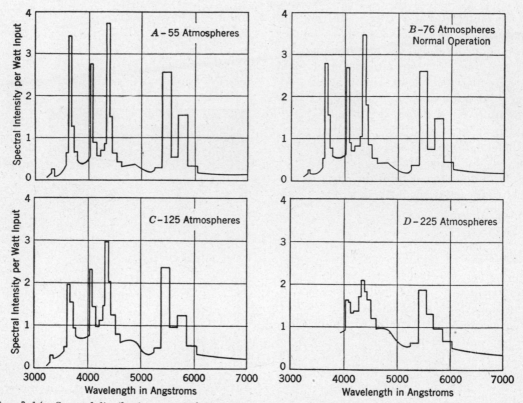

F𝐈𝐆. 3·14 Spectral-distribution curves for a mercury arc operating under different high pressures show-ing the increase in the amount of continuous radiation and the broadening of the lines as the pressure is increased. (W. E. Forsythe, *Transactions of the Illuminating Engineering Society*, Vol. 35, p. 140, 1940.)

sources have important commercial uses. Their normal color is distinctly bluish white.

IRON ARC

A light source having little commercial usefulness, but interesting because of the complexity of its spectrum and very important scientifically since the wavelengths of all its thousands of lines have been deter-mined with high accuracy, is an arc in air between two pieces of pure iron. A photo-graph of such a spectrum over a limited range of wavelengths is shown in compari-son with that of the element europium in Fig. 3·15. From calibrations of the iron lines the wavelengths of the europium lines can be determined. The iron spectrum is used quite frequently both to calibrate the position of the spectrum in a spectroscope and to help in identifying lines in a spec-trum produced by unknown compounds.

The light sources dealt with so far have all been of the type that, as long as condi-tions remain constant, continue to give off radiation of the same quality at a constant rate. The arc lights mentioned are exceed-ingly sensitive to variations in the conditions and tend to "flicker" somewhat, but other-wise will continue to give off light as long as the current flows.

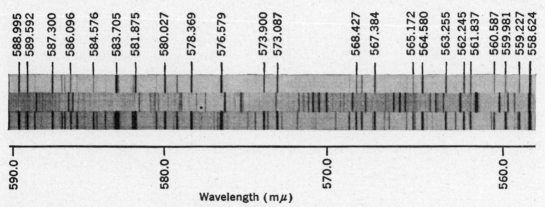

Fig. 3·15 Spectrogram of a portion of the europium and iron spectrums. The europium spectrogram is sandwiched between two of iron so that its wavelength may be accurately compared with the known ones of iron.

CONCENTRATED-ARC LAMP

Another arc source which is very interesting and promises to be of considerable utility is the concentrated-arc lamp recently developed at the Western Union Telegraph Company laboratories.

The lamp consists of two specially designed electrodes mounted inside a glass chamber which is similar to a common radio tube but is filled with the inert gas argon at almost atmospheric pressure. During a preliminary conditioning period an arc is struck, and a large current is passed between the two electrodes. After conditioning, subsequent arcs have a lower current. The spectral quality of this light is continuous in the visible region (it is very slightly contaminated with lines from argon and zirconium from one of the electrodes) with much more discontinuous radiation in the infrared region. The fact that the light source closely approaches a point source coupled with its good light quality assures the lamp considerable use.

FLASH LAMPS

There are several sources, of interest chiefly to photographers, designed to give off a definite *quantity* of light in a brief interval of time and then stop. These are the so-called flashlights of various types. Historically the oldest, but still in occasional use, are the flash powders. They are highly combustible mixtures containing a compound, usually metallic magnesium, which gives off a brilliant light when it burns. The quantity of powder burned determines the total amount of light produced. The time taken for the combustion is of the order of one-tenth of a second. The dense white smoke is the combustion product, magnesium oxide. The typical energy distribution curve for such a flash powder is similar to that of a black body at around 4000° K, although its actual color can be changed by addition of metallic salts.

More recent and less hazardous to use are the photoflash bulbs. Because of their importance to photography and their widespread use, these bulbs have become a highly specialized branch of bulb manufacture. Bulbs may be obtained with various types of combustion rate, so that it is possible to concentrate a lot of energy in a very brief flash, or to have it extend over a sufficient length of time so that a shutter can move across in front of the film while the flash is going on. Curves showing the relative intensities for various times after the start of the flash are given for a number of types in Fig. 3·16.

Since the materials of which these bulbs are made differ with the different bulbs, it is not possible to make any general statement as to the energy distributions which they produce, except that nearly all that are

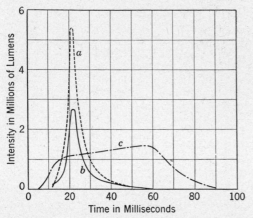

FIG. 3·16 Curves showing distribution of light output during the combustion period of three types of photoflash bulbs: (a) G.E. No. 20, (b) G.E. No. 10, and (c) G.E. No. 31.

made for use in color photography produce energy distributions equivalent to incandescent light bulbs at color temperatures around 3500° K. A number of bulbs are also available that have a blue coating over the outside of the bulb and produce the same result on color films as daylight. They may be used in daylight to throw light into dark shadows and the like. An energy-distribution curve for an uncoated bulb is shown in Fig. 3·17. The shortest duration available with bulbs of this type is of the order of ⅕₀ of a second.

A recent light source invented by Edgerton and Germeshausen at Massachusetts Institute of Technology is capable of producing a brilliant flash with a duration of the order of 1/30,000 of a second. This lamp

has been developed by the Eastman Kodak Company for photographic purposes and is marketed as the Kodatron lamp. The principle involved is the same as in the mercury-

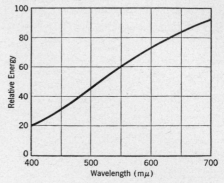

FIG. 3·17 Relative spectral-energy distribution of No. 20 photoflash bulb. (W. E. Forsythe, *Denison University Bulletin, Journal of the Scientific Laboratories*, Vol. 30, p. 113, 1935.)

vapor and neon-gaseous discharge lamps; but instead of passing a current continuously through the gas, a large amount of electricity

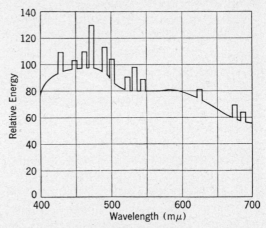

FIG. 3·18 Spectral-energy distribution curve of light from the Kodatron Type II lamp (strong spectrum lines indicated qualitatively only).

is passed through as a single discharge from an electrical condenser. The tube itself in its present form contains, instead of a single gas, a variety of gases mixed in proportions which make the light given off similar to daylight.

A curve showing the approximate energy distribution of the Kodatron Type II lamp is given in Fig. 3·18. Its effect is sufficiently close to that of daylight so that it may be used directly with film intended for color pictures in daylight.

MISCELLANEOUS SOURCES

It may be interesting in passing to note the nature of a few miscellaneous sources of light.

The stars, of course, give off light because of their high temperatures, and there is sufficient difference in their temperatures to make the color of the light a matter of importance to astronomers. The moon, however, is simply a gray object illuminated by the sun and does not give off light of its own. The color of moonlight is essentially identical with that of sunlight.

Certain chemicals when mixed in solution give off a considerable amount of light. The phenomenon is known as chemiluminescence, and the light covers a wide range of colors with sufficient intensity to be photographed with some ease.

Light is given off when some materials are rubbed or struck sharply with a metal, the first being called "triboluminescence" and the latter, usually, "sparking."

Many compounds have the property of coloring an otherwise nearly colorless flame when they are held in it, and the colors produced are used as important indications to the chemist of the nature of an unknown compound. The most common color so produced is yellow from sodium either as a pure metal or in sodium compounds.

Closely allied to fluorescence is a phenomenon often called "phosphorescence," al-though in strict usage the item applies to a different phenomenon. Such compounds have the property of continuing to emit light for a long time after they have received light from some other source. They are familiar in light buttons and the like, which glow for some time in the dark but gradually become dark themselves.

The term phosphorescence strictly applies to the light which is given off by phos-

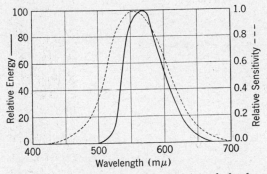

FIG. 3·19 Relative spectral sensitivity of the human eye (broken curve) as compared to the spectral-energy distribution of the light from the firefly (solid curve). (Firefly data: H. E. Ives and W. W. Coblentz, *Transactions of the Illuminating Engineering Society*, Vol. 4, p. 657, 1909.)

phorus and allied substances when they are left exposed to the air and so oxidize at a slow rate, giving off light. It is, effectively, a burning of the material at a very slow rate. It may be seen at times on the surface of the ocean waves, particularly in tropical waters, and is due to the oxidation of minute sea organisms.

Many materials have the property of fluorescing under the action of radiation from minute quantities of radium or from the familiar X-rays, and producing light such as that from the luminous dials of clocks and the like.

Last, and perhaps least, but interesting as a scientific curiosity, is the light given off by the firefly. The cause of this light is not known, and no light source has yet been invented by man which gives off light of the same energy distribution (although, of course, light of the same energy distribution can be produced indirectly with filters). The firefly's light has the peculiar property of being confined entirely to the visible region of the spectrum. It does not radiate energy outside this region and radiates its maximum energy at almost exactly the wavelength to which the eye is the most sensitive. In fact, the shape of its energy distribution curve is very similar to that of the sensitivity curve for the human eye. The two curves are shown in Fig. 3·19.

BIBLIOGRAPHY

Cady, Francis E., and Dates, Henry B. *Illuminating Engineering*, 2nd ed. New York: John Wiley and Sons, Inc. 1928. Chapter II.

Massachusetts Institute of Technology, the Color Measurement Laboratory. *Handbook of Colorimetry*. Cambridge, Mass.: The Technology Press. 1936. Chapter II.

Moon, Parry. *The Scientific Basis of Illuminating Engineering*. New York: McGraw-Hill Book Co., Inc. 1936. Chapters IV, V, and VI.

Parsons, Sir John Herbert. *An Introduction to the Study of Colour Vision*, 2nd ed. Cambridge, England: The University Press. 1924. Chapter I, Section II.

Sears, Francis Weston. *Principles of Physics III —Optics*, 2nd ed. Cambridge, Mass.: Addison-Wesley Press, Inc. 1946. Chapters X and XI.

Illumination

CHAPTER IV

THUS far, light has been considered as originating at a point and radiating outward along straight lines at constant speed so that the light which leaves the source at a given instant travels outward as an expanding spherical surface. While it is true that this is the basic phenomenon, it is also true that there are almost no practical light sources small enough to be considered as actual single points. In almost all cases the size of the source makes it necessary that it be considered as a very large number of points which are side by side and form an area. Each point of this area emits light just as if it were alone, but the combination effect in many instances is so different that it is convenient to establish new rules for the way such areas act.

POINT SOURCES

The most important rule followed by a point source is the so-called inverse square law of illumination, which is illustrated in Fig. 4·1. The *amount* of light which falls on a given surface depends on the distance to the surface. Since *all* the light emitted from the source at any instant lies in the sur-face of a sphere, the fraction of the total emission from the source that falls on the given area depends on the ratio of that area to the area of the sphere of which it forms

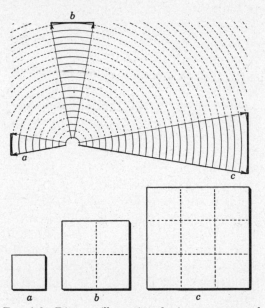

FIG. 4·1 Diagram illustrating the inverse square of illumination at various distances from the source. The three areas, (a), (b), and (c), represent the areas over which the same total amount of light must be spread at one, two, and three units of distance from the source.

37

a part. If this relationship is followed through mathematically, it is found that the illumination on the area decreases with increasing distance according to the square of the distance. That is, if there is a given illumination at two feet, at four feet it will be $(\frac{2}{4})^2 = \frac{4}{16} = \frac{1}{4}$ of that value.

This relationship follows from the fact that the area of a spherical surface increases as the square of the radius of the sphere; and, therefore, the light falling on a *given* area decreases in the same manner. As stated, this is the basic law of illumination. The application of this to a point source also gives the *most rapid decrease* with distance. The illumination from actual sources decreases *more slowly* with distance in all instances.

Before this is considered in more detail and the rules for typical sources are derived, it is necessary to consider the nomenclature of illumination.

TERMINOLOGY

There are six main divisions of the terminology which must be used in discussing a light source. They correspond to the three considered in Chapter I, multiplied by two because each of the three may be applied to the source itself or to the surface which is being illuminated *by* the source. Separate concepts are necessary for the two aspects, and separate words are used. To the beginner this large number of words is apt to be confusing, but, if an attempt is made to learn at the start whether they refer to the source or to its effect, they may be kept straight with little difficulty. A third set of terms is used which takes into account the fact that the light falling *on* a surface is different from that which *leaves* it, but this will be considered in a later section.

It will be recalled that the three main divisions are physics, psychophysics, and psy-

chology. With respect to a light source or its effects, they correspond to the physical quantity and quality of the radiant energy (per unit area at each wavelength in a given direction), to the effect of this radiant energy in terms of standardized eye-response data, and to its psychological effect when seen by a real observer under the conditions. For the present only the intensity aspect of the subject will be discussed, and the quality and color aspects will be considered in succeeding chapters.

The movement of light through space is referred to as a "flux" of light, the term being essentially synonymous with the word "flow." The radiant energy is referred to as "radiant flux"; the evaluation of this with respect to the eye is called the "luminous flux"; and the mental evaluation of it after it strikes the eye is called "brightness."

Under each of these terms come the words or expressions which tell whether the point of view taken is toward the source, toward the light falling on an object, or toward the light after it leaves that object. They are shown in tabular form in Fig. 4·2 and are considered more fully below.

It will be noted that this table is only slightly modified from the Optical Society of America Colorimetry Report given at the end of Chapter I. It has been modified only by the use of the term "brightness distribution" for the term implied by the former table which would be "volume brightness." Since the physical quality of the light reaching the eye from a volume can differ from that from a surface only in its depth distribution, it is felt that for the present purposes this substitution may have more meaning. The two terms "surface brightness" and "surface lightness" are not synonymous, a fact to be considered in some detail under Brightness Perception.

These, then, are the basic words used to describe the concepts. All the physics terms are derived from the word "radiation," the psychophysical from the word "luminous," and all the psychological terms use the word "brightness" except the one case where there are two distinct phases which must be separated as "brightness" and "lightness." The ending "-ance" is used for words indicating the cause, and the ending "-ness" is used for words indicating the effect. These facts,

article, it may be necessary to read very carefully. Whenever the word is used in this book it will refer *only* to the mental evaluation of the light by an *actual* observer.

Two other terms should be mentioned here, although their implications will be discussed again. The first of these is the word "brilliance." In the former literature this word was used frequently to correspond to

FIGURE 4·2

	Physics	Psychophysics	Psychology
	Radiant flux	Luminous flux	Brightness
Source	Radiance	Luminance	Illuminant brightness
To surface	Irradiance	Illuminance	Illumination brightness
From surface	Radiant reflectance	Luminous reflectance	Surface brightness Surface lightness
Through surface	Radiant transmittance	Luminous transmittance	Brightness distribution

FIG. 4·2 Physical, psychophysical, and psychological terms used in describing light phenomena.

if remembered, will prevent possible confusion.

Only with the present report of the Colorimetry Committee has order come out of chaos in this matter, and the beginning reader in the subject can have little idea of how confused the subject has been in the past. Some notion of it will be gained, however, from general reading in the field. The most confusing word which will be encountered is brightness. In the past this word, like "color," was used in all possible meanings. Its present restriction to the psychological response is a badly needed simplification which originated with this committee. It will be found referring to the energy output of a source, to the light falling on an object, and in many other senses. In order to understand its use in any given

the present usage of the word brightness, that is, psychologically. In the present book the word will refer to the contrast of the scene as a whole or of one part with respect to the whole. It is considered the antithesis of "dullness," whereas "brightness" is opposed to "darkness."

The other term involves the word "effective." Throughout this book and much other literature this word will be found in connection with nearly all the other words mentioned above. The psychophysical terminology which has been developed above refers to the eye as the receptor of the light. The word effective refers to the *action* of light in any of its aspects. It is used normally with respect to some specified receptor, but its use includes also the causing of a visual response. Accordingly, whenever it is desired to distinguish between the light itself and its effect, this word is exceedingly useful. It is used also occasionally to clarify the meaning of a more correct but obscure term. Thus the word "chromaticness," which was invented with apologies by the Colorimetry Committee to fill a badly felt want in the terminology, is adequately defined for most (but not all) purposes by the term "effective color," and the term will be so used on some occasions in this book. In this phrase, the word color is being used in its more common sense, i.e., the visual characteristics of light which do not include brightness. This is a situation which the reader must bear in mind. In everyday speech the word color frequently is not intended to include brightness. In the strict terminology of the Colorimetry Committee it does.

This discussion includes all the words that are used in connection with the *concepts* involved in light and its effects. Concepts alone are not sufficient, however. It is necessary that the concepts be tied down by specific measurements, and these measurements must be referred to standardized and well-understood measurements in other fields.

UNITS OF MEASUREMENT

The basic measurements in physics are amounts of energy; those of psychophysics are amounts of effect of this energy on the eye considered as a standardized receptor; those of psychology (unfortunately or necessarily depending on the philosophic tenets which are followed) are measurements of effectiveness *relative* to the other simultaneous elements of consciousness. Of these measurements only the amount of actual energy at each wavelength has a well-defined and generally accepted basic unit, which is called the "erg." In the field of psycho-physics many units have been used. These have been standardized in the Colorimetry Report and will be adopted here. The basic unit is the "lumen." In the field of psychology there are no units, and in the last analysis the reports of observations are in the form "more," "less," or "equal to" some other reference point.

The erg in physics is a very small unit. It is defined as the amount of energy necessary to accomplish a certain small amount of work; 980 ergs are required to lift a single gram of any substance a distance of 1 centimeter. It is not necessary to consider this more deeply for present purposes. The interested reader is referred to any introductory physics text. The important concept is that energy is a capacity for doing work, and the erg is a unit completely defining a small amount of this.

Because this unit is so small, a very much larger unit has been defined, called a "joule" (the name of a famous physicist, as are many terms that will be encountered). The joule is equal to 10 million ergs. One other, more familiar, term should be mentioned. The "watt" is a unit of power defined as the *rate* of doing work. One watt of power corresponds to an energy output of 1 joule per second or 10 million ergs per second. The wattage of a source, therefore, defines the energy output in joules per second; care must be taken to ensure that the term applies to the output and not to the input if calculations are to be based on the data. The input is always equal to or greater than the output; the two are connected by the "efficiency" of the source.

In psychophysics the basic unit is derived in a sense from that of the physics phase, but the derivation is somewhat obscure. The standard unit is the lumen, defined as the luminous flux from a point source of one candle falling on 1 square foot of surface of a screen at a distance of 1 foot.

From the preceding discussion a little thought will show that this definition includes not only the amount of energy radiated by a standard candle, but also its spectral distribution and the sensitivity distribution of the eye. All these have been standardized, or standards have been recommended. Through these standardizations it is possible to define two intensity factors with respect to any non-standard light source. One of these is the luminous efficiency of the source as a whole (all the visible light without modification). It is defined as the number of lumens of light produced per watt of energy radiated (or supplied). The other is the lumens per watt in each wavelength interval (a term which involves the comparison of lights of different colors, a measurement which may be accomplished with suitable instruments). Curves are sometimes seen in which the ordinates are expressed in this unit; the curve expresses the relative brightness of the different parts of the spectrum with respect to the total output of the standard candle. Since the radiation from the standard candle can be specified in the basic units of physics, these factors are derived from the erg and the watt. Other units in common use will be considered as the subject develops.

LARGE AREA LIGHT SOURCES

The light emission from real sources whose areas are too large to be considered as points can now be considered briefly. It was noted at the beginning of the chapter that point sources produce an illumination which decreases as the square of the distance from the source.

When the source is larger than a point, all parts of its area may be considered as individual points, and the effect at a distance is that of the sum of all the points. To visualize the effect thus produced, it is easier to start with the extreme case in which the source is an exceedingly large (infinite) plane surface radiating uniformly over its area.

Consider first the meaning of the term "radiating uniformly." Each point radiates its light spherically. An area parallel to the surface, therefore, receives the same amount of light at each point on *its* surface, since every point has exactly the same relation to all parts of the source. If this receiving surface is moved away from the source, it will still receive the same amount of light as before at each point. In this extreme case, the illumination produced on a given small surface by a very large flat source is *independent* of the distance. It is evident that all sources too large to be considered as points fall somewhere between this extreme and that of a point source. If a source is of intermediate size, say one-fourth of an inch square, the light will fall off more slowly than the inverse square law predicts until the distance is large compared with the size of the source; thereafter it follows this law quite accurately. This may be considered a general property of all sources of light (not including those with reflectors). When the receiving area is parallel to the source, the light varies slowly with the distance as long as the distance is smaller than the width of the source. Beyond this point the light varies more rapidly until, when it is at a large distance (ten times or more), it follows the inverse square law.

Suppose that the source, instead of being parallel to the receiving surface, is at an angle to it. Obviously the surface is still receiving light from all points of the source, but this light leaves the source at an angle rather than perpendicularly. It is an experimental fact that for many sources the received light under such conditions is decreased approximately in proportion to the decreased size of the source as seen from this angle. This is known as the "cosine law of radiation," the amount of light decreasing with the cosine of the angle from the perpendicular of the source surface. If the intensity of the light from such a source is plotted so that distances from a point indicate relative intensities at the various angles, a plot is obtained such as Fig. 4·3.

The light from a flat source, therefore, decreases at the sides of the source, becom-

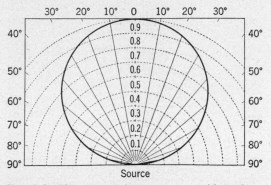

FIG. 4·3 Plot of the relative intensity of light from a small source with a flat surface. The relative intensities are proportional to the lengths of the lines radiating from the source.

ing zero (if it is truly flat) at the extreme sides. If the source is a true sphere, however, the intensities will obviously be the same at all angles. Actual sources vary irregularly with angle, and for most it is necessary to plot curves to describe the angular radiation distribution. Such a plot for a real source (still without reflector) is shown in Fig. 4·4.

This angular distribution of the radiation may be changed at will if the direction of some parts of the light is changed by reflectors or by other optical means such as lenses. It is worth while at this point, therefore, to consider the ways in which the direction of a beam of light may be changed if an object is placed in its path.

In general, only three things may happen to light in its course through space, and they can occur only when it encounters some material object. Light may be absorbed by the object; it may be transmitted, with or without change of direction; or it may be returned into space by reflection. In the first possibility it is converted into some other type of energy, usually heat. In the second, a change of path is produced according to well-defined laws known as the laws of refraction. In the third, a change of path is produced following the laws of reflection. Intensity relations in this possibility depend on the nature of both the surface and the light. All three effects are bases for independent branches of optical science, and

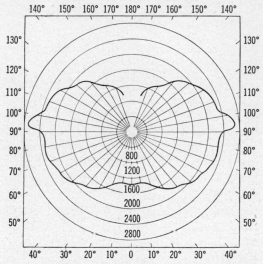

FIG. 4·4 Polar curve of relative intensity of light from a 1500-watt gas-filled lamp (without reflector). (C. Sylvester and T. E. Ritchie, *Modern Electrical Illumination*, p. 181, Longmans, Green and Co., London, 1927.)

their detailed consideration is outside the scope of this work. Certain of the simple principles involved, however, are fundamental to the present subject. The two latter effects will be considered in the present chapter. Absorption is the basic phenomenon of object color and will be considered separately.

Suppose light from a small source at some distance falls on a transparent medium such as a smooth piece of glass. The glass consists of a solid mass of material having the property of transmitting light, and this material is bounded by two surfaces. If these two surfaces are parallel to each other, as in window glass, for example, the path taken

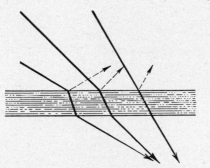

FIG. 4·5 Illustration showing the path of light rays through a piece of glass with parallel sides.

by the light in passing through it is illustrated in Fig. 4·5.

At the first surface there is a change in direction of the path of the light. After this first change the rays are again parallel, but in a different direction, until they encounter the second surface. At the second surface the direction is again changed as the rays pass out into the air, and the light progresses *parallel to its original direction* but displaced sideways by a certain amount, which depends largely on the thickness of the glass.

Two principles are involved in this illustration, and they apply to all instances in which light passes from one medium into another.

1. The direction of light is changed in crossing a boundary from one medium to another, except when the light falls on the surface perpendicularly.

2. The deviation produced on passage back into the first medium from the second

is always the same as the first, but in the opposite direction.

The second principle is important only because the most common instance is a transparent medium in air. The first principle is subject to certain very definite rules which may be stated in two parts. First, light passing through a smooth boundary at a given angle, *from* air into a substance of greater refractive index, is always bent toward the perpendicular to the surface; from a surface of the substance *into* air it is always bent away from the perpendicular by the same amount. The amount of this bending depends on the properties of the transparent medium. Second, the amount of bending depends on both the angle at which the light falls on the surface and the wavelength of that light.

More quantitatively, the rules are as follows:

1. The amount of bending produced at a surface depends on a property known as the "refractive index" of the material. This value is the ratio of the velocity of light in a vacuum to that in the medium. The refractive index of air is 1.000296, and for almost all practical purposes can be taken as equal to that of a vacuum, or one. A table of these values for a number of media is given in Fig. 4·6. Note that the value for ordinary glass is in the neighborhood of 1.3 to 1.6, and that optical glass varies from approximately 1.5 to 2.0.

2. The amount of bending is illustrated in Fig. 4·7. If the distance OB is equal to the distance OC, the ratio of AB to CD is equal to the index of refraction. If this latter value is called η, mathematically this may be expressed as $(\sin I)/(\sin R) = \eta$, where I is the angle of incidence to the perpendicular and R is the angle of refraction, again measured to the perpendicular. If the light falls on the surface perpendicularly,

AB, CD, I, and R are all zero and the light passes through unchanged in direction (although retarded slightly during its passage). The greater the angle at which the light

FIGURE 4·6

Jena O 225 Light phosphate ground glass	1.5159
Jena O 602 Baryt light flint glass	1.5676
Jena O 41 Heavy flint glass	1.7174
Jena S 57 Heaviest flint	1.9626
Rock salt	1.553399
Fluorite	1.43393
Opal	1.406–1.440
Canada balsam	1.530
Gelatin, Nelson's No. 1	1.530
Benzene	1.5012
Ethyl alcohol	1.3695
Water	1.3312

FIG. 4·6 Refractive indices of various substances to Sodium D line radiation. (Smithsonian Physical Tables.)

strikes (the more nearly parallel to the surface), the greater the bending of the light as it passes through.

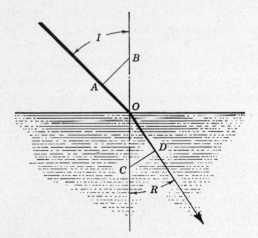

FIG. 4·7 Ray of light passing from air into medium of higher index of refraction.

3. The variation of the amount of bending with wavelength again depends on the nature of the material, and this property is called the "optical dispersion." This prop- erty varies widely with the nature of the material and need concern us here only because it is necessary to know that it does vary. In general, shorter wavelengths are deviated *more* than longer wavelengths, although this is not true for some unusual materials which have what is known as "anomalous dispersion."

4. If the smooth surfaces of the medium are *not* parallel to each other, as in a prism, the light does not return into the air parallel to its original course but leaves the second surface according to the law stated in paragraph 2. The dependence of the angle on wavelength produces an exaggerated separation of the wavelengths and gives rise to a spectrum from a narrow bundle of light. This is illustrated in Fig. 4·8.

5. If, instead of having smooth flat surfaces at an angle to each other, the two surfaces are curved (usually in spherical form), it is possible to make the light which originates at a point on one side of the material return to a point on the other side. The material then becomes a lens, and the result is shown in Fig. 4·9. Because the angular change of direction is different for each wavelength, there is a separation of wavelengths along a path perpendicular to such a lens, and the shorter wavelengths in general come to a "focus," as it is called, nearer the lens than the long wavelength light. This is called "chromatic aberration." In general it may be said that a single material with only two surfaces, as shown, does not bring the light from a single point back to a single point. The light from a series of points representing an actual object, therefore, does not build up a perfect reproduction of the points on the other side of the lens, unless great care has been taken to make it do so by consideration of all the properties of the lens. Improved reproduction usually involves using several kinds of

44

glass having a considerable number of surfaces. The interested reader is referred to the many excellent textbooks on lens optics

The first of these properties is that the further from the lens the point at which the light originates, the closer to the lens is the

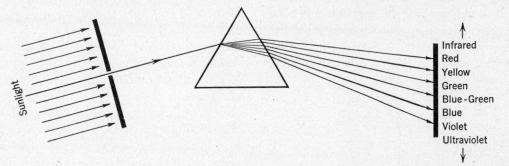

FIG. 4·8 Schematic diagram showing the dispersion of light by a glass prism, forming a spectrum.

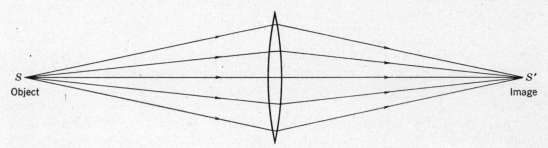

FIG. 4·9 Light rays from the point source S are refracted by the lens with spherically curved surfaces to converge at the image point S'.

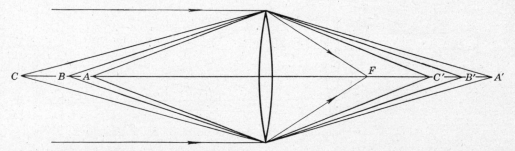

FIG. 4·10 The greater the object distance to the lens, the smaller the image distance. Light originating at point A is imaged at A'; B at B'; and C at C'.

if more information is desired. For present purposes it is necessary to note only a few properties of single lenses and to remember that unless great thought has been put into such lenses the rules are followed only approximately.

point at which the light is imaged. Three conditions are sketched in Fig. 4·10. There is a definite limit to this property, however, because no matter how far away the object is, the image does not come closer than a certain distance which is defined as the focal length of the lens (a property dependent on the material of the lens and the curvature of the surfaces). This condition is reached when the source is so far from the lens that all the light reaching the lens from any *point* of the source may be considered parallel. The second property is that the light from a source placed at this focal length distance

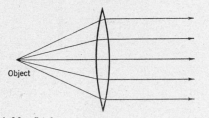

FIG. 4·11 Light originating at the focal point of the lens emerges from the lens as parallel rays.

leaves the lens in such a way that light from any *point* of the source emerges as a parallel bundle, as shown for one point of a source in Fig. 4·11.

These rules have so far been applied only to infinitely small sources with such objects lying on an imaginary line which passes

of extremely small areas of light, each giving off an infinitely great number of light rays. If the lens is perfect all the rays from any given point that strike the first surface of the lens and pass through it will converge at a point on the other side at a position relative to the optical axis and second lens surface which corresponds to the position of the original object point. The aggregate of the points of convergence of all the small object areas will be a reproduction of the original object, and when a white surface is held in the plane in which all the rays converge, the image of the object as formed by the lens is seen. The formation of an image by a lens is illustrated in Fig. 4·12. A ray emanating from any object point as shown in the figure will reach the image at a corresponding position.

It should be pointed out that the assumption that the lens is perfect is by no means a small one and that, when real lenses and objects of appreciable area are dealt with, other considerations are appropriate. These factors which are concerned with inherent

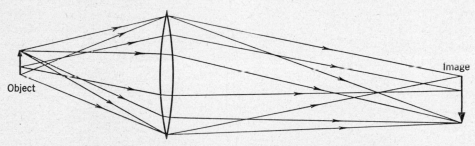

FIG. 4·12 Formation of the image of an object by a lens.

through the center of the lens in a direction perpendicular to its plane. This is a situation that is rarely attained in practice, and most of the objects which are reproduced by lenses have appreciable area. The fundamentals for such an object are the same, however, for any object may be thought of as being composed of a very large number

lens faults, their correction, and so on, have no place in this discussion, and it is sufficient to state merely that for uncorrected lenses, from the optical axis toward the edge of the object, the corresponding image reproduction will generally become increasingly worse and will be characterized by distortion and out-of-focus appearances.

By means of properly calculated and shaped transparent surfaces, the light from a source may be changed so that it will have almost any desired properties, as far as the angular distribution of intensity is concerned. Lenses used in this manner are called "condenser" lenses, because they condense the light falling on the lens along certain definite directions. They are of great use in equipment such as motion-picture projectors, in which much light must be made to pass through a small picture, and in spotlights, in which it is desired to get much light in a small area on the subject. It will be seen also in a moment that their use makes possible the imitation of light sources at distances different from those of the actual source. All such condenser systems, however, have the limitation that they cannot concentrate at a given spot more light than falls on the back of the lens. If the light source is larger than a point, the intensity imaged at a point is limited further by the formation of a definite image of the source which is itself larger than a point.

Concentration of light, however, is not the only change of direction which can be performed by transparent media. Light falling on a surface is always bent according to the laws of refraction. In the above lenses this property was used to concentrate the light. If the surfaces curve the other way, a lens will spread the light as shown in Fig. 4·13. Under these conditions the light acts as though it had originated at point *B* rather than A. It accordingly spreads in space more rapidly than it would from A and gives *less* illumination at a given distance from the lens. Such lenses are known as "diverging" lenses.

If the surface on which the light falls is *irregular*, the transmitted light will still follow these rules for each small area of the surface. If these areas are large and regular, a definite pattern of intensity will be set up in the light which passes through; but if the areas are small enough and oriented at random, the light emerging from the other side

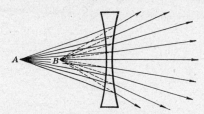

Fig. 4·13 Diagram illustrating the action of a double-concave lens.

will travel in all possible directions. A glass with such a surface is called a "diffuser." Glass whose surface has been sandblasted or ground with sand has this property; such glasses are frequently called "ground glass." A similar effect can be produced by the presence of small particles embedded in the glass. This is caused by deviation of the light by these particles.

REFLECTION

As mentioned earlier, light falling on a surface follows one of three courses. It

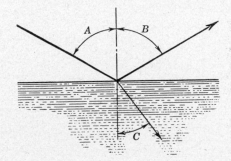

Fig. 4·14 Reflected and refracted light at a flat surface.

passes through, is absorbed inside, or returns directly to the medium from which it came. It is necessary now to consider this third possibility. This phenomenon also follows definite laws which are illustrated for a smooth surface in Fig. 4·14. In this figure the light falls on the surface from the left, making an angle A with the perpendicular to the surface. The law of *refraction* defined the ratio of angle A to the angle C for the transmitted light. The law of *reflection*

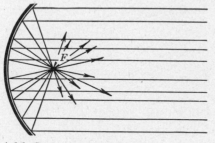

states that the reflection angle B is *always* equal to the angle of incidence A, regardless of the nature of the material or the wavelength of the light. The only requirement is that the area under consideration be *flat*. This very simple law gives rise to a number of possibilities, however, which are essentially identical with those of lenses. The more important may be summarized as follows.

1. Reflected light from a large smooth surface acts and looks as though it had come *through* the surface from behind.

2. By properly curving the surface, as shown in Fig. 4·15, it is possible to concen-

trate the light just as can be done with a lens.

3. If the surface is irregular the same two cases arise as for transmitting surfaces, i.e., the light may be thrown into a definite pattern or it may be *diffused* in all directions. The two cases are illustrated in Fig. 4·16.

By means of the phenomena of refraction and reflection, therefore, it is possible to modify the *directional* properties of light in any manner that we please, except that all modifications follow the principle that no more light may be diverted in a new direction than falls on the material from the source.

To illustrate the paths of light which have left such a modifying material, it is possible to draw a picture in which the intensity is represented by lines of varying lengths for the different directions. Such a picture for light passing *through* a material which has a number of small irregularities is shown in Fig. 4·17. For convenience, only a small beam of light is shown, but the action would be similar although it would be harder to draw for a larger beam. If the surface were

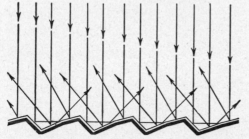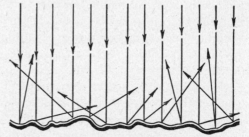

FIG. 4·16 Two surfaces, (a) giving rise to a pattern reflection, and (b) to random reflection.

reflecting rather than transmitting, the light would come from the front but the result would be unchanged. Similar distribution curves for materials which produce more and less diffusion are shown in Fig. 4·18. The first diagram shows what is known as a "complete diffusor," the circular diagram showing the intensity distribution when the tiny facets are at all possible angles. The second and third show the effects of decreasing amounts of diffusion. In these instances

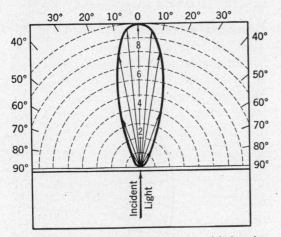

FIG. 4·17 Polar diagram of a beam of light after passing through clear glass, sandblasted on both sides. (M. Cohu, *Proceedings of the International Illumination Congress*, Vol. 1, p. 440, 1931.)

in direction" and is encountered in many usages such as "specular reflection," "specularity," and the like.

After this consideration of the fundamental properties of reflection and transmission, it is convenient to look at the subject of illumination from the somewhat different point of view of the source *plus* the reflector or lens and to consider the *combination* as a source of light.

It is apparent that the main effect of either a reflector or a lens is to alter the way the intensity of the light *changes* with distance. Condenser lenses concentrate the light from the front of the source into a much smaller path than would be the case without it, and the intensity change along this path is greatly decreased. If the light source is small and placed at the focus of the lens, there may be no appreciable change with distance over relatively great distances.

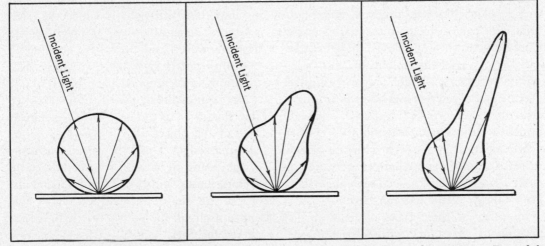

FIG. 4·18 Polar diagrams of light reflected from surfaces with various degrees of roughness. From left to right the surfaces decrease in roughness.

only a certain percentage of the light (portrayed by the bulges) is said to be diffused; the remainder is specularly transmitted or reflected as the case may be. The term "specular" used here means "without change

A typical example of such a combination is a theater spotlight. When this condition is reached, however, the width of the beam of light produced may not be much larger than the lens itself. For the theoretical case in which there is no appreciable change with distance, the beam would be exactly the size of the lens at all distances; and this condition is nearly met by some spotlights when they are set for maximum distances.

In exactly the same way, spherical or parabolic mirrors behind light sources can concentrate the light from the back of a source into a beam of light which is projected ahead. With parabolic reflectors and small light sources such as carbon arcs, very accurately aligned beams of light may be projected which do not decrease greatly in intensities over distances measured in miles. The best-known example is probably the anti-aircraft searchlight, but on a smaller scale a focusing flashlight properly adjusted may be made to project its beam surprisingly great distances. As in the case of lenses, of course, a beam set for maximum distance is nearly identical in diameter with that of the reflector. Since large reflectors are easier to make than large lenses, such searchlights are nearly always of the reflector type.

In either of these types of light, if the position of the source with respect to the lens or reflector is changed, the beam may be made to increase, decrease, or remain the same with distance. By the use of diffusing or semi-diffusing materials over the front of the light, the distribution may be changed still further. All these conditions are used, especially by the professional photographer, to control the quality of his light. (See Fig. 4·19.)

LIGHT SOURCES AND SHADOWS

Any way a beam of light changes its intensity with distance from the source modifies the angular relations of the various parts of the beam to each other. For the intensity relations which are involved when the beam strikes a flat diffusing surface, this

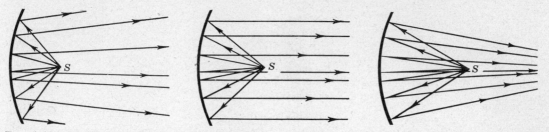

Fig. 4·19 Diagram showing the effect on the light beam reflected from a curved surface as the position of the source is changed.

angular relationship does not matter. There are important situations in which the effect produced depends on this property of the beam, however, and this phase of illumination must not be overlooked. One of these situations is exemplified if an object stands in the path of the light and throws a noticeable shadow. In this case both the appearance of the object and of the shadow may vary markedly. Since the angular relations in the beam are controlled not only by reflectors, lenses, and the like but depend also on the size, shape, and position of the light source itself, all the possibilities may be considered together.

If a light source without lens or reflector is placed near a circular opening in a large piece of opaque material, the amount of light which passes through the opening depends on the distance to the opening (or "aperture," as it is usually called) and on its size. The beam of light passing through spreads out beyond it in a cone-shaped beam, the edges of which are determined by lines drawn from the source through the edges. Suppose now a receiving screen is placed beyond, and then moved back and forth. It is apparent that for such an opening there will be a circular spot of light on the screen which will vary in size with the distance between the two; it will be larger the greater the separation. A similar effect

change in distance is small compared to the total distance.

Exactly the same phenomena are found if, instead of an aperture in a large screen, a round disk of opaque material is placed in a beam of light. Such a disk throws a shadow on the receiving screen. The shape of this shadow and the changes in its size with distance from the source and to the screen follow exactly the same rules as the

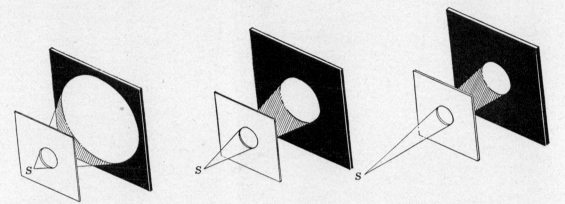

Fig. 4·20 Diagram showing the effect of the source distance on a light beam through a circular aperture.

is produced by moving the aperture and leaving the receiving screen stationary. The angle which the beam makes on passing through the aperture, that is, the rate at which the beam spreads out beyond the aperture, depends on the distance to the source. This is illustrated in Fig. 4·20, where small, medium, and great distances are illustrated. This angle in turn regulates the rate at which the size of the spot of light changes with the distance between the opening and the receiving screen. In the limiting case of a source at a great distance there is no appreciable change in size of spot over considerable distances, and the intensity also remains approximately constant (to the same extent as the size). This is the case with sunlight, for example. The inverse square law is still obeyed, but the

spot formed by the aperture. Cases similar to those illustrated for the aperture in Fig. 4·20 are shown for a triangular disk in Fig. 4·21.

The illustrations of Figs. 4·20 and 4·21 are for small light sources. With such sources the shadows produced are fairly sharp at the edges. If the size of the source is appreciable, however, the edges of such shadows are not sharp, and the larger the source relative to the distance the less sharp the edges will be. The principle is schematically illustrated in Fig. 4·22 for three different sizes of light sources. It is seen that the shadow consists of two parts, a very dark region called the "umbra" and a partially illuminated region called the "penumbra." The umbra is that portion which is completely shadowed, whereas the penumbra is only partially shadowed. The intensity of the illumination in the penumbra gradually falls off from the maximum to zero as one goes from its outer edge to the outer edge

everyday life, however, show that the effect of the size of the source on the edge of a shadow is actually surprisingly great, and Fig. 4·23 shows normal-size photographs of

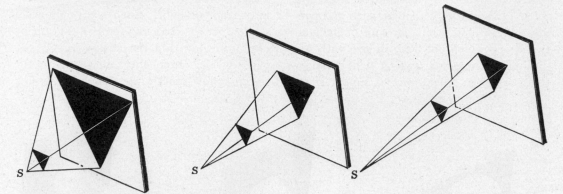

FIG. 4·21 Diagram showing the effect on shadow size of the distance between the source and the object casting the shadow.

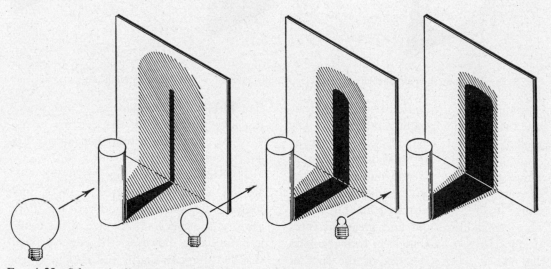

FIG. 4·22 Schematic diagram showing how the distribution of light throughout a shadow changes as the size of the source changes.

of the umbra. The relative size of the penumbra has been shown here only as a function of the size of the source, but it is obvious that it also depends on the distances involved.

The schematic diagram of Fig. 4·22 by necessity is exaggerated. Examples from

the edges of shadows thrown by the sources indicated.

It would seem from geometrical considerations alone that with a small source at a great distance it would be possible to make a critically sharp shadow, even though the object were some distance from the screen.

This is not quite the case, however. Even though the light were to strike the edge of the object in an exactly parallel beam, there would be a very small amount of illumination behind the object due to a phenomenon known as "diffraction," and the shadow edge would still grade off over an appreciable distance. Over short distances this effect is negligible, but if an attempt is made to "throw" a shadow very far it becomes distinctly noticeable.

Shadows, therefore, vary characteristically with the size and distance of the source. From the appearance of the edge illumination gradient and the size and position of the shadow, the nature of the source may be inferred. This inference is always based upon experience and is largely unconscious, but surprisingly strong. Figure 4·24, for example, shows the same object with four types of source as indicated. In most, if not all the cases, the title is hardly neces-

(a)

(b)

(c)

Fig. 4·23 Objects and their shadows with illumination from (a) sunlight, (b) near-by lamp bulb, and (c) overcast sky.

sary. The source, so to speak, can be "felt" from the picture.

In speaking of light sources so far, consideration has been given to the rate of light begins. When light falls on a diffusely reflecting (or transmitting) surface, however, light is scattered in all directions, and this *surface* may be considered as a new source

(a)   (b)

(c)   (d)

FIG. 4·24 Objects and their shadows with illumination from (a) sunlight coming through office window, (b) two lamps, one with reflector and one without reflector, (c) lamp with no reflector, and (d) lamp behind cardboard containing hole ¼ inch in diameter (photograph taken in room with considerable diffuse illumination).

change of intensity of the light with distance and to the size and edge characteristics of the shadows produced. The sources themselves, however, have been entirely what is known as "primary" sources, that is, they have been the materials from which the of light and treated as such. In many cases this is the most significant method of considering such a surface. When the light reaching a particular object is to be evaluated, the light reaching it from all the reflecting surfaces in its neighborhood has to

PLATE I

The nature of the light source affects the appearance of object surfaces.
At top, a small concentrated source gives a glossy finish; center, large diffuse source, satin effects; bottom, diffuse and uniform lighting, a dull and
opaque appearance.

be taken into account. Such light is very frequently of higher intensity, and perhaps of an entirely different quality, from the direct light from "primary" sources, mostly because the illumination from large sources decreases quite slowly with distance. In a room with light-colored walls, for example, a lamp which illuminates the wall to a moderately high intensity may give little direct

Fig. 4·25 Object and its shadow with diffuse reflections from flat wall serving as the source of illumination.

illumination in the middle of the room, whereas the light reflected from the wall may be of nearly the same intensity as it is quite close to the wall. Shadows produced by the light from such a wall are also characteristically "fuzzy" and may determine to a very large extent the appearance of the illumination on any object. Photographs of shadows produced by such a wall are shown in Fig. 4·25.

PERCEPTION OF ILLUMINATION

This discussion of the geometry and the intensity of illumination leads to two important concepts with respect to illumination which can be stated here but must await the development of the subject of perception in later chapters for broader treatment.

When an object or a large collection of objects (as in a landscape) is viewed by an observer, there is, first, a recognition of the objects in the scene. In addition, however, there is a general "feeling" or perception of the illumination on the scene as such. The two responses to the source are closely connected with each other because we both see the objects in their characteristic appearance under the given illumination and simultaneously "see" the illumination as falling on the objects which we recognize. This simultaneous vision of both phases is produced to a large extent by the phenomena discussed above. The two main factors are the "illumination ratios" of various parts of the scene and characteristics of the shadows in and around the objects.

In a landscape there are two main sources of light, the sun and the sky, although this statement hardly does justice to the multitude of effects which the two may produce. It is, perhaps, more accurate to say that illumination in daylight may vary from that of a single source covering the whole sky (overcast day) to that of a single source subtending a very narrow angle (the sun, whose angle is ½ ° at the earth). In between are all possible combinations due to sunlighted clouds in any part of the sky. All these possible conditions, however, have one characteristic in common. In each, the sources are so far from the earth that the *intensity* does not vary appreciably with distance. Illuminations, therefore, are everywhere the same, except where some object is casting a shadow.

The net result in nature is that under a given set of conditions all shadows which are illuminated by the same amount of sky have the same intensities. All the shadows also have the same size relative to the object.

These characteristics have come to be associated directly with nature, and when a setting meets these requirements, daylight is inferred. When an attempt is made, however, to imitate the effect on a large scale by artificial lighting, it is found to be practically impossible, although it can be and is done on a small scale when occasion demands.

The term "illumination ratio" used above may be defined as the ratio of the intensity of the light in those parts of the scene reached directly by the sun to those of the principal shadows. This ratio may vary from exceedingly high values for sunlight coming through a small aperture in a dense forest to unity on a day when the sky is completely overcast and no shadows are being produced.

In artificial lighting there are, in addition to the above factors, the change of intensity of the illumination with distance from the source and the variation of size and edge gradient of the shadows with distance. It is these factors which make an artificially lighted scene characteristically different from daylight. From the illumination standpoint they introduce the concept of "illumination gradients" into the scene in addition to the concept of "illumination ratio."

The combination of all these factors determines the appearance of the scene as a whole and of the objects in the scene. When an attempt is made to describe the visual effect produced in an observer, two words are commonly used; it may be well to consider their meaning more closely, although they have both been mentioned earlier. The first of these is "contrast." As with so many words, it is used in two allied but quite different senses. Every subject consists of a series of different reflectances, and the light reaching the eye varies with these reflectances. Thus, if the deepest black in a subject reflects 1 percent of the light to the eye and the lightest part similarly reflects 90 percent, *when*

these are uniformly illuminated to the same intensity, the contrast of the intensities may be properly defined as 90 to 1. This may be called the "object contrast." Suppose, however, that this object is a checkerboard composed of white and black squares and that a shadow falls over half of it. Suppose, also, that the illumination in this shadow is one-fourth of that falling on the rest of the board. In this *shadow* the light reaching the eye from the blacks is only one-quarter of that from the blacks on the other side of the board. Accordingly, it is one-quarter of 1 percent of the light *falling on the bright side*. The total ratio of intensities reaching the eye is now 90 times 4, or 360 to 1. This may be called the "subject contrast." Since the ratio of the illuminations producing this subject contrast is 4 to 1, this ratio may be spoken of as the "illumination contrast." There are, therefore, three ways of considering contrast, and it is essential in any discussion of the matter to keep the three as distinct as possible. Throughout the rest of this book this terminology will be used, but the reader is warned that no such clear-cut distinction exists in the general literature.

Contrast enters into many phases of color work, and there are many references to it in later chapters. An earlier reference, however, may usefully be repeated at this point since it may be somewhat clarified by the present discussion. The appearance of a scene which is best described by the term "brilliance" is largely determined by the subject contrast. Brilliance is a complex visual reaction to the total light intensity range visible to the eye from a given scene. Accompanying this reaction (and to a great extent part of it) is the unconscious estimation by the observer of both the total *illumination* intensity and the proportion of this light which reaches his eye. *Both* of these are determined in large measure by the *contrasts* of the scene rather than by the *actual* intensities. It will be found later that the eye is largely a "null" instrument indicating "more" and "less" quite accurately, but indicating total quantity of light rather inaccurately. An automobile headlight at night can give as adequate and as painful an impression of intensity as the sun at noon, and properly lighted stage sets can appear to cover the brightness range of both daylight and artificial light.

The eye, therefore, cannot be used as an adequate meter for illumination intensities. In the chapter on brightness perception it will also be shown that the eye cannot be used to judge accurately either illumination gradient or illumination contrast. In order to know definitely what illumination exists on a given scene only two accurate methods are known, both of them involving physical measurements. Either the light must be measured with some instrument not involving the eye, or each of the individual areas must be compared directly (with exclusion of everything else) with a known light source under conditions in which the two may be made to appear equal. The techniques which have been developed to accomplish such measurements and the factors involved are exceedingly numerous. Discussions of them may be found in the books listed in the bibliography which follows.

BIBLIOGRAPHY

Cady, Francis E., and Dates, Henry B. *Illuminating Engineering*, 2nd ed. New York: John Wiley and Sons, Inc. 1928. Chapters V and XIV.

Moon, Parry. *The Scientific Basis of Illuminating Engineering*. New York: McGraw-Hill Book Co., Inc. 1936. Chapters IV, V, and VI.

Sears, Francis Weston. *Principles of Physics III —Optics*, 2nd ed. Cambridge, Mass.: Addison-Wesley Press, Inc. 1946. Chapters II, III, V, and VII.

Wood, Robert W. *Physical Optics*, 3rd ed. New York: The Macmillan Co. 1934. Chapters II, III, IV, V, VI, and VII.

Wright, W. D. *The Measurement of Colour*. London: Adam Hilger, Ltd. 1944. Chapter I.

Colored Objects

CHAPTER V

SO far only light whose spectral-energy distribution is determined by the source has been considered. The modifications have been of types which do not change its energy distribution. Such modification by reflection or transmission is called "non-selective," since its action is not selective with wavelength. Only the direction and the amount of the light are changed, whereas the *relative* amounts of energy at the different wavelengths do not change.

SELECTIVE ABSORPTION

Actually, such non-selective action is relatively rare. Almost all materials absorb some of the light which falls on them and have some selective action since they absorb more at some wavelengths than at others. The net result of this absorption is that the light that *leaves* the material has a different energy distribution from the light that falls on it. In some cases this difference is slight, and in others it may be very great; but, in all cases in which there is no re-emission of the light by processes such as fluorescence, the change is necessarily one of a *decrease* of the amount of light in some regions of the spectrum compared to the others. Since the light absorbed must come from the light falling on the object, the process may be thought of as a subtraction of energy from this light. Accordingly, the action is often referred to as "subtractive," and a surface which produces such a change in energy distribution is called a "subtractive-color" surface.

When an observer looks at the light from such a surface and compares it with the light from the source, he sees in general that there has been a change in color. Both the extent of this change and the actual color which will be perceived depend to a large extent on the circumstances, as well as on the actual selective action. It is customary and entirely reasonable, however, to refer to the change as due to the *color of the object* provided that this is defined as the color the object will appear to have *in daylight amidst familiar and usual surroundings.* Under other circumstances it is necessary to take into account the psychophysics and the psychology of the *situation* as well as the physics of the energy distributions themselves. In order to make a clear distinction between the effects which are due simply to the changes in energy distribution produced by the surface and those due to the observer, only the physics of colored objects will be considered in this chapter and the next. Later the effects of these on the observer will be introduced. This wide separation is introduced here because it is not generally understood what a large part the observer plays in the perception of color and because many writers imply effects due to the observer, when the result can be predicted directly by the changes in the energy distribution of the light. It is hoped that this wide separation may clarify the situation for some readers. It is again necessary to rely almost entirely on energy distribution curves for illustrations. The whole key to the solution of any color problem lies in a knowledge of what has happened to the relative energy distribution of the light, and for describing what has happened such curves are the only adequate means available. The necessity for this knowledge comes from a fact of vision that was mentioned earlier. *Two light sources having completely different energy distributions may look exactly alike to an observer and yet may produce entirely different colors if the light from them falls on the same object.* It is apparent that no description of these lights in terms of *colors* can ever explain the situation, but knowledge of the energy distributions involved may make it entirely obvious.

REFLECTION, ABSORPTION, AND TRANSMISSION

When light falls on any material, three things can occur. The energy is reflected, absorbed, or transmitted. Usually all three occur, but the *proportion of each is different at each wavelength.* Since it is one of the basic principles of physics that energy can neither be created nor destroyed but can only be transformed from one type to another, the above gives rise to what is sometimes known as the RAT law, $R + A + T = 1$; that is, the sum of the reflected, absorbed, and transmitted energies at each wavelength is always equal to that of the incident light. The sum of the fractional parts represented by each is always equal to 1. Since these fractions depend on the wavelength, however, the action of the material can be shown best by curves. In Fig.

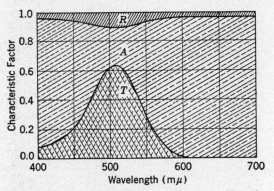

FIG. 5·1 Curves showing the reflectance (R), absorptance (A), and transmittance (T) of a substance dyed with a green dye.

5·1 is shown the distribution with wavelength of the three for a typical dye. Note that it is only the fractional distribution of the *action* of the dye that is shown. This action takes place in this manner *regardless* of the energy distribution of the light that may fall on it. It describes a fundamental property of the material which does not have anything to do with the nature of the incident light.

Although such a set of curves shows rather clearly just how such a material will act, it is frequently more convenient to plot the fractional effects separately as fractions or percentages at each wavelength. Such curves for the material of Fig. 5·1 are shown in Fig. 5·2. In any particular problem usually only one of the three needs to be considered since the problem may involve only the reflected light, and so on. It must always be kept in mind, however, that the rest of the light is distributed between *both* the others, and the reflectance curve does not indicate how much is absorbed, unless the amount being transmitted is known also.

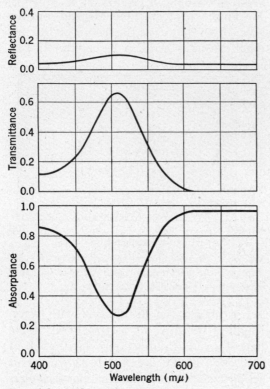

FIG. 5·2 Reflectance, transmittance, and absorptance curves of a green material.

Many materials such as colored glass, for example, do not reflect selectively, although they have selection absorption; the transmitted light from such materials is colored, but the reflected light is the same as that from the source. There are also some materials, notably the metals, in which the reflection is selective, but which in ordinary thicknesses do not transmit light at all. Between these come all possible combinations, and usually the actual cause of the color of an object is quite a complex affair.

Before we consider typical examples and the details of selective absorption in specific cases, a distinction must be made between the total effects of an object and its component parts. A simple example will make this clear and establish the basis for much that follows. It will be followed in some detail, and new principles will be established where necessary.

A SIMPLE COLORED OBJECT

Suppose we have a piece of dyed gelatin, such as is used over camera lenses and theater spotlights, or a thin sheet of colored glass.

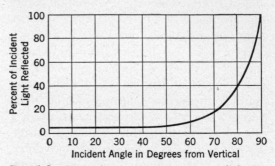

FIG. 5·3 Curve showing the percentage of the incident light reflected from the surface of a material with a refractive index of 1·5.

Such materials reflect non-selectively from their front surfaces but have selective transmission. This surface reflection, although it is non-selective, does vary in amount with the angle at which the light strikes the surface. If the light strikes perpendicularly, about 4 percent is reflected straight along the beam, and the rest of the light passes on through the surface. If the light strikes nearly parallel to the surface, i.e., it just grazes the surface, it is reflected nearly 100 percent and none passes through. Between these angles, the amount reflected increases from the minimum of 4 percent to the maximum. The percentage reflected is plotted against the angle in Fig. 5·3. The amount of light which will pass through the front surface, therefore, depends on the angle at which it strikes. Conversely, if we look at the surface, the amount of light which will reach the eye from the surface will depend on the direction or directions of the incident light. Whatever reaches the eye from this surface, however, will have the same relative energy distribution as the light source.

Now consider the light which passes through this first surface. If the material

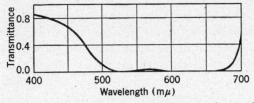

Fig. 5·4 Spectral transmittance of a purple signal glass.

is clear, there will be no deviation of the light other than the simple change of angle caused by refraction in crossing the surface, and it will pass straight through and out on the other side except to the extent that it is selectively absorbed in passage by the dyes it contains. It is fairly simple to measure the percentage change which is produced at each wavelength, and the transmittance curve for a piece of signal glass is shown in Fig. 5·4. This curve gives the percentage transmission of each wavelength region plotted against the wavelength. It may be thought of in another way also. Since percentage transmission is calculated at each wavelength and 100 percent would mean complete transmission with *no* absorption, this curve is also the relative energy distribution which would be passed by the layer if the light falling on the front had equal energy in each region.

Now suppose that instead of an equal energy source, the light falling on the filter is coming directly from an ordinary incan-

descent lamp bulb. The energy distribution of this light is shown in Fig. 5·5. It is seen that it has less than one-quarter as much energy at 450 mμ as at 700 mμ. What will this light be like after it passes through the layer? The transmittance curve of Fig. 5·4 is expressed in percentages passed at each wavelength. The light-source curve is ex-

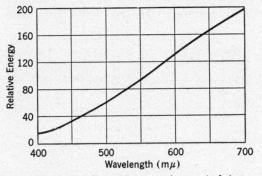

Fig. 5·5 Spectral distribution of a typical incandescent lamp.

pressed in terms of the relative *amounts present* at each wavelength. The final light passed at each wavelength will, accordingly, be the *percentages* shown in Fig. 5·4 of the *amounts* shown in Fig. 5·5. At wavelength 500 mμ, for example, the percentage passed is 10 percent, and the relative amount pres-

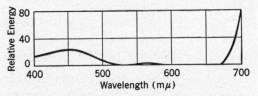

Fig. 5·6 Product curve of Figs. 5·4 and 5·5.

ent in the light is 60. Since 10 percent of 60 is 6.0, this is the relative amount in the light passed. The energy distribution for the whole spectrum obtained in this way is shown in Fig. 5·6. So far, then, the light non-selectively reflected from the outer surface is described by Fig. 5·5, and that transmitted is given by Fig. 5·6.

Now suppose that this filter is laid on a selectively reflecting surface. Suppose that the selective effect of this surface has been measured and can be represented by the percentage reflectance curve of Fig. 5·7. As before, this curve represents the percentage of the light at each wavelength which will be reflected regardless of the energy distribution of the light as a whole. The effect of this surface on the light that passes

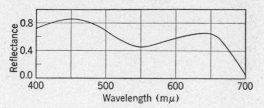

Fig. 5·7 Spectral reflectance curve of a selective surface.

through the filter, therefore, is identical in type with that of the filter itself, and the energy distribution of the light leaving the surface may be calculated as before by considering it one wavelength at a time. The resultant curve is shown in Fig. 5·8.

The filter, however, is in contact with this surface, and for the light to get out into the

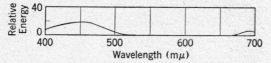

Fig. 5·8 Light of Fig. 5·6 reflected from the surface of Fig. 5·7.

air, so to speak, it must pass through the filter for a second time. The filter, of course, will act in exactly the same way this time as it did before, decreasing the light at each wavelength by the percentages indicated in Fig. 5·4. The light falling on the rear surface, however, is given by Fig. 5·8. As before, the light leaving the upper surface may be calculated and is found to be that given by Fig. 5·9.

Now suppose that an observer looks at this filter lying on the colored surface and illuminated by this light source. The light *reaching his eye* will be a *mixture* of the unchanged light reflected from the surface and the changed light which has twice passed through the filter and meanwhile has been reflected from a colored surface. The light he sees will be not only a mixture but also a mixture that changes in relation to his position with respect to the light source and in relation to the nature (such as size, shape, and position) of the light source itself. Suppose he stands in a position such that 10 percent of the light falling on the surface from the source reaches his eye unchanged. This part of the light is simple to calculate. The energy distribution is given by Fig. 5·5, and the intensity at any wavelength is one-tenth that of the incident light. Another part of the light, however, has been modified

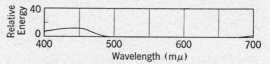

Fig. 5·9 Light of Fig. 5·8 after being transmitted through glass of Fig. 5·4.

three times. In order to calculate exactly how much of this reaches the eye, it would be necessary to know how much *would* reach the eye under the conditions if both the filter and the reflecting surface were not only non-selective but also 100 percent transmitting (i.e., non-absorbing) and reflecting, respectively. This amount would be that remaining after the subtraction from the original light of the amount reflected at the filter surface and the amount reflected in directions away from the eye by the material under the filter. This last value would depend on the directional characteristics of this surface (its diffusion curve). In any given instance it is practically necessary to *measure* the light given off in any particular direction because its calculation is so difficult. To illustrate the principle, let it be assumed that 50 percent of the light is effective in the direction toward the observer's eye. In other words, the surface seen through a colorless filter if the surface were white would be 5 times that reflected from the top of the filter.

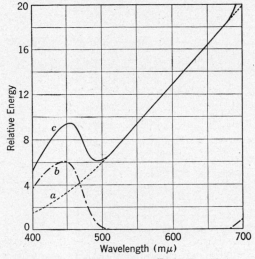

Fig. 5·10 Curves showing effect of addition of surface-reflected light and filtered light.

We return now to the energy distribution as shown in Fig. 5·9. Since only one-half of the light passing through the top surface is effective, this distribution must be divided by two at all wavelengths. We are now in position to consider the energy distribution of the actual light at the eye. At each wavelength the eye receives one-tenth of the light unchanged from the source and one-half of the value from Fig. 5·9. These values, although expressed in percentages, are now percentages of the same thing, i.e., the energy distribution of the source, and may be added directly as percentages. The two curves involved and the summation curve are shown in Fig. 5·10, the curves showing the relative amounts of light from the source

received at the eye (a) from the top, (b) from the bottom, and (c) from both.

It is seen that even in this relatively simple example the calculation is quite complex. For nearly all purposes, however, it is necessary to know only that this is the *way* the action is determined, to be able to predict the effects. For example, suppose we want to visualize what will happen if the observer moves his head. If he moves it so that a *higher* percentage is received from the top, the light will move toward the quality of the source. If he moves so that *less* of this is received relatively, the light will move

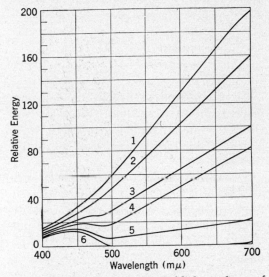

Fig. 5·11 Energy distributions of light made up of different proportions of specularly reflected and filtered light: (1) 100% reflected light, (2) 80% reflected plus 20% filtered light, (3) 50% reflected plus 50% filtered light, (4) 30% reflected plus 70% filtered light, (5) 10% reflected plus 90% filtered light, (6) 100% filtered light.

toward Fig. 5·9, and the source and this latter distribution will represent the two extremes possible at the eye. A series of curves showing the calculated change with varying relative percentages of the two is shown in Fig. 5·11. Furthermore, it is immediately known that changes in the shape and position of the light source would have the same effect, and this series of curves represents all *possible* energy distributions with which the light may leave the object.

SUBTRACTIVE VERSUS ADDITIVE EFFECTS

In addition, this example has illustrated a number of important principles. In the first place, when light strikes an object that has a selective action, whether of reflection, transmission, or absorption, there is a decrease in the relative amount of light in at least some wavelength regions. Furthermore, successive action of several such materials continues to decrease the light characteristically for each material. It has become customary to refer to such successive action as "subtractive mixture," the word *mixture* meaning a mixture of the *effects*. (The term may seem more reasonable if the reader will check for himself the fact that the *order* in which the materials occur does not affect the result.)

The second point brought out was that when lights of two different energy distributions reach the eye they are received as though they were a single light distribution which may be calculated by *adding* the two together. Such a combination of lights of two or more qualities is known as an "additive mixture."

All changes in energy distribution that light from a given source may undergo before it reaches the eye (or any other receptor) may be described as due to one or both of these types of action. They are, at times, exceedingly different in their effects, and, if one is not certain which type of action is involved in a particular case, a predicted result may not occur at all. As an example of what is meant, suppose there is a filter having the curve shown in Fig. 5·12. In normal daylight this would appear deep red.

Suppose this is held up to a sodium light source whose total visible energy is radiated at a position shown by the dotted vertical line of the figure and which normally appears yellow. If it were assumed that the effect would be the additive mixture of yellow and red, which would appear orange, it would be difficult to explain the fact that no light at all would be seen. If it is recognized as a purely subtractive effect, it is im-

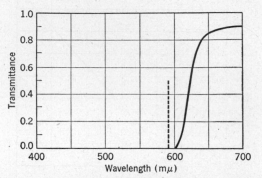

FIG. 5·12 Transmittance curve of a deep-red filter and a line showing the spectral location of the visible energy from the sodium arc.

mediately apparent that the filter does not pass any of the wavelengths that are present in the source and hence no light can get through. This example is particularly obvious, but many cases equally simple are not understood because of failure to consider the type of action involved.

Addition of a solution of one dye or pigment to that of another, as we shall see in a later chapter, may produce almost *any* color because the action is subtractive and depends entirely on the successive (or simultaneous) *subtraction* of energy from the light. That which is *not* subtracted gets through. Only when two *lights*, from whatever sources, are mixed is it possible to predict the final result from the *colors* of the lights. Subtractive action can be understood *only* by reference to the wavelength-by-wavelength action of each component.

It is now possible to consider a number of other means by which selective action may take place and to point out the extent to which they lead to additive or subtractive results. One of the most common phenomena encountered in nature is the scattering of light; and while it does not always produce selective action, it is important because it is the cause of the blue of the sky. To a far lesser extent, it produces this same blue color under conditions in which it may not be expected.

When light passes through a medium that contains large numbers of exceedingly fine particles, the direction of the light that strikes each particle is somewhat changed. If the diameters of the particles are many times as large as a single wavelength of the light, there is only this change in direction and nothing more. The action is then described as "diffusion," and the action is nonselective. There are a number of semi-quantitative terms used to describe the amount of this diffusion: transparent, cloudy, turbid, translucent, semi-opaque, and opaque are fairly familiar and form a continuous series from zero to such a high value of non-selective diffusion that no light leaves the medium. However, if these same particles are reduced in size until their diameters become approximately the same size as a wavelength of light, "scattering" takes place rather than diffusion, and this action is selective with wavelength. Scattering is due to the phenomenon of "diffraction" and may be visualized as a bending of the light around the particles rather than reflection from their surfaces. This scattering follows the well-known Rayleigh law, which states that the amount of light scattered in any direction varies inversely as the fourth power of the wavelength. In effect this means that more short wavelengths are scattered

than long ones; often the long wavelengths are hardly scattered at all. Since under normal conditions the short wavelengths appear blue and the long wavelengths appear red, the light *transmitted* by such a medium is changed toward the red, and the *scattered* light seen from the side becomes quite blue. The blue of the sky is due to this Rayleigh scattering, as it is sometimes called, of the light from the sun.

This scattering effect is also the cause of the blueness of distant haze and the comparative redness of *bright* objects that are seen through distant haze or through fog. A somewhat less familiar, but quite startling, example may sometimes be found in white glasses such as are used for cooking utensils. When these are held up to a bright light such as the sun, they are seen to be a deep ruby red, although the scattered blue is hardly in evidence. Scattering is also the reason for the distinct blue color of diluted milk and a host of other phenomena. Whenever an object appears bluish by reflected light—particularly if viewed perpendicular to the path of the incident light—and brown or red by transmitted light, the presence of scattering may be assumed, or at least suspected.

Selective scattering may be produced also, under some conditions, by particles which are much too large to cause diffraction effects. An interesting example of this type is afforded by the so-called "Christensen filter." This filter consists of small colorless particles such as colorless glass beads, immersed in a colorless liquid. When a parallel beam of light passes through such a system, selective transmission takes place. The action may be explained as follows.

It was noted earlier that reflection from a polished surface occurs in such a way that the angle made by the reflected beam is equal to that of the incident light. Light falling on a small sphere, therefore, is reflected off in all directions, i.e., scattered (Fig. 5·13). The amount of this reflection depends on the angle at which it strikes the surface as was shown in Fig. 5·3. The remainder of the light passes through the surface into the material. The amount for any given angle depends on the index of refraction of the material itself and of the medium outside the surface. Figure 5·3 was given for polished glass (index of 1.5) in air.

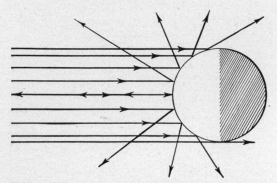

Fig. 5·13 Schematic diagram illustrating reflection from a sphere.

The law that this reflection follows states that the percentage reflected will be greater, the greater the angle between the light and the perpendicular to the surface, and the greater the ratio of the two indices of refraction. For most types of glass in air this ratio is usually about 1 to 1.5. The index of refraction for all materials, however, varies with the wavelength, and the property is called the "dispersion" of the material. Curves showing the index, plotted against wavelength for a number of different media, are given in Fig. 5·14. It is seen that it is possible to find a liquid medium, such as carbon disulfide, and another solid, such as one of the glasses, both of which have the same index at one wavelength only. If beads of this glass are placed in the liquid, and a beam of light is directed toward the combination, there will be no reflection at the wavelength where the two indices are

equal, but there will be increasingly high reflectance for the regions in which they are different. The light transmitted by such a combination, therefore, consists of a rela-

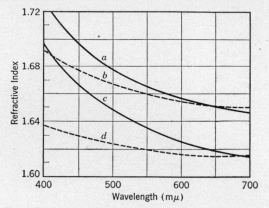

Fig. 5·14 Dispersion curves of highly refractive liquids and solids; (a) l-bromonapthalene, (b) dense flint glass, (c) carbon disulfide, and (d) barium flint glass.

tively narrow region of wavelengths, and almost all the remaining light is reflected out of the beam. Transmission curves for a series of such filters are shown in Fig. 5·15.

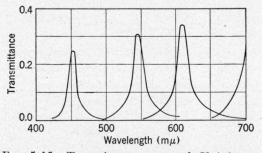

Fig. 5·15 Transmittance curves of Christianson filters consisting of borosilicate crown glass particles immersed in a benzene-carbon disulfide mixture of differing proportions. (E. D. McAlister, *Smithsonian Misc. Collections*, Vol. 93, No. 7, p. 4.)

This effect sometimes plays a large role in the action of pigments and the like when they are ground up in oil or other media, the amount of light reflected from the par-

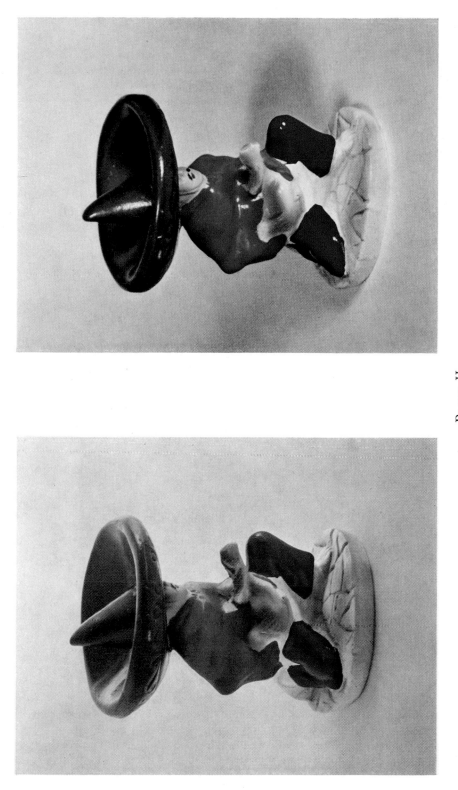

PLATE II

The nature of the lighting affects the saturations of object colors. (*Left*) In this illustration, the lighting is diffuse, giving desaturated colors. (*Right*) The light is directional and gives colors of higher saturation.

ticles being determined by their relative indices.

Selective reflection takes place also at the surface of a metal. Curves are given in Fig. 5·16 for some of the common metals and graphite, but it must be kept in mind that many of these change considerably if

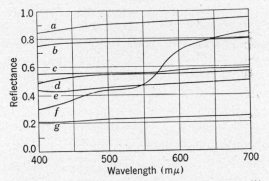

FIG. 5·16 Reflectance curves for: (a) silver, (b) aluminum, (c) steel, (d) chromium, (e) molybdenum, (f) copper, and (g) graphite.

the surface is not clean and highly polished. The presence of a thin oxide coating over the surface may change the color of the reflected light and even introduce new colors. This is particularly noticeable in brass and copper. All the curves given are for clear surfaces.

Most of the customary surfaces other than the metals do not reflect selectively. Such surfaces as glass, oil paints, varnishes, and polished woods reflect in all situations a certain percentage of the light unchanged. Only the part that passes through the outer surface and is reflected again is altered in its energy distribution and therefore changed in color. Some materials that are not metals do show such selective surface reflection, however, and these materials are said for this reason to show "metallic reflection." It is interesting to note in passing why some

materials do and others do not reflect selectively. As already stated, the amount of reflection depends rather markedly on the index of refraction. It was pointed out also that the index of refraction varies with the wavelength of the light considered. When these two statements are taken together, it is apparent that all surfaces should show at least some selective action. The amount of difference with wavelength for ordinary materials, however, is too small to consider, and for all practical purposes we can say there is no selective action unless something is done to make the situation more critical, as in the Christensen filters. Metals have exceedingly high indices of refraction, and the reflection differences with wavelength are accordingly very large so that distinct selective action is shown, especially by copper and gold. There are a few other materials, however, in which the index changes rapidly enough, so that they show the same effect. Whenever a material absorbs light of some wavelengths very much more strongly than others, that is, when it has what is known as an "absorption band" at some region of the spectrum, the index of refraction changes abruptly in this region. If the change is great enough, light in this region will be reflected very much more strongly than in the rest of the spectrum. This is true of many dyes in the solid state. The dye fuschine, for example, absorbs very strongly in the green region of the spectrum and in the solid state appears a brilliant green by reflected light. In former years we frequently encountered blue printing inks that were red by reflected light, and so on. The phenomenon is relatively rare aside from the metals and such dyes, however, and usually reflection from the top surface of an object does not affect the energy distribution appreciably.

For the sake of completeness it should be noted that there are three other ways in which energy distributions may be changed that do not involve selective absorption or reflection. They are "refraction," "diffraction," and "interference." Refraction, the bending of light at a surface by different amounts depending on the wavelength, is the cause of the formation of spectra by prisms, considered in Chapter II. By refraction also colors are produced by diamonds and similar cut stones; they are simply small spectra of high intensity which happen to strike the eye so that only one wavelength region is seen. Refraction, of course, is involved also in the production of a visible spectrum by raindrops in the rainbow. Diffraction, the bending of light around the edge of an object, also can produce changes other than those of selective scattering. An explanation of the mechanism by which this effect produces color is outside the scope of this book, as is that of the interference colors to be described next, but the *phenomena* involved in both may be described as follows. It is convenient to consider interference first.

Light may be considered to be a series of waves traveling at high velocity outward in all directions from a source. Suppose that a source gives off light at only one wavelength and that there is another source *exactly* like it which can be moved with respect to the first. A wave consists of the maximum displacement first in one direction and then in the opposite. These series of displacements repeat each other at a rate equal to the frequency of the wave. If the light from both sources arrives at a point in space so that displacements in the same direction coincide, the displacements will be much greater than they would be from only

one of the sources. The intensity at the point would be greatly increased. If, however, one light source is moved so that the maximum displacement in one direction arrives at the point from one source at the same time as the maximum displacement in the opposite direction arrives from the other, the two waves will cancel each other. Instead of increasing the intensity, there will be no light at all at the point. In principle the phenomenon of interference occurs when two beams of light cancel each other either wholly or partially so that the wave motion ceases to exist. It is apparent that very special conditions must be met before such an effect can produce a visible change in white light, since white light consists of all possible wavelengths over a range of nearly an octave. These conditions are met, however, in a number of familiar instances and are the basis for many scientific instruments.

If a large number of parallel lines (sometimes as many as 40,000 per inch) are scratched into the surface of a smooth transparent material and a beam of parallel light is allowed to fall on it, diffraction takes place at each scratch as the beam passes through. In effect the space between each scratch becomes a new linear light source. If a screen is now placed beyond this "grating," as it is called, a whole series of spectra are formed on this screen, each similar in nature to that formed by a prism. The cause of the spectrum formation is the varying distance from any point on the screen to the various light sources produced by the scratches. From any given point one wavelength region is intensified and all others are decreased or suppressed by interference. (The reader interested in the theory is referred to Sears, *Principles of Physics*, listed in the bibliography at the end of the chapter.) The spectra formed by such diffraction gratings have the interesting property that the spacing along their length is uniform with wavelength so that it is necessary to determine the wavelength accurately for only two points in the spectrum to be able to specify all positions with the same accuracy. This is not true of spectra from prisms and is a valuable property in optical instruments.

In nature a number of objects have a linear structure capable of producing such diffraction spectra and hence of showing brilliant colors which change with the position of the observer's head. Some forms of beetle wings and some butterfly wings appear to owe their iridescent colors to this effect, although as Michelson has shown many of them exhibit metallic reflection. Diffraction colors may be observed by looking at a light source through a feather, a thin piece of cloth, or almost anything that has a regular structure. It should be noted that although diffraction is the source of these modified energy distributions the actual effect is due to interference. For this reason exactly the same phenomena occur when the lines are scratched in a reflecting surface, the reflection at points between the scratches now taking the place of the diffraction.

A related but quite different class of effects is known as "interference colors." When a beam of light strikes a transparent medium, there is both reflection at the surface and transmission into it. Of the light entering the medium, part will be reflected from the rear surface. If the medium is thin, this part will be reflected out of the medium along a path effectively the same as that of the beam reflected from the front surface. If the thickness of the medium is such that a displacement of a half-wavelength (or any *odd* number of half-wavelengths) takes place, the two beams will cancel each other in the same manner as that described for diffraction patterns. If

the spacing is such that a reinforcement for one wavelength region takes place, this region only will be strongly reflected. When many such layers, equally spaced, are above each other this effect results in a strong reflection of a single wavelength. This appears to be the cause of the exceedingly brilliant colors of the fiery opal and of a number of other brilliantly colored crystals. (See R. W. Wood, *Physical Optics*, pp. 198–99.)

The list is complete of the six main phenomena which give rise to color by the selective modification of the energy distribution of light: reflection, absorption, transmission, diffraction, refraction, and interference. These are the physical causes of all changes in energy distribution of light when it has once left the source. In any given practical case the color produced is usually the result of several of these causes, and in some instances all may be present at once. The light resulting from the several effects gives the object its color, and it is apparent that in general this color depends on the direction in which the object is viewed as well as on the geometrical relationships (such as direction, size, and angle) of the source.

The most common type of colored surface—so common that it is almost possible to neglect all others—consists of a nonselective outer surface beneath which there are selectively absorbing materials and some means by which the light not absorbed is reflected through this surface. In general principle each is the same as the filter on the selective surface discussed at the beginning of the chapter. In detail any one may be very different, and a number of examples will be discussed in the next chapter. It is necessary to consider first several further effects which may take place below such an outer surface.

One of the very common differences among colored materials is the nature of the outer surface reflections. The change that is produced in a colored object, such as a piece of wood, if it is coated with varnish or wax is occasionally so startling that it is hard to believe that the coating has not produced some chemical change in the material. The cause of this change is the introduction of multiple reflections under the polished surface, accompanied by simultaneous elimination of a *diffusely* reflecting outer surface. The two can best be considered separately.

If the non-selective outer surface of a material consists of small elements at all angles, light falling on it is diffused by simple reflection, and this light is visible from all directions. Suppose, however, that such a surface is covered with a varnish or wax giving a new outer surface that is flat. If the coating material has an index of refraction approximately the same as that of the original surface, reflection from the diffusing material will be eliminated. Since the coating material is smooth it will reflect non-selectively but only in one direction. Unless the eye is placed so that it sees the reflection, there will be *no* light from the surface and the colored light from below will not be diluted. Since such diffuse surfaces sometimes reflect as much as 50 percent of the incident light, it is apparent that this alone may make a large difference in the quality of the light reaching the eye. Schematic curves for such an illustration are shown in Fig. 5·17.

In addition to this elimination of surface diffusion there is an added effect due to the reflection of light downward from the under side of the new outer surface. In Fig. 5·18 are traced some of the components of a ray of light striking a diffusing surface cov-

ered by such a layer. Light passing through the outer surface strikes the inner one and after selective absorption is diffused in all directions. Part of this light is reflected

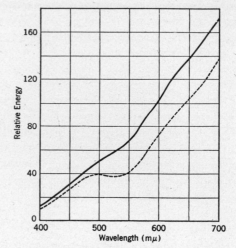

FIG. 5·17 Curves showing the effect of varnish on a diffusing, selective surface. The solid curve represents reflected-light quality before varnishing and the broken after varnishing.

downward and is again selectively absorbed and diffusely reflected, and part of this is again reflected downward. This process of multiple reflection, as it is called, greatly

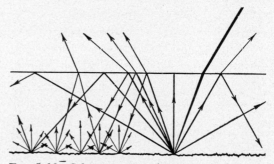

FIG. 5·18 Schematic diagram showing what happens to a ray of light striking a diffusing surface covered by a thin coat of varnish or wax.

intensifies the selective action of the colored material. Energy-distribution curves for the first six multiple reflections from a colored surface are shown in Fig. 5·19. It is apparent that the light quality at the last reflection is much more nearly restricted to a single region than it was at the first reflection. What the eye actually sees is the additive mixture of a fraction of each of these reflections, and the fraction is determined by the amount that passes through the surface each time.

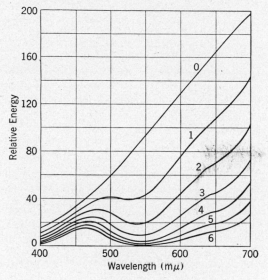

FIG. 5·19 Curves showing quality of light from an incandescent lamp after successive reflections from a selective surface. The graph numerals denote the number of reflections that the light has had.

If the overcoating surface itself is colored there is still further intensification of the color. Since consideration of how such a surface acts forms a good introduction to the effect of the thickness of a transmitting layer, it will be considered in some detail. Suppose in the above example 25 percent of the light diffusely reflected from the bottom is reflected down again from the top and suppose the layer is selectively absorbing but the bottom diffuser is non-selective. These suppositions would be equivalent to painting a colored transparent layer over a white diffuse surface. Each time the light passed through the layer there would be selective absorption. Suppose the transmittance curve is that shown in Fig. 5·20. Each time the light goes up to the smooth surface and down again it passes through this layer twice, and at each passage the percentages indicated are transmitted. Curves for the sec-

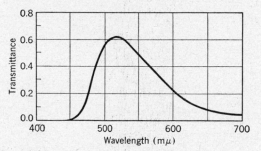

FIG. 5·20 Transmittance curve for a colored transparent layer.

ond, fourth, and eighth passages are shown in Fig. 5·21. If 25 percent is internally reflected from the top surface each time, 25 percent, or one-fourth, will undergo two passages; $\frac{1}{4} \times \frac{1}{4}$ or $\frac{1}{16}$ will undergo four;

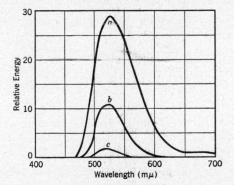

FIG. 5·21 Relative energy of light from an incandescent lamp after it has passed through the selective filter: (a) two times, (b) four times, and (c) eight times.

$\frac{1}{16} \times \frac{1}{4}$ or $\frac{1}{64}$ will undergo six, and so forth. The sum of the first four double passages are shown in Fig. 5·22, and the dotted line shows the effect of a single passage down and back, drawn to a similar scale for comparison. Visually the effect is a considerable deepening of the color compared with the simple doubling of the absorption which would be given by a smooth undersurface. This effect does not take place, incidentally, if there is an air space between the colored layer and the diffusing surface, as was discussed for the filter lying on the surface. The reason for this failure involves a concept known as the "critical reflection angle."

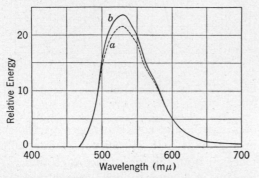

FIG. 5·22 Curves showing the effect of partial multiple transmission through a selective layer: (a) single reflection and (b) combined effect of first four reflections.

When light falls on a smooth surface, the part which passes through is bent toward the perpendicular if the first medium has a lower index of refraction than the second but away from the perpendicular if the first medium has a higher index. Since air has a very low index of refraction (practically equal to that of a vacuum), light approaching any surface from air can always enter, even if for large angles the percentage reflected may be high. Approaching the surface from a material of higher index, however, this is no longer true. At a certain angle the light which passes out is bent so far from the perpendicular that it leaves parallel to the surface, and any light which approaches at a greater angle is totally reflected into the medium. The situation is illustrated in Fig. 5·23. Light entering a

layer with air on both sides, therefore, is transmitted much more freely and with fewer internal reflections than it is transmitted if there is only one air surface. This is particularly true if the lower surface is

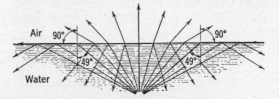

FIG. 5·23 Diagram illustrating the phenomena of total reflection. At an angle of incidence from water to air greater than 49° all light emanating from the source is reflected back into the water.

diffusing since in that event, even if the light enters in a parallel beam, it is reflected to the upper surface at all possible angles. When two surfaces are in close contact with no space between them, they are said to be in "optical contact," and light reflected out from a transparent surface making optical contact with a lower one is quite different from that which is obtained if the two surfaces do not make such contact.

LAWS OF BOUGUER AND BEER

We are now in position to consider what happens when the thickness of a selectively absorbing (but not diffusing) transparent layer is changed. Suppose two layers, one of which is four times as thick as the other but made of identical materials. A single colored gelatin filter compared with four of them in optical contact will serve as an example. In Fig. 5·24 are shown the transmittance curves for the single layer and for the four layers. The curve for the thicker one may be derived from that of the thinner as follows. At wavelength 526 mμ the transmission is 50 percent. This means that $\frac{1}{2}$ the light is transmitted at this wavelength. The same intensity reduction will take place for each layer. For four layers this would be ½ of ½ of ½ of ½. This equals $\frac{1}{16}$ of the original light. Expressed mathematically this is $(\frac{1}{2})^4$. More generally, if the transmission at any wavelength is T and the thickness is n times that of a single layer, the transmission for that wavelength equals T^n, i.e., T multiplied by itself n times. This

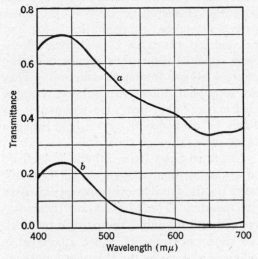

FIG. 5·24 Transmittance curves of (a) one thickness of a substance and (b) four thicknesses of the same substance.

is known as Bouguer's law.* It may be expressed in words by saying that the effect of changing the thickness of a colored transparent layer is the same as if it passed through the equivalent number of thin layers in optical contact. It is important to notice that this law means that a thick layer of a colored material may not have the same kind of curve as a thin layer. Suppose, for example, a transparent material has the curve shown in (a) of Fig. 5·25. The curve for a thickness five times as great for the same material is given by curve (b). The first material, although it transmits light at all wavelengths, passes more energy in the central part of the spectrum than at the long

* Sometimes called Lambert's law.

wavelength end. At five times this thickness, however, the fact that the long wavelengths have a higher percent transmission has reversed the situation, and the ratio of long wavelengths transmitted has become much greater than at the center of the spectrum. This is a very common effect in dyes, known as "dichroism." The word means "two colors" and applies to the fact that in thin layers the above material would look green because so much energy is transmitted in the middle of the spectrum, whereas the thicker layer would look red because much more energy is at long wavelengths.

The equivalent of Bouguer's law for thickness of a colored layer is followed also by

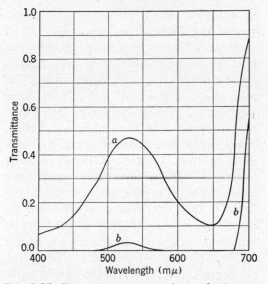

FIG. 5·25 Transmittance curves for a selective material of (a) a given thickness and (b) five times this thickness.

layers of constant thickness when the *amount* of absorbing material is changed. Suppose a glass cell with parallel faces is filled with water containing a dissolved dye. The selective action of this layer is due to the absorption of light by the molecules of the dye. If there were twice as many of these molecules there would be twice as much absorption, just as if the light were made to pass through the layer twice. This is known as Beer's law; namely, the effect of changing the concentration of the absorbing material in a given layer is the same as if the thickness had been changed.

COLLOIDAL COMPOUNDS

A dye in true solution, i.e., divided into the smallest possible particles and hence existing as independent molecules, is an extreme case of an absorbing material in a medium. More often the absorption which takes place below the upper surface is due to larger particles; as the size of these particles increases from molecular dimensions up to visible pieces, the causes and the nature of the absorption also change. If an insoluble substance is ground up into particles which are too fine to be seen directly under a microscope (with dimensions of the order of a wavelength of visible light), these particles will remain suspended in a liquid as if they were in true solution. Such a dispersion of fine particles is called a "colloidal solution," and the material is called a "colloid." If the particles are opaque and non-metallic, the selective absorption produced is due largely to scattering and exhibits a definite color series which depends only on particle size. In general, the coarser the particles are, the less the scattering and, accordingly, the shorter the wavelengths most scattered. Hence, coarse colloids pass all but the shortest wavelengths. These solutions appear yellow. As the particles are made smaller the transmitted light turns orange and finally a deep red, as longer and longer wavelengths are scattered out of the beam. If the particles are metallic, a new effect known as resonance enters, and colloidal solutions of gold and silver and the like have regions of transmission in the spectrum that are due to the fact that light fall-

ing on the particles is absorbed and re-emitted at the same wavelength, giving the effect of transparency. The Christensen filter effect can presumably take place also in colloids; there may be transmission regions due to this effect even if the particles are not metallic.

If the particles are transparent and colored rather than opaque, a colloidal solution will have the characteristic color of the transparent substance, although this color may be modified somewhat by scattering effects. Such colloidal dispersions cannot be distinguished by eye from true solutions. They act somewhat differently, however, because they may not obey Beer's law and may sometimes be observed to scatter light when a beam passes through them.

Larger particles than colloids, ground up in a viscous medium such as oil, form the basis for the familiar oil paints of the artist and painter. The particles are themselves colored and insoluble; the particle materials are known as pigments. Such a pigment in oil owes its color to the fact that light coming through the surface of the oil penetrates the pigment particles a short distance, is reflected out again (perhaps reflects from one or more particles), and finds its way back out through the surface.

A similar result is obtained if the particles instead of being themselves colored materials are white, i.e., diffusely but non-selectively reflecting, but are coated with a transparent colored substance such as a dye. Light falling on such particles is selectively absorbed by the coating and diffusely reflected by the underlying white material. Such a mixture is known as a "lake" and represents a considerable proportion of colored paints. It has the advantages, not possessed by dispersions of transparent materials, of returning a large percentage of the light and also covering up more completely the surface over which it is coated. A third possibility in such a paint is that a soluble color may be dissolved in the oil itself and the immersed white particles may reflect the light. All three, separately and in combination, are found among commercial paints.

2. Most materials other than the metals and some solid dyes reflect non-selectively from their outer surfaces.

3. Overcoating a diffuse outer surface with a smooth transparent and colorless film such as varnish, oil, wax, or water will greatly increase the selective effect of any absorbers

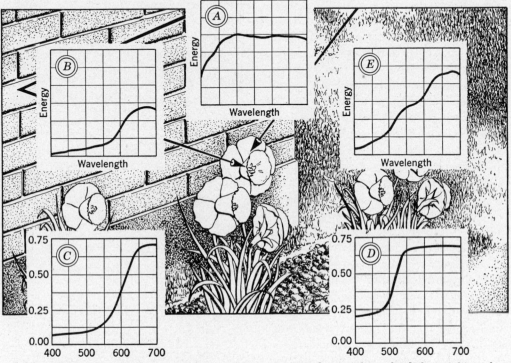

FIG. 5·26 Schematic diagram of a common viewing situation, showing how the light reaching the eye from an object has been selectively modified.

It is difficult to summarize a subject which contains as many variables as the present one. Only a few generalizations are possible; but it might be well to state these briefly, along with a few warnings on what cannot be assumed safely about a surface whose selective action is not understood.

1. It is true of all bodies that do not fluoresce that the amount of light at any wavelength which they reflect or transmit and which can reach the eye *from* them is always *less* than that which falls on them.

below this surface, except in the direction in which the light source is specularly reflected.

4. Increasing the thickness of a layer containing absorbing materials or increasing the concentration of these materials without changing the thickness will increase the selective action and sometimes greatly change it.

5. The total selective effect of a colored surface in general depends on *both* the energy distribution of the light source *and*

its geometrical position with respect to the object. There are a number of exceptions to this, the most important of which are the selectively reflecting metals, in which there is no non-selective outer surface.

6. In *almost* every instance of a colored surface encountered in nature, the cause of the selective action is selective absorption produced below the outer surface by particles varying in size from molecules to those large enough to see with the unaided eye. For these larger particles the effect is greatly accentuated by multiple reflection between particles before the light emerges.

7. Because of the extreme complexity of the light paths in a given instance it is usually not possible to predict precisely the selective action which will be obtained if two pigments are mixed in a medium.

8. A clear distinction must always be kept in mind between the successive or simultaneous action of selective media (subtractive mixture) and the simultaneous addition (additive mixture) of lights having different energy distribution.

It may be well to end the chapter with a diagram (Fig. 5·26) illustrating the general way in which light is selectively modified by a colored object. The inserted energy-distribution curves are intended to indicate the energy distributions of the light following the courses indicated by the arrows. The course of events is as follows: daylight, which has the spectral-energy distribution given by curve A, strikes both the red brick wall whose spectral reflectance curve is given by C and the yellow flower whose reflectance curve is given by D. The light reflected after selective absorption by the wall has the energy distribution as shown in B. Part of the light from the wall strikes the flower, is selectively absorbed by it, and again reflected. This is additively mixed with the daylight which has reached the flower directly, been selectively absorbed, and reflected again. The additive mixture of these two which strikes the eye is given in E. The action of the wall makes this radiation slightly orange, whereas it would have appeared yellow had the flower been isolated from the wall.

BIBLIOGRAPHY

Burton, E. F., and Smith, May A. *The Physical Properties of Colloidal Solutions*, 3rd ed. London: Longmans, Green and Co. 1938. Chapter IX.

Massachusetts Institute of Technology, the Color Measurement Laboratory. *Handbook of Colorimetry*. Cambridge, Mass.: The Technology Press. 1936. Chapter III.

Michelson, A. A. *Studies in Optics*. Chicago, Ill.: The University of Chicago Press. 1927. Chapters II, VI, and XV.

Sears, Francis Weston. *Principles of Physics III —Optics*, 2nd ed. Cambridge, Mass.: Addison-Wesley Press, Inc. 1946. Chapter VII.

Wood, Robert W. *Physical Optics*, 3rd ed. New York: The Macmillan Co. 1934. Chapters VI, XIII, and XVI.

Wright, W. D. *The Measurement of Colour*. London: Adam Hilger, Ltd. 1944. Chapter I.

The Physics of Everyday Color

CHAPTER VI

THE division of the subject of color into physics, psychophysics, and psychology was discussed earlier. In the last four chapters the subject has been surveyed in some detail from the physics standpoint. The treatment has been somewhat sketchy, and the beginner in color should realize that an entire book, a very large one, could (and should) be written on the subject. It is felt, however, that enough of the details have been given so that the careful reader may gain some appreciation of the fact that what we call the "color" of an object is not constant in any sense of the word when considered purely from the standpoint of the quality of the light which reaches the eye. In later chapters we shall consider why it is customary to think of object color as constant and will find, as a consequence, that the energy distribution reaching the eye is often less important than the brain behind the eye. This additional fact, however, makes the subject difficult because it is too easy in any given case to blame an obscure effect either entirely on the eye or entirely on the light quality. The student of the subject needs to know whether the eye or the light quality is more important or the extent to which each enters. It seems well, therefore, before we introduce the visual and mental mechanisms and their effects, to summarize the information given us by the purely physical approach. Persons accustomed to the psychological approach should consider the facts carefully, just as those accustomed to physics should consider the implications of later chapters. Color is neither physics nor psychology; it is *both*. Physics cannot predict the appearance of a given energy distribution nor can psychology predict the color of a subtractive mixture. Both together *should* be able to do both; this and similar aims should be the goal of the science of color.

Rather than attempt an academic summary of the facts already brought forward, we shall consider color as it is encountered in everyday life. If we may presume a little on the subject matter of later chapters, much of the so-called mystery of color comes from the fact that people do not look at color critically. We tend merely to assume that colors are what we think they are and do not verify our assumptions. It is hoped that this chapter may lead some people to look carefully at colors.

It is certain that if they make the attempt many will be surprised at what they see. The present chapter is devoted to energy distributions. If its contents are considered carefully in terms of what is actually seen, the psychological content of color will become apparent.

SHADOW ILLUMINATION

We may make a good start on the subject by considering the illumination of shadows and the quality of light reaching the eye from such areas. If a single-point source illuminates an object, there is behind this object a region of space into which this light cannot penetrate directly. The illumination in this shadow region, therefore, must come from elsewhere. There are only two possibilities, but their implications are tremendous. The illumination in this shadow *must* come either from another primary source or from a secondary source such as an object reflecting the light. In either case there may be little resemblance between the quality of the light reaching the object directly and that reaching the shadows; perhaps it should be pointed out that, if *no* light reached the shadow areas, details in these areas would be invisible to the eye.

In a similar manner, if there are two small light sources, both forming shadows from the same object, there will, in general, be a portion of each shadow illuminated by the other light and an overlapping region illuminated by neither. When such a pair of lights is present the situation is fairly

obvious. Unless the lights are quite different in intensity the double shadows are evident, as well as any differences which may exist in their colors.

A more common and far less apparent situation arises when there is one small source and one large source. In this event the small source forms shadows but the large one may not, with the result that the shadow area may be lighted entirely by the large source. Such a situation exists in daylight, where the sun and the sky are the two sources, and in interior illumination, where reflected light from the walls or a deliberately lighted ceiling may form the second source. In these instances the shadow illumination may vary from practically zero to an intensity value just less than that from the combination of the two; the limit is reached when the light from the small source is so weak in relation to the larger one that no visible shadow is produced. From the standpoint of the physics of color the estimation of the quality of such shadow illumination is often a difficult problem. It must be remembered that, if an object is sending enough light to the eye by reflection so that the object is visible, it is sending the same amount of light in many other directions also. If it is situated near the shadow of another object, it sends this light into that shadow unless there is some obstruction. Accordingly, if there is a single source, all the shadow illumination comes from reflecting objects near by; and if these have selective surfaces, this light will, in general, be colored. When there are several objects of different colors, the shadow illumination is the additive mixture of all of them. All this would be quite straightforward and would be apparent to the eye if it were not for a peculiarity of vision which tends to make these shadow colors far less noticeable than their illumination quality would lead one to expect. This peculiarity will be con-

PLATE III

(*Top*) There is direct reflection of light from the surfaces of the water lilies, all of it having the color of the blue sky. (*Bottom*) In another direction there is no such surface reflection, and the various colors of the water lilies are seen.

sidered in detail under color perception (Chapter XI), but as a preparation for this material it seems well to review in some detail the physics of a few common examples.

Perhaps the most common situation in which we deal with double or multiple light sources is daylight itself. When the sun is shining there are always at least two light sources to be considered: the sun and the sky. The intensity of the direct sun on a clear day at noon does not vary greatly throughout the year when it is measured on a surface perpendicular to the sun's rays. Although the expression "clear day" is a little vague, it is usually correct to assume that if distance visibility is good and the sky is deep blue, the intensity of the sun is about the same the year round (8,000 to 11,000 foot-candles). However, if instead of on a surface perpendicular to the light the intensity is measured on a surface parallel to the ground, the variation is much larger and in the northern parts of the United States amounts to more than a ratio of 3 to 1. If the day is not clear, the direct sunlight may easily drop to one-fifth; similar and lower values may be found before sunset even on clear days. Sunlight, therefore, is not a constant intensity source; its variations are of the order of magnitude of 5 to 1. The light from the sky, however, depends on more factors than its brightness alone. The sky itself is a hemisphere of more or less constant brightness with a deep blue color on a clear day with no clouds. If an object has a shadow behind it cast by the sun under these conditions, the shadow is illuminated by the sky and has an illumination intensity of about one-fourth that of the sun on the object. The color of this light, of course, is just as blue compared to the sun as the

sky appears directly to the eye. In fact, a shadow on a white surface will be found to match the sky if some way, such as with two mirrors or the like, can be found to make a direct comparison.

If the sky contains isolated clouds there are two effects produced. In the first place part of the sky is covered by the clouds, and in the second these clouds, if they reflect the sun, mix sunlight with the blue. Under these conditions the intensity of the light in the shadows may become much higher than before, and the color far less blue. In the extreme case of large numbers of scattered clouds lighted by the sun the light intensity may be quite high in the shadows and the *same* color as the sun. If there is a haze between the sun and the object, this haze will tend to decrease the intensity of the direct sun and increase that of the shadow until a point is reached where the sun is completely obscured and the shadow disappears. We then have what is known as an "overcast sky" in which the sun is not visible. The intensity of the light on such days may vary from a relatively high value (perhaps 3,000 to 4,000 foot-candles) to the very low values for daylight (as low as 100). The color of the light on an overcast day also can vary widely, depending on the conditions existing in the sky. If direct sunlight is obscured by heavy clouds and the rest of the sky is obscured with light mist, the light can be quite blue, nearly as blue as the sky itself. This condition prevails regularly early and late in the day when the sun is low in the sky. If the overcast consists of a low-altitude haze which is heavy enough to obscure the sun, the light may consist of a mixture of sunlight and skylight and be the same color as the sun outside the earth's atmosphere. At sunrise or sunset the usual sunset colors may be diffused by the overcast, and the whole illumination color may move quite far toward pink.

It is seen, therefore, that not only for the light falling directly on an object, but to an even greater extent for the light illuminating the shadows, daylight itself varies over rather wide extremes. So far we have considered only conditions in which light from the sky is not obstructed by other objects and in which no other objects are reflecting light into the shadows. Under other conditions daylight becomes even more complex. The illumination in shadows may reach exceedingly low values, as, for example, in a forest where sunlight comes through small openings in the foliage. Under these circumstances, any light that reaches the shadows at all comes from objects reflecting the sunlight, and this light will, in general, be the same color as that of the objects. If some skylight and some reflected sunlight reach the shadow, the color of the light will be the additive mixture of the two.

Both the color and the intensity of the illumination in a shadow, therefore, may vary greatly, direct sunlight being the limiting intensity. In general, out in the open the shadows will tend to be blue, but blue will not be the predominant color if there are highly reflecting colored surfaces such as brick buildings or trees near by or if the day is not clear. Of the two variables, color and intensity, the intensity factor is by far the more noticeable. The ratio of direct sunlight plus skylight on the object and skylight plus reflected light in the shadow can vary all the way from 1 to 1 on an overcast day when no shadows are thrown, to exceedingly high values—so high, in fact, that no detail can be seen in the shadows unless all directly reflected sunlight is shielded from the eyes. Shadow contrast, therefore, is perhaps the largest single variable in daylight. Next in general magnitude come the variations in shadow color, which theoretically can be any color but usually contain

a fair amount of blue; and third, the variations in general color of the direct illumination, which can be a mixture of sunlight (varying from white at noon through yellow and orange to red at sunset) with the blue of the sky in all proportions. These last variations mean that direct light can fall anywhere in the white, the yellow, the orange, the red, and the pink ranges, but the color is white usually, most of the day.

SURFACE REFLECTION

In addition to these color and intensity changes, the geometrical nature of daylight illumination can vary over an immense range. Direct sunlight coming in a window is essentially parallel light (extreme angle $\frac{1}{2}$ °). As such, when it falls on a selective object with a smooth surface, it gives rise to about the *maximum* selective reflection of which the object is capable. At the other extreme, if such an object is placed in the open on an overcast day, there will be no position in which it can be seen that does not give direct reflection of the sky from the smooth surface. The light from the object under these conditions mixes additively with the maximum amount of skylight, and the object shows *minimum* selectivity. The possible magnitude of the effect can be judged from the two calculated curves of Fig. 6·1. Between these extremes come all possible combinations of the two, such as sunlighted clouds, haze, and clear blue sky. It is not worth while to consider all of them separately, but two facts should be considered carefully. Most objects in nature have a surface which is more or less smooth, and the reflectance of such a surface increases rapidly as the angle at which it is viewed decreases. Any object, such as a leaf in sunlight, therefore, may have a fairly intense selective action if it is viewed perpendicular to the surface in direct sunlight. Viewed in the light from an overcast sky it may show very little selective action because of the high brightness of the reflected source. Viewed across the surface at a glancing angle it may well show *no* selective action at all but may simply reflect the light from whatever is in the proper position. If the light is from red brick, the reflected light will be

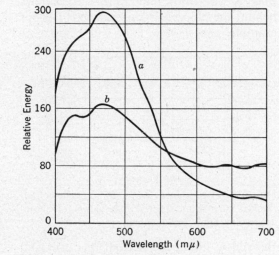

FIG. 6·1 Energy-distribution curves of light reflected from a blue object with a glossy surface when it is illuminated (*a*) by direct sunlight and (*b*) by a uniformly overcast sky.

red; if it is the blue sky which is reflected, it will be blue, etc., without regard to the color of the leaf. The faces of people show this effect quite clearly, even when considerable face powder has been used.

The term "daylight" is obviously to be interpreted as meaning "not-artificial light" rather than as a description of the actual effective light at any given time or place. Determination of the actual quality of light outdoors at any particular spot calls for careful study of all the conditions involved.

INTERIOR ILLUMINATION

Perhaps to an even greater extent these considerations hold true inside buildings

whether the light is natural from outside the building or artificial from inside. Under these conditions the direct light falling on an object, i.e., the light which *causes* a shadow, may be of almost any quality, and the light in the shadow may be the same or very different. A room having one large window beside a large tree with green leaves in full sunlight is lighted entirely, for all practical purposes, by green light. The energy-distribution curve for such light may be almost wholly that given by sunlight on green leaves (Fig. 6·2). On the other hand, if sunlight enters the window and falls on a bright red carpet, all other objects in the room are lighted by *red* light of the color of the carpet. For the room, the green tree or the red carpet are the *primary* sources of

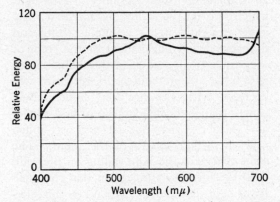

FIG. 6·2 Curve (solid) representing sunlight reflected from a typical green leaf. Light includes both diffuse and specular component. The broken curve is for sunlight alone and is included for purposes of comparison.

light. It does not matter that the light arises by way of a reflecting surface. The point is that all the light illuminating other objects has this source quality, and the tree or the rug may be considered as if it were giving off light. This is a general fact which is encountered in many important situations, and it may be summarized in a general rule. The quality of the light reaching an object is that of the sum of the light qualities reaching it from *all* the points of its environment, and each of these points may be considered as an independent source.

With this in mind it is important to consider somewhat more closely the factors that affect the quality of such reflected light. In particular, it is important to consider the various qualities of light present in a fairly small room lighted by a single source, such as a fairly bright lamp with a shade open at the top so that considerable light falls on the wall and ceiling above as well as directly on objects not obscured by the shade. It is not necessary to consider the direct light carefully; its intensity decreases with distance from the lamp according to the inverse square law and may become negligible at a relatively short distance. The light which falls on the ceiling may cover a fairly large area, and if the ceiling is white and diffusing it will reflect light of the color of the source to all corners of the room. Since it acts as a large source, its intensity will decrease with distance very much more slowly than indicated by the inverse square law; in fact, it may not decrease very much over the whole length of the room. The same is true of the light falling on the wall, with the important exception that the quality of light reflected will depend on the selective action of the wall itself. Suppose, for example, that the wall is a fairly deep yellow, perhaps with the reflection curve shown in Fig. 6·3, in which the energy distribution of the source has been included. Light falling on an object in the middle of the room, therefore, will consist largely of light from the wall and the ceiling and not from the lamp directly; this light will be distinctly yellow compared to that of the source itself. Several complications may arise from this apparently simple conclusion, however, and these must be considered separately. The first of them is the possibility of another

selectively reflecting surface near the object. The second is the multiple reflection of light back and forth between the walls of the room. Both effects are identical in principle but may be somewhat different in the nature of their results.

If a large reflecting surface stands just behind the object and is selective in its action, it will throw light into the shadows behind the object. If the surface is red, for example, the shadow light will be that of

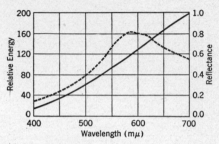

Fig. 6·3 Reflectance curve for a yellow wall (broken curve) and spectral distribution of an incandescent lamp (solid curve).

the yellow illumination from the walls and the ceiling as modified by reflection from the red surface.

In the absence of a large surface lighting the shadow, the light which reaches this point must come by reflection from other points in the room. The largest areas are usually the ceiling and the walls. Light falling on one wall reflects into the room, strikes another wall, reflects again to a third, etc. Even if the walls are fairly light colored, the net result is a very considerable deepening of the color due to this multiple reflection. The curves in Fig. 6·4 show the quality of artificial light as reflected from a cream-colored wall (broken curve) and the quality of the light after the first, third, fifth, and tenth multiple reflection. It is apparent that a great increase in selective action has taken place. The light reaching any object in such a room is the sum of all these reflections, after their relative intensities have been taken into account. This effect enters as an important factor into the visual color of any shadows which may be present in the room. It also is a determining factor in the apparent color of the walls themselves. The common experience of finding that the color of a paint or wall paper has become far more intense *after* it has been placed on a wall than it appeared in a small sample is due largely to this effect.

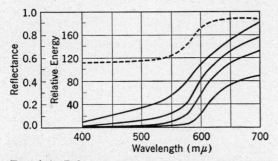

FIG. 6·4 Relative energy distributions of the first, third, fifth, and tenth multiple reflections of light from an incandescent lamp on a cream-colored surface. The solid curves from top to bottom show how the light reflected from the surface becomes darker and redder as the number of reflections is increased. The broken curve is the reflectance curve for the surface.

In passing it may be noted that many objects owe a peculiar type of beauty to this effect. When the interior of any object such as a bowl or box is colored, multiple reflection will very greatly deepen this color, and its appearance will change greatly, depending on the angle at which light enters the opening. This effect is particularly noticeable in objects such as silver goblets which have been lined with gold. Gold has a distinct selective surface reflection as well as a high reflection factor. If the walls of the objects slope slightly, it is possible to get multiple reflections of a high order. The result is a deepening of the color of the gold, sometimes to a deep red. Curves for the first, third, fifth, eleventh, and nine-

teenth reflections of gold are shown in Fig. 6·5.

The illumination in a room, therefore, cannot be specified by describing the lamp bulb or by the statement that it is daylight coming through a window. The light on each separate object and the light in its shadow call for separate consideration. Careful study will often reveal that the light is far different from what might have been expected. Consider, for example, the complexity of the common situation in which daylight enters a window in a room in which artificial light is being used to illuminate dark corners.

The reader may find the foregoing statements at variance with the facts of his every-

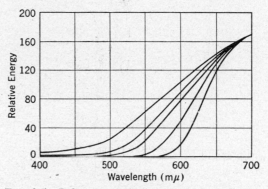

FIG. 6·5 Relative energy distributions of the first, third, fifth, eleventh, and nineteenth multiple reflections of light from an incandescent lamp on a gold mirror. The top curve represents the light quality after the first reflection, and the bottom curve after the nineteenth. All curves have been plotted to the same maxima.

day experience. They have been introduced deliberately to call attention to the fact that such a discrepancy exists. None of the statements is exaggerated, although, of course, in any given situation some of the factors may not be present. Actually in a poorly illuminated room it is almost impossible to calculate the quality of the light at any particular spot; it may vary over exceedingly wide limits. Ordinarily *none* of these differences is more than casually noticed by an observer. Consideration of the reasons for the last statement must be postponed since they come under the headings of psychophysics and psychology, but the facts brought forward should make one at least hesitant about any academic statements concerning the color of shadows under such conditions. Similar situations exist out of doors, especially in shaded spots, and the would-be landscape painter will do well to consider carefully the *actual* appearance of a shadow if he wants to re-create the true appearance of an object. It may be that shadows when lighted by *white* light follow definite rules, but it does not follow that all shadows are so lighted. Much of the character which a painter may wish to capture may be in these very shadows. Perhaps a note of warning is in order, however. It is the *appearance* of such things which counts most either in painting or in daily life. The actual energy distribution is important only when the *effect* of this light is to be calculated or otherwise used.

ATMOSPHERIC DIFFUSION

The appearance of objects out of doors suggests also the next subject which must be considered in this survey. The primary and secondary light sources so far considered have had definite locations and sizes. There is, however, an important group of secondary sources that do not. They may in fact be considered as volume sources. These are the instances so often met in nature of diffusion of the light by particles in the air, known by various names such as haze, mist, fog, and snow.

When the air is filled with particles of moisture, these particles deflect the light, either by the scattering considered earlier or by direct reflection. Their presence in the air also changes it from a clear transparent medium to one which, if it were a liquid, would be described as cloudy or turbid, sometimes even practically opaque. Because of the frequent occurrence of such conditions it is worth while to consider them systematically, if only briefly.

The air is considered to contain haze when a distant view has superimposed on it light which appears to originate in the air between the observer and the distant objects. The color of this light is normally somewhat bluish and owes its presence to sun or skylight scattered by moisture or dust particles in the air. The amount of light scattered by a given volume of air is the same at all places in the view, but the amount seen by the observer depends on the total distance *through* the air to the distant point at which he happens to be looking. Accordingly, the amount of bluish light *added to* the light from a distant object will depend on the distance to that object. If the object is far enough away and sufficiently dark, it may be completely obscured by this added light and so appear blue. At lesser distances and for lighter objects the added blue will play a lesser role, and for near-by objects it will not be apparent at all. The distance of objects, therefore, may be judged by the extent to which they appear blue; this effect is so common that among artists it has received the name of "atmospheric perspective." Producing this effect is a standard technique for the indication of objects at a distance in paintings.

Aerial haze has another equally important characteristic which is frequently overlooked. Since it owes its bluish color to the fact that it scatters short wavelength light *out* of a beam of light, the light which it transmits directly is deficient in these wavelength regions. Accordingly, light-colored objects in the middle distance will send less short wavelength light to the eye than if the air were clear and so will tend to appear of a browner or redder color. At a greater distance this effect may be offset by the scattered light from the sun, and at less distance there may be no effect. When haze is present, pale yellow surfaces at different distances, for example, may be yellow near by, orange to reddish brown in the middle distance, and blue at great distances.

When the moisture particles become larger there may be a condition that we call mist. Such a condition differs from haze because the particles are too large to show selective scattering and objects are seen covered with more and more white light as the distance increases. Near by there may be deep blacks and pure colors, but as distance increases more and more white light reaches the eye along the path until all objects are obscured by a uniform blanket of light. Under these conditions, colors do not change except as they fade into white.

More similar to haze but not ordinarily bluish in color is the exceedingly heavy haze which we call fog. In this circumstance, the number of moisture particles in the air is so high that the observer may not be able to see objects at all, even at relatively short distances, and he feels himself completely immersed in the light source itself. It is only when some other light source bright enough to penetrate the fog, such as a streetlight at night, can be seen, that the resemblance to haze becomes apparent. Under these conditions, there is a strong shift of the quality of the light toward longer wavelengths and a consequent shift of color toward red.

Snow, on the other hand, acts like mist because white light only is added and there is no selective transmission. White light, sometimes in very large amounts, is added to the light from all objects. In a heavy snowstorm objects at 5 or 10 feet may become completely invisible although the brightness of the light may be quite high. One often receives the impression of opacity as if the snow were too dense to see through, but an equally heavy snowfall at night may appear quite transparent.

ADDITIVE MIXTURE IN NATURE

In all these cases of added light it is apparent that the quality of the light reaching the eye depends on the addition of several qualities that are reaching the eye simultaneously. Similar cases were discussed also in the section on surface reflections and occur very generally. In addition to these there is a whole class of additive mixtures quite common both in nature and in daily life which have not yet been mentioned. These are the instances of additive mixture that result when the areas or sources involved are effectively so small and close together that they cannot be separated by the eye. Under these conditions the light may be considered mixed before it reaches the eye, and it therefore acts as if it were a uniform source of the color of the mixture.

In nature this effect occurs often, especially in distant landscapes, and much of the beauty of distant hills arises from the way in which small areas that would be seen as separate colors if near by become fused with other colors to produce a single new color. Sometimes in the fall, especially in the northeastern part of the country, when the leaves have changed color, this process may be seen repeated a number of times in one distant view. At a certain distance the individual leaves will have fused to make one color for each tree. At a greater distance clumps of related trees will fuse to a second color, and far away there will be one color for wooded sections and one for the areas without trees.

This same additive mixing is a common phenomenon in textile materials in which threads of various colors are woven into some sort of pattern. From a short distance the individual threads may be visible, but at a certain distance these become invisible with the pattern still showing. Still further away the pattern disappears. The laws of additive-color mixture are well known and the results of such mixtures can be predicted accurately if the colors of the individual parts are known. Certain reds and blues mix and become purple, for example, and yellow or orange is formed if red and green are mixed. In this respect then, additive mixtures differ from the subtractive effects we have been considering: subtractive effects can be predicted only from a knowledge of the energy distributions involved, but additive ones, independent of their energy distributions, depend only on the colors originally present. This fact is a fundamental property of the eye. It must be emphasized again that additive mixture and subtractive effects are fundamentally different phenomena. It does not follow, however, as is often assumed, that *therefore* the *colors formed* by additive mixture are in themselves different from the same colors formed by subtractive effects. The eye responds to the energy distribution of any light which enters it, and its response is independent of the manner in which this quality is produced. When small colored areas are far enough away so that the individual areas cannot be seen, it is impossible to tell whether the color seen is continuous. The color would look exactly the same if all the small areas were replaced with a single large area having the mixture color. There is a condition, however, under which these additive mixtures are very different from a solid area of color, and this occurs at the distance at which the small areas are almost *but not*

quite fused. Under these conditions the eye sometimes sees the individual areas and sometimes the fusion colors so that there is an interplay of color which gives it a visual brilliance and sparkle not possessed by a single area. This interplay occurs only *at* the fusion distance and is a purely visual effect having nothing to do with the physics of the situation. Closer viewing shows only the small colored areas. For example, a random series of red and green dots covering a surface will be seen as such if the dots can be resolved by the eye, and no trace of yellow will be visible. As the distance from the observer increases, there will be a point at which the mixture color comes and goes (usually as a yellowish brown since a bright yellow cannot be produced in this manner) and red, green, and brown are all visible at once. At greater distances the color becomes permanently brown and cannot be seen in any other way. The production of brown rather than yellow in this example is typical of this sort of mixture in general. It is almost always possible to find a single color which, painted over the same area, will be a brighter color than can be formed by additive mixture. Any advantage in brilliance occurs only at the distance at which it is *not quite* fused.

The factors that have been considered thus far in this chapter have been general in that they apply to all selective surfaces and in that they change the selective action of surfaces. Before we proceed to consider a number of specific examples, it is interesting to consider broadly the implications of what has been covered. It was found that under special circumstances the nature of the illumination in connection with the type of outer surface of the material could cause the selective action to vary from a certain maximum to a completely nonselective action. It was found that this

PLATE IV

Color patches too small to be resolved by the eye fuse to give additive mixtures. The drawing consists of red and green dots which fuse at a viewing distance of about six feet.

outer surface always plays a large part in the color. Since this surface depends also on circumstances it can change materially over a period of time. Dirt and dust will dull a smooth surface and add white light to the color of the object regardless of the type of illumination, as many a housekeeper has learned from experience. On the other hand, rain may wet the outer surface of a leaf and change it from a dull, lifeless thing to a deep, pure green object. The presence of smoke, haze, fog, and the like may add white or blue light to objects at a distance as well as shift their color toward red. Distant viewing of small colored areas may fuse them to an entirely new color. Finally, viewing of surfaces from an intermediate distance may make their appearance fluctuate between the colors of individual areas and the fusion color of the whole. It is apparent that from the physical standpoint there is no such thing as a single quality of light which will describe a given object's action even though we consider it in relation to only one illuminant. It is well to keep these facts in mind. We shall find when we come to consider the psychology of seeing that the naive observer does not see these things and that *no* observer can see some of them without visual aids. When we come to consider the reproduction of scenes it will be found that it is necessary to copy *neither* the appearance (as an isolated area) nor the light quality, but something between the two which can be determined only if we are aware of *both*. In view of this fact, the rest of the chapter will be devoted to a consideration of the physics of certain common colors encountered in life and of the physical properties of some of the media employed by artists. In passing it will be well to consider a few of the other associated factors which properly belong in later chapters.

HUMAN SKIN

Perhaps the most important color of all those encountered in nature is that of human skin. It is also one of the most complex. For our detailed knowledge of the physics of color production by flesh, we are largely indebted to the work of E. A. Ed-

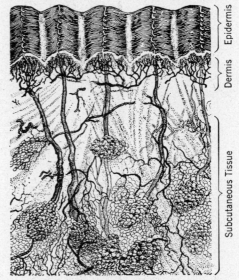

FIG. 6·6 Cross section of human skin showing the three main layers, the epidermis, the dermis, and the subcutaneous tissue.

wards and S. Q. Duntley (see bibliography) at Massachusetts Institute of Technology. The following facts are taken largely from their papers on the subject.

Human skin is made up of a number of layers into which the light may penetrate. The physical arrangement is illustrated in the sectional diagram of Fig. 6·6. An outer diffusing surface, called the epidermis, has below it a layer of skin in which the light is extensively scattered. Below this is the flesh proper, made up of blood cells and the like. Three selective actions take place as far as light is concerned, and the relative amounts of these three actions determine the color as seen from any given direction under the given lighting conditions. The diagram of Fig. 6·6 shows only what might be called the average structure. In some parts of the body, notably the lips, the epidermis is largely missing. In others, such as the soles of the feet, the blood cells are

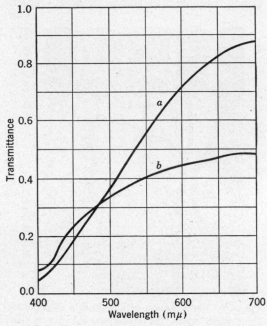

FIG. 6·7 Transmittance curve for: (a) malanin in a 5% potassium hydroxide solution and (b) stratum corneum from a cadaver's heel which displays the spectrophotometric characteristics of malanoid. (E. A. Edwards and S. Q. Duntley, *The American Journal of Anatomy*, Vol. 65, pp. 9 and 13, 1939.)

not effective. The various combinations of all these factors give rise to a variation in color which spreads over the range yellow, red, white, and blue, not to mention the magenta that can be produced by additive mixture of the scattered light just under the surface and the red from below or artificially produced by cosmetics.

In somewhat more detail the selective actions involved are as follows. There is in almost all human flesh (the exception is the rare albino) a yellow pigment called

melanin, the amount of which increases as the skin is tanned by the sun. Associated with melanin, and believed to be a derivative of it, is a second yellow pigment called melanoid. The transmittance curves for melanin and for the stratum corneum of a cadaver's heel are shown in (a) and (b) respectively of Fig. 6·7. The cadaver's heel displays the spectrophotometric characteristics of melanoid. These pigments are present below the outer surface, and the amounts vary between individuals and races. Figure 6·8 shows the reflection curves found

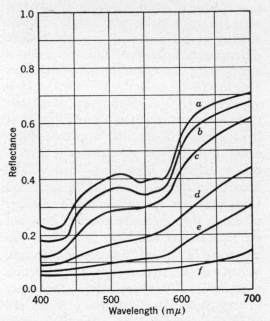

FIG. 6·8 Reflectance curves for buttock region of different races: (a) white blond, (b) white brunet, (c) Japanese, (d) Hindu, (e) Mulatto, and (f) Negro. (E. A. Edwards and S. Q. Duntley, *The American Journal of Anatomy*, Vol. 65, p. 29, 1939.)

by Edwards and Duntley for various races. The immediate color changes resulting from sun exposure are primarily due to an increase in blood concentration near the surface of the skin rather than to the production of melanin. Figure 6·9 shows the result on white skin of prolonged exposure to sunlight.

The absorption due to blood is shown in Fig. 6·10; the two forms of hemoglobin and oxyhemoglobin are shown corresponding to the colors before and after the blood takes up oxygen from the lungs.

The blue color produced by light scattering has already been discussed when consideration was given to the color of the sky and the effect of distance haze.

All combinations of these three basic effects are encountered. The color of the lips and the flesh under the finger nails is due largely to the blood, and tends to be red with little blue or yellow present. Some of the veins run close to the surface skin, and the concentration of the blood red is so high in these veins that it is effectively

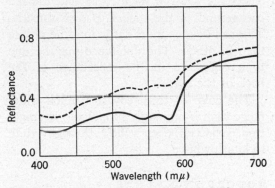

FIG. 6·9 Reflectance curve for skin of sacral region before solar irradiation (broken curve) and eleven hours after a one-hour exposure to August noon sunlight (solid curve). (E. A. Edwards and S. Q. Duntley, *Science*, Vol. 90, p. 236, 1939.)

black. Such veins appear blue since the only color seen is the scattered blue light. Over most of the rest of the body the color shades from red to yellow-orange, or to actual yellow or brown, in accordance with race and degree of pigmentation. Because of the outer diffusing surface with its underlying blue scatter and yellow pigment, however, the appearance of skin is peculiarly sensitive to the size, shape, and positions of the light source. In general, strong parallel light such as direct sunlight or a high-intensity artificial light tends to penetrate the skin deeply, giving it a transparent appearance which disappears more or less com-

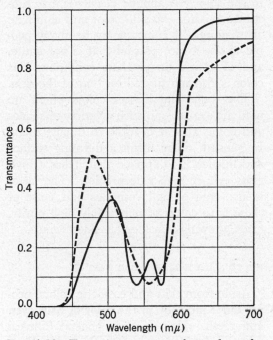

FIG. 6·10 Transmittance curves for oxyhemoglobin and reduced hemoglobin (broken line) diluted one to one hundred. (E. A. Edwards and S. Q. Duntley, *The American Journal of Anatomy*, Vol. 65, p. 15, 1939.)

pletely if the light is from a large diffuse source. In addition, if the skin has a tendency to be at all oily, the outer diffuse surface tends to be replaced by a smooth reflecting one which may eliminate the added white light and greatly deepen the color. As people become older, the skin becomes less and less transparent, and more diffusion takes place below the outer surface. For these reasons it is apparent that the term "flesh color," refers to a range of colors and includes the way in which they shade into each other.

The effect of face powder, of course, is to increase very greatly the surface diffusion and eliminate any tendency for the skin to be shiny. To the extent that the powder is non-selective, it simply adds a large amount of white or nearly white, light to the color. If applied heavily it may substitute this for the skin color and eliminate all shading. It is customary for many people to use a face powder that is not white, and of course under these conditions this color is also substituted for that of the skin.

The rouge and lipstick colors which are used are available in such a variety of shades and colors that it is futile to discuss them. In general, rouge forms a diffusing surface and lipstick is so applied that it has a high gloss surface and a deep color. The latter is also true of nail varnishes and some of these have colors of remarkably high purity, often showing considerable fluorescence.

HAIR, EYES, AND TEETH

Aside from skin and cosmetic colors, people differ radically in the color of hair, eyes, and teeth. Hair color in general forms a complete series from white through yellow, orange, red, and brown to black. Hair differs not only in color but in texture and the sheen of its surface, some being exceedingly shiny and some remarkably diffusing. Probably only one or at most two pigments are involved. White hair is due to effective absence of pigment plus the presence of colorless diffusing materials, probably tiny air bubbles. Black hair seems to be due to the presence of large amounts of pigment plus a smooth surface. The hair that appears blackest is frequently red by transmitted light.

All eye colors appear to be produced by the presence or absence of only one selectively absorbing pigment plus varying amount of scattered blue light. The one

pigment is brown in color and may be melanin. The scattered light is caused by fine particles present in varying amounts or by structure. The series of colors from clear blue through gray is produced by variations in the amount of scatter in the absence of pigment. All other colors are formed by some one of these conditions plus various amounts of brown pigment. Because of the large part played by scattered light some eye colors change markedly with illumination conditions. This is particularly true of those having a tendency toward a grayish green color. In the rare case of the albino, who has no pigment at all, the eyes sometimes may be pink because of the red light reflected by the blood cells at the back of the eye. A similar very deep red color may be seen occasionally in all eyes if the light enters the pupil in such a way that the red background of the eyeball is seen directly. This can be seen more easily in some people than in others. The difference may be due to a difference in the reflectance of the back of the eye.

The color of teeth covers a much wider range than is ordinarily supposed. It ranges from relatively deep yellow through white to bluish white.

COLORS IN NATURE

Among the other important colors in nature are those of water, soil, leaves, and flowers.

The true color of clear water seems to be a pale green, although this color is not seen unless the light passes through a considerable distance of the water. In any given locality, however, the color of the water may be affected markedly by the presence of dissolved materials or of tiny marine life. These effects may change with the temperature of the water and may also be modified by the presence of finely divided sand and the like held up by the motion of the water. Thus the color of water may range from

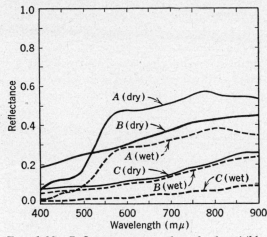

FIG. 6·11 Reflectance curves through the visible and infrared regions of the spectrum of a few typical samples of soil.

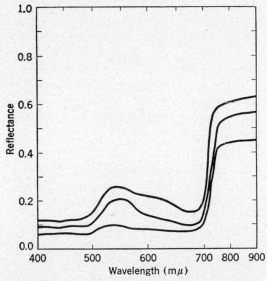

FIG. 6·12 Reflectance curves through the visible and infrared regions of the spectrum of some green leaves.

an exceedingly deep blue through many shades of green to practically colorless. In large bodies of water these basic colors may be modified by surface reflections. On a

calm day when the surface is completely smooth, the surface reflection of the sky and the clouds is obvious and the observer tends to see it as separate from the water color. However, when the wind ruffles the surface or in bodies such as the ocean where the water near the shore is almost never smooth, the sky reflection becomes mixed with the color of the water, and the mixture is seen as a single series of colors. If the sky is uniformly blue, this is the only color added. If the sky is non-uniformly clouded, the colors reflected will change with the

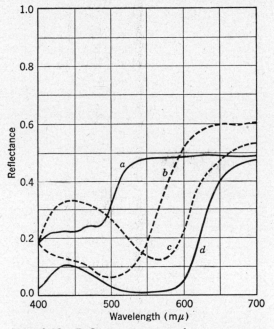

FIG. 6·13 Reflectance curves of some common flowers: (a) desaturated-yellow gladiolus, (b) bright orange gladiolus, (c) pale-violet rose-of-Sharon, (d) wine-colored gladiolus.

direction in which the observer looks. Such reflections do not follow the laws for smooth surfaces in that the part of the sky reflected may be in an unexpected position relative to the observer, even directly behind him, since the determining factor is the angle that the ripples make with the line of sight.

It is quite possible, although only clear blue sky is directly in front of the observer, for the water to reflect no visible blue if the rest of the sky is heavily clouded.

Soil colors vary in hue from red to yellow and cover a wide range of saturations and lightnesses. They include almost all varie-

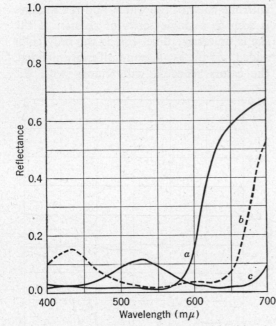

FIG. 6·14 Reflectance curves for dyed felt: (a) red, (b) purple, and (c) green.

ties of brown from those that are nearly black to some that are quite light. Wet soils are always darker than dry soils and are usually slightly more saturated in color. The redder brown soils usually become yellower when wet. Spectral-reflectance curves of a few typical soils are given in Fig. 6·11.

Colors of leaves differ considerably for various types of plants and during different seasons. As with most other objects in nature, leaves have slightly differing colors depending upon the particular direction with respect to the surface from which they are illuminated or viewed. While detailed information on all these variations cannot

be given here, spectrophotometric curves of a few typical green leaves are shown in Fig. 6·12. Of particular interest with respect to these leaves is the high reflectance in the infrared.

The greatest range of selective surfaces in nature, of course, is that of flower petals. These are second only in their selective action to some of the recently detailed textile dyes. Reflectance curves for some of the well-known colors are given in Fig. 6·13. For comparison, several of the more intense textile dyes are given in Fig. 6·14.

OIL PAINTS VS. NATURE COLORS

The complaint is heard frequently from artists that the range of colors available to them in their paints and pigments is far short of that in nature, and that therefore all sorts of compromises and conventions must be employed to produce the effects desired. It is certain that compromises and conventions are a necessity; but before we enter the maze of visual and psychological effects, it may help to investigate these matters from a purely physical standpoint.

We may start with the flat statement that there are very few object colors in nature which cannot be so matched by a capable artist using oil paints that if the two are laid side by side they will look alike except for texture and fine structure. The problem, therefore, is *not* one of being unable to match the surfaces point for point. The difficulty lies in the fact that, whereas the painting is an object in uniform illumination, the scene consists of objects illuminated to very *different* intensities. To the extent that the artist tries to reproduce the scene it is these colors at different illumination *intensities* which he finds himself unable to match. On a dull overcast day he might well find himself able to reproduce exactly all the visible colors and brightnesses, but when the sun is shining and the sky is clear he may have great difficulty in even implying their appearance. Consider the problem for a moment in terms of black and white pigments. In nature the ratio of intensities from a white in full sunlight to a black in deep shadow may easily reach a value of 2,000 to 1. If there are directly visible light sources in a scene, the ratio may go still higher than this. What we ordinarily call a black surface frequently has a reflectance of 4 percent and almost never has less than 0.25 percent (black velvet and carbon black rarely go so low). The best whites seldom exceed 98 percent (good white chalk), and white paper may often reflect as little as 70 percent. The highest ratio that can be attained, therefore, can hardly exceed 400 to 1, and under most circumstances it is difficult to exceed 50 or at best 100 to 1. The range of possible intensities for other colors is even smaller. This is the problem for which the artist must draw on all his resources. Fortunately for the artist (and the observer!) the eye is not effective over brightness ranges of such high magnitude. It will be found later that the eye automatically decreases the illumination contrast in studying a scene, and for this reason, among others, the reproduction which would *look most like* the scene would not involve anything like the actual brightness range of the subject.

Exactly the same considerations apply, of course, to color photography, except that in this case the record is made by the actual intensities in the scene and so, unless actual handwork is done on the picture, cannot be modified deliberately without modifying the subject. Even so, with glossy surface prints and the best dyes, an intensity range in excess of 200 to 1 is seldom found.

Some types of subject, of course, although they are non-uniformly illuminated, can be completely reproduced either in painting or in photography. These are the subjects which have low *object contrast*. Suppose, for example, that the ratio of the highest to the lowest percentage of reflectance in a scene is no greater than 8 to 1. Such a subject could be set up quite easily and would appear to have fair contrast in uniform illumination. Suppose that a single shadow falls across such a subject. As the overall contrast of a scene is the *product* of the reflectance range and the illumination range, the ratio of intensity of the illuminated part to the shadow can reach the high value of 25 to 1 before any of the areas involved exceed the limits that can be reproduced. This possibility is, perhaps, one of the appeals of still-life subjects for the artist. It is quite possible to arrange such a subject so that *all* its values can be reproduced (although in most instances such reproduction plays only an incidental role in what the artist is trying to do).

This compression of the brightness range, of course, is only *one* of the artist's problems. Coupled with it are a host of other factors such as motion, binocular vision, change in relative position due to head motion, and the like which may provide much of the character of a given scene but which must be translated onto a two-dimensional surface if this character is to be captured. Although the writer is not an artist, it seems that it must be true that an accurate knowledge of the physics of color and of the properties of the visual mechanism that will be developed in later chapters will *free* the artist from misdirected preoccupations by presenting the problems clearly and will permit him to devote his whole energy to the creative factors which must be at the foundation of all true art. Fads and mistaken notions may act as inspirations for work of a very high order, but in the long run an accurate realization of the true problems should lead to results of an even higher order.

BIBLIOGRAPHY

Cady, Francis E., and Dates, Henry B. *Illuminating Engineering*, 2nd ed. New York: John Wiley and Sons, Inc. 1928. Chapters I and II.

Edwards, Edward A., and Duntley, S. Quimby. "The Pigments and Color of Living Human Skin." *The American Journal of Anatomy*, **65**:1–33 (1939).

Luckiesh, M. *Color and Its Applications*. New York: D. Van Nostrand Co. 1915. Chapters XIII and XVI.

Luckiesh, M. *Lighting Fixtures and Lighting Effects*. New York: McGraw-Hill Book Co., Inc. 1925. Chapter VI.

Moon, Parry. *The Scientific Basis of Illuminating Engineering*. New York: McGraw-Hill Book Co., Inc. 1936. Chapters VIII and IX.

Color Vision

CHAPTER VII

THE eye is usually described as similar to a small camera, and it is true that there is some resemblance between the two. The actual likeness consists almost exclusively, however, of their having lenses which form images on the rear surface. The results produced by these images and the nature of the images themselves are so different in the two that misconceptions arise from thinking of them as the same.

STRUCTURE OF THE EYE

A cross-sectional view of the eye lens and receiving surface (called the "retina") is shown in Fig. 7·1. Light entering the front of the lens is brought to a focus on the rear surface provided the eye is looking at the object from which the light arrives. The image so formed is inverted, as in a camera.

The focal length of the lens of the eye is variable and is controlled by more or less involuntary muscles which change the curvatures of its surfaces so that objects at a certain distance are "seen" clearly. In common with most single lenses, the distance from the front at which light is brought to a focus depends on the wavelength of the light involved, the shorter wavelengths focusing at a point nearer the lens than the longer ones.

The opening of the lens is controlled by another set of involuntary muscles which

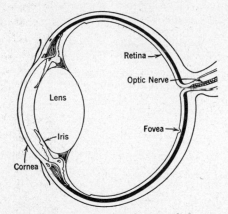

FIG. 7·1 Cross-sectional view of the eye.

change the aperture to a certain extent, in accordance with the intensity of the light which enters the eye. This variation corresponds roughly to the opening and closing of the diaphragm of a camera lens except that the action is involuntary and does not in general cover so great a range. When the diaphragm or "iris" is at its smallest opening, the fineness of detail which can be observed is greatly increased, and physiologically the iris is probably performing its primary function. When the light is very bright the iris closes to get a sharper image. The range over which the intensity of the image is changed is insignificant compared to the ability of the rest of the eye to handle different brightness levels.

The receiving element of the eye, which would correspond to the film in a camera, is a surface consisting of separate sensitive elements of two general types. These may be thought of as small photocells, present in the extraordinary number of about seven million in each eye. When an image falls on this mosaic of nerves each separate cell reacts characteristically, causing an electrical disturbance which is then transmitted to the brain. The details of individual cell response will be considered in a moment. First it is important to follow this response through to the brain to obtain some concept of the physiology of the visual mechanism.

These light-sensitive elements or cells in the retina are connected to nerve fibers which run from the eyeballs back to the base of the brain. In some parts of the retina there is a nerve fiber for every cell, whereas in others, many cells are connected to a single fiber. All the nerve fibers, however, are collected just behind each eyeball into a single cable as shown in Fig. 7·2. The number of nerves in each cable is approximately one million. These cables run back toward the back of the head, where they divide as the diagram shows, and parts of each cross over to the other. The two cables then continue to the base of the brain, each connecting with one half of the so-called occipital lobes as illustrated.

Information about what nerves cross over and how they are divided between the cables forms a fascinating chapter of surgery and physiology. In brief it has been found

that there is a central, roughly circular area in each eye which connects with both halves of the brain. Aside from this the left half (divided down the center vertically) of *each* eye is connected to one side of the brain

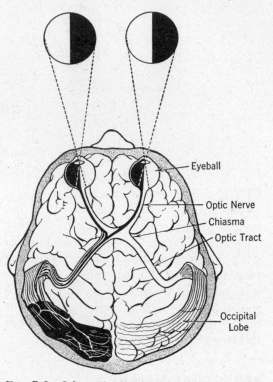

Fig. 7·2 Schematic diagram showing eyes, optic nerves, and occipital lobes of the brain. (Faber Birren, *The Story of Color from Ancient Mysticism to Modern Science*, Westport, Conn., The Crimson Press, p. 277, 1941.)

and the right half of each is, quite independently, connected to the other. Destruction of one whole half of the occipital lobes, therefore, destroys the vision over half of both eyes and weakens central vision but does not destroy it in either eye. Why this should be or how it came to develop is one of the mysteries of vision.

Considering the eye retinas point for point in relation to the occipital lobes we find that approximately corresponding points in each retina have their nerves terminating at roughly the same point in one half of the lobes. The response of the corresponding affected cells in the two retinas, therefore, reaches roughly the same point in the brain. While objects in central vision are repre-

there in even more distorted fashion. What happens when we "see," how "seeing" is related to consciousness, and what the term consciousness itself means are matters of philosophy fortunately outside our present subject. We may discuss it from all stand-

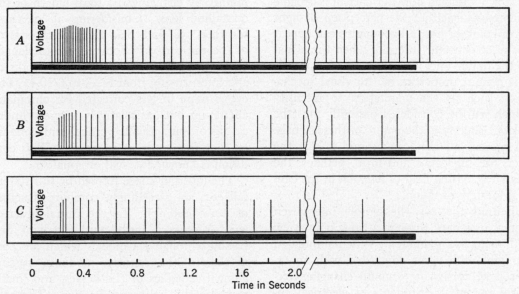

FIG. 7·3 Action potential diagrams of a single nerve fiber of the eye of the horseshoe crab (*limulus poly-phemus*) for stimulus intensities in the ratio of 1:0.1:0.01 for A:B:C. Time is measured from the start of the stimulation period, the duration of this period being indicated by the continuous heavy line. The broken portion of the diagrams indicates time gaps (*a*) of 1.4 seconds, (*b*) 4.5 seconds, and (*c*) 3.3 seconds. Each potential response is approximately 0.3 millivolts. (H. K. Hartline and C. H. Graham, *Journal of Cellular and Comparative Physiology*, Vol. 1, p. 285, 1932.)

sented in both halves, those for the periphery are represented singly. The whole complicated structure indicates that images formed at the back of the two eyes are repeated in distorted and modified fashion over the areas of the two halves of the base of the brain.

With this statement we leave, for the most part, the realm of the known and enter the land of conjecture. The occipital lobes are themselves connected by a complex nerve structure to the higher centers of the brain, and tracing these nerves indicates that the pattern of the lobes is again repeated

points, but the central events are as mysterious as life itself.

From the eye to the occipital lobes, however, science has probed deeply enough to have some inkling of what occurs. In each of the million nerve fibers from each retina a tiny current flows when the cell or cell-block to which it is connected is stimulated by light from an image. The nature of this current has been determined. When a cell is exposed to light an electric current passes along the corresponding nerve. This current has the property of possessing a definite amplitude which remains relatively constant but varies in frequency with the intensity of the light stimulus. The frequency, however, diminishes with time if the cell remains exposed to light and eventually drops to a low value. The effect is illustrated schematically by Fig. 7·3.

It is not known how this current is capable of producing either the perception of light or of color, or how a light source can appear to be of constant intensity when the signal to the brain varies with the time of exposure, but certain properties of the visual mechanism such as the adaptation to intensity which will be considered presently must be related directly to the nature of these signals. At present all that can be said is that the facts are suggestive and form, perhaps, the most fascinating field of research in the general mystery of vision.

Behind the eye the closely interwoven nerves pass back through a cable only a few millimeters in diameter. When stimulated by light each nerve connected with an exposed cell is carrying a rapidly changing electrical potential. Students of electrical engineering will recognize in these conditions the requirements for the production of "cross talk" in telephone cables and will not be surprised in these terms to encounter the phenomena of "simultaneous contrast" and "glare," in which illumination of one part of the eye causes apparent effects in another.

This, in brief, is the manner in which the neural mechanism of the eye operates. Before we consider the over-all characteristics of the eye, attention must be given to the mosaic of nerve endings called the retina.

THE LENS AND RETINA

The distance from the lens to the retina is approximately 14.6 millimeters and is filled with a watery medium, the index of refraction of which is 1.336 and in which objects may sometimes be "seen" floating because of the shadows which they cast. The diameter of the iris varies from 2 millimeters to 8 millimeters, depending on the intensity of the light, and the eye can normally focus objects from about 8 inches to infinity by changing the focal length of the crystalline lens. Considering all of these together, we find that the optical system of the eye can vary between a focal length of 18.7 and 20.7 millimeters and works at apertures varying from f/2.3 to f/10.4. The eye is more or less corrected for chromatic aberration but has relatively severe cylindrical distortions, usually vertical and horizontal, but frequently at an angle. (This condition is known as visual astigmatism.)

The inverted image formed by this system falls on an exceedingly complex structure of nerve endings. To the casual observer this structure is inside out, the light first passing through the nerves which are connected to the sensitive endings, passing along the bodies of the nerves, and finally reaching the light-sensitive tips. The general arrangement in which the light enters from the *top* is illustrated schematically in Fig. 7·4.

The nerve endings themselves may be divided roughly into two types known as "rods" and "cones." It is known from comparative physiology that animals that have only the rod type of nerve ends in their eyes are sensitive only to light *intensities*, while those that have both are sensitive also to color. Because of this fact and corroborative evidence from the distribution of color and brightness sensitivity over the human eye it is assumed that the cones are primarily color-sensitive nerves and the rods are primarily brightness-sensitive nerves without regard to color.

These types of nerve endings are not equally distributed over the retina. Approximately in the center of each retina is an area about 0.5 millimeter (1° 40′) across in which nothing but cones occur and in which they are exceedingly numerous. In this area, the fovea, in each eye there are about 34,000 cones and each of these has a separate nerve which is believed to connect to both halves of the brain. Here is the seat

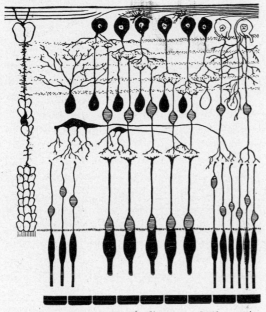

Fig. 7·4 Cross-sectional diagram of the retina greatly enlarged, showing the rods, cones, and nerve connection. (F. E. Cady and H. B. Dates, *Illuminating Engineering*, 2nd ed., p. 233, John Wiley and Sons, Inc., New York, 1928.)

of the best vision. When an object is viewed only the part of the image which falls on the fovea is really seen distinctly.

The remainder of the surface of the retina is made up of a mixture of cones and rods, with the population of cones decreasing continuously as the distance from the center increases. At the outer edges of the retina only rods are present. Since the total number of nerves is far less than the number of cones and rods, and in the central portions there is one nerve to each cone, it is apparent that in the outer parts of the retina

many cells must affect the same nerve. Since in the outer regions the rods predominate, it is equally apparent that sensitivity to color and to form must decrease with distance from the center and that sensitivity to brightness changes (since there are many cells to a single nerve) must increase. These facts are found to be true. Here we are concerned primarily, however, with the facts of direction vision and must pass over these effects as relatively unimportant. It may be noted, however, that the outside areas of the field of vision are used primarily for the detection of *motion*, whereas the central regions are used chiefly for *color*.

In addition to the separation of the nerve endings into rods and cones the areas of the retina differ also in the presence of differing amounts of colored pigments. The nerve endings are immersed in dark-colored liquids which prevent reflection from the back of the eyeball and play much the same role as the antihalation backing on photographic film. Surrounding and covering the central spot in which nothing but cones are present, however, there is, in addition, a rather heavy deposit of a yellow pigment which decreases the amount of blue light that can reach the ends of the cones. This is known as the "macular pigmentation." Its function is probably to increase the resolution of fine detail in this region, but its variation from one person to another is so great that it causes very considerable differences in the color vision of different individuals.

It is apparent that, since the back of the eye consists of individual light-sensitive nerves of finite size, only objects larger than a certain minimum size can be seen in their true dimensions relative to other objects. The cones closely squeezed together tend to form a mosaic of six-sided figures like a beehive. Such a structure is illustrated in Fig. 7·5. The average diameter of the cells of this structure is about 0.003 millimeter, and this measurement corresponds to the image height of a man 6 feet tall at a distance of 5½ miles. However, this statement does not give much concept of the remarkable power which the eye has of reporting to the brain and letting it do the interpreting. A telephone wire may be seen at a distance greater than a quarter of a mile! At this distance if the lens were perfect the

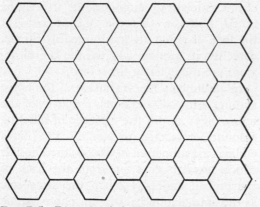

Fig. 7·5 Diagram of the honeycomb structure of the retina surface. Each hexagon is approximately 0.003 mm. across its largest dimension.

image would be 0.0002 millimeter wide. The fact that it extends across a continuous straight row of elements, however, permits a report to the brain that a straight row has been affected, and the brain produces the proper interpretation! Exactly the same effect occurs at all straight edges, and the resolution of the eye for such edges is many times as great as would be calculated from the size of the cells. Some writers believe that all image formation is in terms of such "contours" by the time the image reaches the brain, and there is considerable evidence to support this view. All we can say with certainty is that the constantly moving images which cross the retina as the eye is moved about from position to position do build up in the brain a purely mental construction of the objects in the space before

it. In its detail this mental construction may far exceed anything which can be done with a glass lens and a photographic plate under the best conditions.

In one notable respect, however, the eye may fail badly. If there is a relatively bright area in the field of view, such as may be produced by a headlight at night, or the like, the eye is not capable of seeing *past* this spot. This inability is due to two effects. In the first place, the lens tends to scatter light somewhat, and this "flare" light may be more intense than that from the shadows beyond, so that detail in the shadows is obscured. In the second place, the eye changes its sensitivity in proportion to the total light which enters it and under these conditions may drop to such a low sensitivity that the shadow light cannot affect it at all. Although both effects may be considered as defects for this particular condition, under more normal ones, they represent really valuable properties.

This rough outline of the eye, nerves, and brain will perhaps serve to give a picture of how light can become a mental percept. At best the picture is somewhat vague, and it is not surprising that some of the properties of the eye-brain mechanism do not have a ready explanation in terms of everyday life. However, the properties of the eye have been investigated in great detail for many years. In the next few sections, some of these properties will be presented.

EFFECT OF ILLUMINATION LEVEL

The ability of the eye to distinguish fine detail determines the clarity with which objects in a scene are resolved. Like nearly all the other properties of vision this ability varies with the conditions over a wide range. For ordinary subjects the most important factor is the general illumination level. At exceedingly low intensities only rough form may be distinguished, but vision then improves rapidly and continuously with intensity. Even at levels as low as the light from the full moon, however, detail vision is moderately good, and the eye is able to distinguish separated lines about one-fourth as well as it can in full daylight. At extremely high intensities there is again a decrease for most people, and vision in full direct sunlight in the summer except for dark objects is apt to be about as poor as in full moonlight.

Many factors other than the simple illumination level are involved in this ability of the eye to see fine detail. Most important, of course, is the condition of the individual eye with regard to its ability to form a sharp image on the retina. Assuming, however, that corrective glasses are used, the main variables are the contrast of the detail with respect to its background, the sharpness of the edges, the size of the individual parts of the detail, its motion relative to the observer and the background, and the steadiness of the illumination. Each of these variables has received extensive study, both under restricted conditions and in the more general case of normal vision. The subject is so complex that for the average reader interested in color it is probably better to note simply the general direction of the effects.

High contrast, sharp edges, and the presence of motion and of flicker all tend to make it possible to see finer and finer detail within limits. Extreme conditions of any of them, except sharpness, however, will make it harder to see. Straight lines are easier to see than curved ones, and finer straight lines can usually be seen better in the vertical or horizontal directions with respect to the eye than in the diagonal.

At very low illumination levels the time during which the light is allowed to act on the eye also plays an important part. Under these conditions the minimum intensity and accordingly the minimum detail that may be seen is roughly linear with the time of action. At these levels the area also plays an important role, and for a first approximation the intensity which can be just perceived in the dark is inversely proportional to the area of the object. Both of these rules can be summarized by the statement that at the minimum perceptible intensities the eye reacts to the total quantity of light received rather than to the rate of reception as it does at higher intensities.

In color one is far less concerned with the minimum distinguishable intensity or area than with the minimum differences in intensity or color that can be detected at normal intensities. In fact, at the lowest visible intensities the perception of color disappears entirely. As noted earlier the eye consists of a structure of rods and cones, and the rods are primarily sensitive to light intensities. This fact is corroborated largely by the facts that at minimal intensities only brightness differences are seen and that vision is absent also over the central portion of the eye where only cones are present.

As the intensity level of the illumination on a scene is raised from levels where objects can just be discerned to ordinary daylight values the cones come into action rather abruptly (at roughly 0.1 foot-candles) and there is a transition to color vision in the usual sense of the word. Accompanying this change are a number of changes in the ability of the eye to distinguish brightness differences, as well as in the sensitivity of the eye to radiations of different wavelengths. There is also a marked change in the *range* of intensities over which detail can be seen simultaneously. Since these effects are the very core of the subject of color vision, it may be well at this point to consider them purely from the standpoint of perceived brightness and brightness differences and to disregard for the moment any possible color differences that may occur. The following discussion, therefore, will be restricted to the perception of whites, grays, and blacks in terms of the physics of the

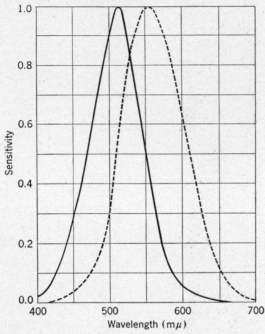

Fig. 7·6 Relative brightness sensitivity of the eye at the scotopic level of vision (solid line) and the photopic level (dotted line). (K. S. Weaver, *Journal of the Optical Society of America*, Vol. 27, p. 39, 1937.)

situation, i.e., in terms of the actual intensities rather than their appearances.

At low intensity levels the maximum sensitivity of the eye falls at a shorter wavelength than at the level of normal vision. This level of vision is referred to as "scotopic." The relative sensitivity of the eye to light of different wavelengths is shown in Fig. 7·6 in which the reciprocals of relative energies necessary at each wavelength to match a fixed brightness are plotted against the wavelength. For comparison the sensitivity curve for normal or "photopic" vision is

shown by the dotted line. Since the maximum of this dotted curve lies in the region of the spectrum usually seen as yellow and that of scotopic vision lies in the green, it is apparent that, if green and yellow are seen as the same brightness in daylight, at levels so low that they may just be seen, the green will appear brighter (although both will be gray!). This is known as the Purkinje phenomenon and may sometimes be seen in late twilight, when green leaves take on an unnatural brightness relative to other yellow and red objects. A red object, in fact, may often be seen as black under these conditions, while green leaves still have considerable brightness and so are seen as gray.

SENSIBILITY CURVES

More important than the Purkinje phenomenon, however, is the way in which the sensitivity of the eye to intensity differences and to a range of intensities changes with the average intensity. If a small two-part field is so arranged that the intensity of each half may be varied it is possible at any intensity level to determine the difference in intensity that is just perceptible between the halves. If after such a setting is made both halves are brought to the intensity of the brighter half and the process is repeated, it is possible to step off the complete range of intensities into just-perceptible differences. This has been done many times by many investigators. While it is true that the results depend to a considerable extent upon the conditions of the experiment there is fairly good general agreement on the result which is obtained under any given set of conditions. When the two-part field is fairly small and circular and is divided vertically through the center, the results obtained may be plotted as the curve shown in Fig. 7·7. For those not accustomed to logarithms this curve may be somewhat difficult to interpret, but there are a number of reasons for plotting it in this manner, notably the fact that it would take a piece of paper several feet long to show it adequately if logarithms were not used. The range of intensities visible to the eye is far in excess of a million to one. If the range from one to two units were to be of appreciable size, a linear scale would have to be

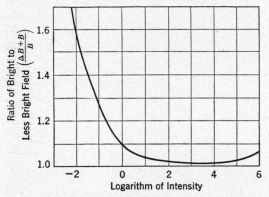

FIG. 7·7 Curve showing the manner in which the ratio of two adjacent fields of just-perceptibly different brightnesses changes for different illumination levels. (L. T. Troland, *Principles of Psychophysiol ogy*, Vol. 2, p. 78, D. Van Nostrand Co., New York, 1930.)

a million times as long to show the whole curve. The intensities, therefore, are represented by their ratios to each other and the whole scale is tremendously shortened. The logarithm to the base 10 of any number is the power to which 10 must be raised (the number of times it must be multiplied by itself) to equal that number. A little thought will show that for any two numbers which have a definite ratio to each other the difference between the logarithms will be the same regardless of the numbers involved. This identity follows from the fact that a ratio is the fraction representing the division of one by the other; if this fraction has the same value for two sets of numbers, then the logarithms of the two fractions are the same because of this identity.

In any case a logarithmic plot of the intensities such as that used in Fig. 7·7 has the property that any fixed distance applied horizontally to the graph represents a fixed *ratio* of light intensities regardless of its position along the base line. The distance from 1.0 to 2.0 on the logarithmic scale represents an intensity ratio of 10, as does also the distance from 5.0 to 6.0. Vertically the value plotted is the ratio of the intensity of the just perceptibly greater intensity $(B + \Delta B)$ to the intensity with which it is being compared (B).

At low intensities a rather high ratio is required for the difference to be detected; this ratio then drops to a relatively low value which remains sensibly constant over a considerable range; it rises again at high intensity levels. In the early days when this subject was first investigated it was felt that over the normal range the ratio or fractional increase that caused a just perceptible change was actually a constant. G. T. Fechner (1801–1887), one of the early investigators in this field, decided that this relationship was a fundamental psychophysical principle and stated what has since come to be known as the Weber-Fechner law. It is that from physical stimuli of all kinds the psychophysical response is constant when the intensity is increased by a definite *ratio*, i.e., independent of the absolute amount. This law has long since been shown to be a special case which holds only approximately over the central range of intensities, but it does give an approximate rule for all conditions. With respect to the eye this rule may be stated as follows. The eye tends to indicate a constant change when the stimulus is changed in a constant ratio. In other words, the eye is sensitive to percentage rather than to absolute changes in intensity. This rule is exceedingly fortunate because of the tremendous changes that the world would appear to undergo with illumination level if it were not so. For example, imagine two shades of gray which reflect 5 and 10 percent of the incident light respectively. At an incident illumination level of 100 foot-candles the difference in the light reaching the eye is 5 foot-candles, with one reflecting twice as much as the other. At 10,000 foot-candles in summer sunlight the difference is 500 foot-candles. That the visual differ-

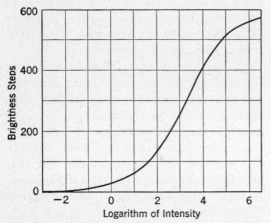

FIG. 7·8 The number of discriminable steps to zero brightness as a function of stimulus intensity. (L. T. Troland, *Principles of Psychophysiology*, Vol. 2, p. 77, D. Van Nostrand Co., New York, 1930.)

ence between the two remains about the same is due to the fact that one still reflects twice as much as the other and that this percentage is what the eye sees, not the absolute difference. At very low or very high intensities the law breaks down, however, and the two look *more* nearly alike than over the middle of the range.

On the assumption that what the eye sees is the number of just perceptible steps from one intensity to another and that the difference between them is judged in these terms it is possible to construct a scale which shows the differential sensitivity of the eye at different intensity levels. Such a curve is shown in Fig. 7·8 in which the horizontal scale is the logarithm of the intensity as

before and the vertical scale represents the number of discriminable steps down to absolute black at each level. Actually this curve has little practical significance and is presented for its general and historical interest.

The data on which the previous curves are based and from which many generalizations have been made with respect to the eye were obtained with a relatively small area of light surrounded by a large field in which no light was present. As soon as light is permitted to be present around the split field and the experiment is repeated, radically different

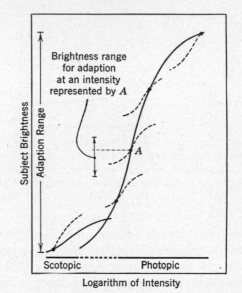

FIG. 7·9 Curve showing brightness range for different levels of adaptation. Above the brightness range for a given level of adaptation added intensity merely tends to cause pain without increasing subjective brightness; below this brightness range, visibility is zero. (W. H. Marshall and S. A. Talbot, *Biological Symposia*, Vol. 7, p. 130, The Jaques Cattell Press.)

results are obtained. Unfortunately there is not a great deal of such data, and generalization is accordingly somewhat risky. It appears, however, that if such data were available curves similar to those of Figs. 7·7 and 7·8 would result, but they would be very much restricted in their intensity range. In other words, the presence of a surrounding intensity (usually called simply a "surround") increases very much the intensity necessary for illumination to be perceived as present at all in the central patch, as well as the difference that must be present to be seen as a difference. The situation is shown schematically in Fig. 7·9.

In practice in a lighted room the range of intensities over which brightness differences may be seen is very much less than is indicated by the curve obtained by successive adjustments of a two-part field surrounded by black. Furthermore, the range from black up *to* the surrounding intensity level is very short at low intensity levels and gets progressively *greater* with increasing intensities up to levels at which the eye is blinded.

ADAPTATION

These facts are due to a property of the eye known as "adaptation." When the eye is exposed to a given illumination level for a sufficient length of time it comes to accept this level as normal, so to speak, and all other intensities are seen relative to the given level. At or below a certain fraction of the illumination level, the actual fraction depending on the actual level, black is seen. Intensities near that of the illumination are seen as white. Intensities above this are seen as brighter than white and usually appear as light sources.

Sudden passages from one illumination level to a quite different one may require some time for the necessary readjustment. Thus, passage from noon sunlight to the levels of a photographic darkroom may require half an hour or more to permit the eye to regain its maximum sensitivity. Passage from this darkroom to bright daylight causes a painful readjustment, but the required decrease in sensitivity takes place in a few minutes or seconds. Thus it is seen that, whereas the eye is sensitive to an intensity range of the order of several million to one, it does this by a change in its overall sensitivity. The total range that it can appreciate simultaneously is of the order of 10 to 1 at the lowest levels and only about 1,000 to 1 at the best possible levels in full daylight.

We shall return to this general brightness adaptation of the eye (it is one of the most important facts of vision) under the general heading of perception. At the moment it is necessary to pass on to a consideration of the sensitivities of the eye as they depend on the wavelength of radiation. It was noted earlier that there are two general regions of vision with respect to response to colored light, the scotopic and the photopic ranges, and that these differ in their relative sensitivities to different wavelengths. It is important to note now that over the photopic range, that in which the colors of surfaces are recognizable as such, this sensitivity is essentially constant, independent of the adaptation level caused by the prevailing intensity and independent of the corresponding color adaptation which will be considered in a later chapter. This sensitivity to wavelengths represents, then, a relatively constant property of the eye.

Wavelength differences, however, are not the only variables which may be recognized by the eye, and we have considered intensity differences only for light which is perceived as white. The eye differs also in the just perceptible amount of monochromatic radiation that may be seen when added to white and in the intensity differences that may be perceived when the light is monochromatic instead of white.

The first of these variables is known as the sensitivity of the eye to differences in purity of colors. Sensitivity to spectral radiation added to white is shown in Fig. 7·10 in which the least perceptible increase in purity is plotted against the wavelength that is added. Purity in this instance is defined as the ratio of the monochromatic component to the total intensity.

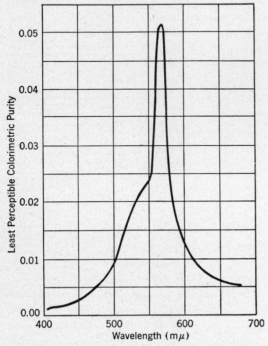

FIG. 7·10 Graph showing the sensitivity of the eye to changes in purity at the achromatic point. The ordinate gives the lowest purity detectable when monochromatic light of the abscissa is mixed with white. (Data from mean values of I. Priest and F. Brickwedde, *Journal of Research of the National Bureau of Standards*, Vol. 20, p. 679, 1938.)

Intensity discrimination of the eye for lights of three different colors is shown by the series of curves of Fig. 7·11 in which it is seen that the increment of intensity that the eye can detect depends not only upon the color of the light but upon the adaptation level of the eye as well. The data completely cover the intensity region in which the Purkinje effect takes place. This region is marked on the blue and green curves by a discontinuous and overlapping

effect as the system changes from cone to rod reception.

With this brief introduction it is necessary to leave this phase of color vision as studied by varying one factor at a time and determining the physical quantity producing a just perceptible difference. The method is one which has been very widely used in psychophysical studies of vision, and reference to the books and articles of the bibliography will introduce the student to a veritable maze of facts. However, one series of facts stands out so clearly that the whole subject of the psychophysics of color in its present state may be said to have originated

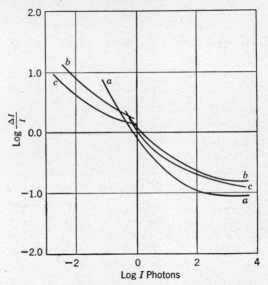

FIG. 7·11 Intensity discrimination of the eye for (*a*) red, (*b*) green, and (*c*) blue light over a wide range of intensity adaptation levels. (S. Hecht, J. C. Peskin, and M. Patt, *The Journal of General Physiology*, Vol. 22, p. 12, 1938.)

from it alone. This is the series of results that have been obtained in the so-called matching experiments for color.

MATCHING COLORS

White light as it reaches us from the sun is a mixture of all wavelengths. From 400 to 700 mμ they are present in about equal amounts. If this light is passed through a slit and a prism to form a spectrum, the band of light containing the wavelengths arranged in order appears to contain only a few separate colors. Newton, who first performed the experiment, divided the colors into seven because of his belief in the mystic properties of the number seven, but most observers see six at normal intensities and as few as three if the intensity is low.

Thomas Young, and later James Clerk Maxwell, pointed out and demonstrated that if only three widely separated monochromatic lights are chosen and these three are projected on top of each other on a white surface it is possible to match the appearance of any of the other parts of the spectrum. Further investigation has shown that this effect has fundamental validity, and from it has arisen our basic knowledge of the color sensitivity of the eye. Without attempting to trace the history of the studies we may state the results briefly as follows:

1. The mixture of any two wavelengths of light will give rise to a color falling between the two in the spectrum, except at the extreme ends where they form a series of purples related to the extreme short-wavelength colors (around 400 mμ in the region known as violet). The exact wavelength matched varies with the relative intensity of the two, being continuous from one to the other as the percentage varies from 0 to 100.

2. There are a whole series of pairs of monochromatic lights which when mixed will give white light. These pairs are called the complementary wavelengths.

3. There are no complementary wavelengths for the central region of the spectrum (the greens).

4. Any known color may be matched by light of a single wavelength mixed with white light, with the exception of the colors which we call purple or magenta.

5. Those colors which cannot be matched by monochromatic plus white light may all be made into white light by the addition of some line from the green spectral region (i.e., they are all *complementary* to some spectral region).

From this series of statements a host of consequences follows. They are the basis of the whole system of the measurement of color as it is known today and may be considered the best-established facts in the realm of color vision. The remainder of the chapter will be devoted to tracing out some of these consequences. The formal measurement schemes which have been established will then be considered in a later chapter (Chapter XII).

Before proceeding it is important to note that the subject under discussion is the *physical* composition of any two lights which appear to a normal observer as *identical*. It is not necessary, except as a convenience, to refer to their appearance. The appearance of the *pair* may change markedly with the conditions. It is, however, possible to calculate the distributions that will appear to match under all conditions, and that is the present subject.

We wish to arrive at the result mentioned earlier: that any possible color may be matched by a mixture of three suitably chosen colored lights. This result is to be derived from the five fundamental facts stated above. We can proceed as follows.

The mixture of any close pair of spectral lines matches for color a line intermediate between the two in the spectrum (Statement 1). If they are far enough apart they form white (Statement 2). If they are still farther apart they form purples which are complementary to light in the green region (Statement 5).

Let us proceed stepwise to see what these mean in the problem of trying to match any color by means of mixtures of monochromatic light of different wavelengths. Suppose we start with a mixture of monochromatic and white lights as illustrated in Fig. 7·12 and proceed to develop a series

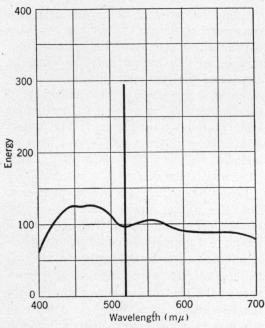

FIG. 7·12 Energy curve of a green light made up of a mixture of ICI Illuminant C and a monochromatic line of wavelength 520 mμ. The energy of the continuous source is per 10 millimicron band.

of colors which will exactly match this mixture.

From Statement 2 it is apparent that the white-light part may be matched by any pair or pairs of complementary lines. The relationship of the complementary wavelengths is shown in Fig. 7·13. Any pair of lines or any group of pairs as indicated by these curves make white light. All the combinations shown in Fig. 7·14 visually match that of Fig. 7·12. In (c) a large number of the complementaries are shown grouped to form continuous regions. In all

of these the original monochromatic light is still present. This is not necessary, however, because adjacent lines also will produce this same color and thus the following groups (Fig. 7·15) also produce matching colors. Again those lines that generate the same color may also be grouped in sets, this time forming a continuous region around the spectral line as in Fig. 7·16.

Since the pairs of lines taken singly depend on the *ratios* of their intensities to produce the exact color and not on their absolute values, it is apparent that such continuous regions may be made to have nearly

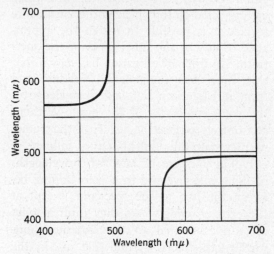

FIG. 7·13 A curve showing the relationship of complementary wavelengths with ICI Illuminant C defined as the neutral white. Any line drawn perpendicularly to the abscissa at any point other than between 492 mμ and 568 mμ intersects the curve at the point corresponding to the complement of the wavelength, the complementary wavelength being located on the ordinate.

any shape provided this condition is fulfilled. This possibility is still further extended by the fact that any pair of lines matches one between them and that this pair can then mix with a similar pair to produce the same result as if *only* the intermediate lines were present, giving the same

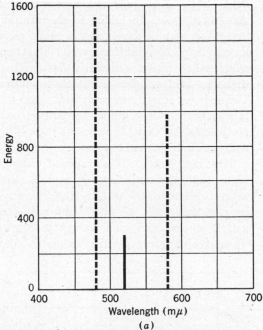

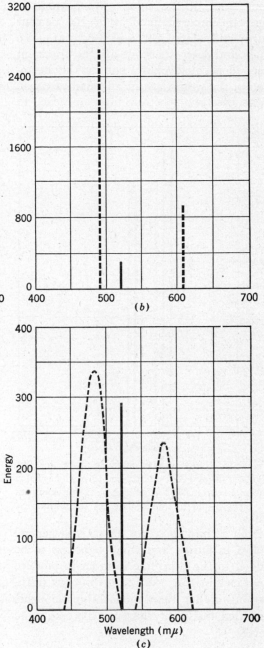

Fig. 7·14 Three different energy-distribution systems which visually match the light of Fig. 7·12, for both chromaticity and luminance. The arbitrary energy units are identical on all graphs so that energy relationships between graphs may be compared. The energy of the continuous sources is per 10 millimicron band.

effect as a single line between each of these two. The possibility is indicated in Fig. 7·17 in which lines (*a*) and (*b*), and (*c*) and (*d*) match lines (*e*) and (*f*) respectively and the resultant mixture matches (*g*).

It is apparent that the mixture of a single wavelength with white light can be matched by an *infinite* number of different energy distributions, all of which will *look exactly alike*. This is a valid generalization. Any color can be matched by an infinite number of other energy distributions.

The only limitation on the variety of such mixtures lies in the "purity" of the color which can be obtained. This purity is defined as the percentage of white light which must be mixed with the required monochro-

matic light to match the given color. Note that this is a purely physical definition as far as the light is concerned and is based on the *matching* condition and not on the appearance of the color. Monochromatic light is simply defined as of 100 percent purity and white light as of 0 percent. We shall find later that not all the spectrum lines *look* equally pure, but for this definition of the word they are all assumed equal. Whenever two spectrum lines are mixed to

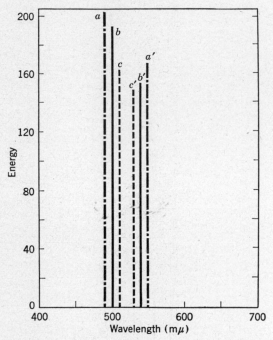

FIG. 7·15 Three pairs of monochromatic lines, (*a*) and (*a'*), (*b*) and (*b'*), and (*c*) and (*c'*), which match the monochromatic line of Fig. 7·12 for dominant wavelength and luminance but not for purity.

match a third, however, there is in general a loss in purity, and white light has to be added to the third line in order to produce an exact match. When continuous distributions rather than monochromatic lights are used this purity loss may become quite severe.

We may proceed to develop a series of systems by which a given color may be matched. In the first place, as stated, a color may be matched by the choice of a proper wavelength and the addition of white

light (or the analogous choice of a complementary wavelength added to the sample). Second, it may be matched if a single wavelength is chosen arbitrarily and then one which when mixed with this wavelength or with the sample gives a match is chosen. Third, if we select arbitrarily any three that taken together in suitable proportions will produce white, suitable ratios of these three will match any possible color.

The last system is of special interest. Note that the *only* requirement is that, taken together in the proper ratio, the wavelengths will form white. They will then match *any possible color* except for purity. This exception means that to match some

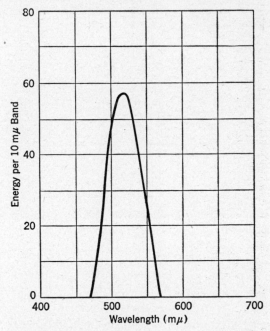

FIG. 7·16 Continuous energy curve which matches the monochromatic line of Fig. 7·12 for luminance and dominant wavelength but not for purity.

very pure colors it may be necessary to add white to the sample. This phenomenon has given rise to all the so-called additive processes of color rendition—those in which the image is formed by the additive mixture of colored lights—and has also been the source of endless speculations on the mechanism of vision itself. It is an obvious, even if not an entirely logical, deduction that if only three colors are necessary to match all possible colors, there must be only three processes in the eye which give rise to color.

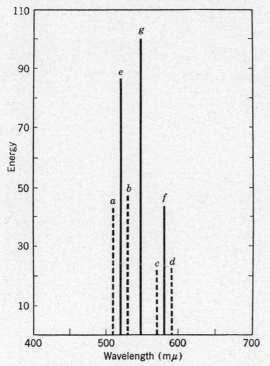

Fig. 7·17 Relative energies of various matching monochromatic line combinations in which lines (a) plus (b) match line (e); (c) plus (d) match (f); and (e) plus (f) match (g). All matches are for brightness and dominant wavelength but not for purity.

The matter has been hotly debated for two centuries, but no conclusive experiments have been devised. Fortunately, it is not necessary that one of the types of theory be accepted in order to understand the empirical facts, and we shall proceed without taking a stand on the issue.

Returning to the fact that any color may be matched by a suitable mixture of only three spectrum lines provided white can be added to the sample, let us proceed to generalize this statement somewhat in the terms used above. It is apparent, from what has already been said, that each of the three spectral lines in a set may be matched by an infinite number of energy distributions. Each line of such a set may therefore be replaced by a continuous distribution which exactly matches it except for its purity (white light content). Since there are an infinite number of sets of three monochromatic lines that will match all colors and an infinite number of continuous distributions that will match each one of these lines, it is apparent that *in theory* there are a triply infinite series of sets of three that meet these conditions. We have now reduced the facts to what amounts to an absurdity, however. Although all these facts are true, the purity of the colors involved becomes so low if the continuous distributions involved are very broad that they are of no practical interest. The subject has been pursued to this point to make it as clear as possible that there is nothing *unique* about a set of three colors that in appropriate mixture will match all possible colors. This clarification has been considered necessary because such sets have come to be called "primary" colors since in any given color mixture in which they are involved the primary colors come first and the mixture color second—*and for no other reason.* The word will be used in the present book because it is the one usually encountered in the literature. In any given instance there is nothing fundamental about "primaries"; they are simply the colors which happen to be used to form a mixture.

COLOR MIXTURE CURVES

In these terms, then, let us look at the so-called color mixture curves for the eye. Suppose we take an arbitrary set of three colors which meet the requirements of forming a white in suitable mixture and are in themselves quite pure colors. By a suitable instrument we can arrange to have pure monochromatic light illuminate one half of a small field and variable mixtures of our three colors illuminate the other half. If we can also add white to the monochromatic half, we know from the previous processes that it is possible to obtain exactly matching fields through the whole range of visible monochromatic radiation. This has been done many, many times in the last fifty years. The result is always a set of data which tell how much of each of the colors was used to produce the match, and these data can be used to plot curves called color-mixture curves for the eye. The actual technique used varies slightly with each experimenter. It is important at the start, however, to realize that these curves are *completely* arbitrary in the sense that if three other colors had been chosen as primaries the results would have been quite different. On the other hand it is equally obvious that *with respect to these particular primaries* these curves describe the color mixture properties of the eye. Since there are an infinite number of sets of such curves, however, each different but each describing the same properties, data of this type provide no way of determining basically what these properties are. Some other criteria are necessary to untangle the eye from the primaries involved, and so far no one has been able to devise such criteria. The visual mechanism by which the eye evaluates color, and so sees these infinities of distributions as matching, is not known. As matters stand at the moment, color-mixture curves are isolated although well-determined facts, and this is true whatever theory of color vision the reader may follow in his thinking, although there is ground for the hope that the work of Wright on color adaptation

may tend to clarify the matter eventually.

A set of color-mixture curves, taken from the standard International Commission on Illumination (ICI) mixture data, is reproduced in Fig. 7·18. Each curve represents the relative amount of one of the three primary colors used. The curves are plotted against the wavelength and are matched in such a way that the heights of the three curves at any wavelength indicate the relative amounts of the three necessary for the match. Where the curves go below the line, that primary was added to the *sample* (i.e., the monochromatic field) to reduce its purity to the point where a match was possible. These particular primaries were monochromatic lights of wavelengths 480, 510, and 600 mμ.

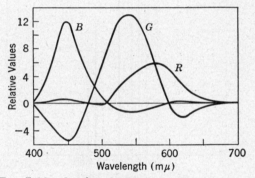

FIG. 7·18 Graphs of ICI tristimulus data transformed to real primaries.

Mixture curves for three other primaries are shown in Fig. 7·19. These sets of curves have an interesting property: if one of them is considered as the reference set, the others can be calculated directly from a knowledge of the energy distributions of the primaries involved. Without going into mathematics, this possibility is apparent from the fact that each primary of the *new* set can be matched by a suitable mixture of the *three* from the standard set and these *mixtures* can be considered the primaries for the *new* one. Mathematically all that is involved is the solution of three simultaneous equations in three unknowns. Since this possibility is true for any set of *real* primaries, it is also true for *imaginary* ones, and it is possible to calculate a set of mixture curves for three primaries that are more pure than any colors in the spectrum. This calculation involves the simple assumption that no one of the primaries ever has to be added to the monochromatic sample. Such a set of mixture curves has no negative components, and calculations when color mixture curves have to be used are very much simplified. One set of this type has received international standardization and will be discussed in some detail in a later chapter (Chapter XIII).

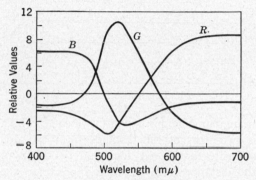

Fig. 7·19 Graphs of ICI tristimulus data transformed to real primaries different than those of Fig. 7·18. The curves of this figure are for highly desaturated primaries, whereas the purity of the primaries of Fig. 7·18 equals 100%.

In the rest of the present chapter it is desirable to note briefly how it is possible to calculate whether two energy distributions will appear to match and to note the general manner in which it is possible to specify colors so that they will be brought to a comparable basis.

Suppose two energy-distribution curves are presented which, as curves, appear entirely different. It is desired to know whether they would match if the lights that they represent could be observed side by side. We can proceed in a great many ways, based on the given facts. Basically, however, all the ways are the same. Each curve is analyzed, wavelength by wavelength, to determine which mixture of some arbitrary set of primaries will be required to match each one. If the results indicate that the same mixtures are required for each, the two match. If different ratios are required, they do *not* match. The failure indicates the direction of the differences between the two. At the present time it does not define the *amount* of the difference except so far as the properties of the primaries may be a matter of visual experience.

To facilitate this matter of evaluating differences, as well as to make it possible to define colors numerically, several systems have become customary. These are basically either a monochromatic plus-white system, such as has been described, or some arbitrary three-primary system. There are obviously an infinite variety of such systems, and only a few have received general acceptance.

Before proceeding to a consideration of the *appearances* of energy distributions and the variables involved in such appearances, it is well to consider the psychophysical variables which have been developed in this chapter so that the difference between a psychophysical and a psychological variable will be apparent.

The infinite variety of ways in which an energy distribution may be constructed so that it will match a given energy distribution makes it somewhat difficult to state generalizations that aid in visualizing the phenomena involved. Perhaps the only legitimate generalization that can be made is that it takes *three* physical variables in the light to produce a match.

What is meant by physical variables is difficult to describe. In the monochromatic plus-white system they are wavelength, ratio of monochromatic to white intensities, and total intensity. In any three-primary system they are the amounts of each of the three primaries or any derived combination of these. Thus, two ratios and the amount of the third, or the total energy and two ratios, etc., are sufficient. In mathematical terms, color vision is a function of three independent variables, and three independent variables are necessary in order to specify a color stimulus.

Any set of three independent variables may thus be made the basis of a color-stimulus specification system, the word system meaning simply a convention by which a series of three numbers defines a stimulus. Historically the earliest of these systems, and from the present standpoint the most obvious, is the numerical intensity values for a set of three arbitrarily chosen primaries.

THE MAXWELL TRIANGLE

James Clerk Maxwell introduced a simplification of this system which has had far-reaching effects on subsequent methods. He suggested that, since one of the most logical variables is the total intensity and since color as such does not seem to vary greatly with the total intensity, the color part of the light could be expressed separately by means of only two variables. He chose as these two variables the ratios of two of the three intensities to the total. However, to make it simpler to visualize the nature of the mixture of the three, he pointed out that three ratios which add up the unity can be plotted simultaneously on a triangular diagram. Such a diagram is shown in Fig. 7·20 and has become known as the Maxwell triangle. The color represented by the point A on the diagram is calculated and plotted as follows. It is found by experiment that one unit of blue, two units of green, and two units of red are necessary

to match the particular color being studied. These units are based on the amounts necessary to match white, i.e., one unit of red, one unit of green, and one unit of blue mixed give white. They are, thus, psychophysical units rather than purely physical energy units. The sum of the units used is five. The blue is one-fifth of this, the green two-fifths, and the red two-fifths. On the

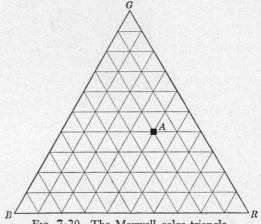

FIG. 7·20 The Maxwell color triangle.

triangular diagram a point is located which is two-fifths of the distance from the side opposite to the red apex and two-fifths of the distance from the side opposite to the green apex. It is a property of an equilateral triangle that this point is also necessarily one-fifth of the distance from the blue side to *its* apex. The sum of the three perpendiculars from any point inside an equilateral triangle is the same for all points. If the sum is equal to unity, triple fractions of unity are represented by every point inside.

The greatest importance of such diagrams comes not from the ability to specify a stimulus in terms of three known lights, although this is important, but from the fact that if two colors come out with the *same* specifications it can be stated with conviction that the two lights will exactly match if they are placed side by side. This statement can be made without having seen the two side by side.

Such matching conditions obviously transgress the limitations of the system. The fact that two lights match is independent of the system because if they match in one system they match in *all*. Thus, it is possible to

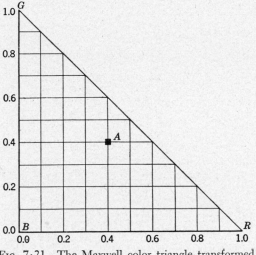

FIG. 7·21 The Maxwell color triangle transformed to rectangular coordinates.

pass immediately from one system to another by the simple procedure of determining the corresponding points of each.

In practice, the systems that are in use today are not plotted on the Maxwell triangle but on a simple right-angled triangle. If the total intensity can be neglected, only two variables are necessary, and two variables may be plotted on an ordinary right-angled plot. The plot of Fig. 7·20 is repeated in Fig. 7·21, and it is seen that this plot has the same effect as the previous one.

It will be seen in a later chapter, in which it will be considered in some detail, that this method of plotting is used in the highly developed ICI system of colorimetry. It

is important, however, to realize just what is meant by a point in such a triangle.

The fact that two colors which plot at the same point will match visually suggests that in some way the point *therefore* specifies the *appearance* of the colors. This is not true, however, except under *fully specified* conditions. The energy distribution from which the point was calculated is one of an infinite number of energy distributions that will be seen to match by a normal observer. No statement is made in regard to the possible psychological effects which may influence the observer. The specification is purely *psychophysical*. It states the properties of the radiant energy in terms of the eye considered as a receptor with fixed sensitivities. It does not in any way take into account the interpretation which may be placed by the observer on the messages from this receptor to the eye. In the next chapter we shall take this interpretation into account and see what systems may be developed from these appearances. It will develop that there is little relationship between the two. The reader should realize, however, that this lack of correlation exists in spite of the fact that it is possible to specify *matches* without regard to *appearance*. It is to be hoped that eventually purely psychophysical specifications will include also the appearance of stimuli. They will do so if some way is found in which *differences* may be specified so that they are comparable for all colors. Progress is being made along these lines at the present time.

BIBLIOGRAPHY

Moon, Parry. *The Scientific Basis of Illuminating Engineering.* New York: McGraw-Hill Book Co., Inc. 1936. Chapters XII and XIII.

Parsons, Sir John Herbert. *An Introduction to the Study of Colour Vision,* 2nd ed. Cambridge, England: The University Press. 1924.

Polyak, Stephen L.   *The Retina.* Chicago, Ill.: The University of Chicago Press. 1941.

Sears, Francis Weston.   *Principles of Physics III —Optics,* 2nd ed. Cambridge, Mass.: Addison-Wesley Press, Inc. 1946. Chapter V.

Southall, James P. C.   *Introduction to Physiological Optics.* London: Oxford University Press. 1937. Chapter I.

Walsh, John W. T.   *Photometry.* London: Constable and Co., Ltd. 1926. Chapter III.

Woodworth, Robert S.   *Experimental Psychology.* New York: Henry Holt and Co. 1938. Chapter XXII.

Wright, W. D.   *Researches on Normal and Defective Colour Vision.* St. Louis, Mo.: The C. V. Mosby Co. 1947. Chapters I, II, and XXX.

Zworykin, V. K., and Wilson, E. D.   *Photocells and Their Application,* 2nd ed. New York: John Wiley and Sons, Inc. 1932. Chapters I and XIV.

The Visual Variables of Color

CHAPTER VIII

UP to this point light and color have been considered either as purely physical in nature, i.e., consisting solely of energy distributions, or as psychophysical, i.e., as energy distributions evaluated by the eye as a fixed sensitivity receptor. In the present chapter it is necessary for the first time to consider the appearance of the colors to the observer.

THE APPEARANCE OF COLORS

Once the consciousness of the observer is included in the subject of color, a whole new series of phenomena must be considered. These lie for the most part in the realm of psychology. It is well to keep in mind, however, that there are many phases of the psychology of color. When light that consists of pure short-wavelength energy is viewed by an observer, he usually sees the color blue, provided he has what is known as normal vision. If the area is fairly small and surrounded by bright green, he will usu-

ally see the same stimulus as purple, and if the area is surrounded by bright purple he will usually see the stimulus as green. As far as we know at present, these effects are just as much properties of the eye as any of its other characteristics, but they are usually considered part of psychology. If the mechanism of the eye were better known they would probably be considered part of psychophysics. The *interpretation* of the messages to the brain as blue or green or purple, however, is definitely part of psychology. On the other hand, there are a considerable number of conditions under which the color that the observer will see is *indeterminate*. That is, the color cannot be specified from a complete knowledge of the physical conditions. These situations arise generally when there are, so to speak, two or more ways of looking at the subject, and the way actually chosen depends on the *intentions* of the observer toward the scene. These effects cannot become part of psychophysics except to the extent that the extreme possibilities may be defined in these terms. They represent one aspect of the true psychology of color. There are many other aspects which are also completely non-physical, such as emotional reactions to color. They can all be classed as the reaction of the observer's *organism* to color as distinct from his interpretive reaction.

The present discussion deals with the interpretive part of the observation of color as such. It is restricted mainly to a consideration of the conditions under which a given stimulus gives rise to a perception of red or green or blue, as the case may be. It is the part of color vision that it is hoped some day may be considered psychophysical, i.e., completely determined by all the light reaching the observer's eye. The phases of the subject that are less determinable in this sense will be discussed in the next four chapters.

HUE, SATURATION, AND
BRIGHTNESS

When light having a given spectral-energy distribution enters the eye it gives rise to a consciousness of some color. If the energy distribution of this light is varied systematically, the color in consciousness varies systematically also. Careful introspective study shows that these observed variations may be described in terms of three mental variables, called hue, saturation, and brightness in the terminology of the Optical Society of America (OSA). Like all mental variables, it is difficult to describe these separately without reference to the physical stimulus variations which cause them. In conversation we can describe a color to another person only by reference to a physical object or stimulus such as green as the color of grass, or red as the color of a rose. It does not follow and is not true, however, that because this reference is necessary there is any simple relationship between the stimulus and the mental variables. For most people this concept is a difficult one to grasp. The viewing conditions are just as important in determining the color seen as is the stimulus itself.

With this word of caution, the three fundamental variables of color as a mental phenomenon may be described. Perhaps the most important of the three for everyday purposes is hue. *Hue* may be described as the main quality factor in color. It is the essential element which leads us to name it red or green. It is the most noticeable factor that changes in the spectrum as the wavelength of the light changes, and for this reason it is the quality that permits us to describe the color in terms of the wavelength of the monochromatic light which it matches. It is not possible to get much closer than this to the definition of any mental variable except by the introduction of words which have little meaning to the average reader. Perhaps we may say simply that hue is the chief (although not the only) characteristic that gives rise to the basic color names. The eye can distinguish about two hundred different hues under the best conditions.

Saturation may best be defined as the percentage of hue in a color. In common speech the saturation of a given color is described by such words as pale or deep, weak or strong, in connection with the name of some hue. The concept is roughly parallel to that of the purity of a chemical compound or the concentration of a solution. Saturation and hue together define what may be called the quality aspect of the mental image caused by light.

Brightness, the third variable, may be defined as the quantitative aspect of the mental image. It describes the appearance of the image in terms of its apparent amount. It is important to point out, however, that this definition is in terms of the mental image alone, without reference to any *estimate* based on the appearance of other objects. It will be seen presently that a direct judgment of brightness made independently without regard to other visible areas may differ markedly from a considered judgment of the situation. In particular, it will be found necessary to distinguish carefully between the brightness of the light coming from an object and the apparent relative reflectance of the object compared to other objects. The difference is purely psychological, i.e., determined by the attitude of the observer, and may be described as a difference in apparent brightness caused by the intentions of the observer with respect to the scene. To avoid confusion when this difference is discussed (Brightness Perception, Chapter X), it will be found necessary to use the additional term "lightness" (OSA nomenclature). This may be defined as the visually apparent reflectance of a surface under a given set of conditions. In general, brightness and lightness differ whenever there is a noticeable non-uniformity in the illumination of a scene.

The three variables, hue, saturation, and brightness or lightness, therefore, define completely the qualitative and quantitative aspects of color as a mental phenomenon. It is apparent that these three may be made the basis of a three-dimensional system for plotting or at least describing a particular color. For example, all possible mental colors may be thought of as distributed through the interior of a solid in which brightness varies vertically; hue varies with the position about the center in a horizontal plane; and saturation varies with the distance outward along straight lines perpendicular to a vertical through the center of the solid. A schematic diagram of such a solid is shown in Fig. 8·1. In this diagram the vertical line through the center of the solid has zero saturation, and hence zero

hue, but varies in brightness from one end to the other. Along any radial line (i.e., a line perpendicular to the brightness axis), saturation increases with distance from the center, and hue varies with the angular position of the line as seen from the top or bottom of the figure. Such a system for the surface colors has been worked out by the

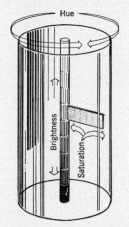

Fig. 8·1 Diagram of a color solid. Brightness varies with position along the vertical axis, hue varies with position around the axis, and saturation varies with distance from the axis.

Munsell Company (now the Munsell Foundation) and will be considered under Specification of Color, Chapter XIII.

COLOR CIRCLES

Just as it was found possible to represent the psychophysical aspects of color, other than intensity, by plotting the ratio values of additive-mixture primaries on a two-dimensional diagram, it is possible also to represent hue and saturation on a two-dimensional diagram, again neglecting brightness. It is a fact peculiar to color vision, first pointed out many years ago, that all possible hues may be arranged in a continuous circle. If all the hues seen in the spectrum plus all the hues which may be produced by mixtures of the ends of the spectrum, i.e., blue and red, are laid out, it will be found that all *possible* hues are present. Such an arrangement is called a "color circle" and is obviously the basis for the angular arrangement of hues in the color solid shown in Fig. 8·1. In such a color circle if saturation is considered to increase outward from the center, any color can be designated by a point on such a circle. This procedure is completely analogous with the method used for the additive primaries in the previous chapters.

In talking about hue and saturation, however, we are discussing psychological variables, that is, *mental* percepts, which cannot be *measured* in any way. In the previous discussions of additive primaries, we could define directly the *amounts* of each primary and their exact ratios. In the present discussion, in common with all mental variables, such measurements cannot be made. We are forced to use in their place a whole group of new concepts in order to develop scales on which to plot our data. There are no words by means of which we can state how blue an object looks except by reference to some other blue object. Even then, all we can say is that it looks *more* or *less* blue, i.e., higher or lower saturation, etc. Nor can we state with any great exactness by *how much* it is more or less blue. Accordingly, in order to have a scale on which such data may be plotted (and so visualized and compared), it is necessary to use a quite different and less satisfactory approach. We *can* state with fair accuracy when two colors seem to differ by the *same amount* as two others, and this judgment may be refined by suitable instruments and practice, provided the differences are fairly small. We can judge quite accurately also what are known as "just perceptible differences" between colors, provided we may vary the differences from zero up to and beyond this condition.

The two methods known as the method of just perceptible differences (j.p.d.) and the method of equal differences are the only methods available by which the *mental* qualities of colors can be stated quantitatively. By the first method, for example, it has been determined that some 125 hues in the spectrum may be discriminated by the average observer, and that as many as 200 steps of saturation may be seen for some hues. By the second method it is possible to imagine a systematically constructed solid in which all possible colors are spaced so that at a given point a distance in any direction is equivalent psychologically to the same distance in any other part of the solid, i.e., the colors at the two ends of two lines of equal length will appear equally different in all parts of the solid. A figure spaced in this manner is discussed in many places in the literature of color. It is probably an unattainable ideal in many respects (i.e., an *incorrect* concept), but it serves as an aid in visualizing the gamut of possible colors. This method has been approached sufficiently by a number of material standard systems to have real practical value.

By the use of either j.p.d. or equal-distance steps it is possible to study many of the variables of mental color and to arrive at a great many conclusions about the way in which the eye-brain mechanism acts in response to the physical quality of a light stimulus. It must never be forgotten, however, that data derived in this way are essentially *different in nature* from those obtained by physical measurements. In particular, they differ in the fact that, whereas a physical scale, such as a series of intensities, is *known* to be equally spaced with respect to some physical variable, the j.p.d. or equal-difference scales do not have such certainty. A j.p.d. or an equal-visual difference may be the same sort of thing for one pair of colors as for another pair or it may not be; there is no way of knowing. It is customary to overlook this difference because we know nothing better to do. That practice will be followed here except for an occasional reminder.

Having considered the three mental variables of color broadly, we may now consider them individually in some detail. In particular it is important to consider in what ways they are and are not related to the physical variables involved in the quality of the light. It has been stated earlier that there is no simple relationship between the light in terms of its physical properties and the mental color produced. The rest of the chapter will be devoted to an amplification of this statement and to a consideration of some of its consequences.

BRIGHTNESS

It is desirable to consider first the general subject of brightness, and it may be said at the start that for this variable there is less connection between the stimulus and its effect than there is for the other two.

Brightness, in a general way, increases with the physical intensity of the light which produces it. If a single spot of light is the only light in the field of view, and this light increases or decreases in amount without changing its spectral-energy distribution, it will appear brighter or dimmer respectively if it appears to change at all. The eye, however, is much more sensitive to the *rate* of change than it is to the absolute intensity. A carefully considered decision as to the physical intensity of the light may be in error by a factor as high as several hundred times the value chosen, the amount of error depending on the recent conditions to which the eye and the observer have been exposed. A change in intensity if moderately rapid may be apparent when the absolute change is of the

order of a few percent or sometimes even a fraction of one percent. A careful decision as to the *intensity* of a constant light as judged by the brightness of the mental image may be in error by a tremendous amount, since comparison is made with the memory of other brightnesses. In the case of brightness there is no way of stating the exact magnitude of the error, however, since brightness is a purely introspective variable. Errors become apparent only when one is surprised by returning to a known situation.

The point of the discussion is the fact that an absolute brightness scale *does* exist as a mental phenomenon but is very vague and indefinite compared to the roughly parallel physical intensity scale. That it does exist must be kept in mind when in a later section the phenomena of brightness adaptation are considered, since it will be found that the eye has a strong tendency to maintain brightness constant under different intensities of light. If this tendency were complete, all fields containing light of a single quality would appear equally bright, and they do not.

In sharp distinction to the vague way in which absolute brightness may be estimated is the exceedingly precise estimation of the *relative* brightness of two lights of the same quality seen adjacent to each other. As stated earlier, the eye is most successful when operating as a null instrument. It can distinguish the condition of equality with great precision; it can detect equal small differences with fair accuracy; it becomes quite inaccurate when called on to estimate absolute values. It has this property in common with all the other human senses, and in much the same degree. Lighter or heavier is an easier decision than absolute weight, warmer or colder than temperature, and louder or softer than total sound volume. This general fact is due to the adaptability of the organism to its environment and is one of the fundamental phenomena of life. Before considering it in detail with respect to vision, however, it is best to consider how colors appear in relation to each other under fixed conditions.

Consider first the relative appearance of two surfaces which are colorless (i.e., without hue) to the eye. It can be stated definitely that, if there is a brightness difference between the two, the dimmer one will appear to contain gray. If the intensity of the illumination is low, both may appear gray, but the dimmer of the two will appear darker gray than the brighter. If the intensity is moderately high (and no brighter surfaces are visible), the brighter will appear white and the dimmer gray. This general phenomenon holds as well for surfaces that do have hue as for those which do not. Whenever two surfaces are seen side by side, the dimmer of the two will appear to contain more gray than the brighter, and it is possible to generalize that gray is a mental phenomenon that occurs whenever light is seen as dim with respect to another light. In addition, gray is sometimes, but not always, seen when the absolute intensity of light is low. In these instances it may be seen as gray or it may be seen simply as a light of low intensity, the appearance depending in part on the attitude of the observer.

It may be added that these are the only ways in which gray may be seen, either alone or in a color. Gray is the mental phenomenon whose presence indicates a brightness lower than another and is not produced by the quality of the light itself. The apparent external reality of gray surfaces is due almost entirely to the fact that in any ordinary situation there is either a visible surface of higher reflectance or at least a clear knowledge of how a surface of higher reflectance would look.

GRAY SURFACES

The concept of a gray surface has added a new phenomenon to the preceding discussion. There is an important difference between the color of a *surface* and the color of *light* of the same quality. The difference arises from the fact that the surface is localized in space. The change in appearance is not so simply explained.

There are only two ways in which light may reach the eye. It may come directly from a light *source* or it may reach it by reflection from a *surface*. If it comes from a surface, the light must somehow have reached this surface from the source before proceeding to the eye, and there are two general ways in which this may occur. The light falling on the surface may be the *same* as that falling on other objects around it or it may be different. There are, then, three general ways in which light may reach the eye from a given scene: it may come direct from a source, be reflected by an object receiving light from the general illuminant, or be reflected from a localized illuminant not shared by the surroundings. These three ways cover all possibilities from the physical viewpoint. Psychologically, it will be found necessary to distinguish one more situation; namely, the presence or absence of *texture* in the reflecting surface. Texture may be defined as visible non-uniformities in the reflectance of a surface which are obviously a physical property of the surface. It may vary from a roughness so fine that it appears simply as a matte surface to irregularities such as exist in coarse textiles, or it may be a simple variation in reflectance. Texture of any kind makes the position and existence of the surface a visible fact quite aside from the fact that the surface reflects light. Complete absence of texture would make it impossible to see the surface directly, even if its existence might be inferred from its edges and a knowledge of the object.

The addition of texture gives five possible conditions under which colors reach the eye. It is possible to increase this number greatly by adding other geometrical and physical conditions, but these five cover all the conditions which affect the mental *color* of the observed light. It is well to list them and consider the possibilities inherent in each condition from the standpoint of brightness alone.

Case 1. Light reaches the eye direct from a light source.

Case 2. Light reaches the eye by reflectance from a surface lighted by the general illuminant and having no texture.

Case 3. Light reaches the eye by reflectance from a surface lighted by the general illuminant and having a clearly visible texture.

Case 4. Light reaches the eye by reflectance from a surface lighted by a separate illuminant and having no texture.

Case 5. Light reaches the eye by reflectance from a surface lighted by a separate illuminant and having a clearly visible texture.

(The case of light transmitted through a diffusing textured or non-textured surface has not been included because it is identical with the reflection case.)

These five *physical* possibilities give rise to *three* general ways in which the light may appear, in accordance with its brightness relative to a reflecting white surface in the immediate neighborhood. They may be summarized as follows:

1. *It may appear brighter than a white surface in the immediate surroundings.* Regardless of its origin, the light may appear either directly as a light source or as a surface having higher than normal saturation.

These two appearances can occur with any of the five conditions; but, in general, true sources and surfaces with no texture will tend to look like sources, and both surfaces and true sources that have texture will tend to appear like surfaces whose saturation is higher than normal. Textured white surfaces will appear simply as brightly lighted white. A true source of high relative brightness will so appear in spite of its texture.

2. *It may appear approximately the same intensity as an illuminated white in the surroundings.* Under these conditions all colors appear either as whites or colors not containing gray, regardless of whether they are direct sources. Recognition of the fact that a particular area is actually a source may change its appearance somewhat, but in general it will still look like an illuminated surface not containing gray. Presence or absence of texture plays little part.

3. *It may appear of lower intensity than a white in the surroundings.* All colors, regardless of their physical quality, will appear to be gray or to contain gray under these conditions, the intensity relative to the illuminated white in general determining the amount of gray.

Note that these observations refer exclusively to areas in a general scene and are stated with respect to the intensity of the light reaching the eye relative to that which would reach it from a white surface in the neighborhood of the area under consideration. The whole matter may be summarized by the statement that any area brighter than an illuminated white contains no gray and may either look like a source or be seen as having higher than normal saturation, whereas anything of lower brightness will appear to contain gray and tend to look like a surface whether or not it has texture. Texture at high brightness tends to prevent the surface from looking like a source.

In this discussion we have referred to whites, super-whites, and grays. It may be well at this point to consider the subject of white, gray, and black from the present standpoint, especially since it affords an interesting introduction to the subject of brightness adaptation to be considered next. White, gray, and black as mental phenomena are associated variables in that they all have zero saturation and zero hue as these words have been defined.

Any attempt to define a physical stimulus that will give rise to one of these appearances, however, is beset by the difficulty that it is necessary to define not only the stimulus itself but also its *surroundings*. In a general way these appearances are produced by *surfaces* that are non-selective with respect to the general illuminant. Gray and black can apply to light sources, but white applies only to a surface. When these conditions are met the brightest non-selective area which is not obviously a light source will tend to look white, although if it has a low reflectance and there are enough familiar objects around it it may be seen as light gray. (The observer's hands can act as such a reference.) Non-selective surfaces having reflectances from as low as 50 percent to 100 percent will look white under almost all conditions when they are the brightest surfaces in the field of view.

Any non-selective surface that is not the brightest area in the field will appear gray, the shade of gray depending on its relative brightness. The same statement applies to the apparent gray content of any color.

The appearance of black is a considerably more complex phenomenon than that of either gray or white, and with this phenomenon we introduce the question of brightness-adaptation level. The eye as a receptor tends to adjust itself to the prevailing illumi-nation level in such a way that the visible range of physical intensities tends to produce about the same range of mental brightnesses for all scenes. The exact relationship which determines the sensitivity level of the eye has not been determined, but it is apparent from the work of Helson and of Judd that it is some complex function of both the general illumination level and the averaged reflectance of the scene being viewed. In a general way the sensitivity level of the eye is determined by the total light which enters it. For any given set of conditions the state of the eye is referred to as the "adaptation level" of the eye. It can adjust over a range of more than 100,000 to 1, in intensity, although the appearance of brightness does change over so great a range. At each adaptation level, however, there is a maximum lower intensity which will appear black provided no lower intensities are present and provided the light has no hue. If the surface or source is colored, a considerably lower intensity is required for it to appear black, but at all adaptation levels there is an intensity level below which *all* stimuli, regardless of their quality, will appear black. This intensity level is usually referred to as the "black point." It rises and falls with the adaptation level and does not bear any simple relation either to the adaptation level itself or to the intensity being seen as white, although both affect it.

It was pointed out in an earlier chapter that intensity discrimination varies with the intensity level and depends markedly on the type of field being observed. By combining this concept with that of the brightness appearance we have been discussing, it is possible to draw a picture, so to speak, of the way the eye responds to intensities at different adaptation levels, if either the number of just perceptible or the number of equally distant steps over the whole intensity range under different observation conditions is determined. The results obtained may be plotted in a diagram such as that of Fig. 8·2. (A similar diagram was given in Fig. 7·9 in Chapter VII.) In this diagram the long curve represents at each intensity level the total number of steps which may be distin-

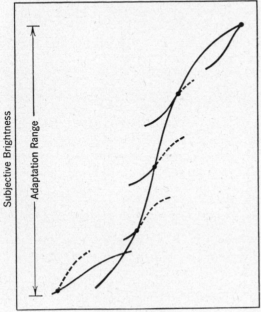

FIG. 8·2 Schematic curve showing how the discriminable intensity ranges vary as the adaptation level of the eye is changed. (W. H. Marshall and S. A. Talbot, *Biological Symposia*, Vol. 7, p. 130, The Jaques Cattell Press.)

guished from zero to that level when the field being observed is small, two-part, and surrounded by black. Under these conditions adaptation is set by the test field itself and rises or falls with its intensity. The shorter curves represent the range of intensities that may be discriminated when the test field is surrounded by a much larger field which is held at the value given by the point where the small curve crosses the larger one. It is apparent that the downward range for each of these surrounding levels is much more restricted than that of the longer

curve. At intensities higher than the surrounding intensity these curves have a different meaning from those for lower intensities. This difference, indicated by dotting the lines, is caused by the fact that a brighter central area tends to take over the eye adaptation and raise it to a higher value than that caused by the surrounding area.

The eye, therefore, is an instrument of variable sensitivity. Its indications as given by the appearance of the stimuli vary with this sensitivity. For scenes taken as a whole this fact is fairly obvious, when the effect is known. The brightness of an incandescent light at night compared with its feeble glow when the sun shines on it is a sufficient example.

BRIGHTNESS ADAPTATION

It is not so apparent, however, that the same phenomenon occurs *within* a uniformly lighted scene under ordinary conditions of vision. The eye changes its sensitivity not only with the general illumination but also with the particular area being observed, and it does this in a way which is dependent on its recent exposure to other areas and to the general illumination level. For explanation of the basic facts involved in this phase of vision, we are indebted to the work of W. D. Wright in England and to J. F. Schouten in Holland. (See bibliography at the end of the chapter.) In brief résumé, the brightness part of the effect may be described as follows. (The effect of colored stimuli will be considered in a later section.)

When the eye is exposed to a lighted area the sensitivity of the eye in the exposed area drops very rapidly to a lower value. The time taken for the change is of the order of 0.2 second and is coincident with the appearance of brightness as a mental phenomenon. (The facts suggest even that the sensitivity drop is somehow the *cause* of the appearance.) This sensitivity drop was measured by these workers by a technique first suggested by Wright. A two-part field was so arranged that one half was observed by one eye and the other half by the other, and controls were provided by which the intensities could be varied rapidly. Another considerably more intense source of light was then provided which illuminated one eye only at any desired intensity, but which when turned on took the place of the half-field normally seen by that eye. The test procedure was to illuminate one eye with this light with the divided field off; then, after the desired time, to turn this off and the divided field on. If the two halves appeared to match before the exposure, they no longer did afterward. The exposed eye then required more light to produce an intensity match. By quickly readjusting the intensity it was possible to determine how much more was needed. It was also found that the effect of the exposure wore off and so called for a constantly changing amount to keep the fields balanced. This effect could be followed, and the rate at which the sensitivity recovered could be measured.

The details of the findings are quite complex but very clear in their implications. They show that exposure of the eye to light almost instantly causes its sensitivity to drop. The amount of this drop depends directly on the intensity of the light and on the adaptation state of the eye at the time of the exposure. The eye, therefore, takes up a new adaptation level almost immediately on exposure to a brighter light, but the new level depends on the old, the dependence on the old level being due to the rate at which the eye sensitivity recovers from the exposure. This rate was found to vary tremendously with the *time* of the exposure, as indicated schematically in Fig. 8·3.

In other words, it was found that for brief times of exposure the eye sensitivity recovers almost immediately, but that for longer exposures the recovery is more and more gradual and requires a number of minutes to return when the exposure is continued as long as a minute. The asymptotic approach of the curves to the upper part of the diagram, of course, is due to the fact that the eye approaches the sensitivity level set by the *test* fields as its new level.

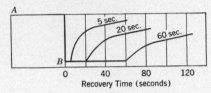

Fig. 8·3 Schematic curves illustrating the manner in which the eye regains the sensitivity it had at low-intensity levels after being subjected to more intense light for the different periods of time as marked. The level A represents the low-intensity sensitivity and B the sensitivity immediately after viewing the intense source.

In terms of normal vision, these facts lead to a picture somewhat as follows. As the eye moves over a scene (jumps would be a better word), one object and then another occupy the center of the field. At each stop the eye sensitivity changes up or down to a new sensitivity level in this part of the eye. Each area, accordingly, is viewed with a sensitivity determined by the previous area. Two factors, however, are operating to make the sensitivity shifts generally small. In the first place, the total *range* of intensity in a normal scene is small compared to the total sensitivity shift of which the eye is capable; and secondly, the eye seldom stops more than a brief time on any one object. The first fact means that the eye gets a long-time exposure to intensities all of which fall in a relatively narrow range. It accordingly takes up an adaptation level at some sort of average of these intensities from which it recov-

PLATE V

The perception of depth is affected by the lighting contrast of the scene. The upper scene has diffuse front lighting. The identical scene, with non-diffuse high-contrast side lighting (*below*), gives a much greater perception of depth.

ers quite slowly. The short-time exposures to individual areas cause sensitivity shifts around this average. Recovery from these depends on the time spent on each area but varies from a time so short that it is complete during the blinking of the eyelids (this introduction of frequent dark periods is probably as important a function of the eyelids as keeping the eyeballs moist) to periods long enough to make a very decided difference in the appearance of the objects viewed subsequently.

In an exactly similar manner these investigators found that exposure to one part of the eye produces an identical, although smaller, effect in regions of the eye adjacent to those exposed. There are, therefore, three types of adaptation which can take place, all of which are customarily present simultaneously. There is the long-time general exposure which sets a slowly changing level and which may be called "general adaptation." There is the short-time local exposure from which recovery is more or less rapid which may be called "local adaptation," and there is the effect of this local adaptation on the adjoining areas which may be called "lateral adaptation."

The everyday phenomena associated with these three adaptation types are familiar to all. General adaptation is the phenomenon of readjustment of vision which takes place when we pass from a light to a dark room and have to wait to see things or, vice versa, is the painful experience of passing from the dark into a sunlighted room. It is also the phenomenon causing the sudden blackening of the windows at twilight when the lights are first turned on in the room, a phenomenon showing nicely the almost instantaneous nature of the readjustment. Local adaptation appears as the well-known "afterimages" and "successive contrast" effects. Lateral adaptation appears as "simultaneous contrast" and as "glare."

The result of these effects on the brightness of a given area may best be described by considering the effects in the cases of one-, two-, three-, and four-part fields. Such fields are shown in (a), (b), (c), and (d) respectively of Fig. 8·4. (Note that an area surrounded by black may be considered a one-part field since adaptation in the sense in which we are using it here is produced only by light.)

(a) The eye adapts to the area. This means that the area contains no gray unless it is of very low intensity or unless a texture is present which is sufficiently variable in brightness to act as an internal reference for white. As the intensity is increased there is some increase in the appearance of brightness but the increase is slow relative to the total intensity change.

(b) If there is a difference in intensity between the two parts of the field several possibilities occur, all but one of which accentuate the difference between the two halves. If the eye looks first at the brighter half its sensitivity is lowered; transfer of the gaze to the other half then makes this look darker. If the darker half is viewed first, sensitivity rises, and the brighter half then looks brighter still. Viewing the dark surround permits the attainment, in general, of a higher sensitivity level and again aids the discrimination of the difference between the illuminated fields. If they are very bright they may produce glare and so tend to mask the difference. Fixed viewing of some point of the figure, however, without blinking, will produce fairly complete local adaptation and greatly decrease the sensitivity.

(c) In a three-part field such as the one shown, the outer surround has little effect unless it is larger and brighter than either of the center areas. If it is, however, this surround produces both a general and a lateral adaptation to an extent which depends on the movement of the eyes. These adaptations then control the sensitivity to brightness differences in the central areas. In general if the central areas are much dimmer, any intensity difference must be relatively large to be visible. The nearer the central intensities approach that of the surround the greater the sensitivity of the eye to the difference becomes. When they become much greater than the surround,

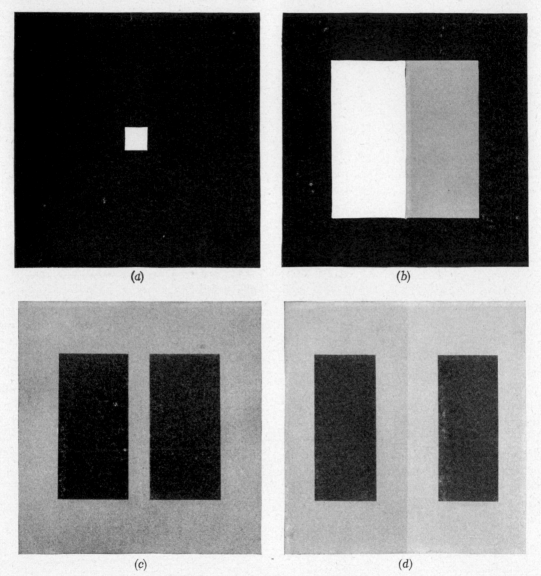

FIG. 8·4 (a) One-part field with black surround; center spot appears brighter than it would without the surround. (b) Two-part field with black surround; the eye is very sensitive to the brightness difference. (c) Three-part field; because of light surround, the eye is relatively insensitive to brightness differences. (d) Four-part field; dark areas are of the same brightness, but the one on the right appears darker because of contrast with its surround.

they tend to take over the adaptation, and the field then acts much as if the outer part were not present. If the outer field is intermediate between the two inner ones maximum sensitivity is present as it would be if there were no surround.

(d) In the four-part field as shown, relations become quite complex. Such a field was studied by Hess and Pretori in 1894. (See Chapter X.) They sought to determine the relationship of the intensities of central squares which would appear to match each other when the surround intensities were varied but kept brighter than the central areas. When the eye was fixated on the center of the central vertical they found that the relationship took a relatively simple form. In brief, if a match of the central squares was obtained for any condition, this match would persist if light were then added on either side in constant ratio to the central square and its surround. The actual *ratio* necessary for a given case was determined by the conditions, but any amount could be added. The appearance of brightness of either central square, therefore, was determined almost wholly by its surround, primarily because of lateral adaptation or simultaneous contrast, in this case, since the eye position was fixed.

This must complete the present survey of brightness but we shall return to it a number of times in later sections and chapters. It will be found that nearly identical phenomena exist in relation to hue and saturation although their effects are not nearly so well known or so easy to see. Moreover, because of the difficulties of observation and measurement of hue and of saturation differences, less work has been done in the field and fewer data are available.

We can start our survey of hue and saturation with a few simple qualitative statements and proceed to consider the consequences of the facts in relation to familiar experience. In the first place colors of different hue but of comparable brightness placed side by side affect each other in such a way that the hue difference is magnified. The same statement can be made with respect to saturation differences with the added fact that they may also introduce a considerable hue difference. Furthermore, both hue and saturation shift with the intensity of the light and with the relationship of the eye adaptation level to the scene.

DEPENDENCE OF HUE AND SATURATION ON INTENSITY

The relation of hue to intensity was studied by Purdy for pure monochromatic

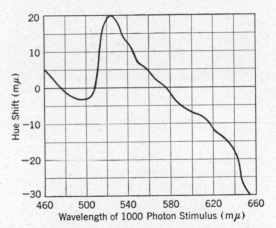

Fig. 8·5 Graph of the change in hue with a change in intensity in which the ordinates represent the change in wavelength required in order to produce the same hue when the intensity is reduced from 1,000 to 100 photons. (D. M. Purdy, *The American Journal of Psychology*, Vol. 43, p. 548, 1931.)

light, and his results for an intensity difference of 10 to 1 between a large test field and a smaller matching field are shown in Fig. 8·5. The curves show the amount by which and direction in which the matching field had to be changed in wavelength to produce a hue match.

Similar but less conclusive data by Abney on the effect of a saturation change in hue over part of the spectrum are shown in Fig. 8·6 plotted in the same manner.

Abney studied also the effect of intensity on hue in much the same manner but over a much wider range and came to the con-

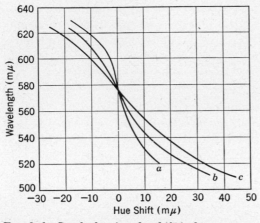

FIG. 8·6 Graph showing the shift in hue, as measured in millimicrons, when the amount of white light added to the colors of the spectrum is (a) 43%, (b) 21.5%, and (c) 15%. Above 577 mμ the hue tends to shift *away* from the red end of the spectrum and below this point the hue shifts *toward* the red end. (W. DeW. Abney, *Researches in Colour Vision and the Trichromatic Theory*, p. 260, Longmans, Green and Company, London, 1913.)

clusion that all colors tend to move toward blue or yellow at high intensities and toward red or green at low, a conclusion not inconsistent with that of Purdy.

COLOR ADAPTATION

The effect of colors of different hue placed next to each other is somewhat better known. It is usually called simultaneous color contrast and was investigated rather thoroughly in the last century by Chevreul in France. In general it may be stated that under these conditions there is a strong tendency for the eye to subtract each color from the other and to intensify the remaining components. The meaning of this tendency will become somewhat clearer when we consider mixture diagrams, but the effect again is to intensify the hue difference. Thus an orange and a yellow placed next to each other will tend toward an appearance of a greenish yellow and a reddish orange, the orange color common to the two tending to disappear. In other words, colors under these conditions have a strong tendency to become complementary to each other, i.e., to approach colors which correspond to those which would make white if they were mixed additively.

If two colors of the same hue but of different saturation are placed side by side there is again a strong tendency for the complementary hue to appear in the area of lower saturation. If both saturations are moderately high, the effect is merely to accentuate the saturation difference. If one is sufficiently low, it may actually appear to have a fairly strong complementary hue.

Perhaps the most startling demonstration of simultaneous color contrast is produced when two colored lights are so arranged that each throws a shadow of the same object on a relatively large white surface. Under these conditions each shadow is illuminated by one light only and the background is illuminated by both. Such shadows *always* appear roughly complementary to each other *regardless* of the color of the two lights, although closely related hues may produce very *low* saturations. This effect was discovered very early in the history of vision and may be repeated in anyone's home. The only requirement is that the lights be of different colors. The most satisfactory results are obtained when the lights give about the same illumination on the screen and when their colors are quite noticeably different. The phenomenon still occurs if these conditions are not met, but the saturations tend to be low if the hues are close and a high brightness difference tends to obscure the colors.

All these effects are due to color adaptation of the eye, and again we are indebted to Wright and Schouten for a clarification of the mechanism. In brief, the color receptor system of the eye acts as if it consisted of three types of receptor, one broadly sensitive to short wavelengths mostly restricted to the blue and blue-green end of the spectrum, one sensitive to a broad band in the green, and one sensitive to the red end but also somewhat sensitive to the short-wavelength blue end (the region seen as violet for this reason). Each of these receptors *independently* follows rules in these regions similar to those that have been discussed for brightness. It is not known whether such receptors really exist, and it is necessary to consider them as *independent* of the brightness phase, i.e., *four* types of receptors have to be postulated to cover all the facts. In that event, however, all the facts fall into a consistent pattern. The hypothesis is not necessarily correct, but it affords a framework for predicting results under stated conditions and is known to be satisfactory, at least qualitatively, for all color adaptation and color-mixture phenomena. The fourth brightness receptor would have the wavelength-sensitivity distribution given in Chapter II and usually called the luminosity function. It does not change appreciably during color adaptation and for this reason must be considered independent of the other three. (It is possible, of course, to imagine that this *is* one of the three and that we see blue as a difference between brightness and red-and-green receptor stimulation but this is not so simple to visualize as four receptors.)

We can now consider the facts stated earlier in the section in terms of the three color receptors and the single brightness receptor simultaneously. The effects are not simple but appear to be straightforward.

The evidence appears to indicate that when the eye is adapted to some spectral quality and intensity of light approximating average daylight the receptors are at what may be called equal sensitivity. Light of this intensity and quality seems always to appear white, and light of any other quality at this intensity will tend to appear colored, whereas light of the same quality at lower intensities tends to appear bluish. A light that appears white at moderately low intensities would tend to appear yellowish in daylight. There is a strong tendency therefore for the mental image induced by a physical stimulus to appear colored if the quality of the light does not correspond to some fixed range. This tendency must be kept in mind when we consider later the adaptation phenomena. Adaptation almost never is complete, at least mentally. There is always a residue which permits the observer, if he so desires, to see the direction of the departure from white of any given stimulus. The adaptation level does, however, have a profound effect on vision.

The facts indicate that if the eye is exposed to a colored stimulus the sensitivities of the receptors are each reduced by an amount which is roughly proportional to the stimulus value for each. Thus, if the eye is exposed to green light, the green receptor and to a much lesser extent the red and the blue receptors are depressed in sensitivity. The duration of this sensitivity depression is governed by the rules for brightness which have been stated before, i.e., the higher the intensity and the longer the exposure, the slower is the recovery of sensitivity after the exposure stops. While the depression lasts, the eye is deficient in response from the green receptor. It will see a low-intensity non-selective stimulus as pink or a yellow as orange, etc. This effect, of course, occurs in all three adaptation forms, general, local, and lateral. As a general phenomenon over the whole eye green adaptation would mean that the stimuli which are seen as neutral gray are those which would appear green under daylight adaptation. True non-selective surfaces illuminated by the green light would have this characteristic, and accordingly they would remain more or less neutral visually. Whereas this effect is true for illumination with light of low saturation, we shall see an exception presently when the Helson-Judd effect for saturated illuminations is considered. (See Chapter XI.)

In the same way a local green stimulus will depress the green receptor locally and produce a spot in the eye which is less sensitive to green with respect to the other receptors than is called for by the illuminant. Transfer of the vision from this area to a non-selective gray area will show a pink spot corresponding to this local change and hence give an afterimage of the first area.

Viewing of a bright spot of color will not only affect the receptors in the eye on which the image of the spot falls, but also depress the sensitivities of those in the immediate neighborhood. Accordingly, if a blue-green stimulus is placed next to a green one, adaptation to the green will affect also the receptors receiving the blue-green, by decreasing the green sensitivity and thus shifting the effect of the blue-green toward pure blue. Obviously this adaptation is the cause of the simultaneous color-contrast phenomena. It works reciprocally also, of course, to increase the apparent saturation of the green by decreasing the effect of any blue light which it may contain.

It is instructive to consider the colored shadow phenomenon in these terms. Suppose there are two lights illuminating a large white projection screen, and an object is so placed that it throws two clearly defined shadows on this screen, one from each light.

Suppose also that one of these lights is pure yellow and the other pure red. Over the whole screen, except for the shadows, there will be a mixture of the red and the yellow forming an orange color. One shadow will be lighted only by yellow light, and the other only by red.

Yellow light affects the red and the green receptors about equally, depressing their sensitivities, but does not affect the blue. Red light affects the red receptor still further, not affecting either the green or the blue. When we look at the screen therefore the blue receptor is depressed very little, the green moderately, and the red by a relatively large amount. With the eye in this condition let us consider the effect of the yellow light. Since neither light has affected the blue receptor it is free to increase in sensitivity to a value approaching that which it might have in a completely dark room. As we have seen this sensitivity may be many thousands of times its value in daylight. Since almost no physical source has so little blue light in it and since the blue receptor does have a slight tendency to respond to longer wavelengths, this sensitivity increase will continue until the blue receptor *does* respond to the yellow and red lights. Meanwhile as stated the green receptor has been depressed somewhat and the red even more. The eye then responds to the yellow stimulus *as if it were a blue-green color*, and the shadow lighted by yellow *looks* blue-green. The red-lighted shadow on the other hand affects the red receptor only, except for a slight effect on the blue, and accordingly it is seen as a deep red slightly tinged with blue. The colors which started as yellow and red have now become blue-green and bluish red and are complementary colors. If this reasoning is carried through for any pair of colors, it will be found that the result is always the same. The colors always appear complementary in hue although, if the differences produced between the receptor sensitivities are small, the saturation of the colors may be low.

GENERAL COLOR ADAPTATION

From the standpoint of normal vision these effects are not very significant although in many special situations simultaneous contrast is an important problem. Even under usual conditions, however, the general adaptation produced by the illuminant has marked consequences. Let us consider it first for illuminants not greatly different from daylight and then for strongly colored illumination. The latter is probably merely an extreme case of the former, but strongly colored illumination makes some phenomena apparent which would not be noticed otherwise and it should be considered separately.

When the eye is exposed for a long time to a scene illuminated, for example, by an ordinary incandescent light, the average color entering the eye is roughly equivalent to that of the light source itself, that is, as the eye looks first at one and then another of the objects the average quality of the light seen tends to approach that of the incandescent light. Since such a light is weakest in the blue end of the spectrum and next weaker in the green relative to the red, the eye tends to become quite sensitive to blue, somewhat less so to green, and least to red, and all stimuli are seen with the eye in this condition because the long exposure makes recovery slow. This eye sensitivity distribution, however, is opposite to the energy distribution of the source. Accordingly, a nonselective surface illuminated by this quality of light *tends to be seen* as white, i.e., it gives the same output to the brain from the receptors as daylight. Furthermore, all normal colors will tend toward their appearance in daylight because the eye tends to compensate for the deficiencies of the source by its own sensitivity readjustments. This phenomenon is known among psychologists as "color constancy" because it tends to make the color of objects constant regardless of the energy distribution of the general illuminant in the scene. Obviously it is of very great importance in daily life since it tends to make color a *property of the object* rather than the variable it would be if the receptor sensitivities were fixed. A white paper illuminated by artificial light would be very yellow indeed if the eye sensitivities did not readjust to the situation.

Because the phenomenon is so important and so little realized by the average observer it seems worth while to consider it in a little more detail and to show the extent to which it does and does not produce actual constancy of object color. We can consider first what would happen if eye adaptation were really complete and then the fact that it is not. This is done to show that even complete adaptation would produce only approximate constancy of object color.

There are four main cases and we may list them and consider them in order.

1. An object color reflecting light at all wavelengths and owing its color to a relatively moderate departure from equal reflectance at all wavelengths.

2. An object color which is produced by a sharply defined reflectance in one region of the spectrum with little reflectance elsewhere.

3. A pair of lights which match in daylight but have different energy distributions, as seen by an eye adapted to some other light quality.

4. Two object colors of different relative brightness, as seen by eyes adapted to different illuminants.

Case 1. Each color receptor of the eye responds to the light to which it is sensitive. The total effect of a given stimulus may be computed by multiplying the energy in the stimulus at a given wavelength by the sensitivity to this wavelength and adding together the products for the whole wavelength range. Suppose the stimulus in question is the pale blue paper (in daylight) shown in Fig. 8·7. This paper reflects light

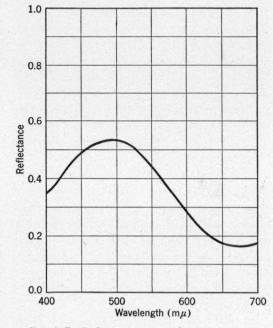

FIG. 8·7 Reflectance curve of a blue paper.

at all wavelengths but more completely in the blue than in the red. Let us assume that in daylight it affects the red receptor half as much as the green and the green half as much as the blue. Now if this paper is illuminated by artificial light rather than by daylight, the light source is weaker than daylight in the blue and in the green relative to the red. Suppose it has one-fifth as much energy in the blue, one-third as much in the green relative to the red as daylight. The eye, however, is assumed to be adapted completely to this light. It is, accordingly, five times as sensitive to the blue, three times as sensitive to green relative to red as it *would*

be in daylight. Accordingly, the blue paper still looks blue since the color of the illuminant has been *corrected* by the sensitivity changes of the eye, and the response to the *paper* is one-fourth as much to red and one-half as much to green relative to blue, just as it was in daylight. This blue, then, with its continuous spectrum and gradual change is seen as of essentially the same hue under incandescent light as under daylight.

Case 2. Suppose, however, that instead of the pale blue with its gradual change of reflectance with wavelength we have a surface which reflects only in one narrow region of the spectrum. The reflectance curve for such a surface is shown in Fig. 8·8. In daylight this surface would affect the green and the red receptors about equally and would be seen for this reason as yellow in color. Suppose now that this surface is illuminated

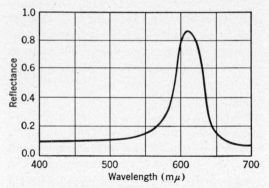

FIG. 8·8 Reflectance curve of a yellow surface.

by the same incandescent light as in Case 1. Because all the reflectance is concentrated in a narrow region of the spectrum, the gradual change of the artificial light with wavelength does not change the spectral distribution of the reflected light from the surface appreciably (it would not change it at all if it reflected only one wavelength of light!). The eye, however, has changed its sensitivity relations to fit the new illuminant. Since this had one-third of the energy in the

134

green that it had in the red, the ratio of sensitivity of green to red is now 3 to 1. Since the quality of light from the paper has not changed and since it affected them equally in daylight, the output of the green receptor is now three times that of the red, and the color is seen as a green-yellow rather than the pure yellow seen before.

Such extreme cases seldom arise in practice, although a monochromatic light which appears yellow in daylight will appear quite green if surrounded by artificial light. Ordinary surfaces vary all the way from this extreme to that of Case 1. The actual color of a surface under daylight and tungsten light, therefore, is not entirely constant but is subject to this error caused by the *way* in which the eye adapts to the illuminant.

Case 3. Assume that a pair of lights with quite different spectral-energy distributions have been so adjusted that they appear to match for color when the eye is adapted to daylight. As shown in the previous discussion the *reason* they appear of the same color is that the three-color receptors and the brightness receptor are stimulated *equally* by the two lights. In somewhat more detail this statement means that the total effective quantity of light for each receptor is the same for the two over the range for which each receptor is sensitive. Mathematically it means that if each wavelength of each light is multiplied by the sensitivity of a given receptor for that wavelength over the sensitivity range to wavelength, the sum of these values is the same for each light for each of the receptors.

Suppose now that the eye becomes adapted to a color of illuminant other than daylight. Under these conditions, as we have seen, the sensitivities, that is, the *outputs* of the receptors, have changed but their sensitivities to wavelength have not. The same amount of energy at any wavelength may produce more or less effect than before

on *a given receptor* but if this receptor were twice as sensitive to one wavelength as to another before the adaptation it would retain this *ratio* of sensitivities. In other words the sensitivity *distribution* does not change; only the amount of response (actually the efficiency) changes.

If the principle involved is considered carefully for a given pair of lights, it will become apparent that no matter how the sensitivity of the receptors is changed in terms of total output, so long as their wavelength sensitivity distributions do not change the ratios of the three receptor outputs will continue to be the same for both the lights. Accordingly, while the apparent colors of the pair may change markedly with the adaptation condition, the lights will continue to match each other whatever condition is encountered. This situation is the "matching condition" stated earlier as an experimental fact. The change in color with the adaptation condition, of course, comes from the change in the relative outputs of the receptors with respect to each other.

REFLECTING SURFACES

Perhaps a word of warning is in order at this point, in view of the literature on the subject. The previous discussion applies only to a pair of matched lights whose spectral-energy distributions do not change with the illumination conditions which control the eye. A pair of reflecting *surfaces* which match in daylight *will* change their reflected energy distributions if the illuminant is changed. While the eye will *tend* to correct this difference, the match, in general, will not continue to persist because of the reasons stated under Case 2.

Case 4. The discussion of the first three cases was restricted for the most part to the color receptors although under Case 3 it was pointed out that the brightness phase of matched lights also persists with adaptation. If we consider the relative brightnesses of reflecting colored objects under different illuminants, however, a quite different situation is encountered. Suppose a red and a green object are equally bright under daylight illumination. The brightnesses may be calculated with respect to each other by multiplying *at each wavelength* the energy in the source by the reflectance of the object and then multiplying this by the sensitivity of the eye to this wavelength as shown by the luminosity curve. If this is done for each wavelength and all of them are added together the result for the two surfaces is a pair of numbers which express the relative brightnesses of the two surfaces (luminances actually, since this is a psychophysical and not a psychological calculation).

When the illuminant is changed to tungsten light, for example, and the calculation is repeated, any difference that exists between the two objects as far as the spectral reflectance is concerned will affect the two sums differently, and there is *no* compensating action on the part of the eye. It is true that the brightness receptor changes its output with respect to the intensity level, but its sensitivity to wavelength does not change appreciably as far as is known at the present time. Accordingly, brightness matches of colored objects, either reflecting or transmitting (the subtractive-mixture case in general), are not compensated by brightness adaptation, and the match does *not* persist. Green objects are usually darker with respect to red in artificial light than they are in daylight simply because there is less energy in the green part of the spectrum of artificial light with respect to the red than there is in daylight.

As a brief summary of the chapter to this point, it may be stated that there is no simple correlation between the physical stimulus producing a colored mental image and the color which is seen but that there is a fairly direct relationship if eye adaptation by way of four independent receptors is taken into account. There is a direct relationship between stimuli that match visually in that such matches persist regardless of the adaptation state of the eye. (We are here overlooking the fact that at extremely low intensities these matches do not always hold. Over the range of normal vision, however, this is one of the few well-established psychophysical relations in the field of vision.)

It follows from this summary that the ratio of the outputs of the eye receptors determines the actual mental colors seen by the observer. This conclusion is not strictly true as will be found in the chapter on color perception. Psychological factors having no relation at all to the stimuli also can affect observed hue. In the absence of such factors, however, it is fairly well established that the color is determined by the receptor sensitivities and their adaptation states. There is one rather interesting experiment, incidentally, which confirms this fact and may be tried rather easily.

It was noted earlier that simultaneous contrast effects modify the hue of a color to a rather remarkable extent. It was also noted that the afterimage produced by staring at a color for a short time and then looking at a neutral surface is always complementary in color to that of the stimulus. However, this afterimage is always complementary to the color originally *seen*, not to that which might be assumed from the stimulus. As one example, suppose that a blue-green is viewed surrounded by a magenta which makes it appear a clear green. An afterimage produced by staring at this area will be magenta surrounded by green, and not the red which would have been produced by the blue-green acting alone.

The discussion of visual color variables will be continued in Chapter XIV. At that point the naming of colors, the detection of color differences, and the mobility of color as ordinarily seen will be considered in some detail, as well as the known facts of color blindness. It seems advisable, however, to consider first the psychology of vision as far as it applies to color, and then to develop the general subject of the measurement and specification of color. In this way both the exceptions to the statements and the quantitative consideration of the differences will be made possible.

It is apparent that color is not a simple subject since it has been shown that there is very little relation between a light stimulus and the mental color except when the physical surround conditions and the physiological condition of the eye are taken into account. In the next few chapters it will be shown that a complete solution of the relation includes also the psychological state of the observer's mind (in particular his intentions in the situation). Having established this point it will be possible throughout the rest of the book to consider the coordinated effects of all three factors in the normal phenomena of color vision.

BIBLIOGRAPHY

Abney, William de W. *Researches in Colour Vision and the Trichromatic Theory.* London: Longmans, Green and Co. 1913. Chapter XVII.

Chevreul, M. E. *The Principles of Harmony and Contrast of Colours.* London: Longmans, Brown, Green and Longman. 1854.

Hess, Carl, and Pretori, Hugo. "Messende Untersuchungen über die Gesetzmässigkeit des simultanen Helligkeits-Contrastes." *Archiv für Ophthalmologie,* **40**:1–24 (1894).

Luckiesh, M. *Color and Its Applications.* New York: D. Van Nostrand Co. 1915. Chapter IV.

Morgan, Clifford T. *Physiological Psychology.* New York: McGraw-Hill Book Co., Inc. 1943. Chapter X.

Parsons, Sir John Herbert. *An Introduction to the Study of Colour Vision,* 2nd ed. Cambridge, England: The University Press. 1924. Chapters I, II, III, and IV, Section II.

Rood, Ogden N. *Students' Text-book of Color.* New York: D. Appleton and Co. 1916 (copyright 1881). Chapters XII and XIV.

Schouten, Jan F. *Visueele Meting van Adaptatie en van de wederzijdsche Beinvloeding van Netvlieselementen.* Utrecht: Drukkerij Fa. Schotanus and Jens. 1937.

Wright, W. D. *Researches on Normal and Defective Colour Vision.* St. Louis, Mo.: The C. V. Mosby Co. 1947. Chapters XVII, XIX, XX, XXII, and XXIII.

Perception and Illusion

CHAPTER IX

IN previous chapters it has been necessary in a number of instances to distinguish between perception and the stimulus which caused it. This was particularly true in the consideration of matched colors in which the match persisted but the colors changed with the conditions. In that discussion only the physical quality of the stimulus and the color phase of the mental image needed to be considered without particular reference to any *object* from which the light might have come. The sole consideration was that of the color perceived. Normal vision, however, is more concerned with color as an indication of a property of an object and usually neglects the light as such. The introduction of an *object* into the discussion makes necessary a whole new series of considerations. The observer who is looking at an object is not concerned with the quality of his mental impressions but with the properties of the object. He is using his eyes to *see* (ascertain) these properties. Furthermore the observer frequently goes a step further and infers properties of the object and its environment which are not directly visible to him, when he *interprets* the facts mentally.

MENTAL PHASES OF COLOR

It is necessary to distinguish three quite different mental phases produced by light although no order of importance can be assigned to them except for a given moment, in accordance with the interests of the observer. Perhaps the simplest of the three, though by no means the most frequent, is the direct decision by the observer of the color of his mental image without regard to its origin. This phase is usually referred to as the simple sensation of color, although the many ways in which this word has been used seriously confuses its meaning. The second and third phases of the perception are concerned with the object that is being seen. Usually the most direct perceptions are the object's color, shape, type of surface, etc. Although they are sometimes referred to as the "appearance" of the object, we usually say that an apple *is* round, shiny, and red or green, not that it appears to be, unless there is some doubt in our minds that it is. In the second phase, therefore, the eyes are trusted implicitly and what is seen is considered to be the object itself and not a mental image. In the third phase the observer not only sees the object but also, by means of what he sees, deduces its properties even when they are not visible directly. This last phase is usually called an "estimate" or an "inference." For example, we estimate a distance, a size, or weight, or infer the presence of a colored object from its reflection on other objects.

In daily life first one of these phases becomes important and then another. They are so much a part of our experience that it is only with some difficulty, and usually after some training, that it is possible for us to distinguish them from each other. The first is usually more easily distinguished than the second and the third. From the standpoint of understanding color, however, it is quite necessary to distinguish each of the three. Each represents such a different attitude toward the light which produces the image that different *colors* are seen with the changes in attitude even if the light qualities remain constant. The details of this change for brightness will be considered rather extensively in the next chapter, and the little we know about the same phenomenon for hue and for saturation is summarized in Chapter XI. The concepts involved, however, are so strange to most people and are so important to complete understanding that the present chapter will be devoted to a study of the way in which the mind appears to react to visual images in general. Because it is a more obvious phase of experience than color and because it is easy to illustrate, space perception has been chosen as the medium for discussing these concepts.

The three mental phases will be called mental image, perception, and inference. Whereas each has a position in the probable chain of events which takes place in vision, it must be remembered that psychologically the observer is seldom conscious of only one of the steps at a time. For him *at the time* what he sees not only is exceedingly real, but also probably seems the only possible *way of seeing*, a phrase which well describes the unitary nature of the experience. We "see" the mental color, we "see" the relative distances, and we "see" the object. The distinction is one dealing with the nature of the process rather than with the nature of the experience.

KNOWLEDGE DERIVED FROM PERCEPTION

Each of the ways of seeing color can represent any one of three types of experience from a quite different point of view without in any way losing its unitary character or the feeling of complete confidence which goes with it. These three may be classified in terms of certainty *after* the event and may be called "knowledge," "illusion," and "hallucination." In other words, the evidence presented to the brain may represent correct knowledge of the external world, may represent incorrect knowledge, or may not correspond at all to an existing object. In this book we shall talk only of the first two but the reader will doubtless realize that an hallucination seen in a dream can be just as real as far as the mental image is concerned as any image produced by a real external object. It is probably not so apparent that an hallucination may be seen as simple color, simple object, or simple object relations. Since such images are not produced by physical means and therefore are not subject to control we shall not have occasion to discuss them further. It may be pointed out, however, that many visual situations in daily life partake exactly of this nature. When we think we know the color of an object and do not look to verify the assumption, we are victims of hallucinations just as real as those in dreams. Rather than try to use such an awkward word for these cases, however, we shall refer to them by the simple statement that the observer did not *look* at the stimulus but relied on his memory.

The other two types of visual experience, knowledge and illusion, need to be considered in some detail and with some discretion. When it becomes necessary to distinguish between real and incorrect knowledge, we enter the realms of metaphysics, philosophy, and mysticism. It seems to be fairly easy to prove that the whole world is an illusion and fairly difficult to prove that anything is real. The difficulty arises from the fact that all our knowledge of the external world enters our minds through our bodily senses and each sense, individually, can be demonstrated to give incorrect reports under certain circumstances. From a rational point of view, however, no serious difficulty is involved. A blow on the foot is convincing evidence of the real existence of a brick seen by the eyes, and on this and similar bases it is possible to develop a real world which is truly believed to exist whether it does or not. For our purposes then, an illusion is a perception of external reality which is not in accord with the evidence derived from other senses and from our knowledge of physical probability. It is most evident in such examples as the geometrical illusions to be considered presently. A simple change of point of view or application of a simple physical principle indicates the error directly. It is not so apparent, however, that perception of depth in a two-dimensional figure is an illusion, and we shall see that such an illusion is so little apparent (or so customary) that it is sometimes used as though it were real.

Knowledge and illusion from the visual senses run through our whole life, and we have oriented our whole lives around them. The problem at the moment is to stand aside and look at these phenomena from a consistent viewpoint. In this way we may get some hint which will explain the rather bewildering array of phenomena encountered in the relationship between the physical nature of the stimulus and the result in mental experience.

DEPTH PERCEPTION IN REPRODUCTIONS

Let us start with the subject of perspective in reproductions. We wish to learn why such reproductions appear to represent space even though they lie on a flat, two-dimensional surface. It is not practical to consider the problem in detail, several books having been written on the subject without

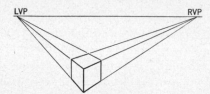

FIG. 9·1 Perspective drawing of a cube showing the vanishing lines merging at the right and left vanishing points.

settling many of the psychological problems involved. It can serve, however, as an excellent illustration of the way in which mental response can be predetermined by the intentions of the observer, by the nature of the stimulus, and by the visual mechanism in general. It can also lead to an understanding of the unique way in which the eye, so to speak, sees what it *wishes* to see almost to the exclusion of the facts.

It is well to start at the beginning. When one's eye is focused on a natural scene, all objects in the scene have certain geometrical peculiarities which are not in accord with our usual knowledge of the objects. Thus a cube, as shown in Fig. 9·1 is narrower at the back than at the front, and the lines of the sides, if extended, are seen to meet in a point on the horizon. The same fact is true of the *image* of a pair of railroad tracks which are seen to converge in the distance. These are simple facts of perspective, caused by the fact that the size of an object in the image formed by the lens of the eye decreases with the distance of the object from the eye.

We have learned to interpret this property of the lens system to mean distance and have gone a step further in our mental processes by seeing this phenomenon directly *as* dis-

In viewing the real scene, however, we are perceiving correctly in seeing the distance, whereas in viewing the reproduction, we are subject, willingly or not, to an illusion since the depth does not exist. As in vision from a high building, however, it is not surprising to find that when the reproduction departs sufficiently from the customary nature of things there is a loss in the direct perception of depth as such and a gain in the percep-

FIG. 9·3 Scene at relatively long viewing distance.

tance. We see the distance *as such* as so real, in fact, that we tend to subtract it from the scene, so to speak, as a separate phenomenon. We do not see a person across the street as much smaller than the one in front of us, but as of about the same size, only farther away. It is not until the situation is unusual, such as seeing people from the top of high buildings or from high up on a tall factory chimney, that we realize that at such distances they "look like ants." Seeing the distance rather than the decreased size becomes, to a certain extent, a habit of vision. It is not surprising, therefore, that when we view an adequate reproduction of a scene we also see the depth portrayed by the converging lines and changing sizes rather than the true state of affairs.

tion of the reproduction as a flat surface. Because this shifting relationship between agelong habits of perception and reality as indicated by direct perception determines the brightness and color of objects in experience, it is worth while to consider in some detail the factors that tend to make a reproduction look like an object in space or like the two-dimensional paper or canvas which it really is. On the relative strength of these two tendencies will depend not only the apparent depth portrayed but also the apparent size and shape of the objects. In color the extreme possibilities may be different in nature, but the concept of an intermediate perception based on a balance of tendencies is equally valid from both points of view.

141

The variables in a reproduction are geometrical perspective, contrast, sharpness, image structure, surface texture of the material, and surface structure of the image. They may be described in photography as visual angle (magnification), high or low contrast, sharp or diffuse image, continuous or grainy tone, rough or smooth texture, and glossy or matte surface. Each of these variables in a "black and white" picture affects the

will soon find examples of his own that will bear out the text in adequate fashion.

Consider first the question of the visual angle of a scene compared to its reproduction. When the eye forms an image of a scene each object in that scene has a certain angular relation to other objects. The diagram of Fig. 9·2 shows an eye forming an image of a box, for example. The eye is at such a distance from the box and the box

Fig. 9·4 Enlarged section of scene of Fig. 9·3, with apparent reduction in depth.

perception of depth. Each will be discussed below and some of them will be illustrated. A note of warning is necessary, however. The illustrations are so mounted that no two pictures of the same scene may be viewed simultaneously. Because it is often possible to recognize geometrical identity in the images, the observer tends to *infer* that the same distance is *represented*. He must view each picture naively and consider the impression of distance in each separately if they are to serve as adequate illustrations of the text. At risk of accusations of fraudulence it is also necessary to point out that too skeptical an attitude toward the effects will produce the same result. The illustrations are intended merely as indications of the *principles* involved; the interested reader

is of such a size that the angle at the eye between the two sides is 10 degrees.

At a distance of 2 feet the box would have to be 4.2 inches across, at 10 feet, 21 inches; and at 50 feet, 8 feet 10 inches to produce the same angle. Suppose now a photograph is made of the scene from the same position, and a print is made with or without enlargement. At some viewing distance from this print the angle at the eye formed by the two sides of the box will be the same in the print as in the original situation. If the picture is much smaller than the object as seen, this viewing distance may be too short for good vision, but there is such a distance for all prints. That position may be described as the "correct" viewing distance for the print. Photographers who are interested may calculate the distance roughly for their own cameras by multiplying the focal length of the lens by the number of diameters of enlargement used for the print. The product is the viewing distance. Thus for a 2-inch (50-millimeter) lens printed at a magnification of four times the correct viewing distance is 8 inches.

F<small>IG</small>. 9·5   Scene with moderately high-contrast lighting.

Magnified eight times the proper distance would be 16 inches, etc.

The correct viewing distance gives the proper perspective, that is, the angular relations seen between objects are identical in the picture with those of the original objects as viewed from the position of the

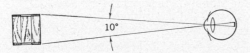

F<small>IG</small>. 9·2   Schematic diagram of common viewing situation in which the image of a box is being formed on the retina of an eye.

camera lens. A satisfactory picture, viewed from this distance, can, in fact, produce a rather startling effect of depth and reality, especially if it is viewed with only one eye. The reasons for this feeling of reality, of course, are that the original perception of depth was due in large part to the geometry

of the visual image and in the reproduction this geometry has been reproduced faithfully.

Suppose, however, that the proper viewing distance is not used. What perceptions are produced by the print? A little experimenting will show that a shorter viewing distance will compress the apparent depth in the subject and a longer one will enhance it, even to the point in extreme cases of altering apparent distances by factors as high as 10. The result comes from the geometry of the image formed in the eye and is a natural consequence of the illusion that depth is present in the first place. It is

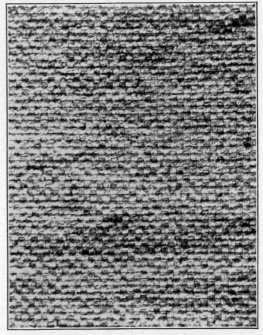

F<small>IG</small>. 9·7   Photograph printed to high contrast.

a transformation of the subject *as seen* in terms of normal experience with respect to lines of convergence and the like. An attempt to illustrate the effect is given in Figs. 9·3 and 9·4.

It has been assumed so far that in all respects except the geometry of the lines the photographic reproduction corresponds to the subject and produces an identical image in the eye. It may differ, however, in many ways, and almost all the ways affect this perception of depth. Almost nothing is known of the effect of color compared to black and white photography other than the universal experience that all color photographs appear to have more depth. Accordingly, we shall consider only the factors other than color.

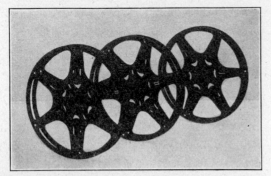

FIG. 9·6 Same scene as that of Fig. 9·5 with low-contrast lighting and therefore apparently less depth.

A small amount of experimenting on the subject indicates at once that one of the most important variables in depth perception is the *contrast* of the reproduction. It does not matter greatly whether this contrast is the result of the lighting or of the photographic process. A high contrast tends to give increased depth; a low contrast tends to give very little. Figure 9·5 shows a subject lighted with moderately high-contrast and Fig. 9·6 shows the same subject with low-contrast lighting. Note that the geometry of the figures is identical except for the shadows but that the apparent depth differs considerably. In Fig. 9·7 a subject is shown in which the contrast has been raised photographically, whereas it has been lowered in Fig. 9·8. There is a considerable change in the detail in the shadows, but otherwise the pictures are identical except for the contrast.

Again the high-contrast picture shows considerably more depth than the low. In photography this effect is so marked that it has received a special name (as so often happens with effects of this sort). Low-contrast prints are known almost universally in the trade as "flat," because they tend to lie flat on the paper, and prints of higher contrast, whether through lighting or handling, are said to show more "roundness." Both terms are truly descriptive and refer to the low and high degree of depth perception. Note, however, that they apply to pictures which are identical for perspective. It is the perception and not the geometry which changes.

FIG. 9·8 Identical photograph as that of Fig. 9·7, printed to lower contrast, and therefore having less apparent depth.

Another variable which will produce the same effect is the sharpness of the image. In Fig. 9·9 a subject is shown photographed with a high degree of sharpness, and in Fig. 9·10 the same scene is shown photographed with considerable "diffusion" over the lens.

PLATE VI

By comparing the illustration at upper left with the one at upper right it is evident that greater perception of depth is given by variations in relative brightness than by variations in color with brightness differences decreased. By comparing the lower illustration with the other two, it is evident that the greatest perception of depth, and by far the best picture, is obtained with variations in both color and brightness.

The effect has been very much exaggerated for purposes of illustration but represents what occurs *to some extent* in all pictures when a print is not sharp. In many cases, particularly in portraiture, the change in depth perception can be so strong that it changes the apparent shape of the head and features. High sharpness, as well as high contrast, leads to more nearly normal depth perception, and low sharpness tends to make

to be seen as the two-dimensional surface which, in reality, it is. In other words characteristics of *prints* as distinct from *subjects* tend to make the perception that of *prints* rather than *subjects*. The important point is that the perception actually produced is neither one nor the other but something intermediate between the two, the actual

Fig. 9·11 Photograph reproduced by normal (133 lines per inch) half-tone process.

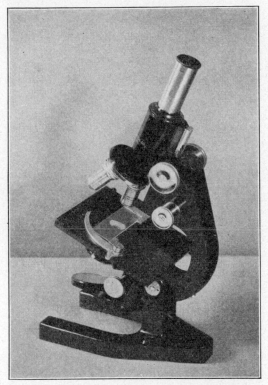

Fig. 9·9 Scene photographed with high degree of sharpness.

all parts of the picture approach the surface of the print.

With this variable we are approaching a generalization which appears to apply in nearly all situations. Whenever a characteristic that is different from normal experience is introduced into a reproduction, the depth perception decreases and the picture tends

point being determined by the balance of the factors involved. We shall see presently that this balance can also be affected markedly by the attitude of the observer, but it may be worth while first to emphasize the point with one further example.

Any factor which tends to draw the attention forcefully to the surface of the paper will have the effect of decreasing depth perception. The three main surface factors involved are texture of the paper itself, the character of the reflections from the surface, and the continuity or lack of it in the structure of the image itself. Since all three effects are due to the same cause they can be illustrated by any one; for convenience,

145

image structure is chosen. The photographer will be able to produce his own examples if he uses smooth or rough and glossy or matte-surfaced printing papers. Figure 9·11 shows a photograph reproduced by the half-tone process, but with a screen fine enough not to be visible at a reasonable distance. Figure 9·12 is an identical picture as it would appear if the half-tone screen were large enough to be visible at the same

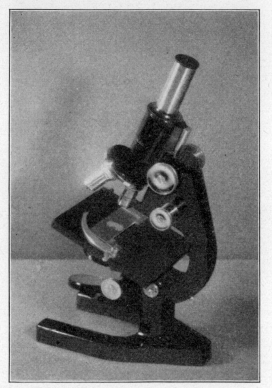

Fig. 9·10 Same scene as Fig. 9·9 photographed with a diffuser over the lens.

distance. The loss of depth can be ascribed to the clear visibility of a structure lying in the plane of the paper. Obviously there has been also some loss of detail and reduction of contrast, both of which affect the appearance in the same direction.

Figure 9·13 shows still another subject and Fig. 9·14 shows the same subject as

it would appear in a very "grainy" photographic process. Again the clear indication of an image lying in the surface of the paper is sufficient to overcome completely the effect of the perspective of the picture with a corresponding decrease in the depth perception; note that the decrease is not in the estimated depth but in the directly perceived *appearance* of depth.

Fig. 9·12 Same photograph as Fig. 9·11 reproduced by half-tone process using only 50 lines per inch.

SIZE ILLUSIONS IN DEPTH PERCEPTION

To some readers this concept of directly perceived depth may be strange and difficult to grasp. Once it is clear, however, it will raise in their minds the question of knowledge vs. illusion which has already been mentioned. It is an illusion that depth exists in a two-dimensional picture, and the perception depends on the strength of the illusion. People differ to such a tremendous extent in this respect that it is difficult to attempt examples but perhaps the following discussion may tend to clarify the issue.

Figure 9·15 shows a photograph taken in a park. The lamp posts on both sides of the street are the same size and the fence posts at the right are all equal. Looking at the picture it is possible to perceive distance from foreground to background directly. It is also possible to see not only that the statements about size are correct but *also* that *in the print* the *images* involved are of different sizes in accord with normal perspective relations. Now the interesting fact is that most people estimate the size relationship incorrectly because the depth perception is so strong that equalizing of the size persists in spite of the conscious attempt to overcome it. Figure 9·16 shows the same picture, but now a *duplicate* of the far lamp post appears beside the larger one and a duplicate of the farthest fence post appears beside the nearest one. To most people these size relations do not seem possible although direct measurement will show that they are. The illusion of depth, therefore, has offset the physical facts and produced a further illusion of size difference between identical objects. Note, incidentally, that it is not the grotesque appearance of the objects which constitutes the illusion but the fact that it is so difficult to see them in their true physical relations as areas on a sheet of paper. Their peculiar appearance comes from the fact that as *perceived in depth* they represent grotesque objects in the scene.

The illusion of depth changes with the photographic variables. It changes also in nature to much the same extent although we are so accustomed to overlooking effects of this sort that it is difficult to see that it is so. On a hazy day, for example, the perception of depth in nature is quite different from that on a clear day; depth and even shapes of objects in clear sunlight are quite different from those on overcast days. In fact it is this variation in appearance of distance, shape, and size that lends such enchantment to the distant view. The reader who has had the good fortune to see a distant landscape change with the days and the seasons will need no illustration of what is meant.

Fig. 9·13 Photograph made by normal process.

One other factor in direct depth and size perception should be pointed out before we consider the question of illusions in more detail. It has been the experience of many photographers and, to a lesser extent, of artists that after a picture has been printed or photographed it appears to represent the object in the wrong size, or shape, or at the wrong distance. The causes of this appear to be twofold. In the first place if factors such as those discussed earlier (i.e., texture, contrast, etc.) affect the direct perception of depth, a picture which has been so affected will have the *wrong* perspective in general. If the perspective is wrong, the *shape* of the objects will be wrong as well as their apparent relative positions. We have mentioned the effect on the apparent shape of the face in a portrait; the effect

FIG. 9·14 Same subject is in Fig. 9·13, but reproduced by very "grainy" photographer process.

on less familiar objects can be even more serious. The second phenomenon involved is somewhat more abstract but none the less real. When we look at an object or a scene some part of that scene attracts our attention to the practical exclusion of all others, and it occupies the whole field of attention. Under such conditions the perceived size of the object or group of objects has a certain mental value. In a reproduction of the scene, however, an exact reproduction of the visual angle of the object as it was seen is *not* sufficient for it to appear the same size. Some subjects require reproduction at very much greater visual angles than the subject

and some at considerably less to appear correct. The phenomenon has not been investigated sufficiently so that quantitative statements may be made, but many subjects require magnification of two and three times more than the correct angle to appear correct, and some require less than the correct value. The obvious question as to how this effect involves perspective has yet to receive study. The illusion of proper size in relation to depth therefore is not a simple matter of perspective, or even of the nature of the reproduction, but depends also on the effect of the original scene on the observer.

It is not strange that we find that many geometrical figures are interpreted incorrectly by the eye and mind. Since we do not know *why* we perceive depth directly in a photograph rather than a flat surface pattern, it is also not strange that usually we do not know *why* we perceive physical relationships wrong in optical illusions. We *do* know that sometimes the incorrect perceptions are due to some peculiarity of the eye which can be demonstrated. They are not, therefore, entirely mental, i.e., due to poor judgment. They are direct perceptions, identical with those leading to knowledge, but leading instead to a false report.

VISUAL ILLUSIONS

One of the most commonly illustrated illusions is that vertical lines always appear longer than horizontal lines. This is illustrated in Fig. 9·17. Note that both the direct perception and the carefully made estimate are incorrect as inferred from physical measurements. The effect seems to be a property of the eye.

Another effect which can be demonstrated as due to the state of the eye or brain is the distribution of parallel lines caused by the presence of lines crossing them at certain angles. Figure 9·18 shows a pair of parallel lines crossed by lines radiating from a point between them. The lines appear to bulge outward around the center. This same effect, however, can be produced in another way. Figure 9·19 shows the two sets of lines separately. If the reader will hold the

been investigated from this point of view.

Köhler in his work on the Gestalt theory as applied to vision has developed a "field theory" of vision which offers an adequate explanation of the effect of radial lines and of many other similar phenomena. The interested reader is referred directly to his

FIG. 9·15   Photograph of a scene with normal perspective relations.

book in fairly strong light and gaze steadily at the center of the radiating lines for 15 or 20 seconds and then shift his gaze suddenly to the dot between the parallel lines, the lines will again appear to bulge, at least for a brief time, even though the radiating lines are not actually present. The effect of the radial lines on the eye, therefore, lasts long enough to become evident in the apparent shape of the straight lines. The evident parallel between this case and the perspective of a picture suggests that the direct appearance of depth may be due to physiological effects. To the best of the writer's knowledge, however, the subject has never

published work listed in the bibliography at the end of the chapter. The important point to bear in mind is that effects such as have been discussed and those to be discussed presently must, *of necessity*, occur in situations where the perceptions are correct as well as in the more spectacular ones where they are wrong. The fact suggests that all illusions are due to useful properties of the eye which normally lead to correct perceptions but sometimes to incorrect ones. Again there seems to be no work which has been done from this point of view. In the absence of a consistent framework for discussion we can proceed to illustrate a few more types with, perhaps, a passing glance at their possible significance. The aim is to show how the eye works rather than to produce any feeling of mystery.

The effect of closely spaced lines at an angle to a straight line seems always to be to distort that line or its position as in Fig.

There are many instances, however, in which it is fairly apparent that we are dealing with higher mental levels, as in ambiguous figures, such as the one illustrated in Fig. 9·24, in which the perspective and detail are correct for two quite different points of view and the perception oscillates, more

FIG. 9·16 Identical photograph as in Fig. 9·15 except that duplicates of distant lamp and fence posts have been inserted in foreground.

9·20. A figure close to another which nearly encloses it is usually seen as larger than when the two are separated as in Fig. 9·21. These and many similar effects are predicted by Köhler's theory. In a somewhat different class is the design of Fig. 9·22 in which the actual physical figure is a series of concentric circles which it is almost impossible to see except as a spiral because of a short diagonal line across each intersection with the background. This diagonal can be seen more readily in the enlargement, Fig. 9·23. Here again we are probably dealing with a direct physiological function of the eye or the lower brain.

or less involuntarily, between the two possibilities.

An extreme ambiguity, so strong with many people that it cannot be reversed and yet apparently based on a pure mental habit (and so missing in many people), is the effect shown in Fig. 9·25. The photograph was taken so that the light comes from the upper right of the observer. The indentations in the curved surface of this figure are so perceived because of the shadows being in the upper portions of the recesses. While this is a direct perception, it is not the only interpretation possible. If the mind were willing to accept the illumination as coming from below, a different perception would result. The fact that this is so is demonstrated in Fig. 9·26, which is identical with the picture in Fig. 9·25, except that it is turned upside down. Here the depressions appear as raised surfaces. The effect is so strong and so general among observers that an architect's drawing has to show the light coming from the upper left (whether or not this is possible for the building), in order that certain of its features will not be seen as reversed in depth.

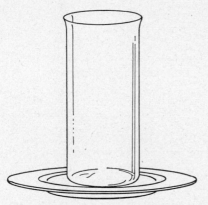

Fig. 9·17 Illusion in which the diameter of the plate is actually larger than the height of the glass.

The point of all this discussion is to acquaint the reader who is new to the subject with the fact that many things are involved in a direct perception of seeming reality. Our visual perceptions, real as they may seem, are made up of a whole series of phenomena, part of which may be considered as properties of the eye or brain but all of which are based on learned reactions cultivated over the whole life of the individual. The naive view that a thing is true physically because the observer can see it visually has no place in the study of color, even though it may be a good subject for psychology. It is necessary first to know the facts physically without reference to the eye, second to note how the facts appear to the observer, and third to see what effect the

attitude of the observer has on the appearance. From this shift of appearance with attitude it is possible to draw correct inferences.

Fig. 9·18 Illusion in which the two heavy lines are parallel.

VISUAL RESEARCH

Such complexity in the visual process has brought about sharp differences of opinion among the workers in the visual field. Every careful worker tries to control his conditions so that the results he obtains are as unambiguous as possible. To do so he sets up a very specialized sort of apparatus or situation. It does not matter whether the set-up

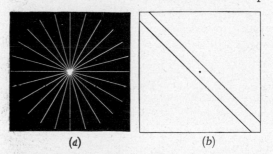

(a)   (b)

Fig. 9·19 If the gaze is fixed steadily on the center point of (a) for 15 to 20 seconds and then transferred to the center point of (b), the parallel lines appear to bulge.

is simple or complex or whether he is working with simple stimuli or the whole situations of the Gestalt school. Always one of the conditions which he tries to control is the attitude of the observer toward the set-up. It follows necessarily that the results apply only to that set-up and only to that attitude. There has been work, of course, in which the shift with attitude has been the subject of study but such studies have been regrettably few. Some of them will be considered in the next chapter.

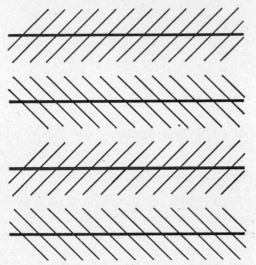

FIG. 9·20 Illusion in which the horizontal lines are all parallel.

Before we start a detailed consideration of brightness perception, however, it is worth while to review the relationships which have been developed here to see if they can be made more explicit. Fundamentally the problem is to review the ways in which an observer approaches a new visual situation and the nature of the results which he obtains.

It was noted that the attitudes toward the subject could be grouped into three general classifications which can be called sensing, perceiving, and inferring. These corre-spond roughly to an introspective study of the mental image as such, to an externally directed study of the appearance of the objects themselves, and to a consideration of the relationships among the objects in the situation, respectively. It was also noted that the observer is not ordinarily aware of his attitude at the moment of viewing and so feels that what he sees is a unique characteristic of the scene, not subject to change.

From these three general observer attitudes there develop three general types of belief which can be distinguished only by

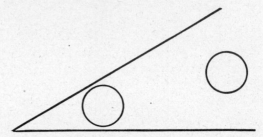

FIG. 9·21 The two circles are the same size.

comparing the belief with further knowledge of the external scene. These three were called knowledge, illusion, and hallucination. From the purely physical standpoint *knowledge, illusion,* and *hallucination* refer to beliefs that are correct or incorrect. Illusion refers to an incorrect belief about an existing object and hallucination refers to an incorrect belief that the object exists.*

As in all such classifications, however, one must be careful not to permit the classification to obscure the facts. If properly used they permit easier thinking about the subject and lead to a clearer insight into the phenomena involved. If adhered to strictly they prevent extension of knowledge, largely

* Throughout this discussion the word "object" has been used to refer to any type of external phenomenon the observer may desire to see. It is intended to include such observables as illumination, contrast, and the like, not ordinarily called objects.

through the shortcomings of the words which must be used. For example, the word "belief" has been used to refer to the result of perception. It is, however, possible to "see" an optical illusion even if one knows that what he sees is not in accord with the physical facts. In this particular case, then, the word is unfortunate since it sounds contradictory (although it can be argued that he *still* "believes" what he sees and simply knows also that it can be proven false). In

use of the words by making the concepts to which they apply more definite.

ANALYSIS OF REAL SITUATIONS

Suppose an observer is facing a landscape containing both near-by and distant objects, and suppose that the day is clear with bright sunlight and blue sky with some white clouds. Such a situation can easily involve all the phenomena discussed above. Sup-

FIG. 9·22 Illusion in which concentric circles appear to make a spiral.

FIG. 9·23 Enlargement of preceding figure, showing true nature of concentric circles.

many other situations, however, it *is* the belief that counts. If he knew that the facts were different he would "see" them differently. This is particularly true of brightness perception and, to a somewhat lesser extent, of color, but it is also true many times for space perception. The point is that if a visual situation is analyzed by reference to the classification, all points of view necessary to an understanding of the results will have to be examined.

We can proceed with the analysis of a few situations in these terms by way of example. It will, perhaps, clarify the author's

pose first that the observer is an artist and suppose further that he is interested particularly in the quality of the light in the scene. He may very probably be much more concerned than the average observer with an introspective study of the light and color reaching his eye from each part of the scene than with the form or the color of the objects themselves. With this attitude he will proceed to analyze in some detail the color of the light reaching him from each area and will be more or less unconscious of the nature of the object concerned. In the terms used he is concerned with the color *sensations* he is receiving, not with his perceptions *of the objects*. Now suppose that, being professionally interested in the matter,

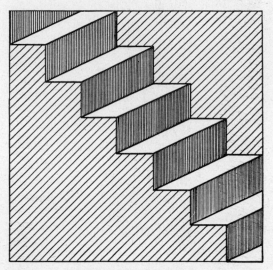

FIG. 9·24 The ambiguous staircase. Is one below or above it?

he is surprised to find that some familiar object, such as a leaf on a tree, is sending bright blue light to his eye. He knows the leaf should be green and proceeds to look at it *as a leaf* to see if it *is* green. He then *sees* that it is green after all, usually because the light from some parts of it at least *will* be green light. He is *perceiving* the leaf as green. The situation becomes fairly obvious at this point since he can see that the leaf is reflecting the blue sky from some part of the surface. This perception, however, involves the *inference* that the leaf is really green and that the blue is due to reflection. He can prove his inference by moving his

head or the leaf and noting that the reflection changes with the angle.

Now let us consider the results of the three attitudes which he has assumed with his changing interest in the subject. His first observation led to the true belief which we have called knowledge that the light was blue. The second observation led to the knowledge that the leaf was green, and the inference led to the knowledge that the sky was being reflected from its surface. We have assumed that all his conclusions were correct but the opposite assumption could also have been made. Suppose in his introspective study of the color of the light he saw it as the same shade of blue as the sky but found when he actually made the comparison by looking at first one and then the other that this was not true, that the color of the mental image from the two was actually different. We could then refer to his first observation as an illusion although the attitude was still introspective. We could have supposed also that when he looked to see what color the leaf actually was he still saw it as blue. This again would have been an illusion since he could have found that the leaf was green by changing his position, but the illusion this time refers to his belief about the leaf rather than the color. He could then have inferred incorrectly some reason why the leaf was blue and could have been under an illusion in this respect also.

Finally, to carry the example through to the end, if the whole thing were to be supposed a dream, none of his reactions would correspond to an external stimulus except by way of memory, and we would call them an hallucination. Although strictly speaking it is probably true that the same classifications used above can be used in hallucinations if we consider that they refer to past

Fig. 9·25 Photograph of a tank showing indentations in the surface and rivet heads protruding from the surface. (Reproduced through the courtesy of the C. H. Stoelting Company.)

Fig. 9·26 Identical photograph as that in Fig. 9·25, but turned upside down. Indentations and protrusions are now reversed. (Reproduced through the courtesy of the C. H. Stoelting Company.)

stimuli, there is no point in doing so for the present purpose.

An artist was chosen as the observer because by training and inclination he is likely to be the most analytical of observers. If a person who was interested chiefly in forestry had been chosen, it would have been logical to assume that the blue of the leaf would never have been seen at all except as one component of a blue-white illumination falling on a tree consisting of normal green leaves. If he did happen to see the blue of the leaf, it would take the momentary form of an illusion, but he would quickly disprove it by examination. Because his interest is centered in the object, he would not consider the mental-image phase, and his inferences would be concerned with the nature and condition of the tree rather than with the light. If the blue were called to his attention and he could not make it disappear by a change of position, he might make inferences as to its cause either correctly or incorrectly, but probably he would not believe that the leaf was blue.

If the observer were a student of color he might see the reflected blue directly in terms of the glossy surface reflectance of the leaf, this glossiness being his inference from the stimulus. His inference might represent knowledge or illusion, depending on the situation.

What is seen and the inferences drawn depend on the attitude, training, and inclinations of the observer. We shall see in the next chapter that these factors lead to changing appearances of objects and that the effects in many instances are quite large.

BIBLIOGRAPHY

Ames, A., Jr. "Depth in Pictorial Art." *The Art Bulletin*, **8**:4–24 (1925).
Köhler, Wolfgang. *Dynamics in Psychology.* New York: Liveright Publishing Corp. 1940.
Köhler, Wolfgang, and Wallach, Hans. "Figural After-Effects. An Investigation of Visual Processes." *Proceedings of the American Philosophical Society*, **88**:269–357 (1944).
Luckiesh, M. *Visual Illusions, Their Causes, Characteristics and Applications.* New York: D. Van Nostrand Co. 1922.

Parsons, Sir John Herbert. *An Introduction to the Study of Colour Vision*, 2nd ed. Cambridge, England: The University Press. 1924. Chapter III, Section I.

Woodworth, Robert S. *Experimental Psychology*. New York: Henry Holt and Co. 1938. Chapter XXV.

Brightness Perception

CHAPTER X

ONE of the fields in which the effect of the attitude of the observer has received attention is brightness perception and its effect on form, depth, apparent surface properties of objects, and the like. In this field the extreme separation which may exist between a physical stimulus and the mental image which it produces becomes apparent. An attempt will be made to present this subject systematically both in relation to the physical nature of the stimulus and to the normal psychophysical properties of the eye. It must be remembered throughout that brightness is one of the most important variables of color. Although its photographic analogue is "black and white," it is still the most important variable in color photography as well.

INTENSITY TERMINOLOGY

To discuss the subject clearly it will be necessary to use a number of words which have been avoided thus far. The facts of the so-called "brightness-constancy" effect are somewhat startling to a person unacquainted with their magnitude. The added necessity for a complex terminology, because of the different types of appearance which may occur from the same stimulus, gives the whole subject a slight air of mystery and abstraction which is not in accord with the definite character of the effects in real life. We shall start, therefore, with a reconsideration of the words which must be used and attempt to make their meaning clear. Because the meanings also involve to some extent the subsequent discussion they will be amplified as the subject develops.

The ways in which brightnesses may be perceived are among the most important facts of the psychological phases of color. It is quite essential that the facts be kept in mind in spite of the present lack of any very satisfactory explanation of the facts.

As seen in the table at the end of Chapter I, many words related to visual phenomena are defined in order to cover the various aspects of light intensity, disregarding its color. As a purely physical phenomenon, light is called "radiant energy." The light falling on a surface is called the "radiance." The effectiveness of this radiant energy for the eye is called the "luminance" to indicate that the sensitivity of the eye has been taken into account. The mental effect of this luminance is called the "brightness" and it may be noted under the table, "Attributes of the Modes of Appearance" (Fig. 10·5), that an alternative word "lightness" may sometimes be necessary. The present discussion involves this distinction between lightness and brightness. One more term defined in the report is also necessary, that which defines the effective *reflectance* of a *surface* for a particular *light* for the *eye*. This is called "luminous reflectance." The word "luminous" means that it is evaluated with respect to the eye and will be dropped in the present discussion. Of this group of terms, four are vitally important to the subject. They are discussed below.

1. *Reflectance* (luminous). Reflectance refers to the fractional part of the light reflected under given conditions by the surface under consideration. It is a calculated psychophysical value, obtained by multiplying wavelength by wavelength the energy of the light source, the percentage of light of that wavelength reflected from the surface, and the sensitivity of the eye for that wavelength of light, by adding them up for all wavelengths, and by dividing the total by the effectiveness of the light *falling on* the surface, evaluated in the same manner with respect to the eye. In effect reflectance is the ratio of incident to reflected light evaluated with respect to the eye *considered as a standardized receptor*. It does not take into account any psychological or other effect of the surroundings, or of the state of the eye at the time. Two equal values mean that the reflecting surfaces would appear equally bright *only if* they were placed side by side in the same illuminant. This equality corresponds to the "matching condition" discussed in Chapter VIII and holds for almost all conditions of the eye. Reflectance, then, is a property of the *surface*, which varies with the energy distribution of the light source (i.e., a "red" surface has low reflec-

tance to blue and green light but high to red light, etc.). In the present chapter we shall deal largely with gray, non-selective surfaces whose reflectance is independent of the color of the light because they reflect the same percentage at all wavelengths. In the next chapter in which colored surfaces will be considered it is important to remember this dependence on the color of the light.

2. *Luminance.* As the word reflectance refers to the effective physical reflectance of a surface for a given quality of light, so the word luminance refers to the effectiveness of a given light *on the eye,* regardless of its origin. Thus the luminance of any light which reaches the eye may be determined by multiplying the energy at each wavelength by the sensitivity of the eye to that wavelength and adding them all together. The total so obtained is the effective intensity of the light as it affects the eye. Its relation to reflectance is apparent if the definitions are compared. Reflectance is the ratio of the luminance of the reflected light *from* a surface to the luminance of the light falling *on* the surface. As reflectance is a characteristic of the surface for that light so luminance is a characteristic of the light *itself* and is a purely psychophysical term which does not take the viewing conditions into account. Furthermore it meets the matching condition in that two identical luminances would appear equally bright if compared with the fields in direct contact.

Reflectance and luminance, therefore, define the stimulus in terms of the eye, not the mental perceptions the stimulus will produce.

3. *Brightness.* Brightness refers to the mental effect of light of a given luminance *as perceived* under the given conditions. It does *not* correlate directly with either luminance or reflectance as we shall see in a moment, except under certain specialized conditions. It is, nevertheless, the mental

reaction *produced by* the light and so is properly described as the *apparent* luminance of the light. The reason for the word "apparent" is obvious. The same luminance does not produce the same brightness if the conditions are varied; two equal brightnesses do not necessarily correspond to equal luminances. Luminance (i.e., intensity of light), however, is the physical variable which the observer is *trying* to see when brightness perception occurs. The relationship between the two is usually so poor, however, that an estimate of luminance based on a mental evaluation of brightness is usually incorrect. Equality of two brightnesses generally means only that the two lights have equal *psychological* intensities and may or may not be equal physically even if evaluated in terms of the properties of the eye.

4. *Lightness.* As brightness refers to the mental perception of luminance, so lightness refers to the mental perception of reflectance. It may be surprising to some readers that it is possible to separate the two phases visually since a surface is obviously seen only by the light that it reflects to the eye. Such, nevertheless, is the case and is the subject to be discussed. Like brightness, lightness refers to the *psychological* phase of vision. Two surfaces of equal lightness, i.e., apparently having the same reflectance, do not necessarily actually have the same reflectance, and, vice versa, two that are equal as determined by physical and psychophysical calculations do not necessarily have the same lightness. Equal lightnesses have the same psychological effectiveness from the standpoint of the property of the surface called reflectance.

Lightness can also refer legitimately to a light source in the somewhat unusual situation in which a source is seen *as if it were* a reflecting surface having a certain apparent reflectance. It is fairly easy to set up

such situations experimentally, but they are rarely encountered in practice.

Luminance and reflectance on the physical side and brightness and lightness on the psychological side, therefore, are the variables we must consider. A grammatical note is perhaps in order. In comparative expressions it is customary to say "brighter and darker" and "lighter and darker," referring respectively to brightness and to lightness. This, however, leaves the reader without a distinction between the two kinds of "darker." Whenever there is chance of confusion the somewhat awkward expressions "less bright" and "less light" will be used.

BRIGHTNESS CONSTANCY

The phenomenon about to be discussed appears in many psychology books under the heading "brightness constancy," and this term will be retained here to avoid confusion. In the more recent terminology it should probably be called "approximate lightness constancy." Briefly, light reaching the eye when it is perceived as apparent reflectance appears *more intense* than it does when perceived as apparent luminance. As mentioned before, in physical terms the effect can be very large indeed. Only our mental habits prevent the effect from being common knowledge.

Perhaps the simplest way of demonstrating the effect is to mount two identical light-gray squares of paper in the center of two larger squares of white cardboard. These cards have the interesting property that there is no way in which the two may be placed in the ordinary room that will make the outside border of either of them appear gray in the ordinary sense of the word, even though from the physical standpoint the light from the gray in a region of high illumination may be many times the intensity (luminance) of that from the white in low illumi-

159

nation. Two concepts are involved in these facts, and it is quite essential that the two be separated clearly in thinking about the subject.

For those who can make the mental separation, introspection will show that, whereas it is true that the border of the card in shadow is still white, the light reaching the eye from this area is less bright than that from the gray (on the other card) in full illumination. This perception, however, is separate and distinct from the perception of the border as white. One corresponds to the attitude of seeing the *light* and the other, that of seeing the *card*. This dualism depending on attitude and mentioned previously runs through nearly all perceptual situations. To carry the example to its conclusion requires the added fact that neither perception is *correct* from the physical standpoint. The brightness (the actual light intensity) will always appear more than it actually is and the lightness (the true reflectance) will always appear too low. What is present seems to be an indeterminate perception which is shifted to one or the other extreme by the observer's attitude and is never sufficiently effective to give either perception accurately. The details of this perception will be developed presently. First, however, it seems advisable to inquire again into the reason that the border appears "white," rather than "gray."

It is quite easy to demonstrate, as has been pointed out by Hering, that gray is a perception that occurs when there is a brighter area in the field of view. In general any light that is considered as non-colored will be *seen* as gray if there is a brighter non-colored light present with which it may be compared. It does not matter what the nature of this light may be, whether it is a radiant source or one produced by reflection. The only requirements seem to be lack of color and higher brightness. It is

an instructive experiment to project a spot of light on a screen at a high enough intensity so that it appears acceptably white to the eye and then to surround this with a brighter area. The area formerly seen as white will immediately appear gray. The same effect will occur also in an instrument field except that the first spot, seen alone, will appear simply colorless, rather than white, whereas it will still change to gray when the brighter border is added.

These experiments demonstrate the fact that gray is the name we give to the unique sensation of a lesser *relative* brightness. In fact the same perception is produced equally well when the lights are seen as colored, and the addition of gray to a spot of colored light when it is surrounded by a brighter border of the same color is just as definite a phenomenon as when they are non-colored.

White and black, on the other hand, are somewhat different perceptions and as unique as gray. White appears to be the perception corresponding to a surface of high reflectance, usually from 75 to 100 percent, and is seen whenever the illumination on such a surface is sufficiently evident so that it may be seen *as such*. Black is the perception which results when the light from a given area is insufficient for detailed vision in that area. In introspection black is just as positive a perception as white and is equally affected by the presence of an area sending less light to the eye, a black that is not too low in intensity being seen as a dark gray if an area of lower intensity is placed beside it for comparison. In Chapter VIII the concept of a "black point" was developed, in which it was pointed out that all intensities below a certain value appear black. As indicated there the exact value at which the black point occurs depends on the environment of the area; this phase will be developed further. The points which must be emphasized here are that white is a phenomenon relating wholly to the perception of a surface, gray is a perception of *relative brightness* sometimes of a surface and sometimes not, whereas black is a positive perception of the inadequacy of the stimulus to produce a visual response.

The perception of a surface as white, therefore, is not inconsistent with the perception that it is less bright than another white which is more strongly illuminated.

approaching white and less and less effective for the lower reflectances.

The conditions under which brightness-constancy effects appear have been investigated by a number of people, notably Katz, MacLeod, Thouless, and Helson. As a generalization it can be stated from their work that the effect is at the maximum when the situation is most normal. The evidence indicates that under customary (and particu-

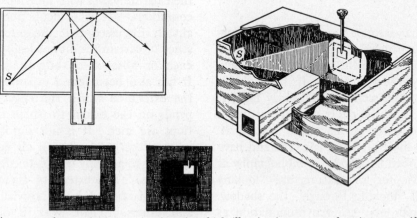

Fig. 10·1 Apparatus for producing perceptions in which illumination on a surface is seen as if it were the reflectance of the surface.

The fact that it is less bright, however, gives the possibility of seeing the light as gray; introspection shows the light intensity as less, i.e., the observer sees gray *light* coming from a white *card*.

When the card itself is not white but gray, the constancy of its apparent reflectance (i.e., lightness) is far less than when it was white, a medium gray becoming much darker in a dim light than a corresponding surface in bright light. The "grayness" of the *light* and the grayness of the *surface* tend to combine as they become greater, a dark gray card eventually becoming quite dark in comparison with the same card at high illumination levels. Brightness (or lightness) constancy, accordingly, is primarily a matter of the direct perception of reflectance but is most effective for surfaces

larly under familiar) lighting conditions the observer tends to see the *surfaces* of objects *and* the illumination in which they are placed as *separate* entities. Thus a piece of white paper placed under a reading lamp is not ordinarily seen as having a graded reflectance which changes with distance from the lamp but as being a uniform sheet of paper with graded illumination. That is, the *light* is seen to change and the paper is perceived as constant and white. Both perceptions are equally distinct.

When the illumination becomes anomalous or invisible to the observer, of course, it is no longer possible to perceive the illumination as such. Under these conditions it is quite simple to design arrangements of surfaces such that reflectance perception (lightness) is very strongly affected. Gelb gives the extreme example of a normally black surface separately illuminated by a high-intensity light source to the point at which it appears white on a dark ground and states that its appearance changes immediately to black if a very small piece of white paper is introduced into the beam of light. This effect can be obtained by means of the apparatus illustrated in Fig. 10·1.

SHADOWS

The other extreme at which the illumination is much more apparent occurs when a visible light source throws a clearly defined shadow across a surface. If the lighting contrast of the scene is sufficiently high, it is easy to note the effect of three attitudes which the observer may take toward it. These are illustrated in Plate VII and have been described by Rood (see bibliography at close of chapter) as "looking at," "looking into," and "looking through" the shadow. The observer may see the illumination as such, in which case the shadow becomes a relatively dark area in the field of view; he may look closely at the objects within the shadow and see their characteristics in more detail; or he may approach them and concentrate attention on them to the extent that he is no longer conscious of the fact that they are in a shadow. In the two latter cases brightness constancy is fairly complete. The three differ in that in the last case attention is directed wholly inside the shadow while in the others it is not.

A fourth attitude of a similar nature is one in which interest is in a surface that passes through the edge of the shadow. Even if the brightness differences on the two sides of the edge are considerable, the observer's concentration on the surface may be so great that he sees only a continuous surface without consciously noting the marked differences in the light coming from the different parts of the surface. This gives the maximum amount of brightness constancy.

Before we consider the relationship of brightness constancy to adaptation, it is desirable to attempt a somewhat more quantitative statement of the effect. In particular it is necessary for the reader to have a clear understanding of the *approximate* nature of the phenomena and the extent to which their nature varies with individuals and with conditions. It is evident from the facts already discussed that the presence or absence of certain conditions leads to the presence or absence of brightness constancy. It has also been found experimentally that the extent to which the effect occurs depends on the extent to which these conditions are met. It is not simply an all-or-none effect but occurs in all degrees from no effect to a nearly complete effect for some observers. The extent of these variations has been studied by Brunswick, Thouless, and others. Their work is discussed by Woodworth. Each of these two experimenters expresses his results in terms of ratios which are derived as follows. There are two extreme types of perception possible, that of the light as such (i.e., the luminance) and that of the reflectance of the surface. These two can be compared in any given situation by considering *the reflectance the surface would have to have in the higher illumination* to send the same amount of light to the eye as it actually does in the lower. If there were no perceptual compensation for the illumination, this reflectance (lightness) is the same as would be seen in the lower illumination. On the other hand, if there is complete compensation the true reflectance is seen. The actual observation in nearly every case falls between the two and the position between the two may be expressed as a ratio. Brunswick developed a ratio which may be applied to the percentage

PLATE VII

(*Left*) In "looking at" a shadow, the shadow is seen as a dark area with little visible detail. (*Center*) By focusing attention within the shadow, or "looking into" it, the shadow appears to lighten, and detail within it is much more clearly seen. (*Right*) By approaching the shadow and focusing attention even more strongly within it, or "looking through" it, the perception of a shadow as such tends to disappear.

reflectances. Suppose that there are two surfaces, A with a reflectance of 80 percent, and B with a reflectance of 20 percent. Suppose also that B is in a fairly high illumination and that to a particular observer, it appears to match A in brightness when A is in an illumination one-eighth as great as that for B. If a true luminance match were to be obtained under these two different illuminations, B would have to have a reflectance of one-eighth of A, or 10 percent. If all this information is applied, the Brunswick ratio for the surface as actually seen is given by:

$$\text{B.R.} = \frac{20\% - 10\%}{80\% - 10\%} = \frac{10\%}{70\%} = 0.143$$

The Brunswick ratio always has a value between zero and one. If, in the above example, the observer had decided that the two surfaces matched when the illumination on A was one-fourth that of B, the Brunswick ratio would have become

$$\frac{20 - 20}{80 - 20} = 0$$

If, on the other hand, no combinations of illumination could be made which would give a match, but on further experimenting it was found that, if B was changed to give a reflectance of 80 percent, a match could be obtained even if the illuminations differed by as much as 8 to 1, the Brunswick ratio would have become

$$\frac{80 - 10}{80 - 10} = \frac{70}{70} = 1$$

The fact that in actual observations neither of these limits is reached, indicates that the brightness-constancy phenomenon associated with viewing surfaces in different illuminations involves an unconscious compromise between identifying the "brightness" of a surface with its true luminance and with its true reflectance.

The Brunswick ratio has the difficulty that it does not correspond to equal perceptual steps and, for this reason, the same value for two different cases does not have the same meaning. A closer approach to the ideal of equal visual differences is given by the Thouless ratio, which is based upon the logarithms of the percentages. Using the same example as first given above, the Thouless ratio is:

$$\frac{\log 20 - \log 10}{\log 80 - \log 10} = \frac{1.301 - 1.000}{1.903 - 1.000}$$

$$= \frac{0.301}{0.903} = 0.33$$

In making various types of comparisons, the eye operates more in accordance with the results obtained by the Thouless ratio than with those obtained by the Brunswick ratio.

In terms of the Thouless ratio the following facts have been observed experimentally.

1. Different conditions may move the observed ratio all the way from practically zero (no brightness constancy) to a value of 1 (complete brightness constancy), and instructions to the observer may even produce perceptions having a value higher than 1 (over-correction for the illumination difference).

2. Different observers vary over the whole range but have a tendency to divide into two groups, one at high and one at low values, corresponding respectively to people who tend to look at *surfaces* and who tend to look at light intensities. There is some indication that the ordinary naive observer (including children) tends to fall in the first group and the trained artist or observer in the second.

3. Instruction to the observer to look for the reflectance or the luminance can in some instances change the observed ratio over a range which is much greater for some observers than for others. Some observers

seem incapable of obtaining anything but the reflectance type of perception.

4. There are few observers and few conditions under which the ratio reaches either zero or one. In other words, even a conscious attempt by a trained observer to see one or the other extreme is almost always unsuccessful to some extent.

5. The ratio is highest for surfaces of high reflectance and gradually decreases as intensities and reflectances are decreased. (This statement is not supported by as much evidence as the previous four.)

If we return now to the nomenclature originally developed, it is possible to express all this in another manner. The stimulus variables are luminance and reflectance. The psychological variables are brightness and lightness. To the extent that the conditions and the skill of the observer permit he may see either brightness or lightness as direct perceptions but the foregoing facts show that the brightness perception in general will be higher than it should be as calculated or measured for the stimulus and the lightness perception will be lower.

Perhaps it should also be pointed out that in the special case of perfectly uniform illumination, brightness and lightness become identical and the brightness-constancy phenomenon ceases to exist. It can occur only when the illumination is non-uniform since it can be described as a direct perceptual compensation for perceived-illumination gradient.

SIMULTANEOUS CONTRAST

It is now possible to consider the relationship between the brightness-constancy phenomenon and the well-known simultaneous contrast effects, and to compare both of them with the brightness-adaptation effects considered in Chapters VII and VIII.

Simultaneous contrast may be described as the effect which makes a surface or a light source of any kind look lighter (or brighter) when it is surrounded by a dark area than when it is surrounded by a lighter one. The effect is illustrated by Fig. 10·2 in which the two gray areas have the same reflectances although the one enclosed by the black is seen as the lighter of the two.

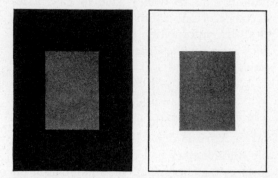

FIG. 10·2 The two rectangular gray areas have the same reflectances, although the one enclosed by the black is seen as the lighter of the two.

Simultaneous contrast for brightness (a similar effect occurs for color) is a general phenomenon. The difference in the lightness of any two surfaces is exaggerated if they are placed next to each other and the effect is at the maximum if a relatively small area of one is completely surrounded by the other. The maximum actual effect is produced when a surface is seen against black on the one hand and against white on the other. Actually, however, the greatest percentage change, so to speak, is produced by the first small differences between two surfaces. The whole phenomenon may be thought of as a mechanism of vision which increases small brightness differences and makes them distinctly more visible than would otherwise be the case.

Not much quantitative work has been done in this field other than that of Hess and Pretori in 1894 which was mentioned in Chapter VIII, but, such as it is, the results of these experiments do form a suggestive link with both brightness constancy and adaptation. While further work must be done to substantiate the conclusions to be reached, they are presented as at least suggesting the possible connections.

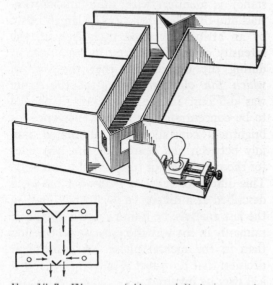

Fig. 10·3 Diagram of Hess and Pretori apparatus with the cutaway portion showing the position of one of the light sources. The intensities of the light reaching the two surfaces on one side of the apparatus are kept constant. On the other side, the light on the front surface is varied systematically, and, for each intensity, the light on the back is adjusted until it appears to match the corresponding surface on the other side.

Hess and Pretori found that when they set up a four-part field, using the instrument shown in Fig. 10·3, it was possible to obtain a whole series of conditions under which the surfaces seen through the central apertures appeared matched. In order to obtain consistent results, however, it was found necessary to take a great many precautions which made the experiment quite different from everyday visual experience. In brief it was found necessary to restrict vision to one eye, to center the eye exactly on the divid-

ing line between the large squares, to expose the eye only for a definite length of time, and (by implication in the published text) to consider the areas as surfaces lying in the same plane.

The results obtained in this manner are shown in the plot of Fig. 10·4 redrawn from their results. They show that if a definite ratio of intensities is set up in the left-hand side, the central area of the right-hand square may be made to match that of the left under a whole series of border brightnesses. When the border is black, a certain

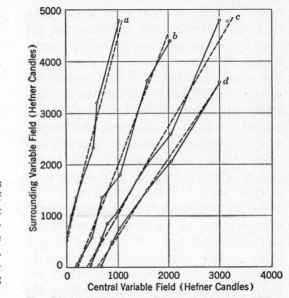

Fig. 10·4 A replotting of part of the data of Hess and Pretori in which the intensities of the surround and central field on the side where they are kept fixed are respectively: (a) 512 and 10, (b) 20 and 200, (c) 10 and 512, and (d) 6.2 and 700, all measured in Hefner candles.

minimum intensity is required in the center. As the border intensity is increased above zero it is necessary to increase the central intensity in order to maintain the match with the central area on the left. The amount of increase required in the center was found to be in constant ratio to the increase of the border, although the ratio depends on the ratio of intensities on the left.

Because of the striking nature of these findings, the writer set up a small-scale model of the Hess and Pretori apparatus to see what effect changes in attitude would have on the results. It was found possible with relatively rough equipment to corroborate the work of the earlier investigators. One fact, however, stood out rather clearly. As soon as the brightness difference between the two surrounds became very large some sort of attitude *had* to be taken toward the figure in order to obtain consistent data. At large differences the appearance of the central squares took on an indeterminate, fluctuating sort of quality, and the observer was equally dissatisfied with the match over a relatively large range of intensities. Binocular vision was used in a room which was not wholly dark. Under these conditions it was quite apparent that there were four surfaces visible, and it became possible to ask the observer to consider their appearances in either of two quite different ways. The whole figure could be seen as a cube viewed from one edge with gray squares on each of two sides, or it could be seen as two apertures through which what appeared to be a single separately illuminated surface was seen. The results obtained by asking the observer to take either one of these two attitudes were quite satisfying. The indeterminateness ceased at once. When the perception was that of a cube with gray squares the matches moved far in the direction of the ratios required by complete brightness constancy. When the perception was that of a uniformly illuminated rear surface seen through two apertures, the results moved equally far toward having *identical* intensities (luminances) on the two sides. These perceptions correspond exactly to the two discussed above for normal situations in which the attention may be directed to reflectance (lightness) or to luminance (brightness) respectively. It seems likely that a careful study along these lines might go far toward a clarification of the whole situation. As far as the experiments go, however, they do suggest that the normal brightness constancy is identical with simultaneous contrast and that the effect may be largely offset by an attitude directed exclusively to the intensity of the stimulus. It was apparent during the experiments that the *way in which the observer looked* at the figure was different in the two cases—it tended to be concentrated *between* the squares for brightness constancy and alternated rapidly between the centers of the two sides for the perception of true stimulus intensity. This difference suggests that what has been described as a difference in attitude may, in the last analysis, be found to be a difference primarily in the way the eyes are used rather than in the mental phase. A consequent decision that the effect is purely psychophysical may be involved.

Such a reduction to psychophysics might also associate the effects with our present knowledge of adaptation. It may be well, therefore, to review adaptation briefly in connection with the present subject before proceeding with a consideration of brightness constancy as it is encountered in daily life.

It was pointed out in Chapter VIII that the eye readily and quickly adapts itself to any new intensity level, if this is brighter than the one to which it has become accustomed. If it is dimmer, a certain time lag enters whose magnitude depends on the time of viewing of the previous intensity and on its magnitude. It was pointed out that this effect occurs not only generally over the field of vision but also locally and laterally. Both the phenomenon of brightness constancy and that of simultaneous contrast can be explained on the basis of this property of the eye but the offsetting of the effect by a *stimulus*-directed attitude cannot be so explained without a rather far-reaching postulate. Let us first consider the explanation and then the possible assumption.

If in moving from the lighted to the shaded part of a scene the eye were to adapt completely to the prevailing illumination, it would be expected that identical relative reflectances would be seen as being in the two parts of the field. Such is the condition of brightness constancy. If vision of a large rectangle surrounding a smaller patch causes adaptation to the brighter-surround area, it would be expected that the center would appear darker than when the same central patch was the brightest area in the field, as it would be if surrounded by black. These explanations seem logical and are probably largely valid for the instances cited. To offset these effects by a change in the mental attitude, however, would call for mental control of the process of adaptation. It seems to the writer that there is good evidence to support such a postulate. It must be remembered that from childhood we have used our eyes to tell us the nature of objects *in spite of* the situations encountered. It would not be surprising to learn that unconscious ways of using the eyes could produce the results described. If so, at both extremes we are concerned only with direct responses of the eye as affected by adaptation, and the whole subject resolves itself on the psychophysical plane.

Whatever the true explanation may be the facts remain that brightness constancy, simultaneous contrast, and brightness adaptation are closely related phenomena, all existing at the same time regardless of how an experiment may be set up, and that probably all are one and the same thing from different points of view.

Perhaps as a final example the three ways of viewing a shadow mentioned earlier may afford an adequate summary. Rood pointed out that an observer may look at, into, or through a shadow. Introspectively, the three may be analyzed somewhat as follows. If the observer is interested in the scene as a whole and perhaps more particularly in the illumination on the scene, a shadow becomes part of the illumination. It is seen simply as a darker area with a certain geometrical shape and certain edge characteristics. In relation to the amount of attention that is directed toward it this appearance may vary all the way from perception of a volume of space which is darker than the space around it to the other extreme, a simple dark spot in the scene as a whole. All these ways can be called looking *at* the shadow. Adaptation is held by the scene as a whole, and the properties of surfaces in the shadow are not noticed.

Suppose, however, the observer desires particularly to see some object lying in the shadow. He looks steadily at it without allowing his eyes to wander out of the shadow; perhaps he also squints his eyes a little and shades them from the rest of the scene. Any of these actions permit the sensitivity of his eyes to increase, and the new adaptation level gives him better vision in the shadow. He now is looking *into* the shadow and is looking at surfaces in that illumination.

If he approaches the shadow and increases his concentration within it, he no longer sees it as a shadow, but as a more or less normally lighted scene, perhaps with a bright fringe of light around it. Looking *through* the shadow seems an appropriate expression for describing this situation.

A fourth variation, which may also be referred to as looking *through*, or perhaps, looking *across* the shadow, involves a shadow which is small, or more particularly, one which is made up of a number of small areas such as those given by leaves on a white house or, perhaps better, on a green lawn. If the observer is interested in the house or the lawn he sees them as continuous surfaces of constant reflectance and pays no attention to the shaded areas. In effect the fourth variation implies perfect color constancy although actually it is rather lack of interest in the shadow than a direct perception.

MODES OF APPEARANCE

So far the perceptions of lightness and brightness have been considered with regard to relative reflectances and light intensities respectively. As encountered in daily life, however, they take on a somewhat different aspect. They are the main factors determining the apparent *shapes* of objects and are the perceptions which give rise to our knowledge of the surface characteristics of objects. Again these perceptions are introspectively direct rather than secondary, that is, an object is seen as spherical and with a dull surface directly and not as a deduction from observed lighting conditions. The perceptions are so direct, in fact, that they have been named by psychologists and are classified under the main heading, "modes of appearance" of objects. These classifications were given consideration in the compilation of the OSA Colorimetry Report, and the part of the table dealing with this subject is reprinted in Fig. 10·5. It is important to grasp the significance of the distinction which has been made in this table between "modes of appearance" and "attributes of the modes." The four modes listed correspond in a general way to what have already been described as types of perception as controlled by the attitude of the observer. The "aperture" mode corresponds roughly to the perception of the quality of the light

from any area considered *as light* without reference to its source. The "illuminant" and "illumination" modes correspond to the perception of the illumination as distinct from the characteristics of the reflecting surfaces as seen, i.e., the light falling *on the*

FIGURE 10·5

Modes of Appearance

(The numbers following the various modes correspond to the numbers of the attributes which they possess)

Aperture (1–5)
Illuminant (1–8)
Illumination (1–3)
Object Modes
  Surface (1–11)
  Volume (1–9)

Attributes of Modes of Appearance

1. Brightness (or lightness)
2. Hue
3. Saturation
4. Size
5. Shape
6. Location
7. Flicker
8. Sparkle
9. Transparency
10. Glossiness
11. Luster

FIG. 10·5 The classification of modes of appearance by the Committee on Colorimetry of the Optical Society of America. (*Journal of the Optical Society of America*, Vol. 33, p. 552, 1943.)

surfaces rather than that reflected. The two "object" modes, "surface" and "volume," correspond to the perception of the *properties of the objects* independent of the illumination in which they stand. The general differences observed in these cases have been discussed for brightness and will be considered for the other phases in the next chapter.

The "attributes" of the modes represent the perceptual variables which can be distinguished when the perception is that of the appropriate "mode" and the numbers in brackets after each mode give the attributes possible for that mode. Thus the aperture mode has the possible perceptual variables 1 through 5, etc.

It is apparent that not all the attributes refer to color in the ordinary use of the word and that most people tend to restrict the subject to the first three attributes. Nevertheless it is true that these perceptual variables so far affect our normal responses that it is exceedingly difficult, even under the best conditions, to make a satisfactory match for the first three attributes unless the other attributes are also matched. This is true even when the comparison is made under the same mode of appearance. For example, it is exceedingly difficult for the untrained observer to tell whether a perfectly plain piece of colored paper which shows little or no texture is or is not the same color as a piece of woolen cloth of coarse weave or a piece of glossy rayon. It is even more difficult to make such a match when the modes of appearance are different, as when the color of a light source is compared to that of a reflecting surface, and many people argue that such a comparison is often impossible.

With these facts in mind it is worth while to consider briefly the physical nature of the light effects that give rise to the attributes when perceived under the various modes. The discussion in this chapter will be restricted to the effects that are dependent on light intensity. It will be necessary to depart somewhat from the terminology which has been used in the earlier part of the chapter but the section will serve as a connecting link between the subject as discussed here and the somewhat more specific nomenclature of the OSA.

The relationship between the physical variables and brightness and lightness has been discussed earlier. As far as the discussion went, perception in the aperture, illuminant, or illumination modes produced an approach to knowledge of the light intensity whereas perception in the object modes produced knowledge approaching true reflectance. The volume mode was not considered, but it corresponds to knowledge of the transmission characteristics of a space-distributed absorbing material such as smoke or milky water.

Perceptions of the size, the shape, and the location of an object or area in a scene are dependent on many psychological variables, some of which were considered in Chapter IX. From the standpoint of the light involved, they represent perceptions based on the geometrical arrangement of the brightnesses of the scene and, in particular, on the abruptness of change in brightness between adjacent areas. (Brightnesses can be equal at such a boundary if hue or saturation changes.) In a sense they are determined by the pure geometry of the image in the eye. In fact, however, the perception of brightness itself, as well as that of lightness, may be affected markedly by the nature of the perception of these variables. An object seen far away through a mist, for example, may give a quite different perception of its lightness from the identical scene perceived through clear air. As with all the attributes, therefore, the fact that the perceptions are physically produced does *not* mean that they are *determined* by the physical conditions. *The psychological result of the situation (i.e., the appearance to the observer) varies in all the attributes when the perception of any one of them is changed by the observer's attitude.* Accordingly no *one* of the attributes can be considered independent of any of the others, and all of them must be taken into account if an attempt is made to predict the observer's perceptions.

This fact of perception makes the attempt to simplify the subject of color exceedingly difficult. When the conditions are so controlled that all the attributes but one of any two lights are the same and they are both perceived in the same manner, comparison becomes a relatively simple matter, and results of high precision may be obtained. As soon as two of the attributes are different it becomes difficult to make a relative judgment about either, and when all of them are different even the experts can make only rough judgments. The legitimate statement, therefore, that the attributes are produced by the physical configuration of the light reaching the eye does *not* mean that this configuration does not affect those perceptions which are based solely on the *quality* and *quantity* of the light. Generally *all* the perceptions are dependent on each other.

Attributes 7 and 8 of the list are "flicker" and "sparkle," and it is apparent that they represent changes in the intensity and perhaps in the quality of the light with lapse of time. They represent perception of the fact that the light reaching the eye is not constant.

Attribute 9 is quite different in nature and corresponds to the perception that the light reaches the eye through the material rather than by reflection from its surface.

Attribute 10, "glossiness," refers to the perception that the surface of the object has a high polish and, accordingly, can reflect light specularly without selective absorption (except metals). This perception is quite complex and has been the subject of a long, acrimonious debate because of a rather unfortunate term used by Helmholtz in describing the effect. If a surface reflection is different in color from the reflection of the same light from the rest of the surface (the reflection of a window in polished mahogany is the usual example), the aperture

mode of appearance, that is, the perception of the quality of the total light reaching the eye, gives rise to a perception of the total light intensity (and color). Perception in the illuminant mode subtracts the intensity and color from *below* the polished surface, and perception in the object mode tends to eliminate the surface reflection entirely. Helmholtz, writing at a time when the subject of perception had not reached its present state of development, described these two latter types of perception as "unconscious inference." It is apparent enough from his book that he realized that direct perception was involved, but the implication of a secondary conscious process carried by the word "inference" was sufficient to bring down on his head (and those of many who have followed him) a torrent of abuse.

THE INTERRELATIONS OF THE ATTRIBUTES AND MODES

Attribute 11, "luster," has been the subject of some debate, but it seems generally agreed that it corresponds to the perception of a surface whose reflection characteristics change sufficiently with the angle of view so that different intensities or qualities of light reach the two eyes of the observer. The equivalent of luster is often produced in a photograph, however, if the gradient of a reflected light source is properly reproduced.

It is realized, of course, that all of this discussion is quite confusing to the person new to the subject of color. It is just these effects, however, which have provoked such endless controversy in the field. After reading a simplified explanation of the variables of brightness, hue, and saturation it seems natural to expect that it would be a simple matter to set up a system showing these variables visually and then to compare all colors to them in some form of numerical

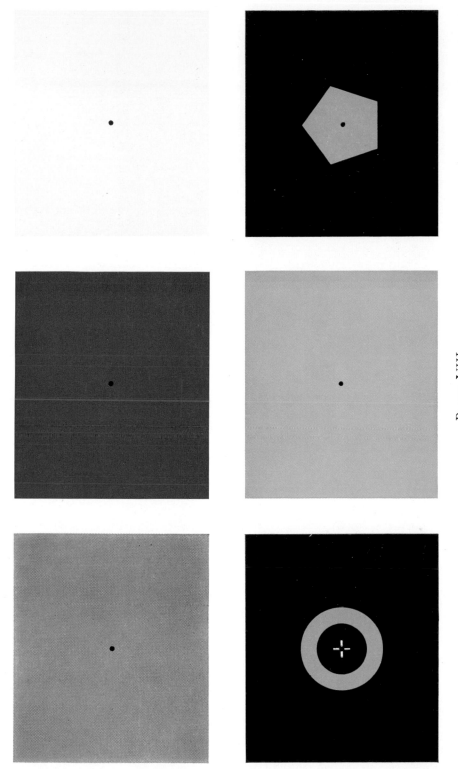

Plate VIII

By looking steadily at the dot inside either the disk or the pentagon, and then transferring the gaze to the dot on one of the other surfaces, an afterimage is seen. The afterimage on the gray surface is complementary to the original color surface. On the other surfaces, it has the color appearance of a subtractive mixture of this complementary color and the color of the surface against which it is viewed.

description. Many such systems have been devised, and a number of them will be considered in some detail in Chapter XII. It is a surprise, when an attempt is made to use one of these systems, however, to find, for example, that the reflectance of a piece of paper cannot be compared easily with the intensity of a light source. It is almost necessary, as will become apparent, to use a different system with appropriate attributes and viewed under an appropriate mode for *every* classification of subject. Those who see only the simplicity of their own system and not the difficulties of its application to fields other than those of their immediate interests are apt to indulge in uncomplimentary remarks which display the lack of breadth of their approach.

Perhaps this chapter may be closed, by way of summary, with two examples suggestive of interrelated attributes.

In the perception of an object in an obvious illuminant such as sunlight or a lamp, variations in intensity caused by the shape of a surface are perceived directly as *shape* and not as intensity changes. In fact this perception is usually so strong that it is almost impossible for the untrained observer to see the "shading" on the objects at all. Yet it is just this shading which the artist must see or the competent photographer must reproduce in consciousness if he is to produce the perception of the shape in the mind of the person observing his reproduction.

Furthermore, the *contrast* of the light on a scene is determined by the geometry of the way in which the light reaches the objects being seen. In sunlight the contrast is determined by the number of clouds in the sky, the closeness of reflecting objects, and the like, since such conditions determine the amount of light which reaches the shadows. In artificial light the contrast is de-termined by the number of lights and by reflection, but again it is largely a matter of the amount of light reaching the shadows. On a bright, clear day out of doors, far from vertical surfaces such as are produced by houses, this contrast can reach very high values. In common speech such conditions are described as "brilliant" sunlight, and this word describes adequately the perceptual feeling of intensity which such a scene conveys to the observer. It is found, however, that much the same feeling of intensity is conveyed by any scene lighted to the same *contrast*, even when the actual intensity is far lower. The perception of the brightness of the illumination (hence in the illumination mode), therefore, is conditioned very largely by the size, the shape, and the location of the light sources, rather than by their physical intensities as such.

The next chapter will consider these same variables as they affect hue and saturation although the discussion will be from a somewhat different point of view. The practical consequence of many of them will be discussed in somewhat more detail in the chapters on applied color which conclude the book.

BIBLIOGRAPHY

Brunswik, Egon. "Zur Entwicklung der Albedo-wahrnehmung." *Zeitschrift für Psychologie*, **109**: 40–115 (1929).

Gelb, Adhemar. "Die Farbenkonstanz der Seh-dinge." *Handbuch der normalen und patholo-gischen Physiologie*, **12**:594–678 (1929).

Helmholtz's Treatise on Physiological Optics, Vol. 2. Edited by James P. C. Southall. The Optical Society of America. 1924.

Helson, Harry. "Some Factors and Implications of Color Constancy." *Journal of the Optical Society of America*, **33**:555–567 (1943).

Hering, Ewald. *Grundzüge der Lehre vom Licht-sinn*. Berlin: Julius Springer. 1920.

Hess, Carl, and Pretori, Hugo. "Messende Un-tersuchungen über die Gesetzmässigkeit des simultanen Helligkeits-Contrastes." *Archiv für Oph-thalmologie,* **40**:1–24 (1894).

Katz, David. *The World of Colour.* London: Kegan Paul, Trench, Trubner and Co., Ltd. 1935.

Luckiesh, M. *Color and Its Applications.* New York: D. Van Nostrand Co. 1915. Chapter VII.

MacLeod, Robert B. *An Experimental Investigation of Brightness Constancy.* Archives of Psychology, No. 135 (Columbia University). 1932.

Rood, Roland. *Color and Light in Painting.* New York: Columbia University Press. 1941.

Sears, Francis Weston. *Principles of Physics III —Optics,* 2nd ed. Cambridge, Mass.: Addison-Wesley Press, Inc. 1946. Chapter XII.

Thouless, Robert H. "Phenomenal Regression to the Real Object. I." *The British Journal of Psychology,* **21**:339–359 (1931).

Woodworth, Robert S. *Experimental Psychology.* New York: Henry Holt and Co. 1938. Chapters XXII and XXIV.

Color Perception

CHAPTER XI

THE word color, as it is used in ordinary speech and as it has been used in this book, has many different meanings. Each of the meanings is associated with one or more of the different phases of the subject, and in any given instance any one may be implied, depending on the attitude at the moment of the person using it. In the present chapter we shall consider color from the psychological standpoint purely as a mental phenomenon, i.e., color as *seen* and the variables which affect its appearance.

THE NATURE OF COLOR

As discussed earlier (Chapter IX) there are three general types of visual attitude which lead respectively to mental images, perceptions, and inferences, and each of these can have one of the three results: knowledge, illusion, and hallucination, depending on its relation to the cause. Unfortunately our present knowledge of the subject does not permit us to carry through such a scheme and to consider the relationships and mechanisms under each heading. It is quite clear in general that all nine phases exist and can be recognized intro-

spectively, but some phases have received little or no study by investigators, partly because of the extreme difficulty of investigation in these fields and partly because some of the phases have been recognized as such only in recent years.

The three types of attitudes may be recognized introspectively, although such analyses are sometimes difficult. Color as a mental image does not necessarily have to have radiant energy as its stimulus since it can arise from pressure on the eyeball, for example, or from memory, either in the abstract or in connection with an imagined object. Thus it is possible to "see" blue as a color or as the color of an object with the eyes closed. It is also possible to compare the color of an actual object with this mental reference system, and in the same way the color of the light from an object can be considered independently of the color *of* the object, just as it was found possible to consider the brightness alone.

Before we attempt to analyze the visual process in this way, however, it will be well to review briefly the properties of the visual mechanism which relate to the colors seen. It does not matter, of course, whether a particular hue is seen because of what can be called a property of the eye or because of an attitude relationship. In the last analysis the two may be the same but it is necessary in considering the subject to try to separate the effects which can be changed by the observer and those which cannot.

As one works with color in a practical or experimental way one is impressed by two apparently unrelated facts. Color as seen is a mobile changeable thing depending to a large extent on the relationship of the color to other colors seen simultaneously. It is not fixed in its relation to the direct stimulus which creates it. On the other hand the properties of surfaces that give rise to color do not seem to change greatly under a wide variety of illumination colors, usually (but not always) looking much the same in artificial light as in daylight. Both of these effects seem to be due in large part to the mechanism of color adaptation mentioned earlier.

When the eye is fixed on a colored area there is an immediate readjustment of the sensitivity of the eye to color in and around the area viewed. This readjustment does not immediately affect the color seen but usually does affect the next area to which the gaze is shifted. The longer the time of viewing, the higher the intensity, and the larger the area, the greater the effect will be in terms of its persistence in the succeeding viewing situation. As indicated by the work of Wright and Schouten it appears that, at least for a first approximation, full adaptation takes place over a very brief time if the adapting source is moderately bright and the eye has been in relative darkness just previously. As the stimulus is allowed to act, however, the effect becomes more *persistent* in the sense that it takes the eye longer to regain its sensitivity to lower intensities. The net result is that, if the eye is so exposed and then the gaze is transferred to an area

of *lower* intensity, the loss of sensitivity produced by the first area will still be present and appear as an "afterimage" superimposed on the second. The effect not only is present over the actual area causing the "local adaptation" but also spreads with decreasing strength to adjoining areas of the eye to produce "lateral adaptation." Also, because of the persistence of the effect if the eye is shifted around from one object to another, all of which are at similar brightnesses or have similar colors, the adaptation will tend to become uniform over the whole eye. In the next paragraphs the phenomena associated with these local, lateral, and general adaptations will be considered with respect to the appearance of colors.

Consider first a simple colored afterimage. Plate VIII shows a colored pentagon and a colored ring, each surrounded by black. Hold the book in a strong light and look steadily at the tiny spot in the center of one of these figures for twenty or thirty seconds; then transfer the gaze to the black dot in the center of the gray area at the upper left. A purple area should appear surrounding the black dot. The effect is cumulative and should increase if one looks back and forth a number of times. Such simple local color adaptation can be "explained" as follows. Assuming there are three color receptors in the eye, one for red, one for green, and one for blue light, the green light stimulus causes adaptation of the green receptor, decreasing its sensitivity to green. Since the figure does not reflect much blue or red, these receptors rise to a considerably higher sensitivity when time is allowed for the adaptation to the white paper to wear off. When the eyes are shifted to the gray area, since this area sends about equal color stimuli to the three receptors of the eye, its effect on the adapted eye is greater on the red and blue receptors than on the green one, and hence the gray area is seen as purple. That this explanation is reasonable can be seen in some of the other colored areas of Plate VIII. If the adaptation to the green figure is repeated and the eyes are shifted to the yellow area, it will be found that this time the spot appears red. This change is because the yellow area does not reflect blue, the eye has low sensitivity to green, and therefore red becomes the effective color. Corresponding shifts in afterimage color should be seen if the red or blue-green areas are used.

That afterimages or local adaptation areas are physically present in some region of the visual system can be demonstrated by developing a rather strong afterimage through continued gazing at a brightly lighted area and then looking at a distant wall in dim illumination. The spot is seen on the wall but, because it does not change physically in size *in the eye*, is seen as tremendously large in comparison with the original image. It is, in fact, possible to measure actual distances if the afterimage is used to get a direct measure of the relative size of the two images in the eye.

In brief summary local adaptation changes the sensitivity of a local area of the eye so that its sensitivity becomes opposite to that of the energy distribution that caused it. The change, however, is roughly in terms of the red, the green, and the blue regions of the spectrum and not wavelength-for-wavelength, a fact to which we shall return in a moment.

The adaptation process also affects adjacent regions in the form that is called lateral adaptation. The effect is illustrated in Plate IX. In this plate there are four vessels, all of which, if isolated, would be seen to have exactly the same green color. As seen with their surrounding colors, however, they appear to differ from each other in all three color variables: hue, saturation, and lightness. A little study will show that the same effect occurs here as in the previous figure except that now it is occurring simultaneously rather than successively and in the area of the eye *not* covered by the stimulus. It is lateral adaptation extending into the center from the outside area and producing the phenomenon usually known as "simultaneous color contrast."

In the "general-adaptation" phase of color vision the eye is exposed for long periods to surfaces all of which are illuminated by light of the same color. If the surfaces viewed are not, in themselves, too highly selective the result is a readjustment of the three eye receptors to compensate for the energy distribution as best they can. If the receptors are thought of as three photoelectric cells—one sensitive to the blue region, one to the green, and the third to the red—it is possible to construct a simple analogy which makes the effect easier to remember. Suppose that for a white surface in daylight each photocell has the same output and the light is seen as white. General adaptation means that to a first approximation for any illuminant and subject the outputs of the three automatically readjust so that the average light from the scene also gives this same ratio of outputs and, by itself, would also be seen as white. As noted earlier (Chapter VIII) this readjustment also *tends* to correct all the colors in the scene toward their daylight appearance. The effect is approximate, for the reasons discussed. Readjustment does not correct some colors as well as it does others. In strongly colored illumination it not only may fail to correct the colors but also may distort them materially, as in the Helson-Judd effect, in which blacks disappear and become complementary to the illuminant color.

In addition to these fairly well-established adaptation effects it was also noted that, when the intensity or the percentage of white light in a stimulus is changed, the visible hue of the color changes also. When the intensity alone is changed, the saturation also changes. It can, in fact, be stated as a generalization that there is no simple physical variable by which the intensity or the quality of light can be changed that does not change all three attributes (hue, saturation, and brightness).

This review has been introduced to emphasize the complexity of the relationship between the physical stimulus which produces a colored appearance and the color which is seen. In spite of the complexity it is possible to calculate the appearance of a color for some simple situations. When an attempt is made to do so, however, a situation is encountered which is exactly analogous to the difficulty involved in the calculation of relative brightness. It was found there that a psychophysical value called the "luminance" could be calculated for any situation but that it corresponded to the psychological "brightness" only in special circumstances. In exactly the same way it is possible to calculate the "chromaticity" of a surface under a given illuminant. This chromaticity completely defines the "colorimetric purity" and the "dominant wavelength" of the light as it would be received by the eye of a "standard observer" under specified conditions. (The bases and the technique of making such calculations will be considered in Chapter XII.) The important point at the moment is that this calculated chromaticity bears the same relationship to the light from a given area as the previous luminance. Just as the luminance represented the calculated effective intensity in terms of a standardized eye sensitivity so the chromaticity represents the other two factors involved in the color of the light.

In the brightness-constancy phenomenon it was found that luminance represented one extreme of the way in which the light intensity could appear to an observer, the other extreme being the luminous reflectance. There is also an exactly corresponding phenomenon with regard to the other color variables. Chromaticity represents one extreme, and the selective action of the surface represents the other. Unfortunately the subject has not as yet received adequate study from this point of view, and no terminology has become accepted.

CONSTANCY OF SURFACE COLOR

The subject usually known as color constancy or as color transformation refers to the perceptual approximate constancy of the colors of objects under differently colored illuminations. It is produced, in part at least, by the general adaptation already reviewed. This phase of the effect, however, is parallel to general intensity level adaptation and not to brightness constancy. The exact parallel to brightness constancy is an effect which takes place in the visual appearance of non-uniformly illuminated colored surfaces. It is a subject of some importance to artists and is usually discussed under the general heading of the color of shadows.

The phenomenon may be described as follows, but we must keep in mind the fact that more adequate study may show that it is somewhat different. It has been noted that both hue and saturation change with light intensity. The light from a uniform surface, however, changes not in quality but only in intensity if the illumination is non-uniform. The carefully trained observer tends to *see* either of these facts. If he *looks for* the color of the *light* reaching his eye, his perception will tend toward seeing the hue shift which accompanies the lower intensity in the shadow. If he *looks for* the *color of the surface*, he will tend to perceive the light from the surface as constant, independent of the intensity differences. The former attitude is in the direction of perceiving the chromaticity, the latter in the direction of seeing the selective action of the surface, the first being analogous to luminance and the second to reflectance.

In addition to these effects there is the final parallel with brightness, that the mental image may be studied introspectively and, to a certain extent at least, the color may be referred to an absolute mental standard of color. This reference is analogous to the perception of absolute intensity level discussed in the previous chapter and is almost equally vague and unreliable. The general color of the illumination in a room can be judged to a certain extent in spite of adaptation and is usually, although not always, correct for direction, i.e., blue, yellow, etc., with respect to daylight. Judgment is frequently incorrect, however, just as it is for intensity, and the inaccuracy may arise from the effects described by Helson and Judd to be considered in the latter part of the present chapter.

First it may be well to outline in somewhat more explicit form the effects and relationships already discussed, even at the risk of too much repetition. So many variables and effects are involved that the beginner finds himself lost in the maze, particularly in the regions in which nomenclature has not yet been developed.

Color in general has three aspects:

Physics
Psychophysics
Psychology

Three types of adaptation have been distinguished by their effects:

Local adaptation
Lateral adaptation
General adaptation

These adaptations were found to take place for both the intensity and the spectral-quality aspects of color apparently by *separate* mechanisms since they were found to differ both in kind and in degree.

Three general observer attitudes have been separated:

Toward the mental image
Toward the light quality
Toward the properties of the object

These three attitudes can each lead to three types of results as distinguished by knowledge after the event:

Knowledge
Illusion
Hallucination

Let us consider these effects and relationships briefly with respect to the perceived color of the shaded side of an object of uniform color which is standing in an illumination different from daylight. The physics of the situation can be specified completely. Let us assume that the same quality of illuminant is reaching the shadow as reaches the more intensely lighted part, although in general this would not be the case, as discussed earlier. In this instance, however, the light reaching the eye from the object has the same spectral-energy distribution from all parts of the object and differs only in intensity. Assume also that the object stands in surroundings which are neutral gray—that is, are entirely non-selective, varying only in reflectance. Physically the light reaching the eye from these surroundings has the same spectral-energy distribution as the illuminant itself.

Psychophysically this set-up may also be calculated completely with respect to a standard observer. The luminance of the light from each part of the surface may be calculated as may the chromaticity. The chromaticity thus obtained may be evaluated with respect to daylight as the reference standard or with respect to the actual illuminant. If we take into account the work of Wright and Schouten on adaptation in connection with the work of Helson and Judd on surface colors and make the extension proposed by the present writer, it is also possible to estimate the general adaptation state of the eye for this subject and to calculate the effect that this adaptation should have, psychophysically, on the colors observed. Since the relative luminances are the same under all adaptation conditions, this calculation gives a correction to be applied to the chromaticities of the various areas.*

The net result of the psychophysical calculations, therefore, would be the luminance, the luminous reflectance of each area, and three chromaticity values for each. The three values, respectively, are those for the reflected light with respect to daylight, with respect to the illuminant color, and with respect to the adaptation color. There is a fourth possible calculation which would give the absolute luminous reflectance for the surface in daylight. It corresponds to the color as it would be seen in white light but does not correspond to a way in which the surface *can* be seen. It may correlate with the memory color if the object has ever been so observed.

These three characteristics, then, disregarding the fourth one, correspond in the psychophysical realm to the causes of the results obtained when the observer takes the three attitudes, looking respectively at the mental image, at the light reaching his eye, and at the color of the object surface. In nearly all cases the three are different—in some cases markedly different.

When a real observer, rather than a hypothetical one, is introduced into the scene and is permitted to take either the one atti-

* See "Visual Processes and Color Photography" (bibliography at end of chapter) for a discussion of this possibility.

tude natural to him or to attempt one or the other of the possible attitudes, his actual perceptions fall into the realm of psychology. The psychophysical calculations indicate what the observer *should* see *if* the postulates on which the calculations were based are *rigidly* correct. As was noted in the discussion of brightness constancy, they seldom, if ever, are. The calculations represent extreme attitudes never completely realized by an observer because of the mutual effect of the possibilities, a factor not included in the calculations. Furthermore the situation may lead either to knowledge or to illusion, and this fact alone may seriously affect both the attitude and the perceived colors. (Hallucination may be neglected since the scene is assumed as real, although it could enter if the observer strongly believed the color to be different and did not look at it to check his belief.)

EFFECT OF THE OBSERVER'S INTENTIONS

From the psychological standpoint, therefore, a considerable number of possible perceptions can result from the scene. They represent the result in consciousness of the various possible combinations of the above variables. Although it is not worth while to consider them all, some of them may be stated to illustrate their general nature. A description from the standpoint of the observer will indicate some of the perceptions. Suppose the object is yellow on a gray background illuminated by artificial light of good intensity (for example, a 100-watt bulb at fairly close range). The observer will be aware of the fact that the light from this lamp is yellowish with respect to daylight and may so observe it if he looks with this intention. Under these conditions he will perceive the light from the background as yellowish. Next if he moves his eyes con-

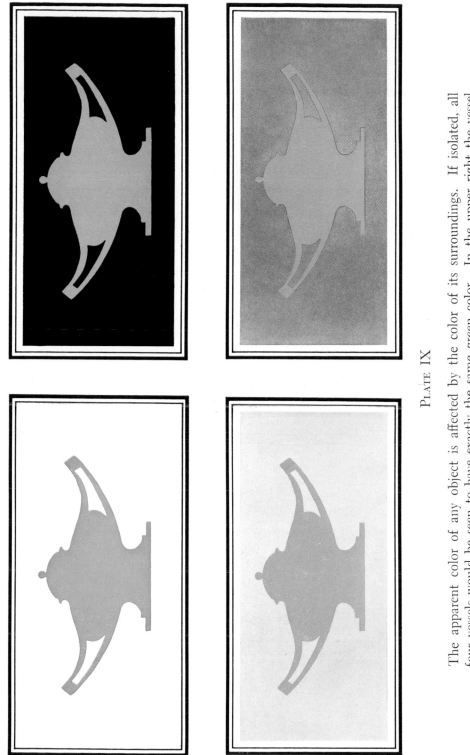

P<small>LATE</small> IX

The apparent color of any object is affected by the color of its surroundings. If isolated, all four vessels would be seen to have exactly the same green color. In the upper right the vessel appears lighter in color and desaturated. In the lower left it is intermediate between the upper two in lightness, and more "bluish." In the lower right it is intermediate in all aspects.

tinuously over the scene for a considerable length of time he will obtain a general adaptation considerably more yellow than that caused by the light on the background. Under these conditions the light from the background will appear somewhat bluish—a difficult observation for these colors but much easier for some others. Suppose he now looks carefully at the background to ascertain its true surface color. As long as he can maintain this attitude, he will see it nearly as the neutral gray we have assumed it to be.

Next the observer may turn his attention to the yellow object and particularly to its lighted side. If he compares its color mentally with that of its former appearance in daylight, he will probably see that it is a somewhat less saturated yellow than before, corresponding to the fact that his eyes are adapted to a yellower light. Long-continued observations of the yellow surface alone would still further increase this adaptation locally and decrease its saturation still further. Transfer of his gaze to a dimly lighted portion of the background would then produce a temporary blue afterimage of the surface.

Suppose next he becomes interested in the shaded side of the object. If he observes the *light* coming from this part of the object, he will tend to see it as distinctly green in hue with respect to the lighted part, especially if it is a pure yellow or slightly toward yellow-green rather than toward orange. Such yellows shift toward green at reduced intensities. However, if he looks carefully at the color of the *object* he will *see* the same yellow continuing around into the shadow with no noticeable hue shift. Finally, if a shadow in the scene is thrown by a hidden object in such a way that it does not appear like a shadow, he may perceive this shadow directly as a greenish-yellow patch. The earlier possibilities represented tendencies of

perception in the direction of true knowledge for each of the instances; this latter example represents an illusion (and a very convincing one if conditions are right). The illusion in this case has produced the perception proper to the *light* when the observer's intention was to see the surface. Similar illusions can exist when colored objects reflect light into shadows and the like and are quite common. They disappear when circumstances permit a complete understanding of the situation and thereby allow the attitude to direct the perception properly.

The suggested set-up and the derived examples were chosen to avoid effects due to local and lateral adaptation, although local effects were mentioned. Presence in the scene of the possibility of hue shifts due to these effects multiplies the number of chromaticities which could be calculated with respect to the adaptation level by the number of possible levels, one for each object and one for each sequence of viewing as well as one for each pair of adjacent colors. The reader may well feel that at this point we have reached a *reductio ad absurdum* but actually we have not. All these effects do exist and may be demonstrated with considerable ease. What we have reached is an explanation of the statement made earlier that investigations in this field of psychology are exceedingly difficult because of the tremendous number of variables and possibilities.

Some of the possibilities inherent in the preceding paragraph will be considered later, and some will be taken up under various headings in the chapters on applied color. It is important for the reader to realize from the foregoing, however, what processes are going on when an observer looks at an object or a scene and makes a categorical statement about his perceptions. If he is a naive observer interested only in the objects and views the scene casually, he may make one statement. If he is a trained artist, he may *see* it quite differently; he may see either the object color or the light color, depending on the directions of his interest. If he is an exceedingly careful observer and is *asked* to state the color of the object, he may (or might if our color terminology were precise enough for such matters) make a still different answer because he has carefully averaged all the effects to form an inference about the color.

This review does not complete by far what might be said on the subject, and it is apparent that a large book could be written from this point of view. What has been said of shadow-hue shifts, for example, holds equally well for hue shifts due to saturation changes, such as those encountered when white light is seen reflected from a polished colored surface and the like. Such light also can be seen as having or not having a hue shift, etc. It can even be seen as a continuous colored surface *under* a white reflection although this is more often in the nature of an inference, as Helmholtz pointed out, than of a direct double perception.

EMOTIONAL RESPONSE TO COLOR

Still another sort of perception, hardly mentioned so far in this book, although its importance in daily life is large, is the relationship, which is not too clearly understood, between color and the emotional or psychical reaction that it produces. Although somewhat outside of our present approach, this phase of color becomes important when the perception is directly that of the state produced rather than that of the color, since the color is not *seen* as such. Perhaps the best-known example is the rather vague subject of "warm" and "cool" colors. To the average observer it is reasonable to de-

scribe all colors from pure yellow through orange and red to and including the red magentas as warm colors, whereas all colors from greenish yellow through green, cyan, and blue to bluish magentas as "cold" (although there is some dispute about the actual divisions). The basis of this division must lie very deep in human experience because it seems nearly impossible to ascribe a reason for the feeling, and yet it is readily agreed to by nearly all observers. Many hypotheses have been advanced, such as the color of fire and the like, and it does seem that the colors of hot and cold objects do have a tendency to divide in the same manner. Perhaps the present writer may add another suggestion to the effect that blue is the predominant daylight illumination color for cold days while yellow is the color of sunlight. Certainly it is true that in the winter in northern latitudes with the sun low in the sky and a tendency for strong haze or overcast days, the illumination on the average is far bluer than in the summer with clear days and the sun high overhead. It is equally certain that a photograph or a painting may be made to represent a hot or cold day by simply shifting the general color scheme toward yellow or blue respectively.

Of direct importance to the immediate subject is the fact that under conditions in which the weather is cold and blue or hot and yellow, the observer is not at all conscious of the color but only of the temperature, whether the viewpoint is a warm house in winter, or a cool shady spot on a hot day.

How far similar effects occur under other conditions or to what extent colors are seen as effects rather than causes is not known. Some studies have been conducted along these lines, and there are many claims to the effect that green is soothing, red exciting, etc. To the best of the writer's knowledge, however, no work has been done on the extent to which these reactions are true perceptions.

There are a number of other not well-understood color effects which, for the moment, should be classified under the psychology of color vision, although it is entirely possible and perhaps likely that increased knowledge will lead us to consider them psychophysical. It may be well to look at these briefly before closing the chapter with a short summary of a rather remarkable attempt made by Judd to derive an equation by which color perception of a given area could be predicted.

SPREADING EFFECTS

One of these little-understood effects was described in some detail by Van Bezold and by Rood before 1900 but seems to have dropped from the literature for want of an adequate explanation. It is described by Van Bezold as a "spreading effect" and was apparently considered just that, in spite of the fact that it runs contrary to our present beliefs as well as to most of those held at the time. The nature of the effect is illustrated in Plate XI. The left and right ends of the design on the second line differ only in the fact that between the red and blue of the right end of the design, black lines have been drawn which are missing on the left. Otherwise the two ends of the design are identical and identical inks were used (the black is printed from a separate plate carrying the lines only and no shading). It is seen that the colors of the part having the black dividing line are darker than the corresponding ones on the left. To many observers the right end also is more saturated, and certainly this end of the figure has higher contrast. It is apparent that black has been added visually to the colors on the right, making them *darker*, and at the same time there appears to be more difference

between them. These effects are so strong to most observers that a hazy line is seen vertically through the figure at the ends of the black-line part of the figure.

The same effect but in the opposite direction is seen at the opposite end of the same figure in which a white line has been substituted for the black. In this case *white* is added to the colors of this end of the design, causing increased brightness and loss of saturation.

Similar types of effects are evident in the other designs shown on the color plate.

It need hardly be pointed out that the brightness changes are directly contrary to what would be predicted from our knowledge of simultaneous contrast. The presence of black borders in a picture should make the colors lighter, and the presence of the *white* should add black and make them appear darker. The writer feels that until this effect can be explained without elaborate assumptions we cannot say that we understand the way in which the visual process operates. Certainly the effects are completely basic to normal vision.

Another sort of effect in the same category which, again, has not received the attention it deserves is the effect of distance on colors. While this can be considered more advantageously under the subject of color harmony in a later chapter, it should be mentioned here.

The relationships between two colors or among any group of small colored areas are far different at short-viewing distances than they are at long. A group of small patches of color seen at a distance of 15 or 20 inches may appear to fit into a harmonious color scheme and yet appear quite disconnected at a distance of 10 feet or more, and the reverse may equally well occur. Again a painting may appear flat and of low saturation at short distances only to arrange itself into a contrasty pattern of moderately saturated colors as the distance increases. In reverse a plain area of color may appear much more saturated and colorful examined in the hand than when it is placed in the same light intensity and viewed from across the room. The reader will understand that the explanation of such effects is not simple. Nevertheless it is a profound statement of our lack of knowledge to read the statement that the colors used by the early miniature painters could be and were of the highest attainable saturation and the accompanying statement that the same colors used in a larger painting would clash and be considered in poor taste. A parallel is, in fact, found in modern experience with color photography in which it appears to be a fact that small prints must be carried to considerably higher saturations than those of medium size whereas very large prints can be made quite dark without being at all objectionable.

JUDD ON SURFACE COLORS

Not many attempts have been made to produce quantitative expressions capable of predicting the appearance of a color. Perhaps the most noteworthy is that of Judd, an account of which was published in January, 1940. In this study Judd derived empirical equations intended to take into account all the known variables involved in the viewing of surface colors in uniform illumination. He was assisted in the experimental phase of the work by a parallel investigation at Bryn Mawr under Helson, who had originally suggested the problem.

Fifteen colors in "irregularly shaped papers of about one square inch" were "spaced out in disarray" on large white and black cardboard backgrounds having reflectances of 80 percent and 10 percent respectively. The observer was requested to arrange these in order of lightness with the lightest at the

top and the darkest at the bottom, and then asked to estimate their lightnesses on a scale of ten, running from black to white. He was then asked to arrange them in order of saturation and make a similar estimate on a scale of ten, running from gray to the strongest color present in the group. Following this he was requested to name the hue of each sample on an eight-point hue scale. Intermediate estimates between the steps were permitted in all instances. The entire procedure was repeated for the two backgrounds in five widely different illuminants (daylight and four strong colors) so that in all 150 sample-illuminant-background combinations were studied. Except for lightness estimation, the samples were kept one-half inch or more apart and the observers were "encouraged to look rapidly from one sample to another in order to avoid as much as possible the influence of any one sample on estimates of the color of another."

The empirical equations which were developed took into account the following assumptions:

1. The "matching condition" as described in earlier chapters was assumed valid. That is, it was assumed that if the calculated chromaticities and luminous reflectances of two samples were the same for a given viewing situation the two would be found to match. This is the basic assumption of the psychophysics of color.

2. It was assumed that it was possible to calculate both hue and saturation from the psychophysical data used to determine the presence or absence of a match, that is, hue and saturation were assumed to depend on the physical stimulus if enough variables were included.

3. It was assumed that lightness was dependent on the luminous reflectance of the sample, taking into account some value related to the luminous reflectance of the field as a whole.

4. It was assumed that saturation and hue each depended on all the factors involved rather than that they were independent variables.

5. It was assumed that the color adaptation of the observer remained constant during each test condition.

The student is referred to the original article for the equations themselves since they are expressed in terms of the Uniform Chromaticity Scale (UCS) developed by Judd. (This system will be discussed briefly in Chapter XIII.)

The results obtained in the work were encouraging in that the equations predicted quite satisfactorily the lightness of some 97 percent of the combinations, 84 percent of the hues, and 73 percent of the saturations. It must be borne in mind, however, that the eleven- and eight-point scales used represent quite large steps in visual color and that observer variation was large. The success of the attempt does indicate, however, that most of the large variables, at least for surface colors in strong illumination, are known, and that a sufficiently painstaking inquiry into all the variables would hold the possibility of exact calculation of the appearance of such colors from the physical characteristics of the situation.

No attempt was made, of course, to introduce the purely personal psychological variables between observers except as a statistical average. It is exceedingly doubtful if such calculations are possible for the general conditions, which would include non-surface colors as well as lighting that is non uniform both for illuminance and for chromaticity.

In any event such calculations would be useful only in specifying the limiting ranges of the appearance of a particular energy distribution. Although it is to be hoped that such calculations may be possible eventually, they will not settle the perennial disputes between those who see a color in one way and those who see it in another.

THE HELSON-JUDD EFFECT

Implicit in these equations developed by Judd is an effect pointed out at some length by Helson. When an observer views a scene illuminated by intensely colored light, his adaptation reaches extreme proportions, and effects which may well be present under more normal adaptation take on proportions which are so strange as to be hard to believe. If a room or a scene is illuminated, for example, by intense red light, the sensitivities of the red receptor, and to some extent the blue, are very greatly depressed compared to the green. The result is a green eye sensitivity far greater relative to the other two than any which is ever encountered under more normal circumstances. The result can only be described adequately in terms of the telephone cross-talk analogy referred to in an earlier chapter. The eye appears to lose all possibility of seeing black. The sensation is one of blinding glare and all shadows and all areas which would normally appear shaded or black become neutral or green. In fact the deeper the black to be expected from usual considerations the more saturated is the green which is observed. This effect is just what would be expected under the analogy. A million or so nerves run back from each eye through a nerve cable only a fraction of an inch in diameter. It is almost impossible to believe that currents passing through some of these nerves do not affect adjacent nerves through which no current at all is passing. If, as must be supposed, red, green, and blue nerves are separate, then it will be the green nerves which are most affected by this "cross talk." The level of excitation will necessarily be low compared with that of the stimulated nerves but two effects will be observed.

First this stimulation will decrease the saturation of all directly stimulated areas and, second, all areas not directly stimulated will appear green. Both effects are clearly demonstrated by the experiments and receive an adequate explanation by the hypothesis. One fact, however, must be borne in mind, and it is crucial to the explanation. For the phenomenon to take place as postulated, adaptation effects must occur, not in the retina as most writers seem to assume, but in the occipital lobes or higher cortex centers. That these and similar effects do actually occur at these levels seems adequately demonstrated by the work of Köhler and others and by the often-quoted fact that binocular color-contrast effects and the like can and do occur under appropriate circumstances.

In any case we are indebted to Helson and Judd for calling our attention to this important effect and perhaps, in spite of Helmholtz, may be permitted to name this phenomenon the Helson-Judd effect. Helson's work demonstrated in unambiguous fashion the presence of the effect at unsuspected levels, and Judd's equations appear to indicate that even under conditions of more or less normal vision this cross talk must be taken into account to calculate the appearance of colors, even to a first approximation.

ATTENTION, INTENTION, AND MEMORY IN COLOR VIEWING

It is to be hoped that the reader, at this point, will realize that the separation of the subject of color into physical, psychophysical, and psychological aspects is no mere artifice that simplifies the writing of a book. The physical stimulus that gives rise to perceived color, the result of the stimulus that would be expected of the normal observer under normal circumstances, and the perception actually resulting in the individual under real conditions are three separate and distinct phenomena, each following its own rules and each distinctly and unambiguously different. The number of possible energy distributions is obviously infinite. Psychophysics recognizes the possibility that perhaps a million different perceptual colors may result from these distributions. Judd calculates that if conditions are sufficiently varied nearly ten million different colors may be recognized in consciousness.

Even Judd's calculation, however, does not exhaust the variations on the theme that life can produce. It was noted in an earlier chapter that the mode of appearance of a color gave rise to a distinct type of perception, different for each mode, and it has already been noted that aperture and surface colors follow their own rules, each quite independently of the energy distribution involved. The matter, however, goes even deeper than this in that the average observer is quite incapable of comparing any two colors if they have markedly different "attributes." Few people, for example, can compare the color of a piece of high gloss satin with that of a piece of dull cotton of nearly the same color, and arrive at a satisfying conclusion regarding their relative colors. Even though precise measurement may indicate that, psychophysically, they are a perfect color match, the presence of different physical attributes is a sufficient block to recognition of their identity. Similar blocks exist with respect to glazed and dull porcelain, powdery substances against transparent materials, and in a host of similar situations. If these psychological difficulties are taken into account in estimating the number of perceptual colors, the number may well become so large as to be considered infinite.

These closing remarks are not intended to imply that the calculation of color is impossible, nor even to suggest that the subject of color is hopelessly complicated. They are intended as a sincere attempt to make the student realize that color as a subject, far from being simple, is exceedingly complex and that, in a sense, the beauty which can arise from natural objects has its origin in the infinite variety of color associated with form which the manifold modes and attributes may produce out of the relatively simple world of psychophysical color.

It is necessary to add one simplifying note to this melange of effects. The average, normal, non-color conscious observer is motivated primarily by a desire to observe the properties of objects. If the writer may be forgiven the remark, this applies also in a slightly different sense to artists and others who strive to "see" nature in one way or another. Viewing of a color in a particular situation is, at best, a peculiar mixture of attention, intention, and memory. Depending on the particular background of the individual, one or the other of these will come to the fore, and with results that are well-nigh unpredictable without an introspective report from the individual concerned. A naive observer will report a leaf as green when the light reaching his eye *must* be pure blue—he hasn't *looked*. An artist will report that the distant view seen through green foliage is pink—he has looked for color, and his adaptation to the foliage has produced pink from the distant haze. The interested layman will report that the shadow side of the box is the same yellow as the illuminated side because he has looked for surface qualities. All are right and entitled to their judg-ments. Color is what you *do* see, not what you should see.

BIBLIOGRAPHY

Birren, Faber. *The Story of Color from Ancient Mysticism to Modern Science*. Westport, Conn.: The Crimson Press. 1941. Chapter VII.

Boring, Edwin G. *Sensation and Perception in the History of Experimental Psychology*. New York: D. Appleton-Century Co., Inc. 1942. Chapters II, IV, and V.

Evans, Ralph M. "Visual Processes and Color Photography." *Journal of the Optical Society of America*, **33**:579–614 (1943).

Helmholtz's Treatise on Physiological Optics, Vol. 3. Edited by James P. C. Southall. The Optical Society of America. 1925. Chapter XXXII.

Helson, Harry. "Fundamental Problems in Color Vision. I. The Principle Governing Changes in Hue, Saturation, and Lightness of Non-Selective Samples in Chromatic Illumination." *Journal of Experimental Psychology*, **23**:439–476 (1938).

Judd, Deane B. "Hue, Saturation, and Lightness of Surface Colors with Chromatic Illumination." *Journal of the Optical Society of America*, **30**: 2–32 (1940).

Rood, Ogden N. *Students' Text-book of Color*. New York: D. Appleton and Co. 1916 (copyright 1881).

Schouten, Jan F. *Visueele Meting van Adaptatie en van de wederzijdsche Beinvloeding van Netvlieselementen*. Utrecht: Drukkerij Fa. Schotanus and Jens. 1937.

Von Bezold, Wilhelm. *The Theory of Color*, American ed. Boston: L. Prang and Co. 1876. Chapter IV.

Woodworth, Robert S. *Experimental Psychology*. New York: Henry Holt and Co. 1938. Chapters XXIV and XXVI.

Wright, W. D. *Researches on Normal and Defective Colour Vision*. St. Louis, Mo.: The C. V. Mosby Co. 1947. Chapters XVII, XIX, XX, XXII, and XXIII.

The Measurement of Color

CHAPTER XII

UP to this point the physics, psychophysics, and psychology of color have been considered broadly. An attempt has been made to present the subject as a whole so that the interrelation of the variables would become apparent. It is necessary now to apply this same approach, by using the material already developed, to the measurement of color. The specification techniques will then be considered in relation to the principles of color mixture in its various forms.

Careful consideration of the material in previous chapters will show that the expression "color of an object" is a rather vague term. There are few physical objects whose colors do not change in some way with direction of viewing or type of illumination, and few viewing situations in which the perceived colors are constant. For the most part, however, these variations are small compared to the gamut of all possible colors even if in themselves they may be very large compared to just noticeable differences. If an object is described as deep red, it is not

likely to appear light green, etc., although it may pass through a range of saturations and brightnesses and the hue may vary enough so that the terms orange or magenta would be more descriptive than the word red. When an attempt is made to determine the color more precisely, it becomes necessary to start restricting the conditions under which it is to be illuminated and viewed in order to cut down the range over which the color may change. Ultimately it becomes necessary, if really precise measurements are to be made, to specify rigidly the conditions employed. This necessity is frequently overlooked. Precision measurements of a color under one set of conditions may be so far wrong when the conditions are changed that it is worse than a direct visual estimate. In particular, for example, a spectral-reflectance curve of a surface defines only the reflection characteristics of that surface *under the conditions used* for the measurement. It is not a description of the surface but of one of its characteristics. If it is

PLATE X

The range of adaptation of the human eye to color is surprisingly great. If the two pictures above were isolated and lighted by daylight, the color balance of the upper illustration with the eye adapted to daylight would be close to that of the lower illustration with the eye adapted to ordinary tungsten light.

not so used the results may be in serious error. In the present chapter the various techniques of measurement will be considered from the point of view of color characteristics. In the two following chapters the proper use of these techniques will be discussed.

REFLECTANCE MEASUREMENTS

The reflectance of a surface, by definition, is the fraction of the incident light which that surface does not transmit or absorb. It can be measured only in terms of the light which *leaves* the surface, and this light must be evaluated in some definite way. The evaluation may consist of a statement of the fractional total energy compared to the incident light or of the fractional energy with respect to some particular receptor. In any event the region of the spectrum included and the type of receptor, if one is involved, are just as important as the surface under consideration. This situation gives rise to a multiplicity of kinds of reflectance measurements. Thus it is possible to speak of a luminous reflectance in which the eye is the receptor, of absolute reflectance with respect to some range of the spectrum, where no receptor is assumed, or of photographic reflectance when some sort of specified photographic material is the receptor, etc. In many instances it is most convenient and accurate to measure the particular property directly in the desired terms. In many other instances it is better to measure relative reflectance in terms of some standardized surface, usually freshly prepared magnesium oxide which has a high reflectance throughout the spectrum with rather little change with wavelength, and to use techniques that eliminate the receptor entirely.

Two general types of reflectance measurement lead to such different results that they must be distinguished carefully. The first of these may be called total reflectance and the second spectral reflectance. The former refers to a measurement in which the entire reflected light is allowed to act on some receptor and the response is compared with that of the same receptor when magnesium oxide or some other standard is used, the results being expressed as a single number, either a fraction or a percent. The latter type of reflectance measurement refers to measurements that result in data for the reflectance of the material at all wavelengths and are usually independent of the receptor.

Total reflectance is seldom measured except with respect to the eye as the receptor. Under this condition a single value is obtained called the luminous reflectance. In practice this measurement may be made in a number of ways, all of them involving the eye of the observer. Perhaps the simplest way, although in many respects the least accurate, is simple comparison of the surface with a series of surfaces of known reflectances and a judgment of the position of the surface in the scale. This is a fairly simple and moderately precise technique provided the *only* difference between the samples is reflectance, that is, if the hue and saturation of the comparison series is identical with that of the sample, the results are entirely satisfactory for most purposes. If the colors are different in hue and saturation, however, the comparison may become quite difficult and, accordingly, far less precise.

BRIGHTNESS MATCHES

The matching of two different colors for brightness has received a great deal of study over the past fifty years. It is known as the problem of heterochromatic matching and is considered to require more experience and skill than any other type of direct match. Any such direct technique of determining reflectance, however, suffers from the defect that the simple value of reflectance so obtained applies exclusively to the one condition under which the comparison was made and to one observer.

Another method by which such total reflectance may be measured is direct comparison of the sample with a field of light of known intensity relative to the light falling on the sample. Instruments in which such measurements may be made are called photometers. It is apparent that when the color of the sample and that of the comparison light are different they call for heterochromatic matching also but in such instruments the conditions may be so controlled that much higher precision results.

PHOTOMETERS AND SPECTROPHOTOMETERS

The general design of all such instruments is illustrated in Fig. 12·1. A light source A throws light on the sample at B, and the reflected light from the sample passes into the eyepiece C where it may be observed. At the same time light from the same source passes through a different channel D and also enters the eyepiece. The eyepiece is so constructed that the light from the two channels is seen through the eyepiece in different parts of the field, and these parts are so arranged as to have a common boundary line. Some provision is then made for altering the amount of light through either path in such a way that the *amount* of change is known to high precision. Before the measurement is started the reference sample (usually magnesium oxide) is placed in the instrument and the beams varied until an exact brightness match is obtained between the two. This procedure gives the 100 percent reflectance reference point. The sample is then inserted and a brightness match again obtained. From the known

change in light intensity required, the reflectance of the sample is then either calculated or read directly from a calibrated scale on the instrument.

Such measurements, of course, may be made also by measuring the light falling on the sample and the light leaving the sample in the desired direction. Techniques for all methods of measuring total reflectance are given in the books on photometry in the bibliography at the close of the chapter and need not be discussed further here. The point which cannot be overemphasized in the present connection is the fact that all such values, however measured, apply only to the sample under the illumination conditions used and in the direction measured, and *only* with respect to the eye as receptor.

The second type of reflectance measurement is that of spectral reflectance or, more accurately, the reflectance of the sample at small wavelength intervals over the range studied. The practical importance of the measurement of spectral reflectance in the field of color is far greater than that of total reflectance and for this reason will be discussed in some detail. Again, however, the reader is referred to the books in the bibliography for details of the instruments in this highly developed field of optics.

Basically all spectrophotometers, as they are called, work on the same principle as the total-light photometers considered above. Light reflected from the sample is compared with a standard light which in turn is compared with the reflectance of the standard white. In this instance, however, rather than a match of the total reflected light with the sample the match is made in light restricted to a narrow region of wavelengths. The process is repeated at definite intervals throughout the spectrum, and the net result is a series of values which may be plotted against the wavelength. They give, when they are connected by a smooth line, the spectral-reflectance curve of the sample.

A careful consideration of this technique will show that such measurements are practically independent of the sensitivity of the receptor used to establish the match. Since only the light in a small wavelength interval is considered at one time and this interval can be so small that the sensitivity of the

be eliminated if the instrument is designed so that the matching condition corresponds to the *same* output for both the sample and the comparison beam.

The advantages of this method of spectral-reflectance measurement have led to its widespread use. The fact that, in addition, total reflectance may be calculated from such data for any receptor whose sensitivity distribu-

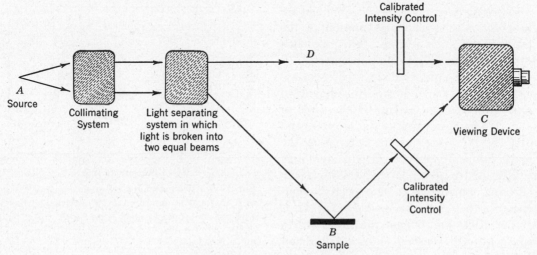

Fig. 12·1   Schematic drawing of spectrophotometer.

receptor does not vary appreciably, sensitivity variations cannot affect the values obtained. The only requirement is that there be sufficient sensitivity at all wavelengths so that a match can be established with good precision. The fact that the sensitivity distribution does not matter has many important advantages. In the first place, it eliminates variations between observers if the instrument is a visual one. In the second place it makes possible the use of physical measuring devices employing photocells or the like without regard to their sensitivities, and in the third place, it is not even necessary to know what the sensitivity of these devices may be, provided it is known that they respond to *intensity* in some measureable way. Even this last requirement may

tion is known has tended to make spectral reflectance the only form of data normally obtained.

Spectrophotometry has become a large and complex subject and there are many different types of instrument capable of producing spectral-reflectance curves. Each of them, however, consists of certain simple elements and produces a definite kind of result. The elements can be considered separately and *must be known* to the person using such an instrument if he is not to be misled by the results.

Two general varieties of instrument may be distinguished. In one the measurements are made by quite pure monochromatic light produced by mechanically screening out of a spectrum all but a very small group of wavelengths. This part of the instrument is called a monochromator and an instrument including such a system may be called a monochromatic spectrophotometer. In the other general class of instrument, measurements are made with light consisting of a much broader band of wavelengths. These broader regions are sometimes isolated with colored filters, sometimes again by mechanical screening of a spectrum. In any event in such instruments the results obtained are those for a relatively large portion of the spectrum for each setting. This approach is called "abridged" spectrophotometry.

The results obtained by the two approaches are characteristically different in some instances and essentially the same in others. The narrowness of the spectral band used for the measurement determines the steepest slope of a reflectance curve that may be measured by the instrument. Suppose a reflecting sample has a true spectral reflectance like that shown in curve *a* in Fig. 12·2. If the spectrophotometer measures with a band width of 20 millimicrons it will obtain curve *b* as the curve for this sample. If it measures with a band width of 50 millimicrons it will, at best, obtain curve *c*. For such samples, therefore, monochromatic spectrophotometers must be used. But if the sample has a very gradual change of reflectance with wavelength, the abridged approach may be entirely satisfactory. The widespread use of abridged spectrophotometers is due to the dual situation that most colors show gradual selective absorption and that such instruments are relatively inexpensive.

The other components of a spectrophotometer that may affect the results are (1) the way in which the light strikes the surface being measured, (2) the way in which the reflected light is picked up by the instrument, (3) the wavelength sensitivity of the

receptor, and (4) the absolute sensitivity of the receptor.

It has been noted many times in earlier chapters that the light reflected from a sample may depend to a great extent on *how* the light strikes the surface in the first place. This is the point at which the usual type of spectrophotometry breaks down. There is a tendency to believe that a curve pro-

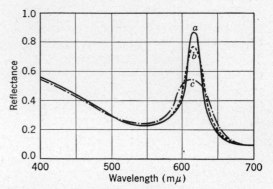

Fig. 12·2 The calculated reflectance characteristics of a material as measured by a spectrophotometer with (*a*) an extremely small band width, (*b*) a band width of 20 millimicrons, and (*c*) a band width of 50 millimicrons.

duced by such an instrument holds for all illumination systems. For some samples such a belief can be described only as a delusion. If the instrument illuminates the sample by completely diffuse light, the light which will reach the eye from the sample when one *looks* at it will be the same *only if at that time* the sample also is illuminated by completely diffuse light. A similar situation, of course, holds for directional illumination and for all other forms.

Exactly the same remarks apply to the way in which the light is picked up *from* the sample by the instrument. Unless the optical system used has the same relation to the sample as the eye, the result will not correspond to the light which *enters* the eye from the sample when it is viewed directly. These remarks are not intended to indicate that spectrophotometry is not a valuable tool. Most of the progress that has been made in the field of color over the last fifty years has been made by this means. No real knowledge of color is possible without its use, and even when conditions are most different from ordinary conditions it still gives a first approximation to the truth which is far more valuable than complete ignorance. When an attempt is made to use it for such purposes as determining whether two samples will match when viewed together, however, it is essential that the viewing and measuring situations give the same results. It is entirely possible, for example, to have a glossy and a dull sample which have exactly the same color to the eye but which measure quite differently on a particular instrument. Colors with these two surfaces if they measured alike on the instrument would *look* different.

RECEPTOR SENSITIVITY

In monochromatic spectrophotometry the wavelength sensitivity of the receptor, whether it is the eye, a photocell, a bolometer, or any other photosensitive device, does not affect the result obtained. The fact that the light used is restricted to a narrow wavelength region means that only this range of the sensitivity is used for any one measurement. If this region is quite narrow, there will be no appreciable change in the sensitivity over any such range, and the results will not change. If the range is larger, however, as it is in most of the abridged spectrophotometers, the change in sensitivity with wavelength will affect each reading differently and the result will no longer be independent of the receptor used. Again it is apparent that the deciding factor is the steepness of the slope of the sensitivity and the reflectance curves. If the change is small over any range in which the measurements

are made, the readings will be affected very little; if it is large, the result may be so incorrect as to be quite misleading. The result is particularly misleading if a sample with a steeply changing reflectance curve is measured. It is apparent that a generalization may be made for all spectrophotometry, namely, that the maximum range of wavelengths that can be used for the component measurements and still give correct results is that over which neither the sample nor the receptor shows any appreciable change in any part of the spectrum. If the sample is completely unknown, it follows that only an instrument with the narrowest possible range can be used for the first measurement. If many samples known to be similar to it are to be measured, a suitable abridged type may then be used. This restriction is not severe in many applications, and abridged instruments, because of their lower cost and high operating speed, have many valuable applications. To avoid serious error, however, they should be used *in conjunction with* a monochromatic type.

The other characteristic mentioned that could affect the result was the absolute sensitivity of the receptor. In general the lower the light intensity to which the receptor will respond measurably the lower is the minimum percent reflectance that may be determined with the instrument, although the minimum also depends on the intensity of the light falling on the sample and the way in which the reflected light is picked up from the sample. Whatever the cause of the limitation the minimum reflectance that can be read determines the degree to which samples may be matched by the use of such an instrument. The ordinary spectrophotometer is not capable of reading less than 1 percent of reflectance in any part of the spectrum. Whereas this limitation is suitable for a good many samples, there are a great many cases for which it is entirely insufficient. Especially in the blue end of the spectrum it may be necessary to reach a reflectance of less than 0.1 percent in order that calculations based on the data will not be misleading. However, the care with which such an instrument must be designed and made makes it too expensive for most practical purposes. Reliable instruments using receptors other than the eye have not as yet been developed to the point where they may be used for such measurements.

For reflecting surfaces the minimum value that may be determined is not so important as it is for transmittance measurements. Not many reflecting surfaces have low enough total reflectance to make such measurements important, and in any case such samples are usually seen under conditions in which the eye is at too high an adaptation state for the low total reflectance to matter. In transmitting samples, however, conditions can be entirely different and transmittances as low as 0.001 may often become of great importance.

It has been emphasized that the illumination and the viewing conditions in a spectrophotometer must be made uniform if comparable sets of readings are to be obtained. Although this necessity is entirely correct as a generalization and holds for all samples of all types, its importance varies from one sample to another. For a few types of measurement uniformity of illumination and viewing conditions is so extremely important that a specially constructed instrument may be necessary, particularly when measurements are made on metallic surfaces or on those which fluoresce under ordinary illumination.

METALLIC AND FLUORESCENT SAMPLES

Whenever a glossy surface of the ordinary type—varnished wood or the like—is illuminated by sunlight, there is a relatively high percentage of the light falling on the surface which is specularly reflected without selective absorption. When such a sample is seen by an observer who wants to look at the wood he turns it at such an angle that he does not see this specular beam. Under these conditions the wood is seen by means of the light not so reflected. However, if such a sample is illuminated by light coming from all directions, as from an illuminated hemisphere, there is no position in which a reflection from this hemisphere can be avoided, and its brightness is seen mixed with the light from the wood itself. This gives a very different appearance and one not characteristic of the wood. Since the more usual condition is the first rather than the second, most, but not all, spectrophotometers are designed to imitate the first kind of viewing. The usual technique is to block out the beam which reflects from the front surface and measure only the light diffusely reflected from the material below. This works satisfactorily for samples in which the color to be measured is produced diffusely. In many cases—such as a colored lacquer over a shiny surface and the like— the color is not produced diffusely, and the instrument gives the wrong answer. A case of particular importance is that of the metals. As noted earlier it is the specular beam that is selectively reflected, and the energy distribution of its color determines the appearance. If a highly polished sample of copper or brass is placed in an instrument which blocks out the specularly reflected beam, it will give either no reading at all or so little as not to be significant, even though the true reflectances may run from 60 to 100 percent. Obviously, in this case it is the *specular* component that should be picked up and measured.

What has been noted here applies equally well to a number of other situations. Often

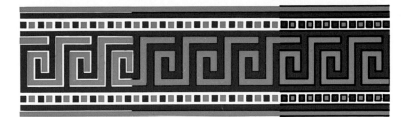

Plate XI

Van Bezold "Spreading Effect." As there is no overlapping of inked areas in these designs, they consist of only three colors in addition to the white of the paper: a red, a blue, and black. The visual appearance of any area of red or blue, however, depends in part on the colors of the adjacent areas. The blues surrounded by black appear darker and more saturated than those surrounded by white, and different in hue from those surrounded by red. The shifts in brightness are opposite to those that would be predicted on the basis of contrast effects. This phenomenon is called the "spreading effect."

colors such as those seen in opals or butter-fly wings appear only when the sample is viewed from a particular *direction*. Unless the measurements are made in this direction the results may have no connection with the visual colors involved. In the last analysis, therefore, illumination conditions and pick-up conditions have to be essentially identi-cal with those encountered by the observer if any assumption is to be made which con-nects the measured energy distribution with the appearance.

A similar situation but one arising from the nature of the illuminant rather than from the way in which it is picked up occurs in the case of fluorescent samples. Many dyes, particularly those used to color fabrics for dresses and the like, have the property of fluorescing when illuminated by ordinary daylight or even artificial light. The color which these fabrics appear to the eye is the additive mixture produced by the spectral reflectance of the fabric *plus* the light pro-duced by fluorescence. A proper curve for the energy distribution of light *leaving* the sample under a given illumination, there-fore, would *include* the fluorescent light. On the other hand the definition of the word reflectance does not include light *emitted* by the surface. Fluorescent com-pounds, however, have the general property that the light which they give off is of *longer* wavelength than that which produces the fluorescence (a generalization known as Stokes' law). There are, accordingly, two separate types of measurement which can be made on such surfaces with respect to the fluorescent light. Unfortunately the ordinary spectrophotometer not only does not measure the light which is *seen* but also gives a false report on the reflectance itself, because most spectrophotometers illuminate the *sample* with light from a narrow region of the spectrum and then collect and read *all* the light from the surface (except for the

specular component which does not matter here). Suppose that a particular dye fluo-resces under the action of blue light at wave-length 410 millimicrons and gives off a band of green light. Such an instrument will receive and record this green light *as though it were blue* and will record a high reflec-tance in the blue although there may be hardly any there at all. On the other hand an instrument that illuminates the sample by white light and then measures the 410-millimicrons component of the light *given off* would measure the true blue reflectance provided there were no fluorescent light at that wavelength. An instrument that illu-minates monochromatically and measures total reflection, therefore, will give false curves for all fluorescent samples. Instru-ments that illuminate with white light and then measure the distribution of the re-flected light will measure the light which would reach the eye from the sample under the illuminant conditions. In order to measure the true reflectance of the sample independent of the fluorescence it would be necessary *both* to illuminate the sample by monochromatic light and to screen out all wavelengths except those in the illuminant when the reflected light is measured. In this way the fluorescence would not affect the results.

To give a proper description of a fluores-cent dye or a fabric colored with such a compound it would be necessary to have a pair or a family of curves, one of which would give the true basic reflectance of the sample wavelength by wavelength and the others the *emitted* light in terms of the wavelengths which caused them. The result would sometimes be plots in which the emitted light was shown for *each* wavelength region capable of producing it. This is, nevertheless, the only way in which the sur-face can be described completely. If the amount of light visible in the green is to depend on the amount of light present in the blue, the effect cannot be shown on a single curve, and no calculation from such a single curve would be valid if the light source were changed, for example, with the *omission* of the blue.

SELECTIVE DIFFUSION

The measurement of transmittance curves has been mentioned already in connection with the importance of using an instrument of high sensitivity. In a number of other respects also transmission is rather different from reflection. Consider a sample having considerable selective diffusion, that is, suppose that when light falls on the sample a considerable portion of it passes straight through, but that a considerable other portion of it is scattered or reflected out of the main beam and that the amount of this scattering or reflection varies with the wavelength. Obviously there are three general types of measurement which may be made on such a sample. Measurements may be made on the light passed, only that scattered, or only that passing straight through. It is equally obvious that the appearance of the sample will be determined by the way in which the sample is seen. Suppose the sample is a typical piece of white glass and this glass is held up between the observer and the sun. In many instances the directly transmitted beam is a deep pure red. Around this directly received beam, however, are a series of regions of increasing angles off the main beam, in which less and less red will be seen. Eventually a point is reached where scattered white or bluish white light only is seen. A measurement of the direct beam will give the *red* spot which is seen. Complete transmission will give a value true for some intermediate region around this spot, and measurement of the scattered light *only* will indicate the

white which gives the glass its name. Other examples of similar phenomena will occur to the reader.

This example is sufficient to indicate the general necessity in *all* spectrophotometry to determine that both the nature of the illumination and the receptor system are consistent with the particular phase of the selective action of the object that it is desired to measure. Data, however precise, have no meaning unless they are based directly on the phenomena under investigation.

EVALUATION OF RESULTS

Turning now to the uses which may be made of properly obtained measurements we find that, in general, they fall into a few well-defined categories. The total effect on some receptor, such as the eye, photocell, or thermopile, may be calculated; the effect of the light on a further-selective transmitter or reflector may be computed; or the energy at one wavelength alone may be considered. In any event the use of such data involves their consideration wavelength by wavelength with respect to the next object in their path and the computation of the final effect.

Most important among such calculations is the evaluation of the effectiveness of an energy distribution with respect to the eye as receptor. It was pointed out earlier that it is possible to compare two energy distributions by considering the amounts of three quite arbitrarily chosen primaries that would be required to match the two samples visually. The only requirement is knowledge of the amounts of the three necessary to match each wavelength in the spectrum. Each sample can then be considered as composed of the sum of these three amounts for each wavelength in each sample, and the final result is the sum of all of them. In practice it works out somewhat as follows. Suppose two samples have the spectrophotometric curves *a* and *b* shown in Fig. 12·3. Suppose also that for three arbitrarily chosen primaries mixture curves for the eye of a standard observer have been determined. (Many people have been tested and the

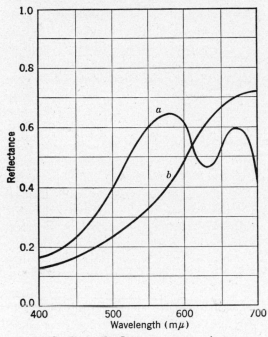

FIG. 12·3 Spectral-reflectance curves of two samples.

average taken.) Such curves are shown in Fig. 12·4. Each curve means that the indicated relative amount of each primary is needed to match a unit-energy amount of light of the monochromatic wavelength above which it is plotted. Curve *a* of Fig. 12·3 states that the sample reflects a certain amount at each wavelength. By computing for each wavelength (or wavelength region over which little change occurs) how much of each primary would be required for a match, a series of values is obtained. The laws of additive mixture state that if two pairs of light sources mutually match, their

mixtures will also match, a proposition easily deduced from the fact that the eye cannot analyze radiation but responds only to its effect. The mixtures of the primaries required to match each wavelength region, therefore, can be added together for all the wavelength regions. The net result will be a mixture ratio which *in toto* will match the light from the total energy distribution. A similar calculation with respect to the second distribution will result in a mixture ratio which will match this color also. If the two ratios are *identical* the two distributions, themselves, will also match. Such is at present almost the limit to which psychophysical calculations may go. If there is a difference

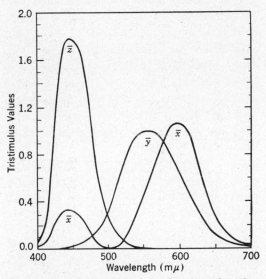

FIG. 12·4 Standard ICI tristimulus data plotted to show the relative amounts of each primary necessary to match any part of the visible spectrum.

in the ratios so calculated, it cannot be evaluated except by considering an extraordinary number of variables not yet discussed. These facts will be discussed in the next chapter under the specification of color. At the moment, however, it is important to note that from a spectrophotometric curve of a given sample it is possible to calculate whether another sample will produce exactly the same color, by simple reference to an arbitrary set of primaries which do not appear in the final results. In the next chapter we shall find that this fact has been elaborated into a system of specification which has become of primary importance in color work.

Before going on with this and allied systems of specification, however, we must consider first the problems which are encountered when an unknown sample of light is compared with a chosen, known distribution. This approach to the study and description of color is known as "colorimetry," the word indicating that the *color* is being measured and not its energy distribution with wavelength.

Direct colorimetry is usually accomplished by means of specially designed instruments, so arranged that the light from the sample is seen as one half of a field visible through the eyepiece. This field, called the "photometric field," is usually of some simple geometric pattern, such as a circle or square, and the two halves are divided by a sharp boundary, usually a vertical diagonal. In some instruments one part of the field is completely surrounded by the other, and occasionally the field may have three or more parts. The configuration is intended usually to increase the visibility of color differences between the parts, although frequently it is the result of convenience in construction. In a good direct colorimeter the dividing line will disappear completely when a match has been attained. Such a disappearance of the boundary increases the sensitivity many times over an identical instrument in which complete disappearance is not possible.

The other half of the field receives light from some sort of optical system in which the physical variables of color may be manipulated in a known manner until a match is obtained. There are a multitude of such possible systems, each convenient for its own purpose. In all of them the eye of the observer plays the same role. When the two halves of the field appear matched to the observer, a known energy distribution has been found which *to him* looks exactly like the light from the unknown. The values of the variables which have produced the color that matches the unknown may then be used to describe the color. The description is valid, however, only within certain definite limitations. In the first place it is probably a match only for that particular individual, and individuals vary tremendously in matching colors. In the second place the match is valid only for the illumination and pick-up conditions utilized in that instrument. In the third place, the description obtained is not that of the visual color of the sample but that of an energy distribution which would match the sample another time if seen under the same conditions.

These restrictions are no different from those which hold when the matching distribution is calculated from spectrophotometric data, except that the results include the properties of the particular observer's color vision. If the observer happened to have vision just like the standardized assumed observer (and the average can almost be described as never occurring in practice) the results obtained would be identical with the calculations. The more he differed from the average the greater the probability would be that the match was unsatisfactory for another observer. It is not realized ordinarily how great is the variation of observers in this respect. A rough estimate indicates that a perfect match by a perfect "average" observer would probably be unsatisfactory for something like 90 percent of all observers because variations between observers is very much greater than the smallest color differences which they can distinguish. Any observer whose variation from the standard was much greater than his ability to distinguish differences would be dissatisfied with the match. It is difficult to describe the range of variation normally encountered. It ranges from total blindness, through total color blindness, partial color blindness of many types, anomalous color vision, and the range loosely called *normal*. Furthermore, observers differ not only in their color vision but also in their sensitivity to energies of different wavelengths. The subject is exceedingly complex and no large mass of facts is available for summary. For detailed discussion of the subject the reader is referred to the articles in the bibliography at the close of the chapter. We may note, however, the following fairly well-established facts.

Some eight percent of the white male population and one-half of one percent of the white female population have color vision which is distinctly different in kind from that of the normal observer. About three-fourths of them may be considered "anomalous" variants of normal vision and the other one-fourth definitely deficient in some phase of the color sense. For a normal observer three variables are necessary to produce a match, and colors vary in three attributes. Hence a normal observer is said to have trichromatic vision. For him any color may be matched by a suitable mixture of three, more or less arbitrarily chosen, colored lights. The amounts of these lights required to make such a match vary appreciably from one observer to another but they fall within certain fairly well-defined limits. The anomalous variants referred to also require three lights to make a match but the amount of one of the lights that is required falls well outside the normal limits. Hence they are called "anomalous trichromats." The one-fourth who are definitely deficient are for the most part unable to distinguish red from green. This type of observer (and some other much rarer forms) needs only two suitably chosen lights to match all the colors that he is able to distinguish. Hence he is known as "a dichromat." A very rare form of color blindness exists in which no color discrimination is possible, only brightness differences being seen. For these people only one light is required and these observers accordingly are known as "monochromats."

From the standpoint of the normal observer one fact stands out more clearly than the others. A color match for hue and saturation between two spectrally different energy distributions made by a normal observer will usually be entirely acceptable to dichromats and probably also to monochromats. To the much greater number of anomalous observers, however, such a match definitely will not be satisfactory. From the opposite standpoint, of course, dichromats are satisfied with many matches unsatisfactory to the normal observer, and no one except a person with the same anomaly will agree with a match made by an anomalous trichromat. Thus some five or six percent of the male population see colors as distinctly different from the rest whereas some two percent simply see fewer colors or none at all.

In brightness distinctions between colors a similar situation exists, although the division is not parallel to the types of color blindness discussed above. Some three-fourths of all people who have defective color vision, whether anomalous trichromats or dichromats, have normal sensitivity with respect to wavelength, that is, they will make the same heterochromatic brightness match between two colors as a normal person. One-quarter of them, however, are definitely deficient in sensitivity to long wavelength energy and require considerably more energy of red light than normal to produce a brightness match to another color.

It seems, therefore, that some ninety-two percent of the males may be considered to have normal color vision, whereas the percentage of females is more than ninety-nine and a half. The figures given must not be considered exact, however, since the demar-

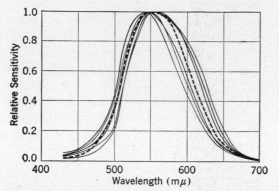

FIG. 12·5 Individual luminosity curves for six different persons compared to the standard ICI curve and showing the large deviations from person to person. (K. S. Gibson and E. P. T. Tyndall, *Scientific Papers of the Bureau of Standards*, Vol. 19, p. 157.)

cation between abnormal and normal observers is extremely diffuse, and an absolute definition of an abnormal person with respect to spectral-brightness sensibility is difficult. The normal range may be considered rather broad, however, for the variations within an average group of individuals are considerable.

The luminosity curves for six of the fifty-two observers studied in 1922 by K. S. Gibson and E. P. T. Tyndall of the National Bureau of Standards are given in Fig. 12·5, and the differences are indicative of the diversity which exists in the general population.

Fewer data on the range of stimuli used by normal observers to obtain color matches are available than on variations in the lumi-

nosity function and are more difficult to interpret when found. It appears that the main differences among observers may be explained largely on the basis of variations in the amount of yellow pigment (macular pigmentation) present in the foveal region.

It is necessary to consider rather carefully what effect such a variation should have on color vision. At the fovea of the eye and for some distance around it a yellow pigment is present through which all light must pass that is to be seen with this part of the eye. Its transmission curve for a representative average observer as given by *Troland* (Vol. II, p. 109) is shown in Fig. 12·6. The dip in the curve at long wavelengths is due to the watery substance of the eye, that at short wavelengths almost entirely to the yellow pigment. This curve represents a moderately intense yellow color. At wavelengths

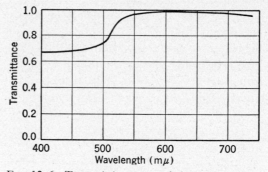

FIG. 12·6 Transmission curve of the ocular media. (L. T. Troland, *The Principles of Psychophysiology*, Vol. 2, p. 109. D. Van Nostrand Co., New York, 1930.)

near 440 its transmission is given as 67 percent. If we assume that the material obeys Beer's law, if there were twice as much present in some individuals as in the average person, the transmission would drop to 45 percent. If half as much were present it would rise to about 82 percent. In view of the tremendous difference in skin, iris, and hair pigmentation in individuals such a range seems not at all unlikely. Skin color gives us the range of people from albinos to Negroes, hair varies from blond to black, the iris of the eye varies from clear blue to an exceedingly dark brown, and the yellow absorption of the macular area like these colors arises from a pigment. Aside from such speculations, however, the facts appear to support the assumption that such variations occur. Suppose then that the internal eye and brain mechanisms of two extreme observers are exactly alike and that they are called on to make a color match using a monochromatic line at 450 as one of the primaries and another line at 540 as the other, the color to be matched lying somewhere between the two. It is apparent that the observer whose pigmentation is double normal will require more of the 450 line relative to the 540 than will the observer whose pigmentation is half normal. The same phenomenon will occur if they attempt to determine the amounts of two complementary wavelengths which together form a white; one will require a greater amount than the other if one line is in the short-wavelength region. It will occur again if these observers attempt to determine the luminosity curve of the eye, that is, if they attempt to determine the amount of energy required of each wavelength to make monochromatic lights appear equally bright. One observer may report much more than the other for some matches.

All three of these types of variation are found when a large number of observers are requested to make such measurements. The feeling has accordingly grown up among workers in this field that the variation in amount of yellow pigment is the major cause of variation in the so-called normal group and that if it were possible to introduce this correction the group would be much more homogeneous and much more clearly separated from the anomalous and the dichromatic observers. In support of this view

Troland points out that if the average curve (Fig. 12·6) is applied as a correction to the luminosity curve for the standard observer it becomes an almost exactly symmetrical probability curve. Whereas there is no known reason at present for expecting this result, the perfection of fit suggests something more than mere accident.

It is seen, therefore, that both the actual observer who may sit down at an instrument and the fictional standard observer who exists only as a mathematical concept will produce results that are not acceptable to a third party when he actually looks at the samples with his own eyes. As a matter of fact many observers, if they were critical, would get different results with each of their own eyes. That this is so does not in the least offset the importance of either colorimetry or spectrophotometry. Variations in the human eye from one observer to another are simply part of the subject of color. Knowledge of their existence, however, should make us somewhat lenient in our estimates of the opinions of others. The standardized observer is, by definition and to the extent that the International Commission on Illumination has succeeded in its goal, the *most probable* basis on which to make calculations.

Several times in this discussion there has been occasion to refer to "heterochromatic" matches. The term refers to the adjustment of the amounts of two colors which are visually different in one or all of their attributes until they exactly match for brightness only. It is apparent that such matches must be made in many of the most fundamental measurements required for theoretical purposes. They are required, for example, in the determination of the fundamental luminosity curve. In these measurements the brightnesses of monochromatic lines must be adjusted so that they appear exactly equal. As pointed out earlier, such measurements are extremely difficult to make if simple direct comparison is used. They may be made quite precisely, however, by a technique known as flicker photometry, based on the experimentally verified fact that if the intensities of two beams of light are alternated at a relatively high rate of speed (some 40 times per second) they will appear to flicker as long as there is any brightness difference between them. If the flicker rate, which depends rather extensively on the conditions, has been set properly, however, no flicker will result from any differences in hue or saturation which may be present. The requirements for setting the critical frequency and the variables on which this frequency depends will be found discussed in any good book on photometry. The method itself has been tested and retested many times, however, and found to be universally valid. The process of matching two monochromatic lights for brightness thus becomes the relatively simple one of alternating them in rapid succession in the field of a photometer, setting the rate of alternation at the critical value for the conditions, and adjusting the relative intensities until the flicker is reduced to the minimum. At this point the two may be assumed to match for brightness.

There are, thus, two generalized approaches to the measurement of color and the specialized method of flicker photometry for brightness only. The two general approaches are both psychophysical in character because they are based ultimately on the infinite number of energy distributions that are capable of producing the same appearance to an observer. In the indirect method this "matching condition" is calculated from the physics of the energy distribution and the known properties of the eye. In the direct method the eye is used to recognize the condition when the physical variables are manipulated. In both methods color is measured by stating it in the standardized units of some more or less arbitrary reference system. The statement of the values so determined is usually referred to as the "specification" of the color. It forms the subject matter of the next chapter. Before we consider it in detail, however, it is desirable to inquire somewhat more deeply into the usefulness of the measurements made by these techniques. In particular these methods must be compared to the obviously simpler method of comparing the color with a collection of standard colors and stating which one is most nearly the same, since such a system has the merit of combining the measurement and the specification in one direct operation. It is not until the limitations of the latter method are realized that there appears to be much merit in the longer and more cumbersome methods. The direct system is indeed used and is exceedingly valuable for certain purposes. The reasons why it is seldom as satisfactory as some form of colorimetry are considered in the following section.

MATERIAL STANDARD SYSTEMS

In the chapter on the perception of color it was noted that while hue, saturation, and brightness may be thought of as the most noticeable attributes of color in the psychological sense, they are not, by far, all the attributes that it may possess. In particular if a color is that of a surface, it may be shiny or dull, it may have sheen, texture, or a number of other characteristics in addition to its hue, saturation, and brightness. It was also noted that these additional attributes could affect the appearance markedly, even at times shifting the visible saturation or hue quite independently of the energy distribution of the illumination. Unfortunately, not enough systematic work has been done in this field to permit more than a sketch of the ways in which these attributes may interfere with the use of a material color system. In brief, however, if a surface color is to be compared to a series of known surface colors with the intention of selecting the one giving the closest match, much difficulty will be encountered and considerable variation between observers will result if the attributes of the surface of the sample and of the set of colors are appreciably different. In other words, if the set of colors has a dull surface with no texture and the sample has a high sheen and a noticeable texture, not many people will be able to find a satisfying match. On the other hand, if the sample is also dull surfaced and without texture, general agreement will be obtained with fair ease. The exact reason for this is not entirely clear, but the guess may be hazarded that different people unconsciously make different allowances for the effect of the type of surface or the perceived color, the allowance being made automatically and unconsciously. The situation is entirely analogous to, but simpler than, the perceptions of color as light and as object color discussed in the previous chapter. Since the intention at present is presumably to match the surface color rather than the light, the object-directed attitude is necessary and calls for direct attention. For some observers this attitude is not easy, and experience and often training are required to make it possible. The presence of texture, with its inevitable variations in brightness, still further complicates matters. It is very difficult to match an area that is uniform to one that is not and feel sure that the brightnesses are alike. Although such a match *can* be made with fair precision, the observer seldom feels any great confidence in his result. Whenever the attributes of the sample and the color system differ appreciably comparison is difficult and often unsatisfactory.

When the modes of appearance also differ, the comparison may become almost impossible. Thus colors seen in the aperture or the volume modes may appear so different from those of a surface-mode system that they may seem hardly comparable. Although the light reaching the eye through a layer of clear water may be the same as that reflected from a white sample, the *modes* of appearance are different and the color seen cannot be described in the same terms. The water may be called clear and *colorless* but the reflecting sample is called white. Again a dark red liquid may transmit the same quality of light as that reflected by a piece of dark brown paper, but few observers without special knowledge of the conditions required could state that they were the same.

Without more examples, most of which the reader could deduce directly from the subject matter of the last three chapters, it is apparent that a system of colors to be used for specification by visual matching is of strictly limited utility. In the last analysis, if such a system is to be entirely satisfactory, its samples of the colors of the system must be seen as having the same attributes and appear in the same mode as those to be matched. The obvious generalization, of course, is that the system should be made of exactly the same *material* as the sample. Although the requirements are not quite so severe as this, since a number of the attributes can be modified by the manner in which the comparison is made and the two can sometimes be brought into the same mode if different viewing systems are used, the generalization does express accurately the limitation involved. The *best* system in any given case will be the one made from materials *most nearly like* the sample. Textile materials are more easily matched to textiles, enameled surfaces to enameled chips, dull surfaces to dull papers, liquids to liquids, etc. The existence of numerous such systems is adequate evidence of the necessity.

The concept of a single set of colored examples to which any color may be compared directly and so be specified is, accordingly, an illusion. The dimensions of color include more than three variables, and many three-dimensional systems of this type are necessary to cover the possibilities.

Such systems can be inter-compared only by way of colorimetry applied to the light from each example. However, colorimetry is not *for this reason* more exact or more directly useful. Colorimetry itself has only three variables and can represent only one of the systems in terms of visual experience. What colorimetry *does* do that the other systems *cannot* is to reduce *all* samples to the same mode with the same attributes. This mode is usually, although not necessarily, the film or aperture mode as seen in unrelated viewing. To translate into terms of normal viewing conditions the results of colorimetric measurements it is necessary to know the connection with a system of *material* standards *like the sample*. In other words, in the last analysis, it is the systems of material standards and these alone that are capable of describing the sample but *only if* the material system has the correct attributes and is to be seen in the correct mode. Much confusion can result if any greater competency is ascribed to any particular system.

It is possible to consider direct colorimetry in this same manner. If a colorimeter is thought of as a device that reduces any sample to the film mode of appearance and removes almost all its attributes except hue, saturation, and brightness, it will be seen that this concept is the equivalent of considering only the *light* without the sample. On the comparison side of the instrument light only is fed in, so that in essence light is compared with light for color. Direct colorimetry thus becomes a material system in which the material is light. It describes the appearance adequately for any sample *when only the light* from the sample is visible, but *not under any other conditions*.

The convenience and utility of colorimetry calculated from spectrophotometric measurements are immediately apparent. The personal factor is eliminated, the light only is considered without object or situation, and variations between observers disappear. It should always be kept in mind as a sobering thought, however, that every one of these will return immediately the moment anyone *looks* at the sample.

When colorimetry, either of the direct or calculated type, is compared from the standpoint of precision to material standards, however, the story is quite different. It seems likely that the desire for precision of measurement on the one hand and the desire for accuracy of description on the other are the forces that drive the advocates of the two techniques so far apart.

The precision with which matches between two light beams may be made on an adequate colorimeter or with which a match may be made between the two fields in a spectrophotometer is greater than that obtainable by direct comparison of samples. In part this precision is due to the fact that it is the exception rather than the rule for two materials to have the same attributes. For the most part, however, it is due to the way in which the halves of an instrument field in totally dark surroundings are used to take advantage of the maximum capabilities of the eye. In the first place the eye almost immediately adapts to the illumination level of the instrument unless it has been exposed recently to relatively quite bright light. When so adapted, it is capable of its maximum sensitivity to brightness differences between the halves. Again it adapts to the color of the field in such a way that hue differences are tremendously exaggerated, hues which are actually very similar being seen as far apart under these conditions. The situation in respect to hue difference exaggeration is exactly analogous to the shadows thrown by two lights in that no matter how small the hue difference between the lights the two shadows tend to take on complementary hues. When they match *exactly* this effect disappears, greatly increasing the sensitivity of the balance. In the same way, lack of a saturation match between the halves will produce a strong tendency for the two fields to appear complementary even if the light on the two sides is identical except in saturation. Addition of white light to one side of a balanced field, both sides of which appear green before the addition, will usually make that side turn pink. This effect again greatly increases the sensitivity of the balance (and the amount of experience necessary to run such an instrument)! Mention should also be made of the fact that a more favorable situation with respect to the observer's attention and continuous rather than stepwise intervals also favor the instrument type of measurement. Although these two latter characteristics could be made part of a material system, very little attempt has been made to do so.

PRECISION IN COLOR MATCHING

Perhaps a word should be said on the need, or lack of it, for precision in measurements of color. Although the eye, under the most favorable normal conditions, can distinguish as many differences as are indicated by the best colorimetric measurements, in everyday life it doesn't, *except* when the most favorable conditions happen to be encountered. It is true that the difference in color that can be detected by an expert between two otherwise identical pieces of paper is, at present, smaller than the difference which can be detected by spectrophotometric measurement and calculation. On the other hand the difference in appearance between identical pieces of paper placed on only moderately different backgrounds is large compared with the precision of ordinary comparison with a set of standard chips. In fact if the background difference is large, the difference in appearance of the samples will be considerably greater than the precision with which each sample can be assigned to such a system by pure *memory!* The precision needed for a given application, therefore, is very much a matter of the use that is to be made of the measurement. Vegetables are not ordinarily weighed to $\frac{1}{10}$ gram nor is an estimated weight accurate enough in the purchase of platinum.

While we are still discussing precision it might be well to consider very briefly the question of colorimetric and spectrophotometric measurements by other receptors than the eye. The general principles involved in such a substitution have been considered in an earlier section. It is dangerous, of course, to generalize, especially when the generalization involves the assumption that there will be no change in a branch of science. For the most part, however, it can be stated that photoelectric measurements and the like are basically *less* precise than the equivalent measurement made by a trained observer. This fact is so frequently overlooked when such instruments are considered that some phases of the subject are becoming confused. Such instruments are convenient, rapid, repeatable, and economical if properly designed and operated. With rare exceptions these are their chief recommendations, however, *not* higher precision. The fact that two instruments will give the same reading whereas two observers may not comes under the head of convenience, not precision.

Visual spectrophotometry will give the same answer, and neither one of them is likely to be exactly like *any* observer, even in the prediction of a match between spectrally different samples. On the other hand the relative ease of design and ultimate probable usefulness of photoelectric direct-reading colorimeters make it seem strange that more have not become available. Colorimetric measurements of only moderate precision are necessary for many practical purposes. Manufacturing tolerances are usually, of necessity, considerably larger than just perceptible differences.

BIBLIOGRAPHY

Committee on Colorimetry. "Colorimetry Report." *Journal of the Optical Society of America*, **34**:245–266, **34**:633–688 (1944).

Gibson, K. S., and Tyndall, E. P. T. "Visibility of Radiant Energy." *Scientific Papers of the Bureau of Standards*, **19**:131–191 (1925).

Luckiesh, M. *Color and Its Applications*. New York: D. Van Nostrand Co. 1915. Chapter XIII.

Massachusetts Institute of Technology, the Color Measurement Laboratory. *Handbook of Colorimetry*. Cambridge, Mass.: The Technology Press. 1936. Chapters I and III.

Parsons, Sir John Herbert. *An Introduction to the Study of Colour Vision*, 2nd ed. Cambridge, England: The University Press. 1924. Part II, Chapters I, II, III, and IV.

Sears, Francis Weston. *Principles of Physics III—Optics*, 2nd ed. Cambridge, Mass.: Addison-Wesley Press, Inc. 1946. Chapters XII and XIII.

Southall, James P. C. *Introduction to Physiological Optics*. London: Oxford University Press. 1937. Chapter VIII.

Troland, Leonard T. *The Principles of Psychophysiology*, Vol. 2. New York: D. Van Nostrand Co. 1930. Chapter XIV, Section 55.

Walsh, John W. T. *Photometry*. London: Constable and Co., Ltd. 1926. Chapters IX and X.

Wright, W. D. *The Measurement of Colour*. London: Adam Hilger, Ltd. 1944. Chapter V.

The Specification
of Color

CHAPTER XIII

THE word "specification" means, or at least implies, accurate description. Its application to the word color raises the question which of the general meanings of the word "color" is involved.

MEANING OF THE TERM

The Optical Society definition of color is based on the psychophysical stimulus, and this definition reflects a trend which has become apparent in recent years. Because of the multitude of systems necessary to obtain an accurate description of a material sample, it is easier to consider the light from the object rather than the object itself. Because of the variations between observers and the uncertainties introduced by mental attitudes and habits, it is easier to consider a standard observer, and the mathematical evaluation that results is called color in the OSA terminology. Under this definition the connection between the specification and the appearance can be obtained by way

of an empirically determined relationship good only for the specific viewing conditions. This necessity exists whatever the starting point for the specification, as was pointed out in the last chapter. Only the use of the word color in this connection will seem strange to those accustomed to working in the field since its use in everyday speech is so very different.

Color specification, therefore, can mean different things to different people, and it is necessary for the reader to decide for himself which of the possibilities is envisaged by the particular writer with whom he is concerned. For the present discussion of the problem let us start with the most seriously and scientifically considered approach of them all, that accepted by the OSA. In this report color as noted, is defined as a purely psychophysical concept obtained by evaluating the physical stimulus in terms of a standard observer capable of reaction only to hue, saturation, and brightness, and these only in a single manner.

FIGURE 13·2

The basis of this system is the series of international agreements commonly referred to as the ICI system (or the CIE system in England and on the Continent). This International Commission on Illumination (Commission Internationale d'Éclairage) adopted as standard for international use a luminosity curve, color-mixture curves for

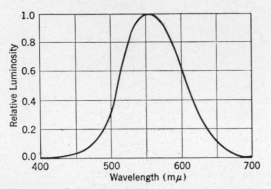

FIG. 13·1 Relative luminosity of the various regions of the spectrum.

Wave-length	Relative Luminosity	Wave-length	Relative Luminosity
380	0.0001	590	0.7570
390	0.0001	600	0.6310
400	0.0004	610	0.5030
410	0.0012	620	0.3810
420	0.0040	630	0.2650
430	0.0116	640	0.1750
440	0.0230	650	0.1070
450	0.0380	660	0.0610
460	0.0600	670	0.0320
470	0.0910	680	0.0170
480	0.1390	690	0.0082
490	0.2080	700	0.0041
500	0.3230	710	0.0021
510	0.5030	720	0.0010
520	0.7100	730	0.0005
530	0.8620	740	0.0003
540	0.9540	750	0.0001
550	0.9950	760	0.0001
560	0.9950	770	0.0000
570	0.9520	780	0.0000
580	0.8700		

FIG. 13·2 Table of relative luminosities of the various regions of spectrum.

three imaginary standard lights, a specific energy distribution for a basic light source, several subsidiary light sources, and a number of allied necessary appurtenances.

The luminosity curve for the standard observer is given in Fig. 13·1, and the values of the ordinates to four decimal places are given in Fig. 13·2.

The amounts of the three ICI primaries required to match a unit amount of energy at each wavelength are given in Fig. 13·3, and the data at the same precision level in Fig. 13·4.

Discussions of the subject in considerable detail and data to much higher precision will be found in the articles in the bibliography at the end of the chapter and in the references to which these will lead the interested student.

The energy distribution of one of the standard illuminants, Illuminant B, is

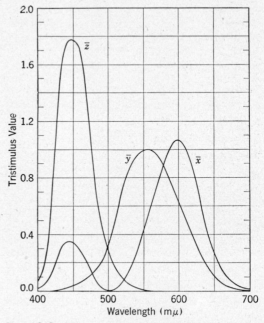

FIG. 13·3 The amounts of the three ICI primaries required to match a unit amount of energy having the indicated wavelength.

shown in Fig. 13·5. The energy distributions of the two other illuminants (A and C)

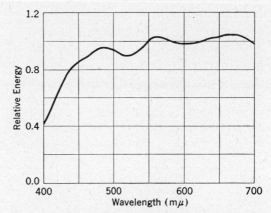

FIG. 13·5 Spectral-energy distribution curve of Illuminant B, the standard ICI light source.

FIGURE 13·4

Wavelength	$\bar{x}$	$\bar{y}$	$\bar{z}$
380	0.0014	0.0000	0.0065
390	0.0042	0.0001	0.0201
400	0.0143	0.0004	0.0679
410	0.0435	0.0012	0.2074
420	0.1344	0.0040	0.6456
430	0.2839	0.0116	1.3856
440	0.3483	0.0230	1.7471
450	0.3362	0.0380	1.7721
460	0.2908	0.0600	1.6692
470	0.1954	0.0910	1.2876
480	0.0956	0.1390	0.8130
490	0.0320	0.2080	0.4652
500	0.0049	0.3230	0.2720
510	0.0093	0.5030	0.1582
520	0.0633	0.7100	0.0782
530	0.1655	0.8620	0.0422
540	0.2904	0.9540	0.0203
550	0.4334	0.9950	0.0087
560	0.5945	0.9950	0.0039
570	0.7621	0.9520	0.0021
580	0.9163	0.8700	0.0017
590	1.0263	0.7570	0.0011
600	1.0622	0.6310	0.0008
610	1.0026	0.5030	0.0003
620	0.8544	0.3810	0.0002
630	0.6424	0.2650	0.0000
640	0.4479	0.1750	0.0000
650	0.2835	0.1070	0.0000
660	0.1649	0.0610	0.0000
670	0.0874	0.0320	0.0000
680	0.0458	0.0170	0.0000
690	0.0227	0.0082	0.0000
700	0.0114	0.0041	0.0000
710	0.0058	0.0021	0.0000
720	0.0029	0.0010	0.0000
730	0.0014	0.0005	0.0000
740	0.0007	0.0003	0.0000
750	0.0003	0.0001	0.0000
760	0.0002	0.0001	0.0000
770	0.0001	0.0000	0.0000
780	0.0000	0.0000	0.0000

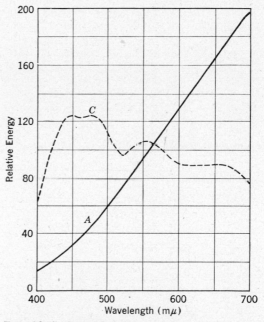

FIG. 13·6 Spectral-energy distribution curves of two other ICI light sources, Illuminants A and C.

FIG. 13·4 Color mixture curve data of the ICI standard observer.

which were specified are shown in Fig. 13·6. The data on which these three curves are based are given in Fig. 13·7.

ICI DIAGRAM

The recommended method of plotting the results obtained in calculating the chromaticity of any color is shown in Fig. 13·8 in what is known in the United States as the ICI diagram.

The values plotted on this diagram are the fractional excitations for the assumed

FIGURE 13·7

Wavelength	E_A	E_B	E_C
380	9.79	22.40	33.00
390	12.09	31.30	47.40
400	14.71	41.30	63.30
410	17.68	52.10	80.60
420	21.00	63.20	98.10
430	24.67	73.10	112.40
440	28.70	80.80	121.50
450	33.09	85.40	124.00
460	37.82	88.30	123.10
470	42.87	92.00	123.80
480	48.25	95.20	123.90
490	53.91	96.50	120.70
500	59.86	94.20	112.10
510	66.06	90.70	102.30
520	72.50	89.50	96.90
530	79.13	92.20	98.00
540	85.95	96.90	102.10
550	92.91	101.00	105.20
560	100.00	102.80	105.30
570	107.18	102.60	102.30
580	114.44	101.00	97.80
590	121.73	99.20	93.20
600	129.04	98.00	89.70
610	136.34	98.50	88.40
620	143.62	99.70	88.10
630	150.83	101.00	88.00
640	157.98	102.20	87.80
650	165.03	103.90	88.20
660	171.96	105.00	87.90
670	178.77	104.90	86.30
680	185.43	103.90	84.00
690	191.93	101.60	80.20
700	198.26	99.10	76.30
710	204.41	96.20	72.40
720	210.36	92.90	68.30
730	216.12	89.40	64.40
740	221.66	86.90	61.50
750	227.00	85.20	59.20
760	232.11	84.70	58.10
770	237.01	85.40	58.20
780	241.67	87.00	59.10

FIG. 13·7 Tabulated spectral-distribution data of standard ICI illuminants A, B, and C.

primaries **X** and **Y**, as indicated by the mixture curves of Fig. 13·3. A convenient and rapid method of calculating these excitations

was worked out by A. C. Hardy and his associates and published as a "Handbook of Colorimetry" by the Massachusetts Institute of Technology Press at Cambridge, Mass. Anyone interested in calculations of this type should refer to this book because of the

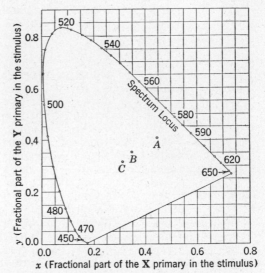

FIG. 13·8 The ICI chromaticity diagram showing the position of Illuminants A, B, and C. The solid curve is the locus of visible spectral radiation with the straight line portion connecting the extremes representing magentas and purples. The ordinate of this graph is in terms of the fractional amount of the **Y** primary in the stimulus and is labeled y; the abscissa is similarly labeled x which represents the fractional amount of the **X** primary.

simplicity of the method set forth and the lucid and straightforward explanation of the system that it contains. In essence the method consists in the use of specified wavelengths, so chosen that if the relative energies of the sample at each wavelength are added together for each primary of the system, their sums will indicate ratios of the primaries which, for the standard observer, would match the sample. In this way the tedious process of multiplying the spectrophotometric curve of the sample by the product curve of the illuminant and mixture curves for each primary and then determining the ratios of the integrals of these curves to the total effective energy is avoided. The whole calculation may be made in a matter of minutes, and the results, if not identical with those of an accurate integration, are at least precise enough for most purposes. Both a "thirty selected ordinate" and a "one hundred selected ordinate" method are described, and the necessary tables and charts are included.

In the present treatment we are concerned not with the technique by which such calculations may be made but with the nature and characteristics of the specification so obtained. Calculations under the ICI system result in three values (as all color specifications must) which are more or less directly in terms of the so-called monochromatic-plus-white system of colorimetry. These three values are defined in terms of the ICI diagram as follows.

Calculation of the fractional excitation values for the sample for two of the three primaries and the total excitation of one of them leads to three numerical results. Two of these are the "trichromatic coefficients," x and y, representing the fractional amounts of the "red" and the "green" primaries necessary to produce a hue and saturation match with the sample, and a third, Y, representing the luminance of the sample. The ICI diagram is plotted in terms of x and y and the value of Y is written beside the point.

Such a calculated point is shown as M in Fig. 13·9. On this same diagram is shown the position of the point for the illuminant C which was chosen as a basis for the calculation of M. Points C and M have been connected by a straight line which has been extended to intersect the locus of spectrum lines at N.

As pointed out earlier, it is a property of such a modified Maxwell triangle that if two light sources are represented by points in the triangle all mixtures of these two lights fall on the line which connects the two, the actual position along the line from either point being inversely proportional to the amounts of the two which are present. Points N and C on the diagram represent respectively a spectrum line and a "white" light. Any point lying on the line connect-

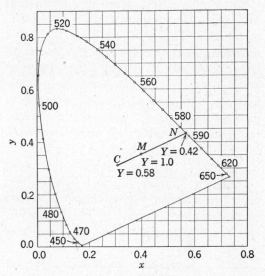

Fig. 13·9 The ICI diagram showing at M the chromaticity position of a light source composed of sodium light and Illuminant C. The relative luminances of the light source and its two components are given beside the points.

ing them may be matched by a mixture of N and C in amounts inversely proportional to the ratio of the distances separating the points from M, with the amount of N proportional to MC and the amount of C proportional to MN. These facts are the basis of the ICI specification. The wavelength determined by the intercept with the spectrum locus of the line connecting the illuminant point and the sample is defined as the "dominant wavelength." The ratio of the distance CM to CN is defined as the "excitation purity" and the value of Y is called the "relative luminance."

These specifications, or appropriate conversions of them to similar coordinate systems, the OSA report calls color. They define rigidly the response of the assumed observer, or perhaps more specifically they completely evaluate the light from the sample in the case of the assumed observer for these three attributes of color.

Since relative luminance is a factor that may depend in obvious manner on the illumination and the like, it is thought of as a separate phase of color, whereas dominant wavelength and excitation purity are combined into a single concept called "chromaticity." The separation is identical in principle and in necessity to that of the common speech separation in sentences such as "The two are identical for color but one is brighter than the other." The word chromaticity, however, refers only to that aspect of color at the psychophysical level and is defined completely by the trichromatic coefficients (or their equivalent) of the ICI system.

Such a chromaticity and luminosity specification for a given surface or transmitting area and the given illuminant define the color in such a way that, if one light were to be placed beside another light having the same specifications, the two would exactly match to an observer whose sensitivities were the same at the time as those of the assumed standard observer. Since such a match would persist over most normally encountered eye conditions (as affected by the surroundings) it has a quasi-universal validity. It is restricted, however, to the *light* from the sample considered as independent of the sample itself as pointed out in the previous chapter.

DISTANCES ON THE TRIANGLE

If calculations for the light from two different samples give two somewhat different values, care must be exercised in evaluating the meaning of this difference. Equal distances in the ICI diagram do not mean equal visual differences. In fact it has been demonstrated that it is not possible to construct a chromaticity diagram in which just perceptible differences are represented by the same distances at each point. This impossibility applies specifically to chromaticity but, if it is recalled that brightness differences also can shift apparent hue and saturation and that such differences do not show on the diagram, it will be realized that bad errors may be made by neglecting the fact.

D. L. MacAdam has investigated the eye sensitivity to differences in different regions of the diagram. He published the diagram of Fig. 13·10 to show the results of his studies. Each elliptical figure represents the locus of equally perceptible distances from its center. For absolute results, however, the length of the axes must be divided by ten since they have been enlarged by this factor for illustrative purposes. It is apparent that there are tremendous variations in eye sensitivity in different parts of the diagram and that at any given point the sensitivity to change in dominant wavelength may be many times that to excitation purity. It is important to note also that these results are psychophysical and not psychological. The data were obtained by direct determination of the *just perceptible* differences in different directions from each point shown. The question of relative *appearance* of the differences was not considered. It may well be that a just perceptible difference in one part of the domain is psychologically comparable to that in another, but this type of comparison was neither reported nor implied. The magnitude of the just perceptible *brightness* differences under the conditions was not reported. The result of this work was the demonstration already men-

PLATE XII

Fluorescent Substances.   All the pictures are of the same flask containing the dye
fluorescein. This dye is yellow and fluoresces green when the light falling on it contains blue.   In the illustration on the upper and lower left the front incandescent
light illumination is not changed but the white background in the upper left seen
through the dye shows its yellow color, whereas in the lower left only the fluorescent light can be seen.   In both center illustrations a yellow filter has been
used which transmits green and red but no blue.   In the upper one it is placed
over the light source, and no fluorescence results.   In the lower, it is over the
eye, and the green fluorescence produced by the white light is transmitted.   In
the illustrations at the right a blue filter is used.   In the upper figure, when the
filter is placed over the light source, blue is transmitted and fluorescence results.
In the lower one, when the filter is placed over the eye, the fluorescence produced by the white light is not transmitted and so is not seen.

tioned that it is impossible to represent these data on a plane surface in such a way that all the loci become circles of equal radius.

It is possible, however, to obtain some compromise presentations which come much closer to the ideal diagram in which all distances are equal than the standard ICI dia-

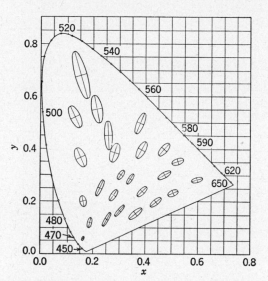

Fig. 13·10 Graphical representation of data by D. L. MacAdam showing the visible effect of chromaticity changes throughout the ICI diagram. The axes of each ellipse have been multiplied by ten for illustrative purposes. (D. L. MacAdam, *Journal of the Optical Society of America*, Vol. 32, p. 271, 1942.)

gram. One of these, made by Judd and called by him the Uniform-Chromaticity Scale (UCS), is illustrated in Fig. 13·11. In place of the right-angled triangle of the ICI he uses the older Maxwell triangle. In Judd's UCS triangle it is more nearly true than in any other at present in use that equal distances have similar significance, at least for chromaticity. The same restriction on relative luminosities still holds.

In making this triangle Judd has used a procedure which illustrates one of the conveniences and important possibilities of calculated colorimetry. The numerical dif-

ferences in different parts of the diagram depend on the choice of primaries for the system. Since any new primary can be expressed in terms of the three ICI primaries, it may be assumed to act like the specified mixture of the three. The same thing can be done for the two others. The net result is a shift to a new set of primaries without the necessity of obtaining new data. Only the distribution of points on the plotted diagram is affected. By careful consideration of the distortions and by careful manipulation it is possible to alter these distortions radically as Judd has done. In his case he obtained a quite good approximation to uniform-chromaticity differences in the dif-

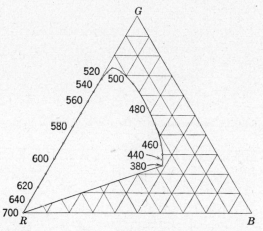

Fig. 13·11 The uniform-chromaticity scale diagram as originated by D. B. Judd. The locus of the spectral colors is plotted with specific wavelengths designated by millimicron units. (D. B. Judd, *Journal of Research of the National Bureau of Standards*, Vol. 14, p. 44, 1935.)

ferent regions of the figure. By this procedure, which may be called either a transformation of the primaries or a shift of coordinates, it is possible to develop a system for any particular application, although the labor involved requires that the application be fairly important. The reader is referred to the books and articles of the bibliography at the close of the chapter for the necessary mathematical considerations.

CORRELATION OF OTHER PRIMARIES

In an exactly similar manner, of course, it is possible to correlate direct experimental work done with any set of primaries, by the simple process of calculating the ICI points for the actual primaries. Mixtures of these as pairs will fall on the straight lines connecting the points. Thus a mixture triangle is formed within the ICI diagram. A specification may then be obtained directly by the simple plotting of a point with respect to the inner triangle and reading the values from the outer one. Such a constructed inner figure is sometimes called a "grid" and is of wide utility. It will be seen later that such grids are particularly important when the ICI system is being used with subtractive mixtures of colorants in which the mixture colors formed by the colorants in pairs do not fall on straight lines. By actual measurement of systematic series of such pairs a grid can be constructed, and the ICI values for intermediate mixtures can be obtained by interpolation.

When such a grid represents actual calculated points with respect to the standard observer the ICI interpolated values, of course, are legitimate specifications. When only the primaries are calculated and an intermediate point is determined by *visual match* of the real primaries, the observer's vision has been introduced, and the coordinates of this point do not represent an actual ICI specification.

The relationship of direct colorimetry to the ICI system, therefore, is dependent on the vision of the observer using the instrument. Departures from the calculated values are due to such differences. They either represent errors in specification or, inter-

preted in another way, they provide a means of checking the vision of the observer. Colorimetric specifications in terms of arbitrary primaries are not interpretable in specific form without accurate knowledge both of the *actual energy distributions* used *and* of the visual characteristics of the observers. It is certainly not legitimate to assume that the average of any small group of observers is similar to the ICI standard observer. In fact it is better, as far as possible, to make no assumptions about the relation of this standard observer to actual vision. The international agreement on which it is based would be about as valuable as a working reference standard if, as it may, it departed rather markedly from a true statistical average for all normal observers. It is not legitimate to assume that a calculated match would be an actual one for a particular observer if there is a marked difference in the spectral-energy distributions of the samples involved.

This fact has been mentioned several times before. It is an important consideration in the choice of primaries for any direct colorimetric method and equally important for a system of comparison standards. It may be stated as a generalization that the more nearly two matching samples have the same wavelength-energy distributions, the more general will be the agreement between observers. In the limiting case of identical distributions all observers would agree, whether color blind, anomalous, or normal. At the other extreme, maximum disagreement may be expected if one sample consists of a few monochromatic lines and the other has a continuous energy distribution extending throughout the spectrum.

SPECIFIC MATERIAL STANDARDS

It follows that a system of material standards having the same energy distributions over the range expected in the sample may be made to give very high precision results which will be accepted by all observers. Such systems, of course, may be correlated satisfactorily with another system such as the ICI because, in effect, these eliminate the observer as a variable.

A number of such systems have been devised, probably many more than is realized since they arise more or less spontaneously in specific applications which often do not get broad publicity. It seems to the writer that such systems should be encouraged for control purposes. Many people not familiar with the broad field of color seem to feel that something worth while has been added if the colors of their products are compared directly with some nationally known standards. Actually in most instances the control would be far more precise if a series were set up covering the expected variations and if control were obtained by direct comparison. If the spectral distributions are similar, it is unlikely that calculation would produce a better result. If it is desirable to correlate such a series with a national set of standards, it may easily be done in terms of the ICI system. Actually the closest tolerance to which a product may be held or to which a color must be adjusted is usually large compared to the precision with which a trained examiner can compare two nearly identical samples under good conditions.

COLOR-TEMPERATURE SPECIFICATION

A specification somewhat different from those discussed so far is that obtained by use of the concept of color temperature. A pure temperature series in a totally enclosed space gives rise to a series of energy distributions of the emitted light which can be calculated by known means. A series of such energy distributions was shown in Fig. 3·3. This is the series actually *approximated* when an incandescent lamp starts at low voltage and gradually increases in temperature. The highest value that can be obtained from tungsten is around 3,700° K because of the melting of the tungsten.

To compare the energy distributions as such it is convenient to redraw this figure so that the same amount of energy is indicated at some one wavelength. This was done in Fig. 3·2.

Each of these energy distributions corresponds to a definite visual color varying from deep red through orange, yellow, and white to blue. It gives a continuous path when plotted on the ICI diagram. This is shown in Fig. 13·12.

It should be noted that the origin of this series is a perfectly definite and clearly defined series of *energy distributions*. Each of the colors which these energy distributions produce, however, could have been formed by any one of an infinite series of distributions and it is these sets of infinite series of lights that are defined by the points on the ICI diagram. It is possible, therefore, to mean either of two things when the term "color temperature" is used. The intention can be to state that the light has the *energy distribution* of a true black body at that temperature *or* that the light *matches for color* that produced by a body at that temperature. The two are, obviously, not equivalent, and yet both meanings are encountered in the literature. Official sanction has in fact been given to the latter meaning, that of the color rather than the energy distribution, by the definition officially adopted by the Optical Society of America in which color temperature is defined as the "color which matches that of a black body at a given temperature." The usage of the term is exceedingly confusing and it appears inevitable that sooner or later a new terminology will appear in which the distinction is made apparent. Obviously a light source whose color temperature is described as 5,000° K will cause a red object to have a *some* scale is almost a necessity *both* for the energy distribution series *and* for the color series. The existence of only one series of designations for two different concepts, however, gives rise to much confusion.

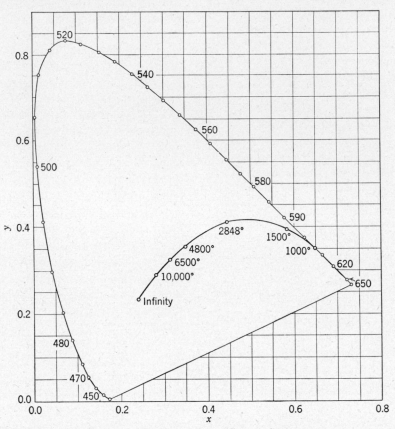

FIG. 13·12 The chromaticity locus of a black body at different absolute temperatures. As the temperature increases the chromaticity proceeds along the curve towards infinity.

very different appearance if it contains *no* red from that which the object will have if the light contains a large amount as does a black body at this temperature. With the advent of practical light sources with discontinuous spectra this question is being brought to the foreground and some constructive action may become a matter of necessity. The basic difficulty involved is the fact that these series of colors are exceedingly important in everyday life and that

The color temperature series has the advantage that it is approximated rather closely by a number of practical light sources such as the usual incandescent lamp and that it is entirely possible to set up a real standard with which such sources can be compared. In a sense, therefore, the color temperature scale may be considered a material standard, applicable primarily to light sources. As such it is one of the few which have been brought forward for this purpose.

A number of material standards have been proposed for transparent materials. Perhaps the best known and best standardized is the Lovibond Tintometer system which has attained considerable importance in the oil industry. This is a form of subtractive colorimetry in which the sample under consideration is matched by means of colored glasses added to the comparison beam until the two present an approximate match. The color of the sample is then designated by the glasses of which the matching color is composed. To the extent that the light transmitted by the colored glass is spectrally similar to the sample under consideration this is an excellent system for such measurements. It does not have the observer limitations of a system such as monochromatic colorimetry and is specific in that definite absorptions are represented by the colored glasses involved. It has the defect, of course, of finite steps and awkwardness of setting. Comparisons are made entirely by instrument, that is, with a dark surround. The eye, accordingly, is at its maximum sensitivity to color differences although the colors seen may bear little relation to the appearance of the sample in everyday surroundings. Making estimates is difficult except on the basis of long experience and many readings with the glasses. It does have the advantage that only the *light* is compared with the standard. Accordingly, it ties in directly with specifications under the ICI and similar systems.

THE MUNSELL SYSTEM

A somewhat different approach to the same problem was made by Munsell. He reasoned apparently that the color appearance of objects was apparent only in objects and so proposed to set up a series of colored papers which varied equally in all directions in the color domain in terms of visual *appearance*. In theory, at least, he was not concerned with the physical variables involved, but only with the color as such, viewed under more or less standardized conditions. With this in mind he and his associates finally succeeded in producing a color atlas containing examples of colors which varied in roughly uniform steps over a large part of the gamut of surface colors.

He defined the three variables of color as hue, chroma, and value—the terms corresponding roughly with our present definitions of hue, saturation, and lightness. These he constructed into a three-dimensional color solid having a vertical black-to-white axis. Around this he arranged the hues in equal angular spacing and defined chroma as the distance from the axis at any particular value level. His published atlas contains colored paper chips arranged according to various sections through this solid, some passing at right angles to the value axis, some including this axis in the plane.

In use it was intended that the sample to be specified should be held near the atlas and the position of the sample with respect to the actual chips determined. The specification of the color then consisted of a numerical statement of its position on the scales of the solid.

The original atlas was constructed on the basis of a number of assumptions that made the spacing neither psychological nor psychophysical in the sense in which we now use the words. For example the constant hue series at various value levels was determined by placing one of the samples on a rapidly spinning disk and whirling it with various amounts of white and black at a rate of rotation higher than that at which the eye can see flicker. This color was then matched by pigments, and the result was *assumed* to be constant in hue. It is now known that this is not true since such a series is psychophysical in the sense that it generates a straight line on the ICI diagram.

In 1943 a committee of the Optical Society of America investigated this spacing of the Munsell colors and recommended a respacing of the colors based on a purely psychological approach more nearly that apparently intended by Munsell. This report appeared in the *Journal of the Optical Society of America* (see bibliography at close of chapter). It represents the nearest approach thus far to a color solid based on the pure appearances of the surface colors.

It should be pointed out again, however, that these small, matte surface chips represent only one *type* of surface, that their energy distributions are unique and hence not suited for comparison with all types of possible distributions by all observers, and that they represent samples exclusively in the surface mode of appearance, unless some technique is used to change the mode during the actual matching.

THE OSTWALD SYSTEM

A very similar type of system, developed in Germany at about the same time, is that produced by Ostwald. It is based on a number of theoretical opinions held by Ostwald about the physical variables of color. He defined an energy distribution, which he called a "semi-chrome" or a "full color," as one which consists of a block of energy in the spectrum bounded by complementary wavelengths and implied that such a distribution would have maximum purity. He considered that the other two variables of color are white and black and advanced the proposition that the sum of the full color plus black plus white in any color is equal to unity. The practical utility of his proposition is not entirely evident and is not, in any event, essential to the system. In the practical reduction of these theoretical considerations to a set of material paper standards it was necessary to use actual pigment colors, and they departed so widely from the theory as to represent a different system.

The implications of the theory and the actual colors used in his published atlases were investigated by Foss, Nickerson, and Granville and were published in the *Journal of the Optical Society of America* as part of

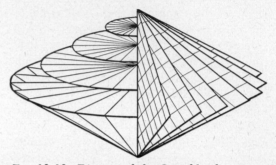

Fig. 13·13 Diagram of the Ostwald color system.

a symposium on the subject (see bibliography at close of chapter).

In the practical atlas published by Ostwald he arranges the full colors around the circumference of a circle in such a way that complementary colors are opposite each other. He uses this circle as the base of two cones with apices on the axis of the circle as shown in Fig. 13·13. The axis represents the white-to-black series. A vertical section through this solid gives a pair of triangles with the black-white axis as a common side as shown in Fig. 13·14. Because of the choice of complementary colors as opposite on the hue circle, these triangles always represent complementary colors. Diagonally in one direction from any point the diamond-shaped sections indicate a series in increasing white and decreasing full color but constant black. Diagonally in the other direction they represent decreasing full color and increasing black with constant white.

The assumption is that in both directions the pigments act as if they were perfect. Foss, Nickerson, and Granville point out that such a system is not possible in actual pigments.

The concept of the system is valuable, however, in that a vertical series in the Ost-

of practical advantages, especially if correlated carefully with a system such as the ICI. Aside from the obvious advantage of permitting direct visualization of such a psychophysical system, these variables are frequently the actual ones encountered in the use of color. A surface color in a series of

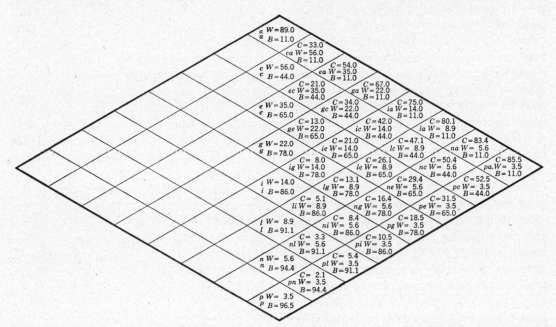

Fig. 13·14 Diagram of a vertical section through the Ostwald color solid. The number given after the letter W in each small section is the percentage of white, after B the percentage of black, and after C the percentage of "full color." The left half of the diagram corresponds exactly to the right half except that the "full color" is complementary to that on the right half.

wald color solid, as the above writers pointed out, is in theory a pure relative-brightness series at constant chromaticity rather than at constant hue. Since the added white series is constant in dominant wavelength also, it represents a series in excitation purity. The Ostwald color solid, therefore, is potentially an arrangement of material standards according to the psychophysical rather than the psychological variables, that is, the related variables are dominant wavelength, excitation purity, and relative luminance, rather than hue, saturation, and brightness. Such an arrangement would have a number

illumination intensities, for example, is physically the same as the vertical path through this solid. Half-tone printing, at least for a single ink, follows the full-color-plus-white mixture series. It would seem that the chief defect of the system is the enforced restriction of the maximum saturation to a circle, with the attendant non-uniformities in purity. It is both theoretically and practically incorrect to assume that maximum pigment saturations are equivalent in any sense.

The Munsell and the Ostwald systems, therefore, offer the attractive possibility of material-surface color systems arranged according to psychological and psychophysical spacings respectively.

At this point it is well to state again, however, that material standards have two quite definite shortcomings. Regardless of how they are spaced they represent real surfaces (or colored glasses, etc.) and have definite psychological attributes, usually in a definite mode of appearance (surface colors, aperture colors, and the like). Therefore they are difficult to compare with any color having distinctly different attributes. Moreover, specification by that system will give a person who has never seen the *sample* little idea of its appearance. Since such is the basic purpose of material systems, the purpose is not wholly fulfilled. To take an extreme instance as an example, a Munsell or an Ostwald specification for an area in a stained glass window would have little meaning to most people because the customary mode and the attributes are quite different. The logical solution to the difficulty, of course, as mentioned earlier, is a series of such systems each system having different attributes. In view of the difficulties encountered in establishing even one system such a solution seems like an idle thought, but the recent advances in colorimetric methods make such systems not only possible but also entirely feasible. As a matter of fact, many such systems *in embryo* are already in existence. When the paint manufacturer wants to show gloss paints he uses glossy samples on his color card. When he is dealing with matte-surface paints he illustrates them as such, knowing that the effective colors are different.

THE TEXTILE COLOR CARD

One of the best examples both of the need for systems with specific attributes and of the extent to which they would be helpful is given by the annual color cards published by the American Textile Color Card Association. An annual card is issued carrying actual textile samples standardized so that all cards are alike. Definite color names are stated for each color, and that color and name are considered standardized by them for that year. The important point for the present discussion is that each of the textile samples is shown in both a dull and a satin finish weave for each color, so that colors of other samples may be matched to the standards with sufficient precision. A similar necessity has been found for the samples of the Color Manual of the Container Corporation of America (based on the Ostwald system) in which the samples are presented with both glossy and dull surfaces without visible texture.

Whereas all possible arrangements are represented by existing material systems, it does not follow that such systems cover the entire field of needed systems. There is much room for valuable work, and many new systems may be expected to develop.

GENERAL LIMITATIONS

The purpose of specification of a color is usually either controlling a product or simple description for literary purposes. For either purpose the assumption is implied that another sample having the same specification would *in appearance* be the same color. The impossibility is generally immediately apparent since all methods of specification necessarily assume a particular energy distribution for the light source. Even with the light source specified, however, the generalization is not valid unless the physical nature of the two samples is identical. The reason can be made apparent by a simple example, but the principle is valid for all cases. Suppose two papers have selective absorption and are identical except that one has a somewhat more glossy surface than the other. Placed in ordinary surroundings these surfaces must necessarily reflect light reaching them from objects in their vicinity. For purposes of illustration let us assume that one surface is matte and the other glossy, and that an equally illuminated red surface stands vertically at right angles to

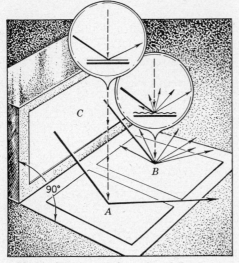

FIG. 13·15 The two surfaces A and B are assumed to be glossy and matte respectively. These surfaces are illuminated by diffuse light from other parts of the room in which they are located and by the light reflected from the red surface C. If viewed from above, little or no red light will be seen from the glossy surface A, but considerable will be seen reflected from the matte surface B.

the two as shown in Fig. 13·15. If the samples are viewed directly from above so that the red surface is not seen, it is possible to arrange the surfaces so that the matte surface reflects a considerable amount of red light to the eye while the glossy surface reflects hardly any. For the glossy surface, nearly all the red light is reflected specularly to one side whereas for the matte surface this light is diffusely reflected, a considerable part of it being reflected toward the observer.

Again, if there is any difference between the selective action of two surfaces, i.e., if the spectrophotometric curves of the matching surfaces are different, even if they lead to the same specification, they are likely to appear of different color in normal surroundings simply because the reflection from them of any *colored* object in the vicinity will, in general, be different for the two.

Carried through strictly and logically, therefore, color specification of any kind is seen to be limited to certain specific conditions and does not give a *general* answer to the problem of describing or controlling a color except in the unique case of two physically identical samples having identical selective absorptions wavelength for wavelength throughout the spectrum.

Nevertheless the usefulness of colorimetric specification is not limited. Such specifications, however, have to be accompanied by more information concerning the materials involved and the conditions under which the measurements were made than has been the usual practice. Furthermore, if a specification is in terms of materials radically different from those with which it is to be used, there is no need for high precision. Such results, at best, will be an approximation, whatever the technique or system.

BIBLIOGRAPHY

Birren, Faber. *The Story of Color from Ancient Mysticism to Modern Science.* Westport, Conn.: The Crimson Press. 1941. Chapter VI.

Foss, Carl E., Nickerson, Dorothy, and Granville, Walter C. "Analysis of the Ostwald Color System." *Journal of the Optical Society of America,* **34**:361–381 (1944).

Judd, Deane B. "A Maxwell Triangle Yielding Uniform Chromaticity Scales." *Journal of Research of the National Bureau of Standards,* **14**: 41–57 (1935).

Lovibond, Joseph W. *Measurement of Light and Colour Sensations.* London: George Gill and Sons. n.d.

Luckiesh, M. *Color and Its Applications.* New York: D. Van Nostrand Co. 1915. Chapter IV.

MacAdam, David L. "Visual Sensitivities to Color Differences in Daylight." *Journal of the Optical Society of America*, **32**:247–274 (1942).

Massachusetts Institute of Technology, the Color Measurement Laboratory. *Handbook of Colorimetry*. Cambridge, Mass.: The Technology Press. 1936. Chapter V.

Munsell Color Company. *Munsell Book of Color*. Baltimore, Md.: Munsell Color Co., Inc. 1942.

Newhall, Sidney M., Nickerson, Dorothy, and Judd, Deane B. "Final Report of the O.S.A. Subcommittee on the Spacing of the Munsell Colors." *Journal of the Optical Society of America*, **33**:385–418 (1943).

Ostwald, Wilhelm. *Colour Science*. Part I, *Colour Theory and Colour Standardisation*. 1931. Part II, *Applied Colour Science*. 1933. London: Winsor and Newton, Ltd.

Sears, Francis Weston. *Principles of Physics III —Optics*, 2nd ed. Cambridge, Mass.: Addison-Wesley Press, Inc. 1946. Chapter XIII.

Wright, W. D. *The Measurement of Colour*. London: Adam Hilger, Ltd. 1944. Chapter III.

Color Differences and Color Names

CHAPTER XIV

THE expression "color differences" has the same range of meanings as the word color itself. For the person to whom "color" means hue, the word "difference" implies a difference in hue only. For those to whom color includes all the attributes that color may possess, a difference includes any visible difference between two objects. The subject, therefore, must be discussed from some definite standpoint. For the present purposes it will be well to eliminate all variables except hue, saturation, and brightness (or lightness).

MEANING OF ''DIFFERENCE''

Even with this restriction, however, it is necessary to consider still further just what is meant by the expression. The difference which a person observes in a photometric instrument is quite a different phenomenon from that which he observes in a reproduction representing a scene he photographed some time before. In the first instance he is making use of the full capacity of his eye to make direct comparison under the most favorable conditions. In the second he is making a mental comparison between a stimulus seen under one condition with another, perhaps quite different, stimulus, seen under different conditions. The comparison in the latter instance has nothing to do with the energy distributions involved but is restricted to the mental perceptions alone.

The variation in the meaning of the word "difference" has given rise to a number of common expressions. In the photometric sense physicists refer to "just perceptible difference" (j.p.d.) or "just noticeable difference" (j.n.d.). To the present writer the first expression seems the more appropriate of the two to represent the smallest discernible difference under the most favorable conditions. In the present book, therefore, "just perceptible" will refer to this type of comparison, and "noticeable" will refer to the much larger differences which force themselves on the observer's attention under ordinary rather than specialized circumstances.

Still another distinction is necessary, however, to cover all the usual meanings which can apply to this quite vague term. This final distinction involves the intention of the observer with respect to the medium and may be defined as the "just acceptable difference." When a prospective purchaser is examining a demonstration of the color variation to be expected in a product, he is moved by two urges. On the one hand he would like maximum constancy of color in the product and on the other he would like to have the price as low as possible. He is aware frequently that these are antagonistic requirements and, accordingly, is willing to compromise his desires by accepting a greater difference than his aesthetic sense dictates. The extent of his compromise, in absolute terms, will depend in large measure on the conditions under which he sees the differences which are involved.

TYPES OF COMPARISON

There are, in general, some five ways in which a presentation of differences may be made. In directly descriptive terms these comparisons may be called photometric, juxtaposed, successive, time lapse, and memory. To each of them a probability of precision may be assigned, and the degree of compromise may be evaluated for each particular case. The first comparison represents the ultimate psychophysical possibilities of the eye, and the last represents the psychology of memory, the others falling in intermediate sequence. The difference between the extremes represents many orders of magnitude, but in every comparison certain definite principles apply, these principles being derived from the psychophysical aspects of

the situation rather than from the details of the particular method.

For example, if a comparison, by whatever method, is made between samples with spectrally similar absorptions, it is the method alone which determines the quality of the judgment. If the samples are distinctly different spectrally, the circumstances play a very different role. In particular, in the first instance the observer is able to make a mental adjustment to the conditions quite aside from the inherent precision to which his visual mechanism is operating and often he is quite successful in this compensation process. In the second instance, however, he is at the mercy of the laws that govern the effective stimulus in terms of the samples which he is seeing. For example, if a person sees an orange surface in daylight and at some later time a spectrally identical surface under tungsten illumination, his eye and his experience are able to compensate to a considerable extent for the difference in illumination and reach a valid conclusion about the difference between the two surfaces, if there is any. If, however, the second illumination condition, although visually identical with the tungsten light, contains little red in its spectrum, the comparison will be strongly biased by this fact, and he may logically decide that the surfaces are quite different.

The term "acceptable" difference, therefore, in an extreme case, can mean a *smaller* color difference in absolute terms than a just perceptible one, if to be acceptable the difference must not appear large under *any* illuminant whereas the "just perceptible" judgment is made under only one. Suppose that two surfaces show a just perceptible difference under the best photometric conditions but their spectrophotometric curves are those shown in Fig. 14·1. It is apparent that if the illumination energy distribution is changed markedly, there will be some conditions under which much larger differences will appear. If this condition is a requirement for acceptance, the two samples would have to be spectrally more similar than the two shown.

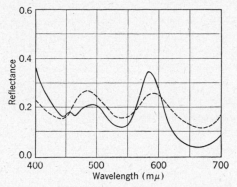

FIG. 14·1 Reflectance curves for two surfaces which match when illuminated by an incandescent source with a color temperature of approximately 4,000° K.

In an extreme case such as that of the pair shown in Fig. 14·2 there may be an exact match under one condition (ICI observer and Illuminant C in this case) and very little similarity between the colors under another

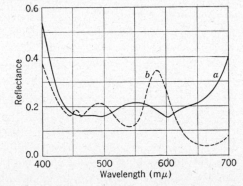

FIG. 14·2 Reflectance curves of two objects which match when illuminated by the standard ICI Illuminant C.

illuminant. The surface represented by curve *a* in the figure would be red, whereas that of *b* would be yellow, if illuminated by orange-colored light consisting of radiant energy in the region of 560 to 700 mμ.

Color differences are not much affected by the mode of appearance under which they are seen if the attributes of the two are similar. They are affected if the color adaptation of the observer is changed, however, since the sensitivity of the eye to color differences decreases for the colors corresponding to the adapting color. Two yellows, for example, may be noticeably different to the daylight-adapted eye but indistinguishable in artificial light, and this could still be true if the energy distributions reaching the eye from the samples were the same in the two cases. The eye apparently is in the state of seeing maximum color differences in a light slightly bluer than daylight, such as the north skylight of the professional color matchers.

PSYCHOLOGICAL NATURE OF THE PROBLEM

Since in the last analysis it is the psychological attributes which determine color differences, we may turn directly to a consideration of the relationships between hue, saturation, and brightness. It must be remembered that, *after* a difference has been determined as a permissible tolerance, the *specification* of this difference *must* be set up in either purely physical or purely psychophysical terms since there is no notation for the purely psychological color space; even if there were it would have no general validity.

There has been much discussion of the relative importance of hue, saturation, and brightness in color differences, and many attempts have been made to set up formulae which represent the facts. Some of these attempts are cited and discussed in the articles in the bibliography at the close of the chapter. The determination and the specification of color tolerances in manufacture are large and increasingly important phases of color work. It is necessary to restrict the present discussion to certain well-defined general characteristics of all this work. We shall consider first the concepts involved in the tolerances themselves and then the methods for determining them for a given example.

Color considered as having only the attributes hue, saturation, and brightness has only three dimensions and can be considered as forming a color space. Within this space all possible perceptual colors have a position, this position depending on the exact values of its three variables. If this color space is thought of as completely filled with points representing possible colors, the position for a particular color is completely enveloped by other points which touch it in all directions. Six of these adjacent points represent simple variations in the sense that they indicate changes of only one of the variables. All the others indicate simultaneous variations of two or of all three. In general, these immediately adjacent points will represent differences which would be too small to see. At a little distance, however, will lie points which represent visible differences. The nearest points that meet this condition will be those that represent the just perceptible differences from that point. All these points taken together form a closed surface around the point in question. The shape of this surface will depend entirely on the spacings chosen originally to represent the three variables. If the scale chosen to represent saturation requires a movement of, say, $\frac{1}{10}$ inch along the direction of increasing or decreasing saturation to obtain a just perceptible saturation change, while a distance of 1 inch is needed for a just perceptible hue change and $\frac{1}{2}$ inch for a just perceptible brightness change, this surface will obviously be of a flat, elliptical shape $\frac{1}{10}$ inch thick, $\frac{1}{2}$ inch wide, and 1 inch long. A color solid with other scales

would give rise to quite different figures having the same meaning, i.e., all points on the surface would represent just perceptible departures from the color represented by the point at the center.

UNIFORM COLOR SPACE

Of special theoretical and practical interest is the possibility of so arranging such a space that these surfaces would be spheres about every point in the space, every sphere having the same radius. Such a color space would have the exceedingly valuable property that all the colors would be in fixed and identical relationship to their immediate neighbors. At first sight such an arrangement of possible colors would appear to be logical and worth while and seems not only possible but plain common sense. There are many reasons to believe, however, that such an arrangement is a purely imaginary concept which could be realized in a practical way only by so restricting its meaning and application as to make it quite useless. In the first place a just perceptible difference in one part of the color solid may not have the same meaning that it does in another. Almost certainly four just perceptible differences in brightness are a different *kind* of difference than four of hue, etc. In other words, whereas such an arrangement has a very logical-sounding basis, it does not necessarily lead to useful concepts. What is really wanted is an arrangement of colors having the property that a distance in one region indicates a color difference which looks like the same difference as that indicated by a line of the same length somewhere else. Much evidence seems to be accumulating that such an arrangement is generally an impossibility. For a particular case, such as artists' pigments, for example, or matte-surface papers and the like, such a system can be imagined and perhaps constructed. At any rate it can serve as a basis for thinking about color difference problems, and it is implied in nearly all discussions of such color differences.

The discussion thus far has been based on just perceptible differences simply because of the ease of visualizing a directly measurable variable. The surfaces surrounding each point, however, might have been obtained by determining the colors about that point which appeared *on direct examination* to show the same difference from the central point. If the space could then be distorted so that all these surfaces were spheres of equal radius, we should have an equal-difference spacing. This spacing also would hold strictly only for the amount of difference chosen but would be far better *for this purpose* than one based on just perceptible differences. Such a system is again found to be implied in many discussions of tolerances and the like. Like the other system it may not be realizable physically, but it at least gives a mental concept around which discussion may proceed.

In practice different small regions of the space are treated separately in direct connection with some practical problem, and little or no attempt is made to organize them to solve the general problem.

There are, of course, many other conceivable distributions having the property of showing the same *kind* of differences in all directions. The one just discussed is for what might be called "equally noticeable" differences. It is possible to imagine spaces that indicate "equally objectionable" differences in all directions and so on. It must be remembered, however, that while such spaces would have valuable properties and are important mental constructs, the arrangement of colors in space is merely a convenience to aid our thinking and *nothing* more. The difference between two brightnesses can never *look like* the differ-

ence between red and green, or between pale and saturated green. The differences can be compared only on the basis of the *reaction* of an observer to them, "noticing," "discriminating," "liking," "disliking," and so on. If they looked alike they could be matched directly and there would be no problem.

SPECIFICATION OF TOLERANCES

Color differences, therefore, even for a restricted region of colors, have to be determined empirically on some aesthetic, or at least arbitrary, principle. Once determined, however, they may be specified to any desired degree of precision by the application of standard psychophysical principles. Such specifications usually take the form of some sort of tolerance limits and are usually restricted to the case of "acceptable" matches to a given standard.

Except the possibility of setting up standardized material sets which illustrate the tolerances or of interpolating the data to determine tolerances for colors intermediate to those especially studied, the tolerances may be specified in any terms. A specification of tolerances on the Munsell system is no more *valid* than the ICI or any other. All mean the same thing and differ only in convenience. In the last analysis their purpose (and it is an important one) is to make it possible to state definitely whether a color falls inside or outside the set limits by reference to a *standardized* and repeatable system. The likelihood that tolerances set for the manufacture of tile will be applicable to the color of porcelain for dental work or of lacquer for nail polish seems remote, but the same principles and the same method of expressing the results apply to all.

Tolerances are usually expressed in some units convenient to the system employed and differ, usually markedly, for different colors. Thus a specification on the Munsell system may state that for a color which should match green at G 6/2 (hue, green; value, 6; chroma, 2) the variation should not exceed plus or minus 2 chroma steps, plus or minus ½ value step, and plus or minus ½ hue steps. On the ICI system a specification may read that dominant wavelength is not to vary more than plus or minus 20 mμ, excitation purity more than plus or minus 5 percent and reflectance more than plus or minus 5 percent. An alternative would be to give the actual values of the limits which may be stated as between 590 and 610 mμ in dominant wavelength, 50 percent and 55 percent in purity, and between 0.4 and 0.45 in reflectance, for example.

DETERMINATION OF TOLERANCES

Having seen what may be meant by color differences and the tolerances which derive from them, as well as how they may be expressed, we shall consider ways and means of determining tolerances and differences for practical examples.

It is apparent that tolerances must be determined by direct observation, preferably by a large number of people. It is apparent also that the method of presentation of the samples, the conditions under which they are viewed, the instructions to the observers, and the quality of the light source will all play an important part. If the tolerances are to determine limits of acceptance in manufacture there may be additional economic factors which will increase the tolerances by affecting the observer's attitude.

The method of presentation of the samples has already been considered briefly. In general the size of the just noticeable difference will be determined by factors such

as the size of the sample, the way in which the samples are compared with each other, the intensity of the illumination, its geometrical nature. It is a necessary requirement if the results are to be significant in terms of a final product, that these factors be comparable to those which will be encountered in practice with the final article. Perhaps the best way to describe the nature of these variables is to consider actual examples.

Suppose it is desired to hold successive batches of some transparent material such as glass or plastic to very close visual tolerances. A sample is chosen to represent a particular color desired. An apparatus can be set up which will present this sample and others which are slightly different as two halves of a photometric field at a moderately high intensity level. Under these conditions maximum sensitivity to differences is obtained, and a set of variants may be selected which will represent just perceptible differences. These tolerances, of course, will be exceedingly close, and the samples representing maximum permissible differences will be seen not to differ at all under most ordinary conditions.

If such exceedingly close tolerances are not necessary, the test may be set up by giving the observers samples which may be held in the hand and viewed side by side against a white background. The physical difference which is just noticeable under these conditions is far larger than before, and the selected tolerances will be increased accordingly. If this method is more nearly comparable with the way the articles will be seen in practice, the tolerances will be more reasonable. Still larger differences will be selected if just noticeable changes are selected on successive viewing, i.e., if the observers are given the samples one at a time and are asked to select those that look alike. Such tolerances, in general, will be so large that quite noticeable differences will exist when the products are placed beside each other. The *way* in which the comparison is made, therefore, determines the differences which will be seen.

Again, the geometry of the illumination under which the samples are studied will have a considerable effect on the colors seen and the tolerances selected. Suppose the product is a material with very little texture and a glossy surface. To take an extreme case, suppose also that the samples are judged in a room lighted indirectly by means of an illuminated white ceiling and that the room has white walls. Under these conditions the saturation of the colors of the samples may be so low because of white-surface reflection that quite large actual differences in the samples cannot be seen at all. On the other hand, if they are viewed in a dark room in pairs under strong light which strikes the samples so that no direct reflection reaches the eye, differences may be apparent which are comparable to the differences seen in a divided photometric field.

Aside from the geometry and the intensity of the illumination there is also the matter of its spectral distribution. As seen in earlier chapters, two light sources may have the same visual color but widely different energy distributions. If a source is used for determining the tolerances which is quite different from that under which the manufactured articles will be seen, the tolerances may not relate directly to the facts. This difficulty is sometimes encountered with artificial sources intended to imitate daylight. If artificial sources are weaker in energy in any part of the spectrum than daylight, differences in some colors will be less noticeable than in daylight and in others more noticeable. In fact a perfect match under such lights may show large differences in daylight and vice versa. For differences

to appear the same under two illuminants it is *necessary* that the relative spectral-energy distributions of the two are the same as well as that their visual colors match. In fact, small visual color differences are considerably less important than differences in energy distribution.

Closely allied to the question of energy distribution but involving a different kind of tolerance which must be determined by different methods is the matter of differences that appear under *several* illuminants. There are two types of tolerance involved when objects are examined under several illuminants. The first and most important type, of course, is the variable difference between two samples which are supposed to match. This difference, as already pointed out, is controlled by the difference in the spectrophotometric curves of the samples. If the curves are identical, the colors will match under all illuminants. If they differ, the observed color difference will depend on the illuminant. Such an instance seldom arises in the manufacture of a product if the colorants involved are reasonably repeatable. It does occur in a very serious manner when one material is matched to another colored with different materials. In this event if the coloring materials are distinctly different, the match may not hold for other illuminants.

The second type of tolerances involved when samples are viewed under several illuminants is quite different in nature and rather difficult to determine. It was pointed out earlier that the human eye tends to adapt to the color of the prevailing illuminant in such a way that the colors of objects are at least partially restored to their daylight appearance. Two rather drastic exceptions to this "color-constancy" phenomenon were noted. No color constancy exists for monochromatic light or for colors whose energy distribution approaches monochromatic light in character, and the relative brightnesses of different parts of the spectrum are not affected by color adaptation. It remains to consider these two effects on tolerances set for a single color with respect to the illuminants under which that color may be seen. Such a tolerance is in the nature of a limitation on the spectral reflectances of the coloring *materials* which may be used to produce the required color, rather than on variability of manufacture. Thus, if it is intended that a material appear blue in daylight, it is not desirable that it should appear purple in artificial light, particularly if the blue color is intended as a sort of trade-mark for the product. The phenomenon due to energy distribution mentioned first may, however, produce this effect, and the extent to which it may be permitted to occur is a proper subject for tolerance standards. The second effect, that of persistence of relative brightnesses, will cause the blue to look darker relative to red in artificial light compared to daylight. This latter phenomenon, however, is completely general and is so little affected by spectral reflectance that little can be done about it. Fortunately the very generality of the effect means that all people are accustomed to its occurrence and do not notice it. Shifts in hue, however, can be avoided to some extent by a proper understanding of the subject.

When the eye adapts to colored illumination it apparently does so through a shift in the sensitivity of the receptors of the eye for color. Each of these receptors appears to have sensitivity over about one-third of the spectrum. The adaptation process simply shifts the effectiveness of whole regions of the spectrum at a time until the net result is that the *illuminant* color appears white or nearly so. It follows that, if a color has energy only in a narrow region of the spectrum, or if it has an abrupt transition in amount of energy at some wavelength, the

ratios of effective exposure to the receptors after and before adaptation will be different. This is best seen for monochromatic light but is true to some extent for all colors with abrupt changes. Suppose R, G, and B in

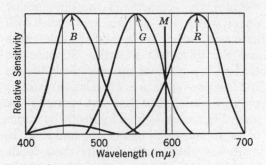

Fig. 14·3 Schematic eye-receptor sensitivity curves with a monochromatic line stimulating the red and green receptors equally and causing a yellow sensation.

Fig. 14·3 are the three eye receptor sensitivities under daylight conditions and that the eye is viewing the monochromatic light indicated by line M. If the eye is adapted to an incandescent light that is relatively or-

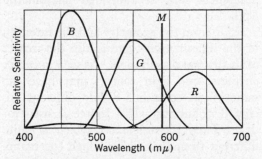

Fig. 14·4 Schematic eye-receptor sensitivity curves after the eye has been adapted to an orange source. The red receptor is now less sensitive with respect to the green receptor than before, and the monochromatic line will appear slightly more green than before adaptation took place.

ange, readjustment of the absolute sensitivities of the receptors will take place with a result that the relative sensitivities may now be represented as in Fig. 14·4. The same monochromatic line at M now affects the

228

receptors in different ratio than in daylight even though the illuminant itself which affects *all* wavelengths of each receptor gives the same ratio as the daylight.

Control of the hue shifts caused by this effect is obviously a matter of avoiding colorants which have sudden intensity changes with wavelength. In general the broader the absorption curve and the gentler the slopes of such curves the less the shift will be. With sharp curves two daylight colors produced by different colorants may differ markedly, for example, one blue turns purple and the other remains blue in artificial light.

Determination of the tolerable limits and hence of the colorants which can be used must depend, obviously, on the average tastes of a number of observers seeing the samples successively under all the illuminants intended. Unfortunately the prevalence of fluorescent lights with energy distributions markedly different from either daylight or tungsten light has made the "instability" of colorants with the illumination a relatively serious matter. An attractive oak table which has a satisfactory and appealing color in both daylight and tungsten light ceases to be commercially satisfactory when it turns green under fluorescent light, and not much can be done by the manufacturer of the table.

It is equally apparent that the manufacturers of light sources also have a problem in setting the tolerances on variations which various light sources will permit in ordinary colored objects as compared with more normal illuminants of the same color. Art objects, meat, eggs, familiar woods, and many other objects appear about the same color under tungsten and daylight but change markedly under an illuminant of the same visual color that has most of its energy confined to the blue and the orange regions of the spectrum. Only greatly decreased operating cost and decreased heat radiation have permitted the general acceptance of such illuminants.

Color differences and the acceptance tolerances which they generate, therefore, depend on a large number of circumstances peculiar to each instance. In the last analysis they can be determined and set only under conditions closely allied to the particular case considered. Once determined, they may be specified to any desired degree of precision by well-known and readily repeatable psychophysical methods. The precision necessary for the *specification*, incidentally, does not determine the size of the tolerances involved since the legal status of a borderline case or some such matter having no relation to color vision or tastes may control the decision.

COLOR NAMES

Closely allied to the subject of color differences is the matter of color names. As in many other fields, the major differences in the subject are marked off by the words that have developed to describe them. However, only the *major* differences are marked off and form such a good criterion of a particular kind of difference that it might well be called the "naming difference" between colors. To the naive observer two colors are different if he calls them by different names, and the fact that he does is a sufficient indication of his tolerances. There are, however, two kinds of color description, and they are somewhat difficult to distinguish. There is one terminology that describes color on an absolute basis, i.e., with reference to the mental color system. The other set of expressions describes differences between two colors and forms the basis of the coordinates of the psychological color domain. These terms apply directly to direction and amount of change in hue, saturation, and brightness. There are, according to Judd, some ten million distinguishable color differences, and they can be described in words which indicate directions of their differences. There are, however, far fewer color names than this would suggest. The Maerz and Paul color dictionary, based on an exhaustive study, lists very large and it will be found presently that a workable system has been developed for systematic naming of surface colors which has only 319 divisions.

In common usage the number of color terms is far less than any of these. A recent

FIGURE 14·5

	Single Terms	Modified Terms				Plural Terms		
	A	B	C	D	E	F	Total	Percent
White	933	None	10	14	None		957	21.7
Black	689	None	1	3	1		694	15.7
Blue	390	44	21	2	25		482	10.7
Red	448	9	8	8	4		477	10.7
Gray	368	11	12	7	2		400	9.1
Green	243	34	14	22	6		319	7.2
Brown	157	11	3	8	6		185	4.2
Gold	176	1	None	3	None		180	4.1
Yellow	147	8	5	3	1		164	3.7
Pink	111	2	None	None	2		115	2.6
Silver	60	None	None	1	None		61	1.4
Purple	44	1	None	1	1		47	1.1
Miscellaneous	300	10	3	1	3	18	335	7.6
Total	4,066	131	77	73	51	18	4,416	

FIG. 14·5 Color terms used in seventeen modern novels. Each column gives the number of times a certain type of color term was used: *Column A*, single terms, e.g., black, blacker, bluest; *Column B*, terms modified by words denoting saturation, brightness, etc., e.g., dark blue, bright red, pale green; *Column C*, terms modified by objects or substance, e.g., ice blue, milk white, cherry red; *Column D*, terms modified by other color terms, e.g., pinkish white, blue-green; *Column E*, terms modified by suggestive words, e.g., violent blue, dull red, intense green; *Column F*, plural color terms, e.g., black and white, red and blue.

tionary, based on an exhaustive study, lists less than 4,000 and the greater part of these are fanciful, having color context only for a season or in a restricted locality. Some 36 of them represent single words having direct color meaning; about 300 of them are compound words consisting of a color name and a modifying adjective; and about 90 of them are the names of common colored objects. The total number of colors considered distinctly different, therefore, is not survey of seventeen best sellers made by Pauline Evans discloses the fact that of the total of 4,416 color terms used, 4,081 are accounted for by only 12 terms. White, black, and gray alone represent nearly half of the total number, 2,051. The actual figures are given in Fig. 14·5. It is interesting to note that of the twelve color terms listed, only two of them, gold and silver, are object or substance names. The remaining 10 are straight color terms, and such terms include 87 percent of those found in this study.

Thirty-three color terms of the Maerz and Paul system are color terms only, independent of objects and substance. These terms are listed in Fig. 14·6 with the number of times they occur in the seventeen books of the study. Eight of the terms were not used

FIGURE 14·6

Auburn	3	Magenta	6
Azure	0	Maroon	4
Black	694	Mauve	9
Blond	16	Orange	25
Blue	482	Pink	115
Brown	185	Purple	47
Brunette	0	Red	477
Buff	1	Russet	1
Cyan	0	Scarlet	12
Cerise	1	Sepia	0
Crimson	24	Tan	9
Dun	0	Taupe	0
Ecru	0	White	957
Gray	400	Yellow	164
Green	319	Violet	23
Henna	0	Khaki	1
Indigo	2		

FIG. 14·6 The numerical occurrence of the thirty-three pure color terms of Maerz and Paul in the literature covered in the survey.

at all and four of them were used but once. It is significant that 90 percent of the total number of color terms used are accounted for by those listed in the table.

It is, perhaps, more instructive to develop the color names starting with the spectral hues and to see the directions in which the terminology branches to take care of the important differences, as is done in the following section.

PSYCHOLOGICAL PRIMARIES

If a projected spectrum at good intensity is studied carefully, it is found that of the whole gamut of colors there are four hues which are distinctly different from each other, and only four. They are red, yellow, green, and blue. All other colors may be seen to contain more or less of two of these. There are, thus, four fundamental spectral hues, and they are sometimes called the "psychological primaries." It is possible, at least theoretically, to describe all colors by these four color names in pairs with the use of modifying adjectives or phrases. Thus orange may be described as a red-yellow, etc. The intermediate colors, however, are sufficiently distinctive in themselves to have received separate names and if we write the above four with their intermediate colors between them, we might have something like the scheme, red, orange, yellow, green, cyan, blue, violet, magenta.

At this point a distressing fact becomes apparent, the extent of which is seldom realized unless a person is acquainted with several fields in which color is used. The color *terms* which are used by one group may be the same as those used by another but they may refer to decidedly different *colors*. In the above list, for example, the term *cyan* for the color between *blue* and *green* and the term *magenta* for the color between *red* and *blue* are taken from the terminology of subtractive color photography, and the use of the word *red* to indicate the long wavelength end of the spectrum is itself largely restricted to physicists and the like. The *cyan* of the artist is a much bluer color, the *red* of the artist would be called a *red* magenta in the above scheme, etc. *Violet* is here used to describe the appearance of the extreme short-wavelength end of the spectrum, at which point both the blue and the red receptors are excited by the light. The same color is produced by mixing longer wavelength blue light with a little red. The color so formed is usually called *purple*. No widely accepted term exists for the intermediate color between green and yellow, the colors shading continuously from one to the other without a distinctive color between. As a matter of fact it is unlikely that there would be a name for the color between blue and green if it were not for the fact that it is encountered frequently in subtractive color mixture as the primary which does not transmit red. In art it usually is known as *blue-green* just as the other is known as yellow-green. The fact must be faced, therefore, that although the spectral hue names are basically few and simple, common usage does not agree even for the four basic ones. The fact that different groups name them differently, however, indicates that far more than four names are necessary as far as the color differences are concerned.

This discussion has concerned the projected spectrum and the mixtures of red and blue light. When the possible range of surface colors is considered many new names are encountered. Basically we have been considering hue and the variables saturation and lightness have been neglected by the use of a spectrum projected in a dark room. In surface colors these variables are introduced and become important.

Consider first the colors that arise when pure pigments are mixed with white. Purples mixed with white give lavender and orchid and the like and magenta gives pink. For the most part the remaining colors when desaturated are described as *pale*—as *pale green, pale blue,* and the like—or are described by the color of some object which they resemble such as *sea green* or *pastel blue,* although either of them might be quite saturated colors, or the first might refer to the hue.

When pure pigment colors are mixed with black several quite new colors are produced. Yellow and black, for example, produce the *olive greens*, and combinations of yellow-orange, orange, and red with black make the series of *browns*.

If the colors containing black are also mixed with white another new series of colors is produced which includes the *tans* starting with brown, and the *khakis* starting with more yellow colors.

It is seen, therefore, that in the "related" viewing of colors, to use Ostwald's term, several new kinds of color are introduced that are not present in the spectrum, and that these are important enough to call for special terms. The total number of such names is quite small, however, and for the most part the gamut of distinctly different colors is handled in ordinary speech by the use of modifying adjectives as in expressions like "pale gray-green," or "bright pure red," or "medium reddish orange."

ISCC-NBS COLOR NAMES

In 1939 an attempt was made to standardize this method of designating colors so that they would be understandable without use of reference samples and yet sufficiently defined so that rigid specification would be possible if necessary. This attempt originated in 1931 when the U. S. Pharmacopoeial Revision Committee requested the then newly formed Inter-Society Color Council to consider the naming of drug colors on some system which would be universally understandable, and it crystallized in the publication of a paper by Judd and Kelly from the Bureau of Standards. (See bibliography at close of chapter.) Basically this system consists of a hue name from the series *red, yellow, green, blue, purple, olive, brown* and *pink*, modified by the terms *weak, strong, light, dark,* and the use of the word *very*. For convenience, the combining terms *pale* (light weak), *brilliant* (light strong), *deep* (dark strong), *dusky* (dark weak), and *vivid* (very strong) are used; thus the necessity for such terms as *very light weak* was avoided. Intermediate hue names are handled by combining forms such as reddish purple, etc. This system results in 319 designations for the entire domain of surface colors.

In the original paper describing the system the Munsell notations are given for the entire series of names. Since the Munsell system has now been specified in terms of the ICI system, the ISCC-NBS color names may also be expressed in these terms if desired. The whole represents a workable and logical system for naming colors which can be adapted to many uses and can be understood without reference to a color chart. Like all such systems, of course, it has the limitation that one encounters bor-

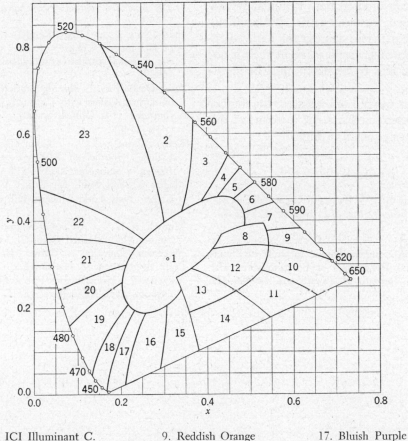

Fig. 14·7

1. ICI Illuminant C.	9. Reddish Orange	17. Bluish Purple
2. Yellowish Green	10. Red	18. Purplish Blue
3. Yellow-Green	11. Purplish Red	19. Blue
4. Greenish Yellow	12. Pink	20. Greenish Blue
5. Yellow	13. Purplish Pink	21. Blue-Green
6. Yellowish Orange	14. Red-Purple	22. Bluish Green
7. Orange	15. Reddish Purple	23. Green
8. Orange-Pink	16. Purple	

Location of the various chromaticity regions into which any light source must fall. The color names for light falling in these regions have been suggested by Kenneth L. Kelly of the National Bureau of Standards. (K. L. Kelly, *Journal of Research of the National Bureau of Standards*, Vol. 31, p. 274, 1943.)

derline colors, which can be said to lie between two of the designations.

When an attempt is made to apply these names to the colors of transparent substances, many of them have to be changed, of course, because the designations for the lighter surface colors lead to *white* for zero saturation and maximum lightness, whereas for solutions they lead to *clear* and *colorless*. With certain modifications a similar system may be used to name actual self-luminous light sources. The sources for dark colors such as brown have no place in such a nomenclature and by necessity must be eliminated.

Kelly has worked out a system for sources and has expressed the result in terms of the ICI system as shown in Fig. 14·7.

BIBLIOGRAPHY

Balinkin, Isay A. "Industrial Color Tolerances." *The American Journal of Psychology*, **52**:428–448 (1939).

Helson, Harry. "Color Tolerances as Affected by Changes in Composition and Intensity of Illumination and Reflectance of Background." *The American Journal of Psychology*, **52**:406–412 (1939).

Helson, Harry, and Jeffers, Virginia B. "Fundamental Problems in Color Vision. II. Hue, Lightness, and Saturation of Selective Samples in Chromatic Illumination." *Journal of Experimental Psychology*, **26**:1–27 (1940).

Judd, Deane B. "A General Formula for the Computation of Colorimetric Purity." *Bureau of Standards Journal of Research*, **7**:827–841 (1931).

Judd, Deane B. "Specification of Color Tolerances at the National Bureau of Standards." *The American Journal of Psychology*, **52**:418–427 (1939).

Judd, Deane B., and Kelly, Kenneth L. "Method of Designating Colors." *Journal of Research of the National Bureau of Standards*, **23**:355–385 (1939).

Judd, Deane B. "Hue, Saturation and Lightness of Surface Colors with Chromatic Illumination." *Journal of the Optical Society of America*, **30**:2–32 (1940).

Kelly, Kenneth L. "Color Designations for Lights." *Journal of Research of the National Bureau of Standards*, **31**:271–278 (1943).

Maerz, A., and Paul, M. Rea. A *Dictionary of Color*. New York: McGraw-Hill Book Co., Inc. 1930.

Munsell, A. H. A *Color Notation*, 9th ed. Baltimore, Md.: Munsell Color Co., Inc. 1941.

Nickerson, Dorothy. *Color Measurement and Its Application to the Grading of Agricultural Products*. Miscellaneous Publication 580, U. S. Department of Agriculture. 1946.

Mixtures of Colored Lights

CHAPTER XV

THE representation of colors and color mixtures on triangular diagrams has been discussed in previous chapters. In the present chapter the use of such triangles to predict the result of additive mixtures of colors will be considered. In the two following chapters color triangles will be applied to the description of subtractive mixtures. The discussion will be restricted almost entirely to the ICI system but it should be understood that the principles involved are quite general and hold for all such methods of presenting the facts.

ADDITIVE MIXTURE TRIANGLES

A color triangle is a means of plotting the relative amounts of three additive primaries. A point in such a triangle indicates the relations of the three to each other for a particular case. Although the point is unique, i.e., it represents a definite energy distribution as far as the primaries are concerned, there are an infinite number of other energy distributions that will produce a match. There are, accordingly, an infinite number of sets of primaries which may be used, and the choice of a particular set is a matter of convenience. (The statement that there are an *infinite* number involves the assumption of infinitesimal differences between them. If the differences are assumed to be discriminative, the number becomes finite and not very large.) Points on the ICI or any other color diagram, therefore, define infinite domains of matching spectral-energy distributions for the standard observer. The important point is that it is colors which are defined, and not colored objects or selective absorbers or reflectors of any kind. The diagram deals, therefore, exclusively with *light* and only from the standpoint of the energy distributions which match each other. In the ICI system the calculated point representing the mixture of the hypothetical primaries can be interpreted directly in terms of the monochromatic-plus-white system of colorimetry. By means of correlation charts or graphs it can be interpreted also in terms of any other color mixture system which has been computed in this manner.

There are no rules known, however, by which it is possible to calculate an energy distribution which matches a given point, although such rules would have considerable utility. The lack of rules is due in part to the extreme freedom of choice presented. For any color of moderately low purity it should be possible to invent an energy distribution which has any desired value at any single wavelength and yet matches exactly for the standard observer.

However, since the diagram deals with light and, in particular, with the mixture properties of a given set of primaries, there are certain exceedingly valuable rules for predicting the results of light mixtures. When light of a given energy distribution illuminates a non-selective surface and reflects to the eye, there is no change in its energy distribution. If two or more such lights are projected on top of each other they all act independently, and the eye receives the simple sum. Simple sums of this type may be expressed in simple fashion on any color triangle of the type described. It is a fact, which follows from the geometry of such figures, that mixtures of lights corresponding to any two points fall on the straight line connecting these points in the triangle. (The geometrical derivation of this fact is quite complex and outside the scope of the present book. The interested reader is referred to J. P. C. Southall's "Introduction to Physiological Optics" in the bibliography at the close of the chapter for a mathematical treatment of the subject.) Thus in Fig. 15·1 M and N represent mixtures of a definite ratio of primaries, in this instance the hypothetical ones of the ICI system, which will match any of an infinite set of energy distributions. If any of the energy distributions represented by these points are mixed together additively, the color resulting from this mixture may be represented by a point on the straight line connecting the two. Furthermore, and of great importance for purposes of calculation, the exact point on this line may be calculated by the ratio of the intensities of the

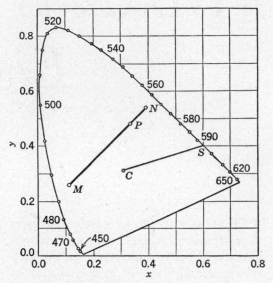

FIG. 15·1 Chromaticity diagram showing the resultant chromaticity of an additive mixture of two light sources having the chromaticity as marked by points M and N and mixed in a ratio of four parts of N to one part of M.

two colors. "Intensity" in this instance is measured in terms of special units called "trichromatic units," and for any light source the number of trichromatic units may be determined by dividing its luminance by the y coefficient of its color as plotted on the chromaticity diagram. If two parts of one color and one of the other, as measured in these special units, are used, the point falls two-thirds of the way from the *less* to the *more* intense of the two. In other words the position along the line is inversely proportional to the relative intensities of the two lights. Thus the point P in Fig. 15·1 represents a mixture containing four parts of N and one of M and is accordingly four-fifths of the way from M to N.

Once this property of the triangle is fully appreciated the possibilities for prediction are innumerable. One such type of prediction is at the basis of the customary description system and has been discussed earlier.

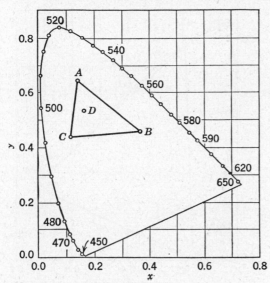

FIG. 15·2 Triangular chromaticity gamut formed by the three primary sources of chromaticities A, B, and C. By varying the proportions of these sources any chromaticity within the triangle whose apices are A, B, and C may be matched.

If some point on the triangle represents white light, however it is defined, the line joining this point with the point that represents pure monochromatic light of any wavelength describes all the mixtures of white light with this wavelength. In the ICI system this line defines all energy distributions with the same dominant wavelength, that is, any color may be defined by saying that it would match a mixture of this wavelength with the specified white in the proportion indicated by its position along the line connecting the two. The fractional distance which the calculated point occupies between the white point and the spectrum locus is

defined as its "excitation purity" under the ICI system. Such a line is shown as CS in the foregoing figure.

Another valuable property of such diagrams, which follows from the simple rule of straight line mixtures, is the possibility of predicting the result of the mixture of any number of colored lights. Suppose three lights may be represented by the points A, B, and C in Fig. 15·2. Mixtures of these in pairs will generate straight lines connecting the corresponding points as shown. Any point such as D inside the triangle may be considered as the light produced by a mixture of two of them with a suitable amount

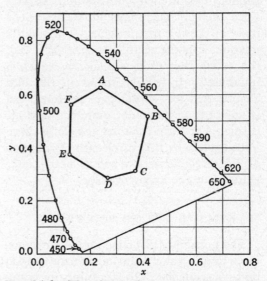

FIG. 15·3 The chromaticity gamut obtained by using six primaries. All chromaticities located within the hexagon are obtainable by varying the proportions of the different primaries used.

of the third. If all three of them are present in equal amounts, for example, the mixture will be indicated by the centroid of the triangle, i.e., the point at which lines from the apices to the centers of the opposite sides intersect.

More complex figures than a triangle are formed if more than three sources are involved. Thus Fig. 15·3 represents as *A, B, C, D, E,* and *F* the mixture diagram for six sources. The maximum purities that can be obtained from any mixtures of the six lie on the hexagon which joins the points taken in pairs. The point representing the mixture of any amount of any number of them may be determined directly by considering them systematically, the point determined by any first pair being combined with a third, this point with a fourth, etc., until all have been considered.

A color triangle, therefore, predicts additive mixtures of colored lights and indicates that the result of such mixtures is independent of the energy distributions as such, since each of the points represents an infinity of possible distributions. For additive mixtures it is the relative "appearance," i.e., the colors that each will match, which is important. It will be found in the next chapter that for "subtractive" mixtures, that is, mixtures of colorants, quite the opposite is true. For them the mixture color is determined *solely* by the wavelength distribution of the selective action and is nearly independent of the apparent color.

MAXIMUM COLOR RANGES

The possibility of predicting additive mixtures from a color triangle has many important consequences. It is possible, for example, to predict the required colors which, used as primaries, would probably include the largest possible range of natural object colors. This has been done by Hardy and Wurzburg, and their results are shown in Fig. 15·4. This range is obtained by the mixture of three monochromatic lights of wavelength 700 mμ, 535 mμ, and 400 mμ as shown. The actual color gamut extends at right angles to the plane of the triangle formed by connecting the three to include a wide range of brightnesses.

By the use of similar concepts and the fact that reflection colorants cannot reflect more than 100 percent at any wavelength it is possible to calculate the maximum theoretical excitation purity for a reflecting colorant at a given luminance level. MacAdam has made the necessary computations and

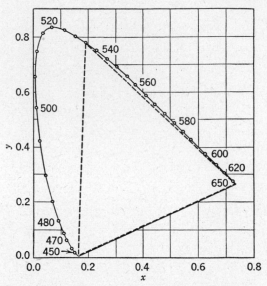

FIG. 15·4 The maximum additive triangle of Hardy and Wurzburg showing the largest possible gamut of chromaticities consistent with positive considerations for chromaticities with dominant wavelengths above 570 mμ. (A. C. Hardy and F. L. Wurzburg, Jr., *Journal of the Optical Society of America,* Vol. 27, p. 231, 1937.)

his results are shown in Fig. 15·5, which is self-explanatory. These results have been examined critically in relation to the appearance of real dyestuffs in an article by T. Vickerstaff, in which he finds it necessary to redefine the term "brightness" as applied to real dyes. He prefers the term "lightness" for the concept used by MacAdam, since purity as well as its luminance is important in the psychological evaluation of a color.

In addition to these applications of the concept of additive mixture it is possible to derive from the concept a complete theory for additive three-color photography. The theory has been stated in full by MacAdam (see bibliography at close of chapter). In essence it indicates that, if a color is analyzed

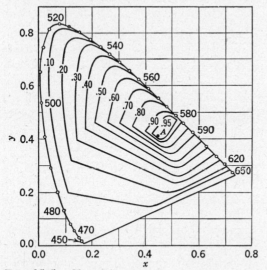

FIG. 15·5 Chart showing the chromaticity loci under ICI Illuminant A for surfaces with different visual efficiencies with visual efficiency defined as a function of the reflectance. The chart gives the physically maximum visual efficiency for the chromaticities lying on the various loci and also indicates the maximum excitation purity that a surface can have under this light if a given visual efficiency, or surface lightness, is to be maintained. It is seen that yellow surfaces may be both light and quite pure, but blue surfaces must be relatively dark if a high purity is to be maintained. (D. L. MacAdam, *Journal of the Optical Society of America*, Vol. 25, p. 365, 1935.)

into three components by a photographic system that acts exactly like the eye, the three components may be used to control three colored lights so that the results inside the triangular gamut which they represent will be identical with the subject. Outside this gamut all colors will be represented by points along the lines connecting the appropriate pairs of primaries. The required sensitivity curves for the photographic process are the color mixture curves required to

match the points on these connecting lines with the primaries of the process. This is discussed somewhat more fully in Chapter XX.

COMPLEMENTARY COLORS

Another consequence of this straight-line additivity principle in color triangles is the ease with which it is possible to predict complementary colors. If the line connecting two points on the diagram contains the point which represents white, it is apparent that in suitable ratio the two colors represented will form white (or gray, depending on the viewing conditions). Such pairs are said to have complementary dominant wavelengths. It is apparent from an inspection of the spectrum locus on the diagram that only part of the spectrum at each end is complementary to other parts of the spectrum; there is a gap in the green region where it is necessary to use a mixture of long and short wavelengths to obtain a complementary mixture. The spectrum-dominant wavelengths which do have complementaries were shown in the graph of Fig. 7·13.

Implied in the discussion but frequently overlooked is the fact that the mixture of two lights, except for a short range in the long-wavelength region, always has lower excitation purity than either light alone. Consequently in transmitting or reflecting selective absorbers the width of the transmission or reflection region in the spectrum determines the excitation purity of the color produced. The wider this "band" the *less* saturated is the color. Maximum purity or saturation, of course, would be produced by monochromatic light.

SATURATION

This is, perhaps, a reasonable point at which to consider again the relation between the psychophysical variables as shown on a color mixture triangle and the associated color perceptions. Whereas it is true that monochromatic light represents the highest physical excitation purity that can be obtained with real light sources, it is not true that the direct perception of such a source gives the highest possible saturation that can be produced in the eye.

If the eye is exposed for a considerable time to light which is complementary in color to that of a given wavelength and if this wavelength is then viewed, it is found to be of higher saturation, at least for a brief time, than it would have been if viewed originally. The process is obviously adaptation as discussed earlier but is usually referred to in the literature as "fatigue," although the term would hardly lead one to expect *higher* saturations from monochromatic light.

The result is easily verified by viewing a patch of magenta light at moderately high intensity and then looking at a projected spectrum. If the afterimage of the spot is positioned in the green region of the spectrum, the saturation of the green will be greatly enhanced. Although the mechanism by which this effect occurs is not actually known, it can, as usual, be described on the three-receptor hypothesis. Magenta light excites about equally the blue and the red receptors, decreasing their sensitivity. Long exposure makes recovery of this sensitivity slow. The green receptor, not having been exposed, increases in sensitivity to a semi-dark-adapted state; its sensitivity becomes quite high relative to the other two. This high ratio, by itself, would not affect saturation except that the green lines in the spectrum normally affect all *three* receptors. Accordingly, a maximum saturation for the daylight-adapted eye is set by this overlap of the sensitivities. When the sensitivities of the blue and the red drop, however, a

much higher ratio of excitation is possible between the green receptor and the other two with the result that a much *higher* saturation of green is seen.

ADAPTATION

Whether this is the "correct" explanation does not matter; it *does* describe the facts as seen. Furthermore, the same approach is capable of extension to many other similar phenomena. Any adaptation to colored light may be considered a shift in the "white point" of a color system. In terms of a definite color triangle the white point is shifted toward the adapting color, and all hues and saturations are modified *in the direction indicated* by the shift. This modification was pointed out by the writer some years ago in an article entitled "Visual Processes and Color Photography" (see bibliography at close of chapter) and follows directly from the work of Wright on color adaptation. In the article referred to, MacAdam contributed a note, pointing out that under the assumption involved (general nature of Wright's specialized results) there is only one set of primaries that can lead to correctly calculated shifts. The primaries must lead to mixture curves that are identical with the "true" sensitivity distributions for the assumed three eye receptors. As pointed out in the article, the curves deduced by Wright from his work, and the much earlier König-Dieterici curves which they confirmed, are a good approximation to this ideal. The interested reader is referred to the writer's article for a rather complete discussion of the subject, including a suggested Maxwell-type triangle and a method of calculation which should permit the approximate calculation of the selective appearance of all colors under all states of color adaptation. The suggestion remains untried to date on any large scale and therefore is somewhat outside the scope of the present treatment.

It is of interest, however, to consider the general subject of color adaptation from the standpoint of the ICI diagram. It must be kept in mind that, when the *appearance* of colors is discussed with respect to this purely psychophysical system, a questionable extension of the concepts on which it is based is being made. The color appearances of the system, of course, are considered to be those of the system of monochromatic colorimetry, viewed in unrelated fields. (In spite of all these warnings and reservations the concept of a moving white point on the ICI diagram is quite useful as a first approximation method.)

When the eye adapts to an illuminant of a given color some intensity of this light always appears white or gray. Since intensity does not appear on the ICI diagram the calculated coordinates of the energy distribution of the source locate this point on the diagram. For first approximation purposes this may be assumed as the visual white point, and any departures from this white point of points calculated for this illuminant may be interpreted as for the true white point.

Suppose, for example, that the illumination color to which a person is adapted is that of the A point in the ICI diagram of Fig. 15·6. If full adaptation has taken place, energy of the quality corresponding to this point will be seen as white at some intensity. A point which lies between it and the C point, as point M, however, will be seen as blue, as will lights which calculate to the C point itself. Seen under C adaptation, M would appear yellow, as would A. Over moderate distances from the C point in all directions good approximations to perceived colors are obtained by this method. As greater and greater departures from daylight are considered, the approximation be-

comes progressively poorer and the variations introduced by the *intensity* of the light become more and more important. (See the Helson-Judd effect, Chapter XI.)

Even for extreme illumination colors, however, this technique does predict the approximate colors which will be seen if allowance is made for the intensity effect. Suppose,

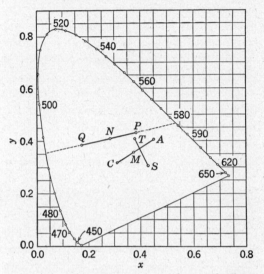

Fig. 15·6 Chromaticity plots of several illuminants which demonstrate hue shifts with adaptation changes.

for example, that two lights may be represented by points P and Q in Fig. 15·6. These lights would appear cyan and yellowish-green, respectively, in unrelated viewing. If both lights are allowed to fall on a white screen and an observer looks at this screen in a dark room he will adapt to the mixture color N. If, now, an object is so placed between the lights and the screen that two colored shadows are produced, each of these shadows will be illuminated by one light only. As noted in an earlier chapter these shadows will not appear to have the unrelated color of the two lights but will appear roughly complementary to each other. (The word complementary here refers to the usual complementary sets with respect to daylight.) In this instance the colors seen may be described roughly by assuming N as the white point and extending the lines through P and Q to the spectrum locus. The colors seen will be similar to the unrelated colors of these spectrum lines. The indication, however, refers only to the hues and not to the saturations. The colors seen are blue and yellow of rather low saturation. If the lights were at S and T, the two lights would be red and yellow as seen separately and the shadow colors after adaptation would be green and magenta.

It is interesting that when the experiment is performed in the manner described the appearance of the *mixture* color is that to be expected for the unrelated viewing of the midpoint, i.e., a greenish cyan in the first and an orange in the second, in spite of the evident adaptation indicated by the appearance of the shadows. The explanation, presumably, is in terms of the Helson-Judd effect; a lower intensity than that represented would appear gray. It has always seemed to the writer that a careful examination of this effect in quantitative terms might clear up many of the mysteries of color vision and perhaps lead to a psychophysical evaluation of all effects except those related directly to the psychological factors not connected with the energy distributions (Chapters IX and XI).

The foregoing discussion will seem somewhat strange even to the expert. It is hoped, however, that the reader, when he encounters some of the apparent anomalies of color vision, will find some assistance from this method of organizing his thinking. There is one point of confusion, however, which appears to be so widespread that it will be well to discuss it again at this point in spite of the fact that it has already been covered in previous chapters.

We have been discussing the movement of the white point with adaptation and have mentioned the possibility of judging the appearance of colors from the ICI diagram. The question arises frequently in practical work how to calculate a particular pair of selective surfaces under an illumination other than daylight. For example, to determine whether two samples of colored paper match under an artificial light that matches the ICI A point has nothing whatever to do with eye adaptation. The illuminant-sample products and integrals are obtained as usual, using the A illuminant energy distribution. If the two points coincide, the samples match to the standard observer regardless of eye adaptation conditions. The confusion arises in part from the problem of determining the dominant wavelength in such an example. It is apparent from the mixture properties of such diagrams that the lack of prescribed method is unimportant as long as the method is made clear. Dominant wavelength is defined as the monochromatic light which, when mixed with white light in proper proportions, will match the given color. If a line through the color point from the C illuminant is extended to the spectrum locus, a wavelength is obtained that will match the color when mixed with C illuminant. If the line is drawn from A, the wavelength indicated will match the color if mixed with A illuminant, and the same thing holds for any of the other points in the triangle. The dominant wavelength does not define a color perception but a physical mixture which will match the calculated point. It is only when an attempt is made to deduce the color *perception* involved that questions arise in regard to the legitimacy of one or the other *specification* of the calculated color.

Therefore, under all possible conditions an adequate color triangle, such as that of the ICI system, will describe completely the psychophysical result obtained by the mixture of two or more lights. In the next chapter it will become equally apparent that a color triangle has little to do with the appearance of actual colored objects in a colored illuminant.

BIBLIOGRAPHY

Evans, Ralph M. "Visual Processes and Color Photography." *Journal of the Optical Society of America,* **33**:579–614 (1943).

Hardy, Arthur C., and Wurzburg, F. L., Jr. "The Theory of Three-Color Reproduction." *Journal of the Optical Society of America,* **27**:227–240 (1937).

Luckiesh, M. *Color and Its Applications.* New York: D. Van Nostrand Co. 1915. Chapter IV.

MacAdam, David L. "Maximum Visual Efficiency of Colored Materials." *Journal of the Optical Society of America,* **25**:361–367 (1935).

MacAdam, David L. "Subtractive Color Mixture and Color Reproduction." *Journal of the Optical Society of America,* **28**:466–480 (1938).

MacAdam, David L. "Photographic Aspects of the Theory of Three-Colour Reproduction." *The Photographic Journal* **81**:333–351 (1941).

Massachusetts Institute of Technology, the Color Measurement Laboratory. *Handbook of Colorimetry.* Cambridge, Mass.: The Technology Press. 1936. Chapter IV.

Morris, Robert H. "Metameric Formulation." *Journal of the Optical Society of America,* **37**:669 (1947).

Parsons, Sir John Herbert. *An Introduction to the Study of Colour Vision,* 2nd ed. Cambridge, England: The University Press. 1924. Chapter III, Section II.

Rood, Odgen N. *Students' Text-book of Color.* New York: D. Appleton and Co. 1916 (copyright, 1881). Chapter V.

Southall, James P. C. *Introduction to Physiological Optics.* London: Oxford University Press. 1937. Chapter VIII.

Vickerstaff, T. "The Brightness of Present-Day Dyes." *The Proceedings of the Physical Society* (London), **57**:15–31 (1945).

Effects of Illuminants

CHAPTER XVI

IT has been shown a number of times in previous chapters that there are an infinite, or at least a very large, number of energy distributions which correspond to each point on a color triangle. This statement, of course, refers to light which has originated in any manner, whether it comes directly from the source or by devious reflection or transmission channels. If two lights, whatever their energy distributions, calculate to the same point, they will be seen to match.

It is sometimes loosely assumed that, if two illuminants match to the eye, colored objects which they illuminate will appear the same to the eye. Although this is obviously false, the notion is so widespread that it seems advisable to devote a brief chapter to an analysis of this sort of color difference, even if in a sense it will repeat much that has already been stated.

When two light sources appear the same to an observer, these light sources excite his eye color receptors in the same ratios. Since the mental perception of any color depends essentially on these ratios and not on the energy distribution itself, these lights are *identical* to the eye in every way. There is

no way in which the observer can distinguish between them without the aid of some effect external to the eye. The color adaptations, afterimages, contrast effects, and every other purely visual effect are identical for both lights.

They are also not distinguishable to the observer in *additive* mixtures. Either of them will mix additively with any third light to produce the identical color as far as the observer is concerned and he cannot tell them apart.

These facts, of course, are the basic principles of all colorimetry in which one light may be described or specified in terms of known lights, as in the monochromatic-plus-white system employed by the ICI system.

The moment any selective absorption of such matched lights takes place, however, differences may become apparent immediately. Since all colored objects normally encountered owe their colors either to selective action or to fluorescence or to both, it is apparent that a visual color match between two *illuminants* gives very little concept of the appearance of objects under them. The one exception, of course, is that non-selective, non-fluorescent surfaces will

PLATE XIII

The color of an object seen under two different illuminations may change, even though the illuminants themselves visually match each other. The scene above is illuminated by the white light of an incandescent lamp. The light in the scene below is also white and would appear exactly the same as that in the scene above, but consists of narrow bands of energy in the blue-green and red portions of the spectrum respectively.

appear identical under each. Even this exception, however, has to be modified in practice if the lights are quite different, because the colors of objects around the nonselective areas may change so much that simultaneous contrast effects may change their appearance.

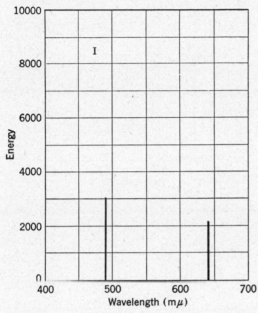

FIG. 16·1 Monochromatic lines which together match ICI Illuminant C.

Artificial light sources for so many purposes are becoming available and the importance of having them adequate to the purpose in hand is so great that it seems worth while to assume three or four more or less arbitrary matching energy distributions and to show graphically how they affect various colors by computing the points that each illuminant gives with each of the colors. For the sake of completeness fluorescent colors are also considered at this point by the inclusion of an assumed fluorescent material. Since the ICI system does not give uniform spacing for colors that appear equally different, that is, since it is difficult to judge the magnitude of some of the ef-

fects from such a chart, where possible the differences are expressed also in the respaced Munsell system. The purpose of this Munsell notation is to aid the reader in his at-

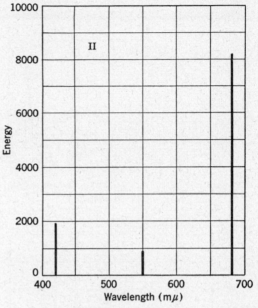

FIG. 16·2 Monochromatic lines which together match ICI Illuminant C.

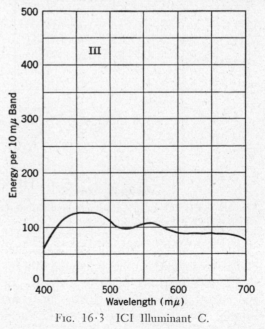

FIG. 16·3 ICI Illuminant C.

tempts to visualize the differences. The Munsell colors themselves are assumed to be viewed in daylight, and the indicated differences are approximate only.

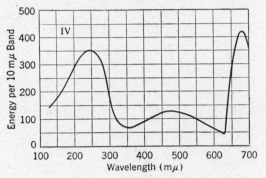

FIG. 16·4 Hypothetical spectral-energy distribution which would match ICI Illuminant C.

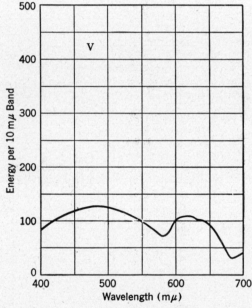

FIG. 16·5 Hypothetical spectral-energy distribution which would match ICI Illuminant C.

For the sake of clarity it may be well to elucidate somewhat the following illustrations. Figures 16·1 to 16·6, inclusive, are the energy curves for six visually matching illuminants. In Figs. 16·7 to 16·12, inclu-

sive, are given the reflectance characteristics of six non-matching surfaces. The chromatic coefficients x and y given in Fig. 16·19

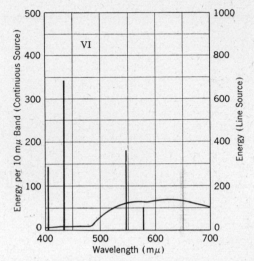

FIG. 16·6 Combination of monochromatic lines and continuous spectral-energy distribution which together would match ICI Illuminant C.

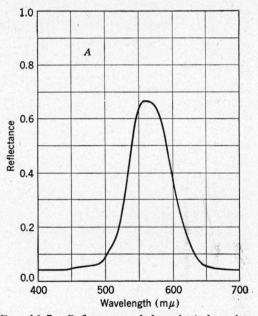

FIG. 16·7 Reflectance of hypothetical surface.

were obtained by computing the chromaticity of each individual surface when independently illuminated by each one of the six illuminants. The Munsell notations given in this table were obtained by converting the ICI trichromatic coefficients to upon the use of ICI Illuminant C as the source of illumination. If use is made of an illuminant that consists of a few monochromatic spectral lines, much higher color

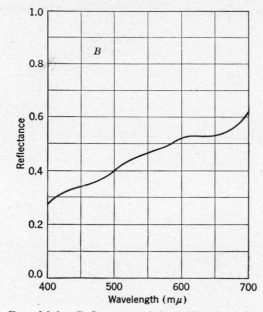

FIG. 16·8   Reflectance of hypothetical surface.

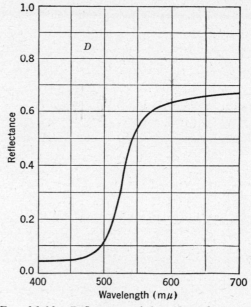

FIG. 16·10   Reflectance of hypothetical surrace.

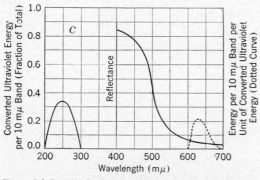

FIG. 16·9   Reflectance of hypothetical surface.

the Munsell re-notation, using the data published by the OSA Subcommittee on the Spacing of the Munsell Colors. It will be noticed that in three cases no Munsell notation is given. The reason is that the tables available for converting ICI trichromatic coefficients into Munsell notations were based

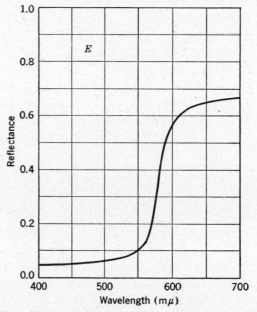

FIG. 16·11   Reflectance of hypothetical surface.

247

saturations at higher reflectances are possible, even if the illuminant used visually matches Illuminant C. The fact that Munsell notations cover only a limited region is not due to a failure on the part of the dye makers to secure a full range of colors. It is inherent in the nature of the dyes themselves in that, for any dye of a particular

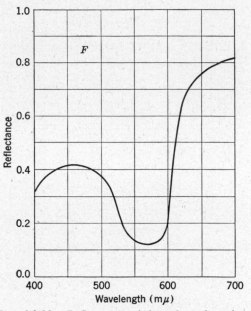

FIG. 16·12 Reflectance of hypothetical surface.

hue and saturation, there is an upper limit to the reflectance that it can have if it is illuminated by a light source of broad and continuous radiant energy distribution, such as Illuminant C. Additional limitations result from the lack of a wide enough range of available pigments, but the limitation already mentioned would apply even if all pigments that were theoretically possible were available.

In order to show more graphically the shifts in the chromaticity of each sample as the illuminant is changed, the ICI diagrams for the six individual surfaces in combination with the six illuminants of Fig. 16·19 are given in Figs. 16·13 to 16·18, inclusive.

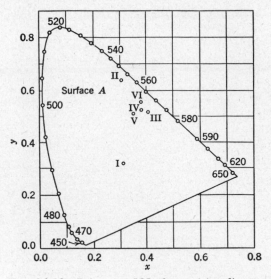

FIG. 16·13 Points on ICI chromaticity diagram corresponding to the light reflected from Surface A (Fig. 16·7) under various illuminants matching ICI Illuminant C.

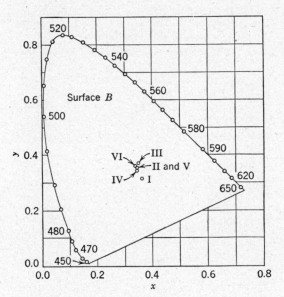

FIG. 16·14 Points on ICI diagram from Surface B (Fig. 16·8).

Directly allied with the energy distribution of matching sources just discussed is the problem of the so-called unstable or sen-

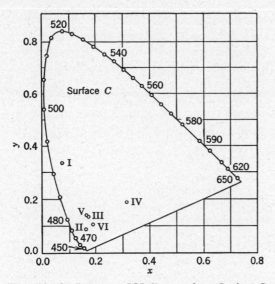

FIG. 16·15   Points on ICI diagram from Surface C
(Fig. 16·9).

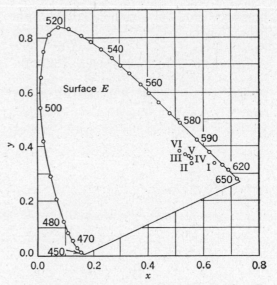

FIG. 16·17   Points on ICI diagram from Surface E
(Fig. 16·11).

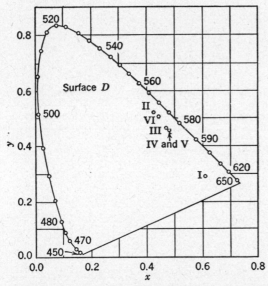

FIG. 16·16   Points on ICI diagram from Surface D
(Fig. 16·10).

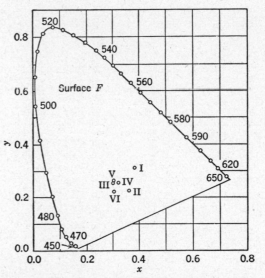

FIG. 16·18   Points on ICI diagram from Surface F
(Fig. 16·12).

sitive colors. This has been discussed in an earlier chapter, but it may clarify the issue somewhat if it is treated here in the same manner as lights have been treated. The succeeding illustrations in this chapter represent an attempt to show the color shift when surfaces are taken from one illuminant to another.

Figures 16·20 to 16·22, inclusive, are the spectral-energy distribution curves of three light sources which correspond respectively to daylight—(ICI Illuminant C), artificial tungsten light, and slightly blue fluorescent light. Figure 16·23 is the ICI plot of these three sources.

Figures 16·24 to 16·26, inclusive, give the reflectance characteristics of three pairs of samples all of which are neutral in illuminant VII, with the samples in any given pair matching each other for relative luminance as well as chromaticity under this illuminant.

The degree of chromatic instability of the three matching pairs may be illustrated by computing their ICI trichromatic coefficients under different sources. Thus when pair G is viewed under illuminant VII the chromaticities of both samples will plot at the illuminant point as will those of pair H.

FIGURE 16·19

Surface	Illuminant	x	y	Luminance Relative to MgO	Munsell Notation
A	I	0.3103	0.3170	0.0775	0 3.26/0
A	II	0.3026	0.6308	0.5575	9.6 GY 7.81/19.6
A	III	0.4029	0.5153	0.4233	3.7 GY 6.95/10.7
A	IV	0.3817	0.5271	0.3934	5.6 GY 6.74/11.0
A	V	0.4005	0.5117	0.3963	3.8 GY 6.76/9.9
A	VI	0.3800	0.5544	0.5160	6.4 GY 7.56/13.9
B	I	0.3628	0.3117	0.4468	2.6 R 7.11/5.8
B	II	0.3499	0.3677	0.4902	6.2 Y 7.41/2.9
B	III	0.3447	0.3511	0.4824	2.5 Y 7.35/2.1
B	IV	0.3467	0.3493	0.4815	1.5 Y 7.34/2.0
B	V	0.3458	0.3498	0.4814	1.4 Y 7.34/2.2
B	VI	0.3413	0.3612	0.4872	8.5 Y 7.38/3.0
C	I	0.0732	0.3368	0.3803	. . . ./. . . .
C	II	0.1649	0.0888	0.1239	7.4 PB 4.06/24.0
C	III	0.1704	0.1371	0.1784	6.6 PB 4.78/17.0
C	IV	0.3108	0.1851	0.3290	7.8 P 6.24/17.4
C	V	0.1684	0.1418	0.1843	6.0 PB 4.85/16.7
C	VI	0.1906	0.1016	0.1396	8.7 PB 4.28/20.0
D	I	0.6067	0.2906	0.2951	. . . ./. . . .
D	II	0.4266	0.5210	0.5676	1.8 GY 7.87/12.8
D	III	0.4719	0.4623	0.4898	2.5 Y 7.39/11.8
D	IV	0.4799	0.4527	0.4754	1.1 Y 7.30/12.2
D	V	0.4784	0.4542	0.4767	1.4 Y 7.31/11.9
D	VI	0.4385	0.5045	0.5425	9.4 Y 7.72/12.1
E	I	0.6394	0.2878	0.2733	. . . ./. . . .
E	II	0.5621	0.3352	0.1752	7.5 R 4.74/13.6
E	III	0.5409	0.3688	0.2447	0.2 YR 5.49/12.7
E	IV	0.5587	0.3523	0.2378	8.6 R 5.42/14.2
E	V	0.5506	0.3616	0.2473	9.5 R 5.51/13.4
E	VI	0.5191	0.3844	0.2226	2.4 YR 5.27/10.6
F	I	0.3776	0.3105	0.5920	0.4 R 8.01/7.5
F	II	0.3618	0.2277	0.3179	2.0 RP 6.15/14.3
F	III	0.3031	0.2528	0.3457	6.4 P 6.37/7.6
F	IV	0.3243	0.2561	0.3703	9.6 P 6.56/9.0
F	V	0.3078	0.2573	0.3591	7.2 P 6.48/7.5
F	VI	0.3022	0.2317	0.3004	6.6 P 6.04/10.0

FIG. 16·19   ICI chromaticities and Munsell notations for various hypothetical surfaces as they might be seen under different illuminants matching ICI illuminant C.

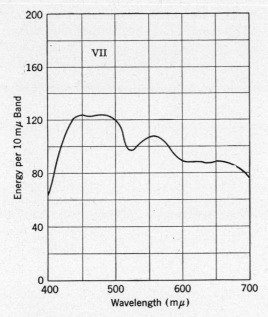

FIG. 16·20 Spectrophotometric curve of ICI Illuminant C (which closely matches one form of daylight).

When viewed under illuminant VIII, however, pair G will still match each other quite well as shown in Fig. 16·27, whereas pair H shows a rather large color difference between the two surfaces as shown in Fig. 16·28. It can thus be concluded that pair H is considerably more unstable than pair G so far as illuminant VIII is concerned.

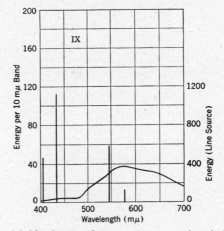

FIG. 16·22 Spectrophotometric curve of a slightly blue fluorescent light.

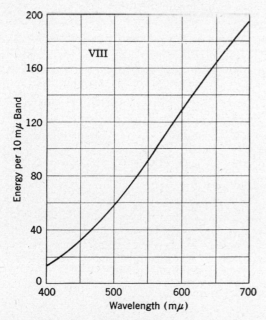

FIG. 16·21 Spectrophotometric curve of a tungsten-filament light source.

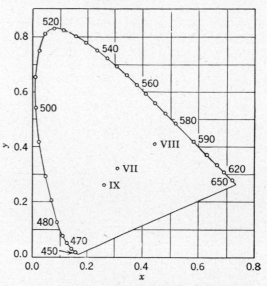

FIG. 16·23 Points on the ICI chromaticity diagram of three light sources whose spectrophotometric curves are shown in Figs. 16·20, 16·21, and 16·22.

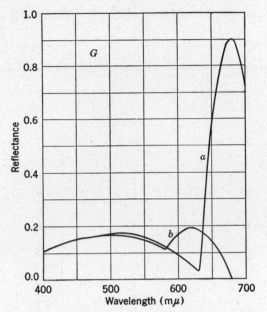

FIG. 16·24 Reflectance curves of surfaces (pair G), which match under daylight.

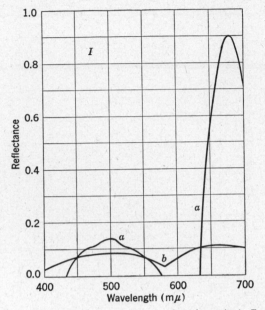

FIG. 16·26 Reflectance curves of surfaces (pair I), which match under daylight.

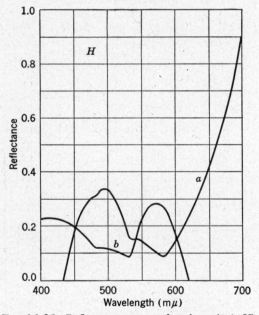

FIG. 16·25 Reflectance curves of surfaces (pair H), which match under daylight.

The possible instability of a sample when viewed successively under illuminants VII, VIII, and IX is illustrated by using the surfaces of pair I. When the samples are viewed under illuminant VII, they are both neutral as already noted. When taken into illuminant VIII, however, their chromaticity changes as shown in Fig. 16·29 and, when viewed under the slightly blue fluorescent light of illuminant IX, the match between them breaks down completely as shown in Fig. 16·30. This plot shows the very marked instability of the pair to fluorescent light.

The results of the computations are tabulated with the relative luminance and Munsell notation in Fig. 16·31.

In finishing this chapter it might be well to qualify slightly the illustrations just described and to caution the reader in regard to their proper interpretation. All the examples are intended only to illustrate the problem and were designed deliberately for this purpose. In order to simplify the examples further all adaptation considerations have

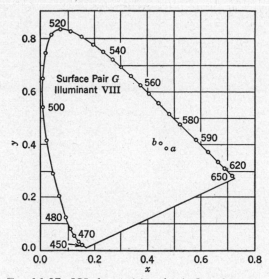

FIG. 16·27 ICI chromaticity of pair G under tungsten light.

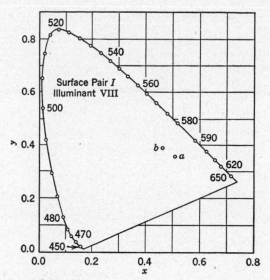

FIG. 16·29 ICI chromaticity of pair I under tungsten light.

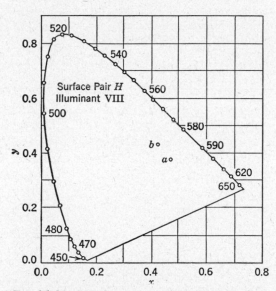

FIG. 16·28 ICI chromaticity of pair H under tungsten light.

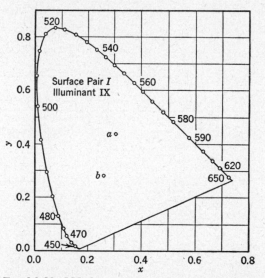

FIG. 16·30 ICI chromaticity of pair I under slightly blue fluorescent light.

been neglected, although it must be remembered that they play a large part in any practical situation. A detailed discussion concerned with the more common colors is given by Miss Nickerson in one of her papers on the subject (see bibliography at close of chapter).

FIGURE 16·31

Illuminant	Surface	x	y	Luminance Relative to MgO	Munsell Notation
VIII	G a	0.4657	0.3933	0.1573	5.9 YR 4.52/6.6
VIII	G b	0.4500	0.4038	0.1555	8.5 YR 4.50/6.0
VIII	H a	0.4721	0.3750	0.1826	2.6 YR 4.83/7.4
VIII	H b	0.4226	0.4327	0.1834	4.9 Y 4.84/5.4
VIII	I a	0.5033	0.3535	0.0718	0.4 YR 3.14/6.5
VIII	I b	0.4599	0.3945	0.0697	6.6 YR 3.09/4.9
IX	I a	0.3033	0.4421	0.0573	9.9 GY 2.80/5.0
IX	I b	0.2599	0.2769	0.0655	10.0 B 3.04/2.3

FIG. 16·31 ICI chromaticity and Munsell notations for three pairs of surfaces which match under daylight, but which do not match under tungsten or fluorescent light.

BIBLIOGRAPHY

MacAdam, David L. "Maximum Visual Efficiency of Colored Materials." *Journal of the Optical Society of America,* **25**:361–367 (1935).

Munsell, A. H. *A Color Notation,* 9th ed. Baltimore, Md.: Munsell Color Co., Inc. 1941.

Newhall, Sidney M., Nickerson, Dorothy, and Judd, Deane B. "Final Report of the O.S.A. Subcommittee on the Spacing of the Munsell Colors." *Journal of the Optical Society of America,* **33**: 385–418 (1943).

Nickerson, Dorothy. *Color Measurement and Its Application to the Grading of Agricultural Products.* Miscellaneous Publication 580, U. S. Department of Agriculture. 1946.

Transparent Colorant Mixtures

CHAPTER XVII

THE general principles underlying the mixture of transparent colorants may be stated quite simply but the consequences of these principles in practice become apparent only with careful consideration of a number of real colorants.

SUCCESSIVE ABSORBING MATERIALS

Subtractive mixture of two colorants, as the term is applied to the subject of color, takes place whenever light is affected by two or more selectively absorbing materials. In most instances whether this action takes place simultaneously or successively in any order, the results are usually identical if all factors are taken into account. Exceptions to this statement are encountered when the materials involved scatter light to an appreciable extent, are fluorescent, or affect each other chemically when mixed.

The basic principles involved in calculating such successive effects were considered

in an earlier chapter. They consist of successive applications of the percentage transmission or reflection data at each step to

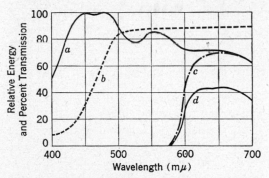

FIG. 17·1 Curves showing results of successive filter action on ICI Illuminant C.

the energy distribution of the light source. The calculations may be made successively, whether the light action is successive or simultaneous. Thus in Fig. 17·1 suppose curve a represents the energy distribution of the light source, curve b the transmission curve of a filter, and curve c that of another.

The relative energy distribution of the light from the source *a* after it has passed through the filters *b* and *c* is that shown by curve *d*, the result having been obtained by successive multiplication of the energies in each wavelength region as shown by *a* by the percentage transmissions as shown in *b* and *c*.

From the fact discussed in some detail in

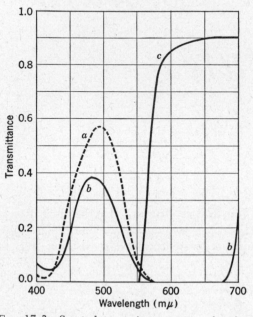

FIG. 17·2 Spectral transmittance curves for three Wratten filters, (*a*) No. 44, (*b*) No. 68, (*c*) No. 22.

the last two chapters that the visual color of an object gives no indication of its spectral absorption distribution, it follows that the result of such successive action of two colored objects or colorants on the light is completely unpredictable in terms of the visual appearance of the colored objects involved.

This unpredictable result may easily be demonstrated by using three common Wratten filters. Thus in Fig. 17·2 are shown the spectral transmittance curves of, *a*, the No. 44 and, *b*, the No. 68 filters. Visually these filters are very similar when viewed by transmitted daylight. If the filters are held side

by side towards the light rather close to the eye and then covered by the No. 22 filter whose curve is shown by *c* a startling transformation is made. The light transmitted through the No. 68 plus 22 combination becomes a deep red whose spectral quality is given in curve *b* of Fig. 17·3, whereas the light transmitted through the No. 44 plus 22 combination is given in curve *a* of Fig. 17·3 and is a dark green color. The effect described here is even more pronounced when the demonstration is made in a darkened room over an ordinary Kodachrome illuminator. Similar examples could be mul-

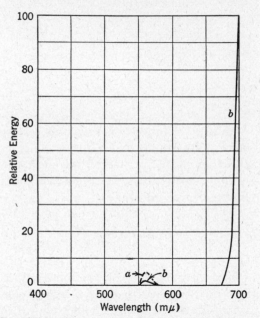

FIG. 17·3 Relative spectral-energy distribution of daylight after passing through Wratten filter combinations, (*a*) No. 44 plus No. 22 and (*b*) No. 68 plus No. 22.

tiplied in great number. The color of light resulting from a subtractive mixture depends (*a*) on the energy distribution of the light source involved, (*b*) on the absorption distributions of the colorants, and (*c*) on the conditions under which the final light is viewed.

These facts must be borne in mind constantly by the person who desires to understand color phenomena. Perhaps the first question that must be decided in the approach to any color problem is whether the conditions are producing additive or subtractive color mixtures.

The result of any color effect, no matter how complex or difficult to understand, may be calculated in terms of the ICI or an equivalent system and plotted on a two-dimensional diagram if it is possible to obtain or calculate the energy distribution of the light reaching the observer's eye. The *results* of subtractive mixture, therefore, may be plotted and studied in relation to other phenomena. If the points for the colorants are shown individually, however, it must be remembered that *except* for the additive case their mixture color is indeterminate from such a chart alone.

BOUGUER'S AND BEER'S LAWS

Two of the basic laws of selectively absorbing materials, as have already been briefly discussed in Chapter V, are Bouguer's and Beer's laws. Bouguer's law, it will be recalled, states that if the transmission at any wavelength is T, and the thickness is n times that of a particular layer, the transmission for that wavelength is T^n, or T multiplied by itself n times. Thus if each layer transmits 10 percent of the light at a given wavelength and there are three such layers in the total thickness, the total transmission at this wavelength will be 10 percent of 10 percent of 10 percent or $\frac{1}{10}$ of 1 percent of the light of this wavelength reaching the first surface. If the thickness is changed to four layers, i.e., if a similar layer is added, the transmission becomes $\frac{1}{100}$ of 1 percent, etc.

Beer's law states exactly the same thing except that it is in terms of the concentration of a colorant in a given thickness. Suppose a dye is dissolved in a solvent such as water or a plastic. The total amount present in a given volume may be thought of in terms of some unit of concentration such as grams per liter, or the like. If, in these terms, there are three units present in a given thickness and each unit *at this*

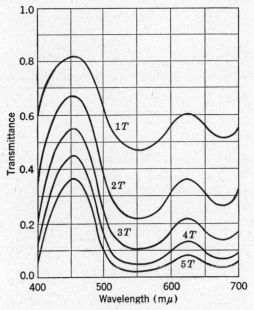

Fig. 17·4 Transmittance curves of five thicknesses of a dyed transparent material.

thickness transmits 10 percent at a given wavelength, the transmitted light is $\frac{1}{10}$ of 1 percent of the incident light as before. Increase of the concentration to four units without change in thickness would drop it to $\frac{1}{100}$ of 1 percent, etc.

These laws have been investigated extensively. Although there are many exceptions for numerous causes, they do describe in essence the action of all transparent materials. As such they are basic to the present subject.

Both laws may be illustrated in a way which makes them readily usable. If a series of concentrations or thicknesses is

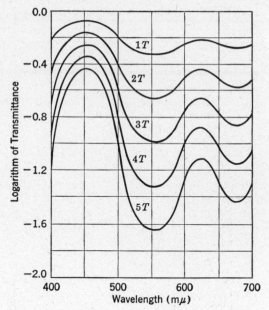

FIG. 17·5 Curves of the logarithms of the transmittance as plotted in Fig. 17·4.

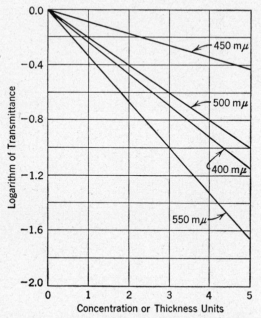

FIG. 17·6 Graph showing the linear relationship between thickness or concentration and transmittance for several different wavelengths.

plotted against the logarithms of the transmissions, the result is a straight line for each wavelength, the slopes of the lines being, in general, different for each wavelength. The type of relationship is shown for an arbitrary transmitting medium in Figs. 17·4 to 17·6. Figure 17·4 shows the transmission curves for a series of thicknesses of the solution. Figure 17·5 shows the same series with the logarithm of the transmission plotted rather than the transmission. The spacing has become more regular. Figure 17·6 shows the same data replotted to show how the logarithm of the transmission depends on the thickness for various wavelengths.

BEER'S LAW SERIES

Transparent colorants, accordingly, follow rather definite laws with respect to changes in thickness or concentration. Once the spectrophotometric curve for one condition has been obtained, it is possible to calculate the curve for another condition by means of these relations. A series of conditions for such a colorant, therefore, passes through a well-defined set of colors, and such a series, which may be called a Beer's law series, is basically important to the subject of color. The colors which such a series generates, however, are not simple in any sense other than those mentioned.

Suppose a dye has the transmission curve shown in Fig. 17·7 and that this curve corresponds to some definite concentration and thickness. The color of the light transmitted by this dye for Illuminant C may be calculated on the ICI system, and the point may be plotted on the diagram. It is shown as M in Fig. 17·8. At zero concentration or thickness the transmission of the solution would necessarily be 100 percent at all wavelengths; therefore the zero point coincides with the Illuminant C point. Intermediate and greater values will fall along the line as shown with point N representing the chromaticity of eight times the concentration represented by M. Note that the line is curved rather than straight. This is a general property of such series. In general, when the thickness or concentration of a transparent colorant is changed, all three of the color attributes change to a degree that can be predicted only by calculation. They are not apparent from simple inspection of the material. Since there are an infinite number of possible spectrophotometric curves which will represent a given color for a given illuminant, the shapes of these Beer's law traces on the ICI diagram may be made to take nearly any form within the limitations that they (a) start at the illuminant point and (b) move progressively toward the spectrum locus along a continuous path.

Several different typical Beer's law traces with the spectrophotometric curves and relative luminosities of the corresponding dyes are shown in Figs. 17·9 through 17·14. The broken portions of these traces are extrapolations extending from computed data, which end at points corresponding to a dye concentration of eight times unity, with the wavelength of the maximum point of the unit-concentration curve being taken as the other terminus of the trace.

While the dyes shown in these figures are not real in that they do not represent actual measurements, they are real in the sense that the energy distributions shown would produce the colors plotted on the diagrams. The curves again illustrate the fact, mentioned so often, that the properties of a dye cannot be determined from its visual color.

Mixtures of transparent colorants act exactly like single colorants as far as their Bouguer's and Beer's laws properties are concerned, that is, whether a colorant is chemically simple or complex, if the ratio of the

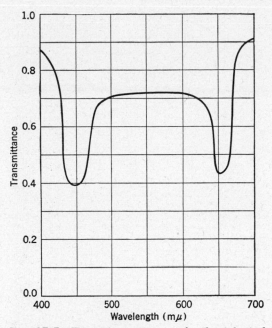

Fig. 17·7 Transmittance curve of a hypothetical dye at unit concentration.

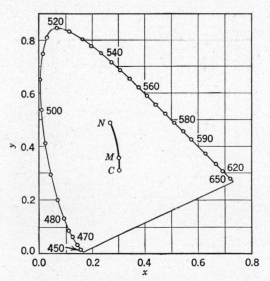

Fig. 17·8 Chromaticity locus of the dye whose transmittance is shown in Fig. 17·7 between zero and eight times the concentration represented by the curve of that figure.

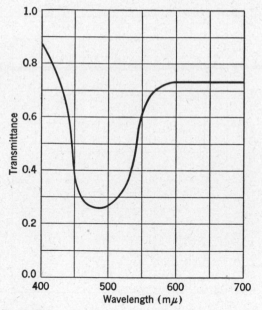

FIG. 17·9a Transmittance curve of hypothetical red dye at unit concentration.

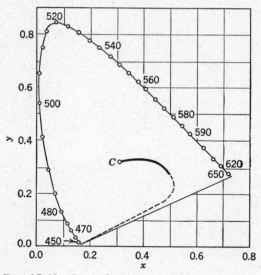

FIG. 17·9b Beer's law trace for the dye of Fig. 17·9a.

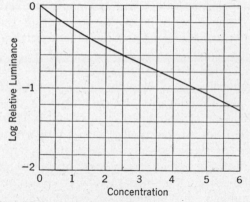

FIG. 17·9c Relative luminance curve for the dye of Fig. 17·9a at various concentrations.

colorant makes the color approach the chromaticity of the spectrum. In general the wavelength so approached is that of the maximum transmission of the solution, regardless of how small a part this transmission may play at low concentrations. The ICI diagram, however, does not show the fact that at these higher concentrations the total amount of light which the dye transmits may become exceedingly low. To illustrate this point the relative luminances at various concentrations of the light transmitted by the dyes have been included along with the other figures. The relative luminances have been plotted on a logarithmic scale, partly to get more of the curves in the graphs, and partly because the corresponding visual brightness differences are more nearly proportional to their logarithms. It should be noted that the lines are not straight. The total transmission of a colorant does *not* obey Bouguer's or Beer's law. The laws apply only to monochromatic transmission.

LIGHT INTENSITY

The curves for dye transmittances illustrate a point that is often overlooked in colorimetric calculations. If such a curve

constituents remains constant, the mixture will act like a single dye.

The curves show also that increasing the concentration or thickness of a transparent

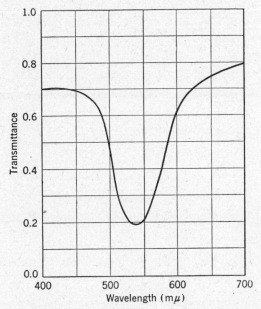

FIG. 17·10a Transmittance curve of hypothetical blue-purple dye at unit concentration.

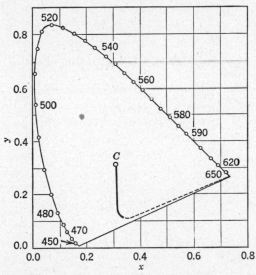

FIG. 17·10b Beer's law trace of the dye of Fig. 17·10a.

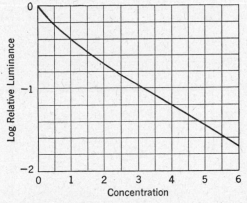

FIG. 17·10c Relative luminance curve for the dye of Fig. 17·10a.

for a dye is plotted on a linear scale with the maximum of this scale at 100 percent, transmittances lower than 1 percent will hardly show on the graph. If the thickness is then increased, nearly the whole curve may drop below the 1 percent line. It should not be assumed that, therefore, the shape of the dye curve is unimportant. A dye layer may show very strong color and still have no transmittances higher than 1 percent. The difficulty arises from the fact that it is the total energy transmitted which is seen and this total depends in part on the intensity of the light source, which does not show on such curves. For transmittance curves to show their true characteristics it is necessary to plot them on an expanded scale which will make the maximum transmittance nearly fill the scale. That this is a legitimate procedure will be seen at once if relative transmitted *energy* rather than transmittance is plotted. In Fig. 17·15, for example, curve *a* shows the relative transmitted energy for a given filter used with a light source of arbitrary intensity. Curve *b* shows the same combination at double the intensity of the source, and curve *c* at four times the intensity. The eye sees all of them as the same except that the intensity changes. Accordingly a very dense dye may give a highly saturated color. It is purely a question of the intensity of the transmitted light compared with the adaptation state of

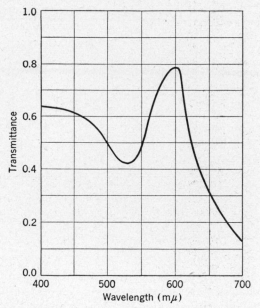

FIG. 17·11a Transmittance curve for hypothetical magenta dye at unit concentration.

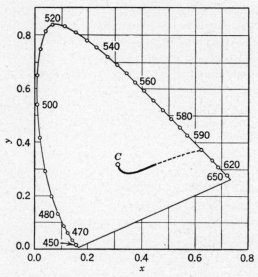

FIG. 17·11b Beer's law trace of the dye of Fig. 17·11a.

the observer's eyes. Unless this factor is taken into account it is possible to make serious errors in calculation of dye mixtures.

One way in which spectrophotometric

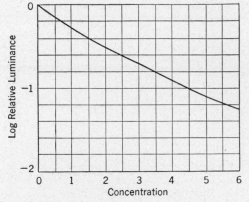

FIG. 17·11c Relative luminance curve for the dye of Fig. 17·11a.

curves may be drawn that tends to avoid such errors and has many other advantages is used in the Wratten Filter Book of the Eastman Kodak Company. In one of the curve sets discussed earlier in the chapter and in a number of other cases, the logarithm of the transmission was used rather than the transmission itself. The logarithmic scale has the great advantage that a fractional difference has the same height regardless of the actual figures involved. Thus, if the transmittance at one wavelength is half what it is at another, the vertical distance between the two will be the same whether one is 90 percent and the other 45 percent or one is 1 percent and the other ½ percent. It is more convenient when such a scale is used, however, to think of the *absorption* of the material rather than its transmission. Accordingly it has become customary to plot such curves with the logarithmic scale inverted and to define the units of the scale as *density* rather than logarithmic transmittance. (For those familiar with photographic sensitometry this will be seen to be the same as the *density* used in that subject.) Zero on the logarithmic scale is equal to *one* on the transmittance scale, one to one-tenth, two to one-hundredth, three

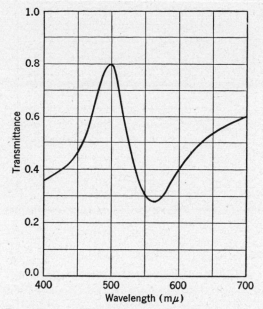

FIG. 17·12*a* Transmittance curve for hypothetical blue-green dye at unit concentration.

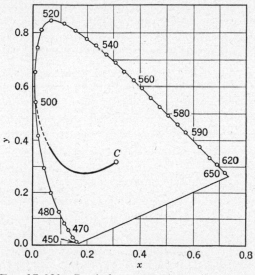

FIG. 17·12*b* Beer's law trace of the dye of Fig. 17·12*a*.

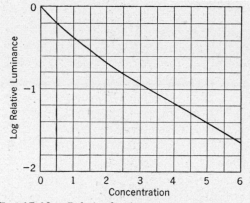

FIG. 17·12*c* Relative luminance curve for the dye of Fig. 17·12*a*.

to one-thousandth, etc. Transmittances for densities up to six are shown in Fig. 17·16.

It is thus seen that the density of a dye to radiation of any given wavelength is dependent upon two variables, these being the spectrophotometric characteristics of the dye and its thickness or concentration. An attempt to show the relationship of these three quantities for the dye of Fig. 17·4 is given in Fig. 17·17. This diagram shows the linear relationship between density and thickness as well as the spectrophotometric characteristics of the dye.

The relationships of spectrophotometric curves plotted in the various ways described are illustrated in Figs. 17·18–17·21, in which the dye of Fig. 17·15 at three concentrations is plotted in terms of transmittance (Fig. 17·18), relative energy of ICI Illuminant C transmitted (Fig. 17·19), logarithm of the transmitted energy (Fig. 17·20), and density (Fig. 17·21) at each wavelength. At the highest concentration, at least, it is seen that the density curve gives the best picture of the selective action of the dye. The relative energy curves of Fig. 17·19 are really the best, however, since they show directly the nature of the light which is affecting the eye. They, however, have the serious disadvantage that different scales are required for wide variations in concentration.

There is another technique for plotting such series which has many advantages and

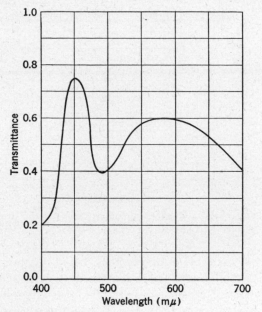

FIG. 17·13*a* Transmittance curve for hypothetical violet dye at unit concentration.

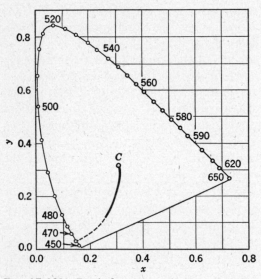

FIG. 17·13*b* Beer's law trace of the dye of Fig. 17·13*a.*.

will be found in many parts of the literature. It combines the advantages of the relative-energy plot and that using densities, but is confusing in that it gives no indication of

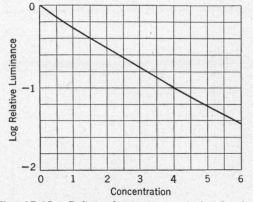

FIG. 17·13*c* Relative luminance curve for the dye of Fig. 17·13*a*.

how dark the material would appear to the eye. The method is to multiply or divide all the relative transmissions of each curve by a figure which will make the value at some one wavelength the same for each. This wavelength can be selected quite arbitrarily, the main aim being to keep all the curves on the paper so that they may be compared directly. Two such transmittance curves are shown in Fig. 17·22.

This particular mode of representation also finds extended application in comparison of light sources. An illustration was given in Fig. 3·2 in which the radiation from a black body at different temperatures is plotted so that the relative energy of all the curves is equal to 100 at a wavelength of 560 mμ.

In either case it should be remembered that such sets of curves are to be interpreted in terms of what would be seen if the *total energy* represented were so adjusted for *each* curve that each had the same *absolute* energy at the chosen wavelength.

There are, thus, many ways of plotting the energy distribution curves and of indicating the selective absorptions of materials. It must always be borne in mind, however, that all mean the same thing. Furthermore,

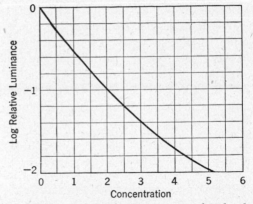

FIG. 17·14c Relative luminance curve for the dye of Fig. 17·14a.

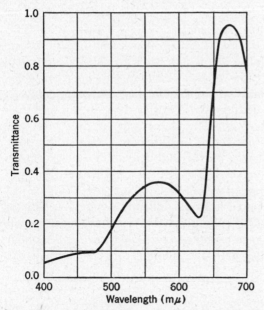

FIG. 17·14a Transmittance curves for hypothetical yellow dye at unit concentration.

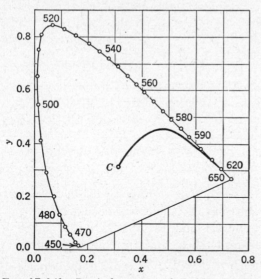

FIG. 17·14b Beer's law trace of the dye of Fig. 17·14a.

it must be remembered that the eye adds up the absolute energy at each wavelength and sees the whole relative to the visual adaptation level. For this reason the *relative*

curves of Fig. 3·5 and of Fig. 17·22 are most like what is seen, provided intensity adjustments are possible. When two colorants are seen under conditions in which no intensity adjustments are possible, as in reflecting materials in normal surroundings, such readjustments are confusing and it may be better to use straight percentage transmittance curves like those of Fig. 17·18. In any case it is the *answer* which is important and no method of plotting will act as a substitute for knowledge of the subject.

It was mentioned that the density method of plotting has many advantages aside from the possibility of covering a greater range in a small space. It may be well to note some of these advantages before considering further the properties of concentration series and of colorant mixtures. It is one of the properties of logarithms that if two numbers are multiplied, the logarithm of the resulting product is equal to the sum of the logarithms of the two numbers. Thus $2 \times 4 = 8$, log $2 = 0.3$, log $4 = 0.6$ and log $8 = 0.9$. Beer's law states that an increase in concentration above unity is the equivalent of multiplying all the transmissions by themselves a number of times equal to the increase in *unit* concentration. In terms of density this becomes simply a multiplication of the density by this figure at every wavelength. For example, suppose at a given concentration and wavelength the density is 0.7. If the concentration is doubled, all densities double and this one becomes 1.4. If the concentration is increased 50 percent, the density

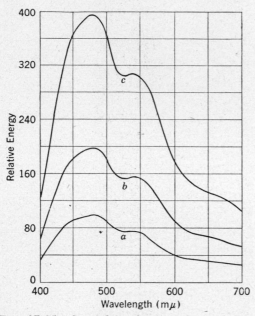

FIG. 17·15 Spectral-distribution curves of light from Illuminant *C* after having passed through a blue-green dye of arbitrary concentration. Curves (*b*) and (*c*) show the result of increasing the intensity of the incident energy by a factor of two and four respectively over that for (*a*).

is increased 50 percent to 1.05, etc. In other words, the density is linearly proportional to the concentration or to the thickness as was noted earlier. Density curves (for monochromatic radiations), therefore, have a simple relation to concentration or thickness.

Another valuable property is due to the same fact and is perhaps even more important. If light is made to pass through two or more colorants, the net effect of all of them may be determined by simple addition of the densities of each at corresponding wavelengths. This is a much easier process to visualize than multiplication, and once one is familiar with density curves it is easier to see what will happen when colorants are mixed if they are represented by density curves rather than by transmittance curves. The same pair of dyes and their subtractive mixtures are shown as transmittance curves in Fig. 17·23, and as density curves in Fig. 17·24. Again the warning is necessary, however, that the resulting density curve is more difficult to interpret visually *as a color* than the transmission curve and requires much more experience and familiarity with the method. In the last analysis

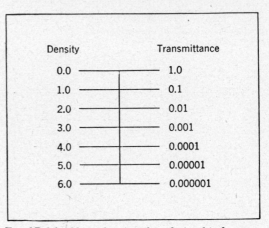

FIG. 17·16 Chart showing the relationship between density and transmittance.

the method of plotting involves convenience only, but the student of color *must* be able to understand the methods used if he is to read the technical literature on the subject intelligently.

SPECIFIC MIXTURE PAIRS

The rest of this chapter is concerned with the subtractive mixture of colorants and the expression of these mixtures by colorimetric methods. As in the earlier part of the chapter, the ICI diagram will be used. In accordance with the foregoing discussion the absorptions of the dyes involved may be shown either as transmittance or density.

tains light in this region of the spectrum. Whichever way the matter is considered it is essential to keep in mind constantly that there is little relation between the mixture

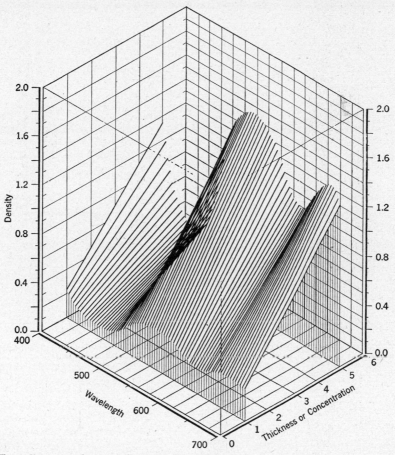

FIG. 17·17 Three-dimensional diagram graphically showing the relationship between wavelength, thickness or concentration, and density for dye.

The light passed by two or more colorants acting simultaneously or successively is described properly in physical terms by saying that it consists of the remainder of the light of the source after each colorant has subtracted its characteristic share of the energy. In mixture pairs it is also convenient at times to think of it as the *mutual* transmission of the two provided the source con-

color produced and the colors of the colorants themselves. This point has already been emphasized but it is of interest to note and illustrate the extent to which it is true. In theory, at least, it is possible to have a color of any hue which *also* has any, arbitrarily set, relative energy at any wavelength. It is possible, therefore, to design transmission curves for two dyes so that each of them

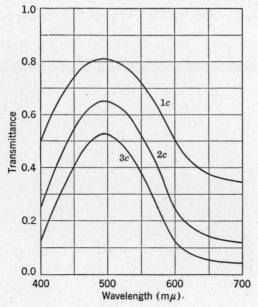

FIG. 17·18 Transmittance curves for the dye of Fig. 17·15 at three concentrations.

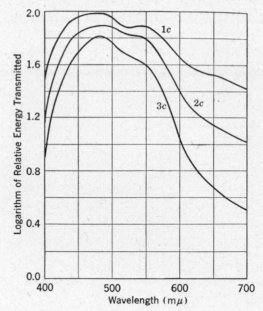

FIG. 17·20 Logarithms of the relative energy distributions of Fig. 17·19.

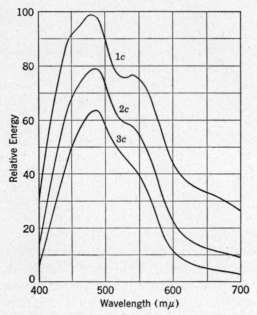

FIG. 17·19 Relative energy of ICI Illuminant C after it has passed through the dye concentrations as shown in Fig. 17·18.

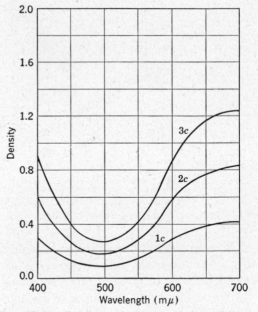

FIG. 17·21 Densities of the dye of Fig. 17·18 at three concentrations.

will have any color that we please and at the same time have identical transmissions at a given wavelength. In this way colorants giving *any* two colors may be made to yield

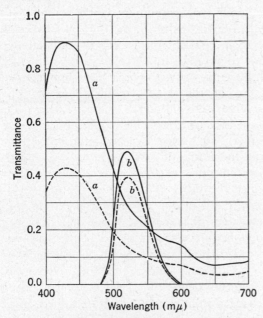

FIG. 17·22 Spectral transmittance curves for two filters, (a) Wratten Filter No. 78 and (b) Wratten Filter No. 58A. Solid lines show transmittance adjusted so that transmittance of each filter is the same at 560 mμ, while the dotted lines show the transmittances before adjustment.

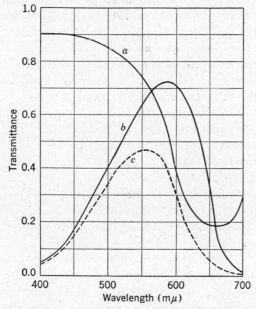

FIG. 17·23 Two dyes (a) and (b) and their mixture (c) plotted in terms of transmittance.

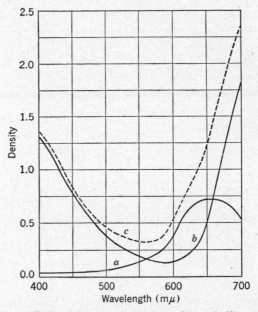

FIG. 17·24 The same two dyes, (a) and (b), as shown in Fig. 17·23, and their mixture, (c), plotted in terms of density.

any third hue when mixed. This broad generalization applies only to hue, or more strictly, to dominant wavelength, but it applies over a surprisingly great range of colors if total transmission is not important. In some practical instances, of course, the result could be obtained only at exceedingly low total transmittances.

The transmittance curves labeled *a* and *b* in Fig. 17·25, for example, represent calculated spectrophotometric characteristics of two dye solutions at a concentration which may be arbitrarily taken as unity. At this concentration the respective dyes individually transmit quantities of blue and yellow light from Illuminant C which are complementary to each other, that is, when light transmitted by *a* is mixed with light transmitted by *b*, Illuminant C of identical intensity for each being the source, the resultant radiation will again match Illuminant C for chromaticity.

To the person unfamiliar with dye characteristics it might seem logical on this basis to expect that a one-to-one mixture of the blue and yellow dyes in various concentrations would yield a series of neutral solutions varying only in density. That this is not the case, however, is illustrated graphically in Fig. 17·26.

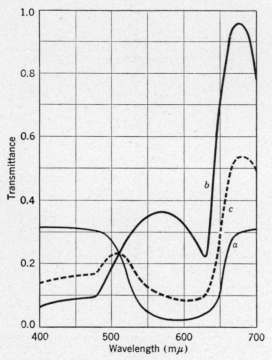

FIG. 17·25 Spectral transmittance curves for an (a) blue and (b) yellow dye at unit concentrations which, when illuminated with ICI Illuminant C, produce lights which are additively complementary. The broken curve (c) gives the transmittance characteristics of a one-to-one mixture of the dyes, also at unit concentration.

In this diagram the heavy curved lines extending from the illuminant point are the chromaticity loci respectively of the concentration series of the blue dye and of the yellow dye and are identical in nature to the Beer's law series of Fig. 17·8. The points labeled B and Y on these loci represent the chromaticities of unit concentrations of each. By combining equal volumes of the individual dye solutions at unit concentration one obtains a solution containing the dyes in a one-to-one ratio, and the solid curve labeled 1/1 is the chromaticity locus of the concentration series of this solution, i.e., it is the locus of the dyes held in a constant one-to-one ratio to each other, but varied in concentration. If a one-to-one mixture of the two dyes yielded neutrals, this curve would be non-existent since the locus of the concentration series would fall at the illuminant point on the diagram. It is seen, however, that a one-to-one mixture does not give a neutral, but instead that it varies from the illuminant point through blue-green, blue, and purple to a very deep red as the concentration is changed from zero to a limiting value, which in this case is twelve times unity.

The rough prediction of the mixture color of the dyes in ratios other than one-to-one is, however, often possible with the accuracy of the prediction depending upon the ratio of the dyes to each other as well as upon the concentration of the dye solution. At low concentrations and high ratios the effect of the lesser dye may be small, and the mixture color may fall close to that of the dominant dye. At high concentrations, however, the relation between dye ratio, the color of the mixture constituents, and the color of the mixture again is very small, and the mixture may assume a chromaticity very different from that of either dye. This property of dye mixtures is also shown in Fig. 17·26 in which has also been plotted the chromaticity loci of the concentration series of blue-to-yellow dye ratio of three to one and one to three.

If a sufficient number of constant-dye-ratio concentration series are plotted for any two dyes, it is possible by connecting the chromaticity points for equal concentrations of all the mixtures to obtain a smooth line representing the chromaticity locus of the two dyes at a constant concentration but at varying dye ratio.

These constant-concentration lines have

duced by varying the ratio of the two dyes at that particular concentration through all possible values.

To summarize briefly, it is seen that the

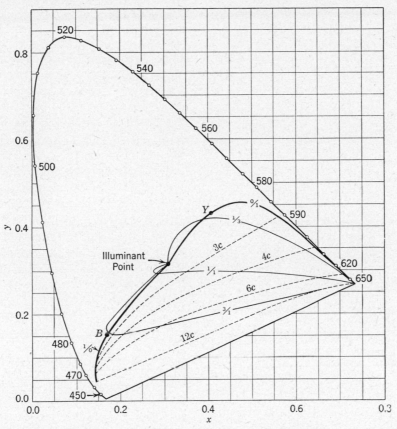

Fig. 17·26 An ICI chromaticity plot of blue and yellow dyes at various concentrations both individually and in mixture of various ratios. The heavy solid lines represent chromaticity loci of a concentration series of the dyes individually. The light solid lines are the same chromaticity loci for the dyes mixed at various constant ratios with the fractional labels on these lines representing the constant blue-to-yellow ratio for that series. The broken lines represent chromaticity loci of constant total dye concentration for the various dye combinations.

been drawn in broken form for four different concentrations in Fig. 17·26. By starting at the intersection of a constant-concentration locus and the constant-ratio locus of the pure blue dye and continuing along the former line to its intersection with the locus of the pure yellow dye one can note the complete series of colors which would be pro-

diagram incorporates both the physical variables in a two-dye mixture, that is, the effect on the chromaticity for changes in both concentration and composition of the mixture are shown. Although it is rare that either the constant-concentration or constant-ratio lines are straight, the fact that their curvature is usually small over most of their range combined with the practice of plotting a relatively large number of them enables one to interpolate at points between them with acceptable accuracy. Thus from a diagram of this type one can tell at a glance the total gamut of colors which can be produced by the two dyes in any proportion and at any concentration within the upper limit

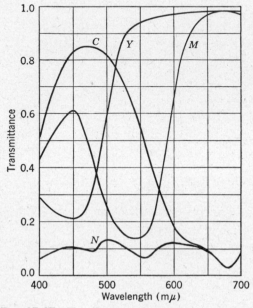

Fig. 17·27 Transmittance curves of a typical set of three dyes used in a modern color photographic process.

set by computation, and also, theoretically at least, one can closely determine the actual concentration and composition of the dye mixture necessary to reproduce a particular chromaticity.

Such a diagram for any given dyes is usually called an ICI grid for the dye system. Diagrams of this type are understandably confusing to the beginner, but they are none the less significant and manifest considerable utility in comparative dye studies and practical color problems.

The blue and yellow dyes just considered were hypothetical and the ICI mixture grid

was computed mathematically. When considering real dye mixtures it is also possible to determine a grid if actual physical concentration changes in conjunction with spectrophotometric measurements are used, and this may often be the only one which gives usable results.

In work with real colorants such extremes as have been illustrated may seldom be met but the principle illustrated is of universal validity. A very large number of dyes have high transmission at long wavelengths, and red is a common mixture color at high concentrations. Dyes ordinarily have only one, or at most, two absorption peaks in the spectrum, and these peaks usually grade off rather gradually in both directions. Even so, the trace representing the mixture of two of them is usually far from the straight line between the two.

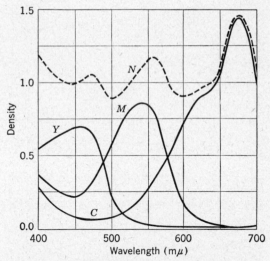

Fig. 17·28 Density curves of the dyes whose transmittance curves are given in Fig. 17·27.

The usefulness of the dye grid is in no way limited to two-dye mixtures but may easily be extended to polydye combinations by considering the dyes in pairs. In color photography the usual practice is to investigate three-dye mixtures, the addition of the extra dye greatly extending the range of producible colors with a given illuminant. Such a three-dye grid is shown in Fig. 17·29 for the three dyes shown in Fig. 17·27. The of the colorants is of equal importance. When this total is taken into account, a very different picture sometimes emerges, for as the concentration increases the luminous

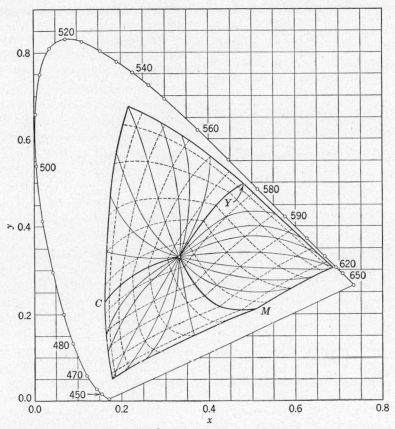

Fig. 17·29 Three-dye grid computed for the three dyes given in Fig. 17·27. Each solid line represents a constant proportion of two dyes with varying concentrations whereas each dotted line represents a constant amount of one dye and a varying amount of another.

densities of these dyes are shown in Fig. 17·28. This is a conventional three-color combination which will produce gray in suitable proportions and will produce all dominant wavelengths at any purity up to that indicated by the boundaries of the figure.

So far only the chromaticity of the mixture has been considered. In any practical instance the total luminous transmittance of mixtures which determines the brightness

transmittance often decreases rapidly. Figure 17·30, for example, is a plot of the logarithm of the luminous transmittance of the one-to-one dye mixture concentration series shown in Fig. 17·26 which may be taken as representative of the brightness distribution throughout the grid.

It is seen that whereas the JCI diagram indicates a great range in purity and hue, in actual fact such a series would be so dark over most of its range under normal viewing conditions that it would appear black and of little importance. Many such series would be dark as was shown also in Figs. 17·9 to 17·14. Such results lead one to the more or less valid generalization that, whereas it is possible to make the ICI traces of a single colorant or mixture of colorants follow almost any path on the ICI diagram, the actual colors that would be seen from such a series would be increasingly darker as the colorants were called upon to perform more tricks.

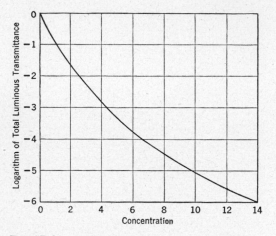

FIG. 17·30 Logarithmic plot of the total luminous transmittance of the concentration series of the one-to-one mixture of the blue and the yellow dyes of Fig. 17·26.

PRACTICAL LIMITATIONS

Whereas the theoretical limitations on the results of dye mixtures are very few, the practical limitations are many and exacting. If dyes are mixed whose traces follow complex colorimetric sequences, the result, expected or not, will be only a dark brown or a black, unless the viewing conditions are so designed as to make the actual transmitted light apparent to the eye at its normal adaptation levels. It is not surprising, therefore, that to the artist and the dyer of textiles, colorant mixture "laws" appear simpler than they really are. A mixture that produces an unexpected or unusual result is simply thrown aside and more useful pairs are sought. The net result is a fictitious appearance of simplicity for the whole subject.

This apparent simplicity has led to endless and unavailing disputes over the last half century concerning the nature of the "true primaries" for this and that purpose. Starting with the pioneer work of Young and of Helmholtz on the results of additive mixture and the fact that the maximum range of mixed additive colors can be produced by red, green, and blue lights, workers in *subtractive* fields have felt that the theory left much to be desired. It is just as apparent to a painter that what the physicist would call cyan, magenta, and yellow *colorants* will give the maximum range of colors on mixture. Thanks to the confusion of terminology by which a bluish cyan becomes "blue" and a reddish magenta becomes "red," it appears that the whole controversy has centered around green vs. yellow. Actually, as this book has attempted to demonstrate, there is not the slightest cause for argument between the two groups. They are simply, and sometimes plainly, talking about two quite different subjects. When the artist mixes his blue and yellow to make green, he is performing a very different operation from that of the scientist who produces a yellow by additively projecting red and green. For that matter both operations are different from that of the psychologist who surrounds a gray with green so that we see the gray as magenta. The chief reason the effect produced by the psychologist is not confused with the others lies in the fact that we do not call it a "mixture," although, heaven forbid, it really might be considered a mixture of sensations due to adaptation.

When the artist talks of "primaries," therefore, he is employing the word in a very different sense from the sense in which the physicist uses it when he talks of additive mixtures. This does not mean, however, that the concepts with which the artist works are any less valid or important. We must not make the mistake of applying to his concepts rules which have been established for the other type of mixture. The artist conventionally arranges his colors around a color circle. In this circle he considers that his hues are more or less evenly spaced. He realizes that saturation varies with the colors as the hue changes, but he thinks of this as a property of his colorants and not as a failure of his system. Blue is inherently dark, yellow very bright, and reds and greens are intermediate. He is not contradicted in this view either by the colors of nature or by those of the spectrum, and if a color exceeds the apparent saturation of his palette he thinks of this as a failure of the colors at his disposal and yearns after the "perfect palette" that would permit him to range over all the splendors he sees before him. In this viewpoint he is both logical and practical, and the Ostwald system of color nomenclature appeals to him the more for its very defects in that it appears to him the way he sees his own problems.

The color circle, thus, is the obvious arrangement for the artist. He must lay out his palette, and since blue joins red through magenta and purple, the ends must tie together. He is also confronted with the problem of complementaries. Since to his practical eye, these show the greatest color opposition or contrast, it is also only logical that they should be opposite in the circle. This arrangement involves some little compromise on equal hue spacing but turns out to be the most important consideration. His color circle is then complete. He must now shade the colors down to gray or black and up to white. The former gives him a series in brightness, the latter a series in saturation, just as does the Ostwald system, and he finds many suggestive harmonies on the way. The "catch," if it may be so called, comes in the fact that, for a given series using given pigments, he finds no simple relations to guide him on his way. As will be seen in the next chapter, mixture of black with white is likely to produce blue or perhaps yellow; addition of white to blue is apt to produce a higher saturation; mixture of cyan with yellow may produce one kind of green but is just as likely to produce another, etc. All these effects are peculiar properties of the particular colorants he is accustomed to using. To work with them it is necessary that he learn their individual idiosyncrasies. The trained artist, however, is a past master at the game and produces the result he desires with a twist of the wrist which is the envy of his less trained adherents. From the present standpoint it is necessary to inquire just what he is really doing.

In the first place it is apparent that the artist must necessarily compensate for the particular mixture series his particular colorants follow, and this is simply a matter of familiarity. In the second place and more important, it is necessary that he have some definite goal, some preconceived notion of the color he desires to produce. These aims may come from the color circle he imagines or from the object at which he is looking, but ultimately in any event they are psychological in nature. He tries to place on his paper or his canvas the *particular* color which he has in his mind's eye. To find the color *roughly* he follows certain empirical rules. To find it *exactly* he follows exclusively the dictates of his experience. It becomes worth while, therefore, to examine briefly the origin of these "rough" rules, and leave to the next chapter consideration of the causes for the necessary refinements.

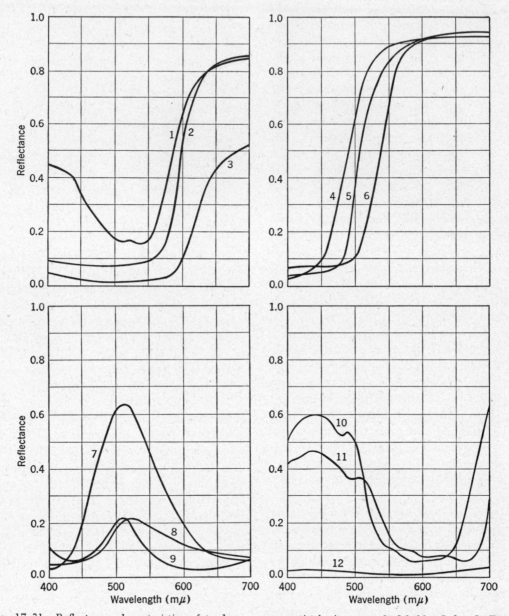

Fig. 17·31 Reflectance characteristics of twelve common artists' pigments: 1. Madder Lake, 2. English Vermilion, 3. Alizarin Crimson, 4. Zinc Yellow, 5. Chrome Yellow Medium, 6. Cadmium Yellow Medium, 7. Emerald Green, 8. Chrome Green Medium, 9. Viridian, 10. Cobalt, 11. Cerulean, 12. Prussian Blue. (N. F. Barnes, *Journal of the Optical Society of America,* Vol. 29, pp. 208–214, 1939.)

MIXTURES OF COMMON PAINTS

Most common colorants are characterized by rather broad, gradually sloping reflectance or transmittance curves. Furthermore these curves generally have only a single, or at most, a double peak. Reflectance curves for twelve common artists' oil paints are given in Fig. 17·31. Those for other media such as water colors are sometimes more abrupt; these represent the character of the reflectance curves of paints used by the artist who works in permanent colors. Mixtures of such colorants to a first approximation are quite safely predictable. It is apparent that a mixture of cyan and yellow will *necessarily* produce a green. Just what green is not predictable, but it will be green. If the cyan tends toward blue it will, in general, be a bluer green. If the yellow tends toward orange it will be a yellower green, etc. In other words, as soon as practical colorants with broad absorptions are used, the *general* colors of mixtures *may* be predicted roughly from the colors of the components, and rules develop accordingly. When an attempt is made to tie down these rules to a precise system, however, the person working with one set of "primaries" develops a different set of rules from the one who works with another set. Thus one pair of cyan and yellow colorants will give a good green, another set much like it gives an exceedingly bad one, etc. All colorants follow the simple rules of *subtractive* mixtures, but they are not predictable from the visual *colors* involved.

BIBLIOGRAPHY

Barnes, Norman F. "A Spectrophotometric Study of Artists' Pigments." *Technical Studies in the Field of the Fine Arts* (Harvard University), 7:120–138 (1939).

Eastman Kodak Company. *Wratten Light Filters*, 17th ed. Rochester, N. Y.: Eastman Kodak Co. 1945.

Wright, W. D. *The Measurement of Colour*. London: Adam Hilger, Ltd. 1944. Chapter IV.

Paints and Pigments

CHAPTER XVIII

IN the preceding chapter the results of mixing two or more transparent colored materials were considered. It was shown that they could be predicted from the spectrophotometric curves of the materials involved but not from their visual colors. When an attempt is made to extend this to non-transparent materials, however, it is found that simple laws are no longer followed and that precise calculation is generally impossible. This is particularly unfortunate as some of the largest users of colored materials deal exclusively with colorants of this type. Almost all commercial paints and the great majority of artists' materials are in this category. Water colors and colored varnishes are usually sufficiently clear to permit fairly accurate calculation, but home and floor paints are designed deliberately to hide the surface over which they are painted and the artists' tempera and pastel colors are naturally opaque. Artists' oil colors cover the complete range from transparent to opaque but for the most part are quite opaque except in very thin layers.

NON-TRANSPARENT MIXTURES

When a colorant tends to hide the surface over which it is coated, rather than merely change its *selective* absorption for light, we are dealing with a material which will not follow in detail the principles laid down in the previous chapter. Although the principles which are involved are quite clearly understood and will be set forth in some little detail in the present chapter, it is well to start with the realization that the subject is so complex that calculation is no longer a simplification. In the extreme cases and whenever a precise mixture color is necessary, nothing will take the place of intimate familiarity with the *particular* colorants involved. The artist and painter must know what results he will obtain when he mixes any two of the paints of the particular brand he is using; the same pigments compounded by a different manufacturer may very well give different results. Therefore, all such mixtures must be made empirically, small amounts of one or the other being added until the desired color is obtained. For this reason the artist works in some sort of scheme which is expressed in terms of the visual result itself, and not in terms of the proportions of the colors that he must mix to get this result. In this process, however, he is aided greatly by knowledge of certain more or less general considerations which help him achieve his goal more quickly.

For this reason and for the inherent interest of the subject, we shall deal with these general principles broadly without attempting a study of the possibility of calculating the results of such mixtures.

PAINT

We may well start our survey of paint mixtures by a more or less detailed consideration of the properties of a single paint as its make-up is changed.

A paint ordinarily consists of solid matter ground up into fine particles in some transparent medium such as oil. To these are added other liquids to produce the physical properties necessary for its application. As far as the color and color-mixture properties are concerned, it is necessary to consider only the two general types of material, the solids and the liquids. There are three general possibilities from the color standpoint: (a) the particles are colored and transparent, (b) the particles are colored and opaque, (c) the particles are opaque and colorless but the liquid is colored. All possible combinations of these exist, and there is a fourth source of color if the particles are ground so fine that they are colloidal and scatter the light selectively. Such materials appear transparent and were treated in Chapter VI under the physics of color. The particles to be considered here are moderately large compared to colloids and can be seen readily under a microscope.

There are two general kinds of opaque particle which are used in paints. To the first of these is given the name "pigments" (although this is also used for the transparent variety). They consist of opaque colored solids. To the other is given the name "lake." Lakes consist of an opaque material, usually white, but sometimes itself colored, which has the property of adsorbing to its surface colored materials such as dyes or colloidal pigments which are themselves frequently transparent. In this way the surface of the original material becomes selectively reflecting but the paint as a whole has properties given to it by the opaqueness of this material. It does not matter greatly so far as color is concerned whether the selective action is due to adsorbed material, or whether the particle is opaque and selectively reflecting.

The percentage reflectance at a *boundary* between two materials (in this case oil and pigment) depends on the relative index of refraction of the two media. This dependence was seen earlier in the case of the Christensen filters. If there is no difference in index, there will be no reflection as far as the boundary is concerned. Such *surface* reflection from the particle is always *non-selective*, and only the light which passes the boundary and returns is *selectively* absorbed. If there is a large difference in index between the oil and the *outer* surface of the particle there will be relatively high nonselective reflection from this boundary. Light that crosses the boundary and enters the particle, however, will be selectively reflected through the boundary, and color will result. Increase in the ratio of indices of the two materials, therefore, will decrease the amount of color produced. Some liquid mixtures used for paints on drying show relatively large changes of index which usually increase as the drying proceeds. Since the index of the particles is almost always higher than that of the oil, the selective action usually increases with drying so that the color becomes intensified, although frequently this effect is offset by a change in the outer surface of the paint which may occur at the same time. With water colors, whether composed of colloidal materials or in true solution, the reverse process takes place since the index of water is greater than air and evaporation of the water *increases* the difference at the boundary and causes a *loss* of selective action of the material.

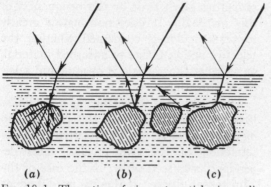

FIG. 18·1 The action of pigment particles in modifying light in different ways.

The situation is reversed if the paint is intended to be white since maximum non-selective reflection is desired from the particles and the greater the difference in index the greater this reflection becomes; the effect

three possible paths, depending on conditions. It may (*a*) enter the particle and be absorbed or (*b*) be reflected out toward the outer boundary of the paint or (*c*) be reflected to another particle where the possibilities are repeated. These three are shown separately in the figure. Which of the latter two will predominate depends, of course, on the size and the number of particles per unit volume of the paint. The first variable to consider, therefore, is the concentration of particles in the medium. An attempt to illustrate the effect of concentration has been sketched in Fig. 18·2 in which a few of the possible light paths have been indicated for three concentrations. Increase in concentration decreases the distance between particles and accordingly increases multiple reflections between particles. Since there is selective action at each reflection, the total selective action is greatly increased and, in general, the saturation of the color produced is increased. If the absorption of the particles is sufficiently high, however, saturation

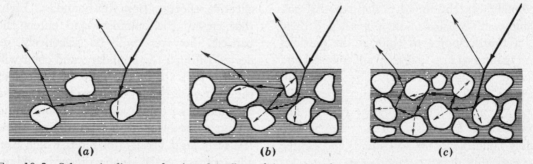

FIG. 18·2 Schematic diagram showing the effect of increasing the pigment concentration in a medium.

is negligible, however, if the particles are truly opaque and of large size.

The characteristics of the paint as a whole may be considered next. A greatly enlarged section showing opaque particles suspended in a medium is shown in Fig. 18·1. Light entering such a mixture through its outer surface strikes a particle and follows one of

may actually be *decreased* since a higher percentage of light is reflected out of the medium from the particles near the surface. Thus the statement is verified which was made earlier that the situation in paints is so complex physically that prediction of results is exceedingly difficult without intimate knowledge of the particular paint. The statement will apply also to nearly all the variables discussed below.

EFFECT OF SUPPORT

It is apparent that the transmission of such a layer will depend on the extent to which the light is able to penetrate the range of particles and reach the back surface of the material in which they are suspended. In a dilute paint containing relatively few particles per unit of volume there will be relatively high transparency, and a fair percentage of the light will reach the rear surface. The same amount of light will be transmitted if the particles are the same in *number* but smaller in size. The amount of light transmitted, therefore, depends on particle size, concentration, and thickness. The effectiveness of this transmission as far as apparent color is concerned will depend, however, on the layer on which the paint is coated. If this layer is black, it will absorb the light; if white, it will reflect nearly all of it up into the paint; or if it is selectively absorbing, some wavelengths will be reflected more than others. The extremes are given by black and by white surfaces and these are considered next.

On a black surface the light which reaches an observer consists entirely of that which is reflected outward by the particles of the paint. The larger the size of the particles, the greater their concentration, the higher their surface reflections, and the greater the thickness, the larger is the amount of light that is reflected and seen as color. On the other hand, if the paint is coated on a white-reflecting surface all the transmitted light is returned toward the observer and thus passes again through the paint in his direction. Similar considerations apply, of course, to a selectively reflecting surface, except that the facts are different at each wavelength.

It is instructive, therefore, to consider a pigment paint coated first on a white and then on a black surface and to see the effect of the variables in the two instances. Suppose the paint is coated on a black surface. Increased particle size, increased concentration, increased reflecting power, and increased thickness will increase the total light reflected outward from the paint. The extent to which it makes no difference whether the paint is coated on a black surface is called the "covering" or "hiding" power of the paint. If a paint reflects upward to such an extent that it does not matter whether it is coated on a black or on a white surface, it may be said to "hide" completely or to have 100 percent "covering power." To the extent to which the black or the white will "show through" it has less of this property.

On a white surface the reflected light passes through the paint twice and therefore is subjected twice to the multiple reflections which increase the saturation of the color. It is not unusual therefore for a paint to show a *higher* saturation when painted over a white surface than when painted over a black.

Both the hiding power of the paint and the saturation of the color, of course, are affected by the thickness of the coating. The greater the thickness the greater the chances for complete absorption or reflection upward and, accordingly, the less the chance that any light will find its way through to the support. On a black support increased thickness is more or less comparable to increased concentration or particle size. On a white support increased thickness at low concentration may give a much more saturated color than increased concentration because the low concentration decreases the reflection from upper layers.

The maximum concentration, of course, is reached when the pigment is used without a liquid medium. In this event the pigment particles touch each other and, if they are truly opaque, no light is reflected except that from the outer layer of pigment particles. Pastel colors, for example, in sufficient thickness to cover the surface physically hide it completely. The customary low saturation of such colors is due to the lack of multiple internal reflection, most of the light coming exclusively from the upper layer of particles. The other extreme is found in paints that have complete transparency due to small particle size. These paints are colorless on a black surface and colored on white. Their characteristics were covered in the previous chapter.

TRANSPARENT VERSUS OPAQUE PARTICLES

This discussion has been restricted to opaque particles. Suppose now that the particles owe their selective action not to reflection but to transmission. Colored glass ground up in oil would be an example. This situation is complicated by the fact that the only mechanism by which light can turn around and head toward the observer is non-selective reflection at the outer surface of the particles. The result is obvious. Such paints would have very low hiding properties. Their hiding properties would be increased by an increase in the difference in index between the particles and the medium but would be decreased as the particles became larger because the ratio of surface to the volume which they occupied would be decreased. In such media the effect of the surface on which they were coated would be large, and, in general, they would occupy a position intermediate between the transparent solutions of the previous chapter and the opaque pastels just mentioned. Increasing the thickness would increase the saturation on a white support but have little effect on a black. On white, however, a great

thickness would absorb all the light and hence appear black.

We come, then, to the third type—that of reflecting particles in a colored medium. An illustration would be an opaque white pigment in an oil carrying a dissolved dye. Again more light will be reflected outward if the difference in index is great and if the concentration is high. Greater saturation, however, may sometimes be produced if the paint is coated on a white support than if the concentration is increased because by this means the light which is seen has traveled farther through the selectively absorbing medium. A range in thickness on white actually may or may not have any effect, depending on the extent to which the opaque material permits light to pass through the medium twice. If no such light is visible there will, obviously, be no change with thickness. Under the same conditions there will also be no change if the paint is on black rather than on white.

EFFECT OF OUTER SURFACE

It is apparent also that the outer surface of the paint medium may play a large part in the final result. Consider the single example of a paint so applied that it has a high glossy surface. As noted before, this paint will show low saturation regardless of the selective action below the surface if it is viewed in a room with highly illuminated white walls and ceiling. On the other hand, if it is viewed by a single light close by and in such a position that no light is reflected directly toward the observer it will show maximum selective action. Paints that dry down with a diffusely reflecting matte surface, however, will have a large percentage of added white light regardless of the position or the nature of the illuminant. Often these purely surface effects are more important than the depth and concentration effects just considered.

In addition to this external effect of the surface there is the frequently large effect of multiple reflection internally. As pointed out in Chapter V, only about 75 percent of the light diffusely reflected under a glossy surface passes directly into the air. The remainder is reflected into the medium and reaches the surface again only after traversing the same path as that followed by the light from the illuminant itself. The varnishing of a painted surface, therefore, may substantially change the selective action of that surface. If an initially rough surface with rather highly diffuse outer surface reflection is replaced by a smooth, glossy varnish surface, the effect may be surprisingly great. Perhaps the most familiar example is the darkness of a spot of water on a concrete sidewalk or pavement, the water substituting a glossy surface for the previous matte one. The effect on oil and pastel colors is no less great but somewhat less familiar.

It is apparent from the characteristics of the individual colors that mixtures will not follow the rules for subtractive colorants that were stated in the previous chapter. However, such mixtures are not completely unpredictable. The subtractive action of a paint is described by its spectrophotometric reflectance curve, and to a *first approximation* it will continue to act in this manner in mixtures. The point is simply that for mixtures no such exact prediction of the result may be made as for clear transparent colorants. In some instances the result of a mixture may be quite close to the expected color and in others it may be quite different. One seldom encounters a mixture that goes in a different direction from that indicated by the two curves.

The simplest type of mixture from the viewpoint of color is made by the addition of white or black to a color originally at full intensity. It may be pointed out that we meet white as a colorant here for the first time. There is no such thing as a transparent white. By definition, a white paint is a non-selective, *diffusing* reflector or transmitter. In particular, white paint consists of a large number of particles of highly reflecting white material ground up in oil or other carrying medium. To have good hiding power the concentration of particles must be high and the particles quite opaque. Addition of such particles to a colored paint produces a number of effects which can be considered separately but take place at the same time. Before discussing these systematically, however, we must consider briefly *why* white or black would be added to a paint. The answer of an expert in paint mixing would probably be that he wants to make the paint whiter or blacker, and this answer of course is literally true. For the present purpose, however, it is necessary to be a little more precise to see just what is expected. White and black, as we have seen, are relative terms and, in the case of transparent colorants, they exist only under certain conditions. Thus, if transparent colorants are seen in unrelated fields, i.e., if they are the only objects in the field of view and all other light is excluded, there is no such thing as a white or a black. The corresponding variables in these circumstances are saturation and brightness, but they are not *seen* as white content or black content of the color. They appear simply as *quantity* of colorant and *intensity* of light respectively. If, however, the same transparent colorants are viewed in ordinary surroundings so that they may be seen in relation to a diffuse white surface, the perception changes immediately to that of white and black *content* of the color.

The paint mixer, whether he is an artist or a house painter, since he always sees his colors in relation to natural objects and almost never in unrelated fields, thinks of colors in these terms. In addition, however, he knows that black and white neutralize each other so that by using both he can desaturate his colorants and at the same time control the apparent amount of added white. It is this direct perception of added white and black, of course, which has made the Ostwald system appeal to people who deal with mixtures of pigments. In the last analysis the painter is working with the psychological variables of color, and his results are interpretable directly in terms of hue, saturation, and lightness. To produce the desired color, however, he must deal with white and black as pigments. This is especially true if the final paint is to be one that has good hiding properties and therefore is more or less independent of the surface. The water-colorist can obtain decreased saturation by diluting his color with water because his colorants subtract from a constant white. The painter in oils has white as a variable and, although it may be argued that the final result may be the same *color* in water and oils, the techniques of arriving at the color may be so different as to make the two people involved think of the subject in a wholly different manner.

It is important to consider, therefore, the effects obtained when opaque white pigment is added to a paint with already good hiding properties. Physically, two things occur. First, the paint is diluted, and, second, highly reflecting but opaque particles are introduced throughout its thickness. ——

The dilution of the paint simply moves the original particles farther apart than they were before. If it is a lake or a pigment paint in a clear medium, this effect alone would tend to produce less color. If it is a paint with a colored oil and white particles, the dilution of this oil gives it less selective action per unit of total paint thickness and thus lowers the saturation in this instance also.

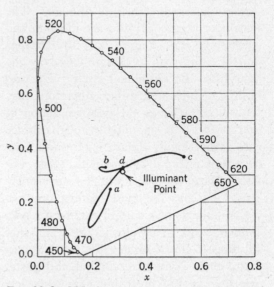

Fig. 18·3 ICI chromaticity traces of mixtures of (*a*) ultramarine blue, (*b*) viridian, and (*c*) cadmium orange, each mixed with (*d*) zinc white in varying proportions. The traces of the darker pigments, viridian and blue, show a distinct increase in excitation purity up to a limit as white is added to them, but upon the addition of more white they again are reduced in purity.

Addition of a white pigment tends to hold the total concentration of all particles constant for a paint of fairly high concentration but may greatly increase the concentration of a low-concentration paint. The opacity of the added white gives a paint good hiding properties. If hiding power was high before there will be little change; if not, there may be a large improvement. Such a change in hiding power may, of itself, tend to obscure light of high saturation which originally reached the observer from the depths of the paint. This effect would tend to desaturate the color. More important as a general effect is the fact that white particles introduce non-selective reflection throughout the whole depth of the paint. The maximum effect of this sort occurs at the top of the layer, where it causes a large increase in the percentage of light which

but absorbs nearly all the light so that little gets out.

These effects are illustrated in Fig. 18·3 which shows the ICI traces for several oil paints mixed with white. Coatings were of approximately uniform thickness on white paper and were made on cards dipped in suspensions of the pigments.

Similar considerations apply to the addition of black paint to a color, except that, in addition to the dilution and the obscuring of light from below, high non-selective absorption is introduced between the other particles. The result may be a considerable

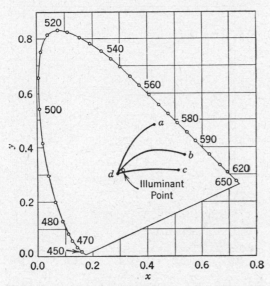

FIG. 18·4 ICI chromaticity traces of mixtures of (a) zinc yellow, (b) cadmium orange, (c) deep cadmium red, each mixed with (d) ivory black, in varying proportions. In all three cases the addition of black reduces the saturation of the mixture.

can pass through a thin layer only. This effect again is in the direction of desaturating the color. On the other hand, the presence of highly reflecting particles may greatly increase the chances that light which has struck a selectively absorbing particle will be "turned around" and reach the observer. If the paint is very dark to start with this effect may offset all the others; there is a distinct and sometimes quite large increase in saturation, particularly if the original paint, instead of having good hiding power because of the opacity of its particles, covers because it is so dark, that is, it is transparent

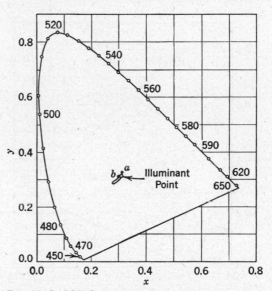

FIG. 18·5 ICI chromaticity trace of (a) zinc white, (b) lamp black mixed in varying proportions. As the black is added to the white the trace passes through the illuminant point into the blue region and then almost back to neutral.

decrease in the saturation of the color as well as a general darkening, because again the effect of the upper layers is increased over the lower and, in addition, there is a decrease in the amount of multiply reflected light which can leave the surface. ICI traces for a number of such mixtures are shown in Fig. 18·4; they were made under the same conditions as for the white.

An interesting situation arises when white is added to black with the intention of making gray. Two important properties of white and black pigments become apparent. Many white pigments are ground fine enough so that when they are diluted they show selective scattering of the same type as that which produces the blue of the sky. When diluted with a good black this property sometimes results in an amazingly pure blue color. This fact actually led Leonardo da Vinci to postulate that the blue of the sky was due to a mixture of the black of

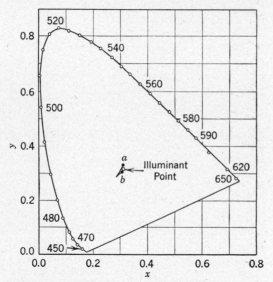

Fig. 18·6 ICI chromaticity trace of (a) zinc white mixed with (b) ivory black. As black is added the trace passes into the blue region, then reverses toward neutral.

outer space with the white of light. The other effect is due to the fact that many so-called blacks are not truly the non-selective absorbers that the term suggests but are really very dark, desaturated colors. When sufficiently diluted with white pigments which increase the internal multiple reflections the colors become apparent.

Two series of different blacks mixed with white are shown in Figs. 18·5 and 18·6.

COLORANT MIXTURES

When paints of different colors are mixed for the purpose of producing a new color,

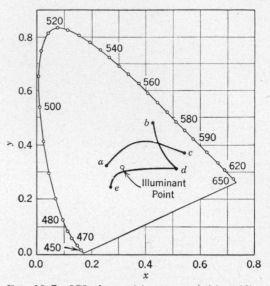

Fig. 18·7 ICI chromaticity trace of (a) viridian mixed with (c) cadmium orange, (b) zinc yellow mixed with (d) deep cadmium red, and (e) ultramarine blue mixed with (d) deep cadmium red in various proportions.

the situation becomes so complex that there is little point in attempting to consider the various possibilities in any great detail. The results will depend, obviously, on the absorption distribution of each paint with wavelength, on the nature of the paint with respect to the *way* in which it absorbs light, on the relative transparencies of the two paints, and on the nature of the surface over which the mixture is to be coated. In certain instances the mixture may follow the relatively simple laws of transparent subtractive colorants. In others the departure may be quite extreme. In any event, only knowledge based on experience with the actual colors will make possible any accurate prediction of the results. In Fig. 18·7 is shown a number of mixture traces for artists' oil paints. The curves which would have been followed if the paints had been transparent and obeyed Beer's law differ slightly from those shown.

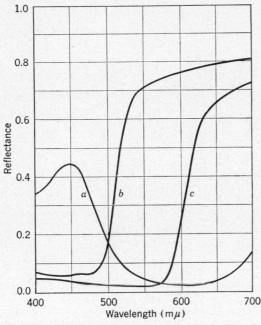

Fig. 18·8 Reflectance curves of (a) blue, (b) yellow, and (c) red powders.

There is one other possibility in pigment mixtures which is interesting to consider in passing. If the particles are themselves selectively reflecting and opaque and are used as *dry* powders, intimate mixture will distribute them uniformly throughout the mixture. If the top of such a layer is pressed until it is completely smooth, light will reach the observer only from the top layer of particles. Under these conditions the color formed will be the *additive* mixture of the two colors and will then become independent of the nature of the particular spectrophotometric curves of the individual pigments. A mixture of blue and yellow will

produce cyan or gray rather than green, for example. Some of this action is seen when pastel colors are mixed on a surface by rubbing them together. The effect is illustrated in Figs. 18·8, 18·9, and 18·10.

As we have pointed out many times the surface of a colorant plays a large part in the color which is observed under different conditions. Because paints in general have more body than other colorants and because the nature of their surfaces, to a large extent, is determined by the way in which they are applied, it is appropriate to consider these effects more quantitatively at this point.

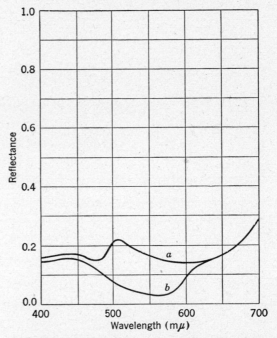

Fig. 18·9 Reflectance curves of mixtures of approximately equal amounts of (a) the blue and the yellow powders of Fig. 18·8 and (b) the red and the blue powders.

Paints may be so designed that they give either a glossy or a dull surface, and the possible range is very large. In addition the surface may be so applied that it is smooth or rough, it may have directional characteristics such as brush marks, or it may exist as small patches set at various angles with respect to the rest of the areas. Each of these surface types has its own peculiarities, and each affects in a different manner the colors that will be seen under different lighting conditions. Under all these conditions, however, the only effect involved is that of adding more or less white light to the colored light reflected from the body of the paint below the surface. Such white light as its only effect desaturates the color produced, as long as the illuminating light is white. The extent of this desaturation under quite ordinary circumstances, however, is seldom realized by the observer and may

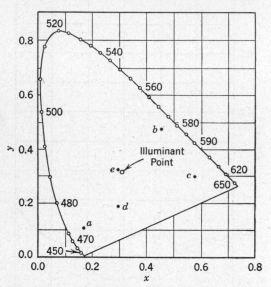

FIG. 18·10 Chromaticity plots of the powders of Figs. 18·8 and 18·9. Points (a), (b), and (c) are for the blue, the yellow, and the red powders respectively, (d) is the point for the red-plus-blue mixture and (e) for the yellow-plus-blue mixture.

result in a mixture which is quite different from that intended.

This desaturation was discussed in some detail in the previous chapter in connection with concentration series in transparent colorants. Its application to pigment mixtures may be described briefly by spectrophoto-

metric curves. Suppose two paints at a given concentration are described by the hypothetical curves of Fig. 18·11. These curves have included in them the white surface reflections of each surface. Suppose that each effective surface reflection is 5 percent (a not unreasonable figure even for

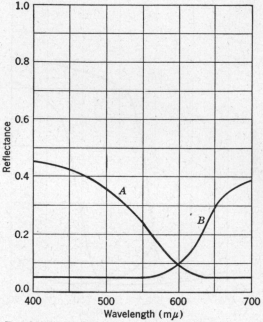

FIG. 18·11 Reflectance curves of deep red and blue paints with surface reflectance included.

a fairly glossy paint). The actual subtractive action of the paint below this surface is, therefore, represented by the curves of Fig. 18·12 calculated from the former curves by simply subtracting 5 percent at each wavelength. Now it is apparent that if these paints are mixed, the main reflection will fall in the region of overlap of the two, that is, around 600 millimicrons and that the total reflection will be quite low. The assumed mixture curve *below* the surface is that given as *a* in Fig. 18·13. Note that the scale has here been multiplied by 10 to show more clearly the shape of the curve. The maximum reflectance at any wavelength

288

is now less than 1 percent. If this paint is coated on a surface, the outer paint surface will again have a reflectance of 5 percent at each wavelength and this reflectance adds to the reflectance from below. The result is that shown in *b* of Fig. 18·13. It is at once apparent that this is a color of very low

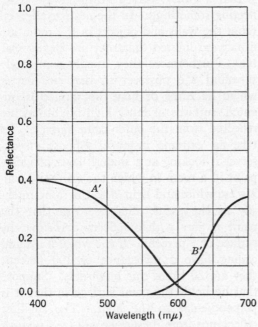

Fig. 18·12 Reflectance curves of the paints in Fig. 18·11 without surface reflectance.

saturation. The extent of the loss is shown in Fig. 18·14, in which the ICI points are given for the two paints with the surface reflection included (points A and B), the same without the surface reflection (points A′ and B′), and the same two conditions for the mixture color (points C and C′). Whereas the paints themselves had fairly saturated colors, the mixture color had *high* saturation below the surface but most of this was lost by addition of the surface reflection. This example may be generalized to the statement that all dark colors under a reflecting surface have low saturations if the observation conditions permit the surface

light to reach the observer. However, if such colors are so illuminated that the surface light does *not* reach the observer they may show very high saturations. This will be discussed further after a brief consideration of the magnitude of surface reflections in general and the conditions which control them.

Any glossy non-metallic surface will reflect non-selectively a portion of any light which falls on it. The laws involved are clear cut and fully understood. The angle which the reflected light makes with the surface is equal to that of the light falling on it but

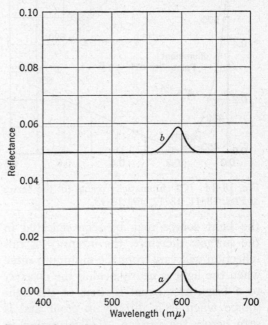

Fig. 18·13 Reflectance curves of a mixture of the paints, (*a*) without surface reflectance and (*b*) with surface reflectance.

on the opposite side of the perpendicular at that point. The percentage that is reflected varies slightly with wavelength but usually too little to be seen, and the total percentage reflected varies quite markedly with the angle the light makes with the surface. For glass and for most paint surfaces or the like, the reflection is of the order of 4 percent for light that falls vertically on the surface, and this percentage increases, at first slowly, and then more and more rapidly as the light falls more and more nearly parallel with the surface. When it just grazes the surface, there is 100 percent reflection. If such a surface is held so that

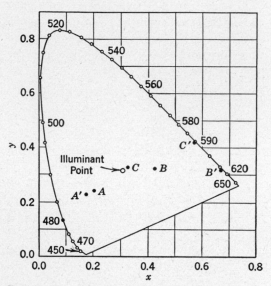

FIG. 18·14   ICI chromaticity points for the curves of Figs. 18·11, 18·12, and 18·13.

the light source may be seen reflected in the surface, therefore, the intensity of this reflection will vary from the minimum value when the light is nearly behind the observer to a brightness equal to that of the light source when it is directly in front and is seen *across* the surface. This variation in percentage of reflectance means that there is a corresponding variation in the amount of light which *penetrates* the surface and re-emerges to mix with the white light. The saturation of the color observed under these conditions, therefore, varies from a moderately high value to zero. If the reflection of the light source is not seen directly and *the surface is not reflecting any other light,* only the light from below the surface may

be seen, and saturation is at the maximum obtainable, although there may be some slight variation with the angle at which the light penetrates the paint. (This effect can become very large if the surface is *not* smooth and glossy.)

The point that is not ordinarily realized is that a glossy surface nearly always is reflecting something. In the ordinary lighted room the walls and objects in the room are usually so lighted that they are clearly visible. Furthermore they usually completely surround the observer so that no matter where he turns or how the surface is oriented, surfaces of fairly high brightness are reflected from the outer paint surface. To take an extreme instance, suppose an observer is looking at a smooth layer of glossy paint in a room in which the walls and ceiling are white and lighted to the same intensity as the paint. Suppose also that the paint is gray with a reflectance *below* the surface of 5 percent. If the white walls and ceiling have a reflectance of 100 percent they are 20 times this brightness. Suppose that he holds the paint surface so that it is perpendicular to the light. The smallest reflectance from its surface will be 4 percent and the total reflectance is now 9 percent. If he holds it at any other angle the reflection will be greater still. The difference will not be great in a gray because the change is seen as pure brightness and not as saturation, although 4 percent is the deepest glossy black that can be seen in such a room. If the paint is colored, however, and its *maximum* reflectance is 5 percent at any wavelength, it follows that 4 percent is the *lowest* reflectance at any wavelength regardless of the paint and low saturation results.

Under most conditions this type of reflection is not severe, and glossy paints in general show the highest saturations except when reflecting the light source directly. Even these, however, are seldom seen at the maximum saturation that they are capable of developing (directly lighted from the side in an otherwise completely dark room). If the surface is glossy but not smooth it may become impossible to place a light source so that it is not reflected directly from some part of the area. If the irregularities are small in area the directly reflected white light may easily reach 30 and 40 percent of the light falling on it. Under these conditions severe desaturation takes place.

The limiting case, a rough but glossy surface, is reached in a "matte" or "dull" paint. In such surfaces the irregularities are too small to be seen and are oriented at all possible angles. The reflection tends, therefore, to become independent of both the viewing and illuminating angles, and a more or less constant but high surface reflection is present under *all* conditions. In an extreme surface of this type the surface reflection may become as high as 50 percent.

In either the extreme type or the intermediate type, therefore, the percentage of white light added by the surface may affect profoundly the saturation of the observed color. In glossy paints this is controllable by the lighting conditions but in matte surfaces it tends to be constant and quite high.

These considerations are not purely academic and of interest solely to the person desiring to mix paints—they are of vital concern to all who illuminate or look at painted surfaces. Perhaps the clearest example is an artist's oil painting. When the artist paints his picture he *sees* his paints with the surface reflections dictated by the illumination condition he is using. He can vary the saturation of his colors by the *nature of the surface* which he produces with his brush and by the *angle* at which he places the various small areas. *Under any other conditions it is not the same picture* and not what he intended to paint. Areas of different texture and angle will have different saturation relations from those he saw when he applied the colors, unless he paints the whole picture smooth and flat, perhaps ending with a thick coat of varnish. Even then, however, the saturations of all colors, and particularly of the dark ones, will change if the painting is placed in a room lighted quite differently from the artist's studio. The same considerations to an even greater extent, of course, apply to viewing or photographing a painting by polarized light so that surface reflections are eliminated.

OTHER METHODS OF MIXING COLORS

Having considered the results of physically mixing colorants in the form of paints and the like, and having seen the effect of surface reflection on such mixtures, we must consider a number of other techniques by which colorants may be combined. Some of these have been considered for transparent colors in the previous chapters but require reconsideration here for paints. There are three types of paint mixtures other than those already considered: simple reflection of light from one surface to another, simple superposition of two or more layers, and juxtaposition of the colors in minute areas.

The first type, reflection of light successively from several surfaces, is identical for paints with superposition of transparent layers. The result may be predicted directly by calculation from the spectrophotometric curves, paint layers being no different in this respect from any selective reflector. The third type, juxtaposition of small areas, may be disposed of in like manner. As shown earlier, juxtaposed small colored areas that are too small to be seen by the eye mix additively like superimposed projected lights on a white screen. The often repeated statement that colorants mixed in this way have higher saturations is not true; most such techniques lead to distinctly desaturated colors obtainable equally well by direct mixture. Note, however, that other factors not considered here enter when the areas are large enough to be just seen as separate. (See Chapter VI.)

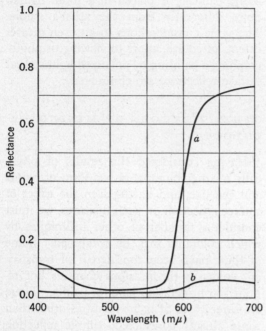

FIG. 18·15 Reflectance curves of alizarin crimson on glass over (a) a white background and (b) a black background.

The second type, however, superposition of paint layers, calls for careful consideration. A layer of paint, because of the particles that it contains, reflects light outward toward the surface from various depths, and the color that is seen is the mixture of the light from the various depths. Paints with good hiding or covering properties reflect upward all the light which falls on them, so that the color of such a paint is independent of the surface on which it is coated. To the extent that a paint as coated is transparent and *does* let light through, however, the color observed is affected by the layer beneath. If such a paint is quite transparent, the color seen approaches that of the subtractive mixture of the two colorants. The principles involved in the mixture, however, are somewhat different.

The curves of Fig. 18·15 show the reflectance curves for an artist's oil paint (alizarin crimson) coated in a layer of moderate thickness on glass and placed over (a) a white surface, and (b) a black surface. The reflection curve on the black background gives the distribution only of the light from the surface and that internally reflected. Coated on white, the transmitted light is reflected through the layer. In this second

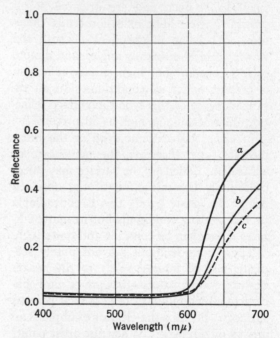

FIG. 18·16 Reflectance curves of alizarin crimson on white paper; (a) one, (b) two, and (c) three thicknesses.

passage, however, it is the absorption as it would be indicated by a transmission curve and not that indicated by the reflection curve on black which is added. Such a transmission curve is greatly affected by the thickness of the layer. Similar curves for three thicknesses of a thinner layer are shown in Fig. 18·16. Changes in thickness, therefore, change the color of the light reach-

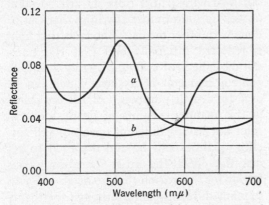

FIG. 18·17 Reflectance curves of (a) viridian coated over alizarin crimson, and (b) alizarin crimson coated over viridian.

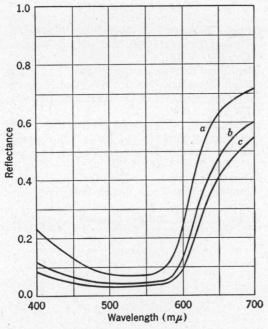

FIG. 18·18 Reflectance curves of alizarin crimson mixed with zinc white in the following crimson-to-white ratios (a) 1 to 3, (b) 2 to 2, and (c) 3 to 1.

ing the surface below more than they change the main component of the light reflected and therefore change the effect of this lower

surface. This fact and the fact that the transmitted light is of different quality than that reflected have two important conse-

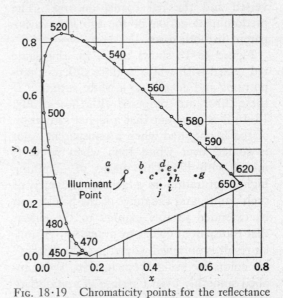

FIG. 18·19 Chromaticity points for the reflectance curves of Figs. 18·15 through 18·18, as indicated:

(a) Fig. 18·17(b) alizarin crimson over viridian;
(b) Fig. 18·17(a) viridian over alizarin crimson;
(c) Fig. 18·16(c) alizarin crimson, three thicknesses;
(d) Fig. 18·15(b) alizarin crimson over black;
(e) Fig. 18·16(b) alizarin crimson, two thicknesses;
(f) Fig. 18·16(a) alizarin crimson, one thickness;
(g) Fig. 18·15(a) alizarin crimson over white;
(h) Fig. 18·18(c) alizarin crimson plus white (3:1);
(i) Fig. 18·18(b) alizarin crimson plus white (2:2);
(j) Fig. 18·18(a) alizarin crimson plus white (1:3).

quences. In the first place the result of superimposing two such layers is very different if the order of the layers is changed and the lower one is coated over the upper; and in the second place, the upper one always contributes more to the final color than the lower. On the other hand, to the extent that the upper paint is transparent, it is possible to take advantage of the fact that the transmitted light is usually of higher saturation than the reflected part, and thus to increase the range of colors which can be obtained. The curves of Fig. 18·17 show the paint of Fig. 18·15 coated (*a*) under a layer of transparent (green) paint on a good white surface, and (*b*) with the order reversed and the red coated on top. The predominant action of the top layer is apparent in both cases.

Figure 18·18 shows curves for this same red mixed with white in three different proportions and coated on a white surface. If these curves are compared with those of Fig. 18·16 it is apparent that a higher saturation of red is obtained when a transparent color is coated over white than when white is mixed with it. This means of obtaining higher saturation is a general property of such paints, and the range of the palette can be extended in this manner to the extent that transparent colors are available. A similar result is obtained when the artist "glazes" his colors by using them in thin layers applied smoothly over a surface of appropriate color.

The ICI points for the curves of the last figures are shown in Fig. 18·19.

The mixing of paints, therefore, is an art rather than a science, since it requires an intimate knowledge of the peculiarities and properties of each individual paint if the desired result is to be obtained. Whereas in transparent colorants it does not matter greatly whether they are mixed or superimposed and thickness and concentration series produce much the same result, the same rules are not followed by paints. On the other hand, the effects which can be obtained with paints from an artistic point of view far outnumber anything that can be done with other media. The facts that light is reflected internally and that the transmitted light is of different quality give each paint a character of its own which can be used for artistic purposes. Artists use paints in this manner. Paints of nearly identical color but having different opacities and covering qualities can be and are used to get just the effect the artist demands. It is largely for this reason that he needs and uses so many different paints although the theory of subtractive mixture suggests that he might get along with a very much smaller number.

BIBLIOGRAPHY

Gettens, Rutherford J., and Stout, George L. *Painting Materials*. New York: D. Van Nostrand Co., Inc. 1942.

International Printing Ink Corporation. *Color as Light*, Monograph No. 2. New York: The Research Laboratories of the International Printing Ink Corp. 1935.

Merwin, H. E. "Optical Properties and Theory of Color of Pigments and Paints." *Proceedings of the American Society for Testing Materials*, **17**, Part II: 494–530 (1917).

Richmond, Leonard. *The Technique of Oil Painting*. New York: Pitman Publishing Corp. 1931.

Weber, F. W. *Artists' Pigments*. New York: D. Van Nostrand Co. 1923.

Color in Photography

CHAPTER XIX

IN recent years color photography has become available on a scale that permits its use for many purposes under a wide variety of conditions. For many of these purposes it is sufficient for the result to contain colors recognizably like those of the subject, usually if the named hue of the colors would be the same.

The student of color, however, who is accustomed for any reason to observe colors carefully, at once encounters the fact that color photographs differ from the subject in many ways. If he is only casually concerned in the matter, he overlooks the differences as defects of the particular product, and this attitude gains support from the considerable variation encountered in all such processes. To the person who is seriously concerned in the matter, however, it soon becomes apparent that much more is involved than the peculiarities of a particular process. To understand the results and to use photography intelligently it is necessary that he understand not only how color photography works but also how a two-dimensional reproduction compares, in general, with a lighted three-dimensional object. In this latter phase the color photographer and the artist have many problems in com-

mon. The present chapter deals with both phases in bare outline form. The following chapter takes up the same problems from the standpoint of the artist.

SENSITIVITY OF SILVER HALIDE

Color photography in all its forms is based on the response to light of the silver halide photographic emulsion. Silver halide crystals suspended in gelatin under the conditions of manufacture have the amazing property of being sensitive to light in such a way that they may be differentially reduced to metallic silver in direct proportion to the extent to which they have been exposed. In particular an emulsion, as it is called, consists of a tremendously large number of tiny crystals, each of which has a slightly different sensitivity to light. When any one of them has received a sufficient exposure it can be reduced to metallic silver by treatment with a chemical reducing agent with special properties known as a developer. The statistical aggregate of all the crystals produces the over-all characteristics of the emulsion to light.

In general only two of these characteristics need be considered here. The first is the relationship of response to exposure, and the second is the nature of the sensitivity itself.

If a graded series of exposures is given to a photographic material and the material is then developed, the result is an increasing concentration series in metallic silver increasing with exposure. A typical response curve of this type is shown in Fig. 19·1 in which

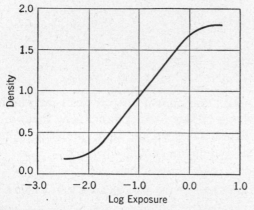

Fig. 19·1 Characteristic curve of a typical photographic emulsion.

photographic density is plotted against the logarithm of the exposure. Photographic density, to a first approximation, may be considered the same as silver concentration. It is measured by determining the light transmission properties of the deposit (specifically the logarithm of the reciprocal of the transmission). Visually, density is closely allied with the darkness of the deposit, equal density differences appearing almost the same under similar conditions.

The exposure is plotted on a logarithmic scale for two reasons: first, because the range covered (frequently as high as 10,000 to 1 in intensity) is too great to plot conveniently in any other manner; second, because logarithmic scales more nearly approach the scale of brightnesses involved in vision, equal logarithmic exposure (log E) differences

tending to appear as equal brightness differences under similar conditions.

If the response curve of a given emulsion is a straight line with a slope of one (at 45° if the same scale of units is used on both axes), a proper exposure on the material produces an exact reproduction of any brightness scale with the order of brightnesses reversed, i.e., the darkest part corresponds to the lightest in the subject and vice versa. The result is called a "negative." It can then be used as a subject and photographed or "printed" on the same kind of material to give an exact reproduction. This result is called a "positive."

If what is known as a "reversal" technique in the original development is employed it is possible to arrive at the final result directly and to obtain the correct reproduction or positive in the same emulsion originally exposed. In the present discussion only this positive phase need be considered, since any negative stage is simply a means to the end.

In color photography of the subtractive type the silver image which is produced by development is replaced by a dye at some stage of the process. The replacement takes place in such a way that the dye concentration produced varies with that of the silver. The final result in all such processes, therefore, is a dye concentration series which has the same type of relationship to the exposure as the silver. The curve of Fig. 19·1 may be thought of as such a dye image. Exposure of an emulsion in a color process of conventional type, therefore, gives rise to a concentration series in a dye.

Silver halide is sensitive normally only to the short wavelengths of the spectrum, the exact sensitivity depending on whether the particular halide is the chloride or the bromide, or a mixture of these, and whether iodide is also present. Under any circumstances, however, pure or mixed halides are sensitive only as far as the short-wavelength green regions of the spectrum. Their sensitivity, however, may be extended throughout the visible spectrum and beyond by the use of special dyes, known as "sensitizers" (or sometimes as "optical sensitizers") which have the property of absorbing light and transmitting its effect to the crystals so that they become developable.

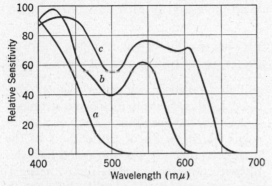

Fig. 19·2 Relative sensitivity curves for three types of emulsions: (a) a blue-sensitive or unsensitized type, (b) an orthochromatic type emulsion or one sensitive to both blue and green regions, and (c) a panchromatic type emulsion sensitive to blue, green, and red radiation.

The relative sensitivity of an emulsion to different wavelengths may be plotted in the same fashion as the sensitivity of the eye. Figure 19·2 shows such sensitivity curves for (a) an "unsensitized" or "blue-sensitive" emulsion, (b) one sensitized for the green region (orthochromatic), and (c) one sensitized throughout the spectrum (panchromatic). By a combination of such sensitized emulsions and the use of transparent colored "light filters" it is possible, therefore, to restrict the region of the spectrum which causes the exposure in any given emulsion.

RECIPROCITY AND ADDITIVITY
LAWS

Photographic materials have another property without which they would be of little use. They respond not to the intensity of the light which falls on them but to the total *amount* of energy which reaches them in the time over which the exposure continues. To a fairly good first approximation the final result obtained from exposure to light depends on the *product* of the intensity and the time of exposure, an exposure of $\frac{1}{10}$ second to light of one intensity giving the same result as an exposure of $\frac{1}{5}$ second to a light of half the intensity, etc. This is known as the reciprocity law, namely, that time and intensity are interchangeable. Under extreme conditions the law breaks down, and the materials exhibit "reciprocity failure."

An interesting extension of this law, which is of more direct consequence for color photography, is the fact that photographic emulsions also obey what is known as the "additivity principle." This law states that, if two different wavelengths of light at a given time of exposure have their intensities so adjusted that each will give rise to the same density on development, one-half of one may be mixed with one-half of the other or one-tenth with nine-tenths, etc., and the same density will be produced. In other words, once equivalent amounts of lights of different colors have been determined it is immaterial to the emulsion in what proportion they are mixed; the result will be the same (Van Kreveld's law).

The consequences for color photography are far reaching and important. A little thought will show that the response of an emulsion to colored light becomes simply the sum of the effects at all wavelengths. Furthermore, the wavelength regions of a color, which in themselves would not be sufficient to produce a developable image, do affect the result. Consequently, to calculate the result of an exposure to colored light it is necessary only to multiply the energy distribution of the light wavelength by wavelength by the sensitivity of the material and to add the results. This process is essentially identical with the nature of the response of the assumed individual eye responses in the three-receptor system hypothesis and makes photographic materials strictly analogous to the eye in this respect.

Just as for the eye, therefore, there are an infinite variety of energy distributions, each

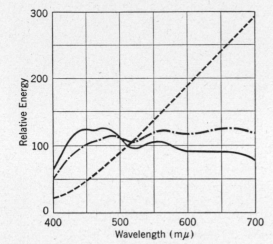

FIG. 19·3 Spectral-distribution curves of three different light sources which will give identical exposures on the panchromatic film of Fig. 19·2 (c) when the time of exposure is the same for all three sources.

of which in a given length of time will produce a given amount of developable density in a given emulsion. Furthermore, once this density has been produced, there will be no indication whatever of the nature of the radiation which produced it. Three such equivalent distributions are plotted in Fig. 19·3.

The following are the fundamental properties of the photographic process around which color photography is built. A logarithmic exposure series in either time or intensity, or both, gives rise to a roughly linear concentration series in dye or silver, i.e., doubling the exposure increases the concentration by a roughly constant fraction.

There is a minimum exposure below which no response is produced and a maximum above which there is no further change. These regions are connected with the constant response ratio region by regions of increasing and decreasing response ratios respectively. Emulsions respond to the total quantity of light which falls on them over the time of exposure and to the effectiveness of all the energy in each wavelength region.

THREE-RECEPTOR
PHOTOGRAPHIC SYSTEMS

It was noted in an earlier chapter how the eye, having sensitivities in three general regions of the spectrum, could distinguish colors by the ratios of the outputs of the three receptors. It was also noted how this three-receptor type system led to the existence of matching colors with different energy distributions and to the gamut of recognizable colors as a whole. Because a photographic emulsion is the same *sort* of receptor, it is possible to combine three such emulsions into a similar three-receptor system with much the same result and the same consequences.

A typical three-color process uses three emulsions which are so designed that they are effectively sensitive each to one-third of the spectrum. A typical set of such effective sensitivities is shown in Fig. 19·4. The word "effective" is used here because, as a matter of expediency, the result is produced partly or wholly by light filter action rather than wholly by the sensitivities "per se."

Now if each of these emulsions is exposed to the same subject, each will record the total effectiveness of the different areas of the subject with respect to its own region of sensitivity, and a definite ratio of densities will be produced for each color which is distinguishable by this system. If each emulsion produces a dye image rather than a silver image and the three dyes are different, each distinguishable color will be represented by a different ratio of the three dyes. If the three images are superimposed the color of the transmitted light, therefore, will differ for each distinguishable color.

The situation has been described deliberately in general terms because fundamentally a photographic color process of this

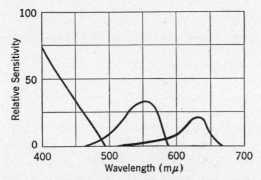

FIG. 19·4 Effective spectral-sensitivity curves of a typical three-color photographic process.

type is a new three-receptor system similar in principle to that of the eye. Its response is a series of colors determined by the relative exposures produced in the three emulsions by the energy distributions of the subject. The actual colors that will be produced by a given set of sensitivities depend on the mixture properties of the three dyes involved and the relationships between the amount of exposure and the amount of dye for each emulsion.

AIM OF COLOR PHOTOGRAPHY

It can be assumed that the aim of color photography is to make a photograph appear as much like the object as possible. While no complete theory exists as to how this may be done, it is theoretically possible with such a system to obtain colors which will appear the same to the eye as the objects, provided

they are seen under exactly the same circumstances. To disregard for the moment the problem of viewing the final picture, the dye colors as produced should appear the same color to the eye as the objects. In other words, for the standard observer the transmission of the dye mixtures should calculate to the same points on the ICI diagram as do the reflectances of the objects.

It has been determined empirically that an approximate solution of this problem is obtained if the three dyes involved in the process meet two specific requirements. First, the combination in some definite ratio must produce a neutral gray, and, second, the dyes must absorb, roughly, mutually exclusive thirds of the spectrum.

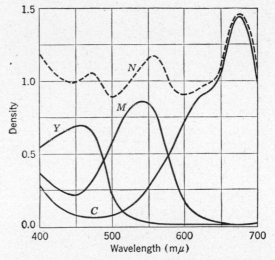

FIG. 19·5 Density curves for three dyes and their neutral.

Although no rigorous proof appears to exist, it seems probable that any set of three dyes, each of which absorbs approximately one-third of the spectrum will, in some ratio, produce a visual neutral in a specified illumination. Color photography makes full use of this possibility. The set of dyes of Fig. 19·5, for example, in the concentrations shown, will produce the neutral indicated by their sum, the wavy line above marked N.

The three emulsions of a color process if exposed to a neutral area will respond to the energy distribution of the light source illuminating that area. If the dye response

As stated before, no theoretical basis exists by which the response of a given dye set may be judged. It is possible, however, to calculate the response under a given set of conditions and to compare the calculation with the stimulus which caused the result. The

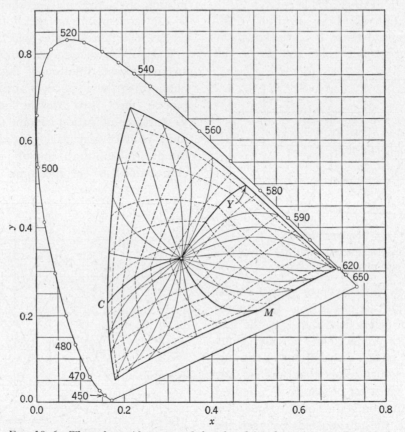

Fig. 19·6   Three-dye grid computed for the three dyes given in Fig. 19·5.

of the individual emulsions are so set that a neutral is obtained from such an exposure, one condition for correct color reproduction has been met. It is necessary, of course, that the same fact holds for all intensity and exposure levels. In a practical process, however, this condition is usually well fulfilled. To what extent a system meeting this condition is likely to meet the requirement that chromaticities also are reproduced with accuracy remains to be considered.

possible visual colors which will be produced by all practical ratios of response of the three emulsions are calculated and plotted on some such colorimetric system as that of the ICI.

Suppose, for example, that exposure of a given set of emulsions to white light produces the three-dye absorptions shown in the preceding figure. From these absorptions it is possible to calculate the ratios of exposure to the three emulsions which will produce any given color by assuming ratios of the three dyes and calculating the response of the standard observer to the light transmitted by these dyes. The results for varying ratios of the dyes are shown in Fig. 19·6 in

Obviously if the emulsion sensitivities which are to control these dyes are the same as for the previous set, the colors that will be produced will, in many cases, be different for the same stimulus. We have to consider,

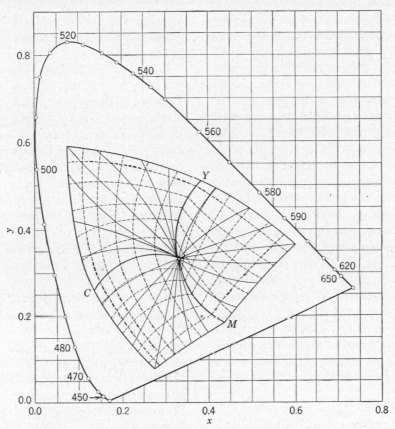

FIG. 19·7 ICI grid for three dyes different from those of Fig. 19·5, but whose concentration ratios are controlled by the same set of emulsion sensitivities that controlled those dyes to produce the grid of Fig. 19·6.

which the chromaticities produced by all possible ratios are shown as a grid superimposed on the ICI diagram. Obviously a fairly large proportion of the visible color domain is obtainable from these dyes. However, any other set of similar dyes might easily produce a somewhat different pattern of colors with the same ratios of concentration. For comparison the grid on the ICI diagram of such a set is shown in Fig. 19·7.

therefore, what the conditions are that will produce the chromaticity of the object from a given stimulus and what conditions will produce the same result from all objects which appear the same to the eye.

In the last analysis both these requirements are the same. They reduce to the requirements that the three emulsions have the same ratios of output for all energy distributions as the three theoretical receptors of the eye and that, given these ratios, the concentrations of the dyes produce an absorption which gives the same result to an observer.

It can be demonstrated that the first result can be met only if the sensitivity curves of the three emulsions involved act in the same way as the sensitivities of the three eye receptors. This condition follows from the simple fact that there are an infinite number of energy distributions for each possible color which look alike to the eye, and this same requirement must be met by the emulsions. In the general case identity in sensitivity distribution with wavelength is required. The second requirement, that the dyes themselves in these concentration ratios should produce exact color reproductions of the original energy distribution, cannot be defined at present although some theoretical dye sets are known which would meet the requirement. As can be seen from the two previous figures, many dye combinations will meet this requirement for neutral exposures which will not meet it for the general case. However, a surprisingly satisfactory result is obtained with any set of dyes which controls roughly the same regions of the spectrum as those effective for the three receptors of the eye.

ERRORS OF EXISTING PROCESSES

For present purposes it is not necessary to pursue this approach further. Existing color processes consist of empirically discovered systems which, on the average, give good reproductions of the colors of natural objects. It is important to realize, however, that the errors of such processes will be of two distinctly different types. First, the colors that will come out identical will not, in general, be the same energy distributions that appear identical to the eye, and second, the color of the reproduction of a particular energy distribution will not be identical with the visual response caused by the energy distribution itself.

The second of these facts is, perhaps, more noticeable and hence more important than the first. The requirement of exact color reproduction for all objects, however, requires that the first condition be met as well as the second.

It need hardly be stated that existing color processes meet neither of these requirements. The true tri-receptor sensitivity distributions of the eye are not known and may turn out to be impossible to match with emulsion sensitivities. Existing dyes have severe limitations in regard to their absorption distributions with wavelength. Every color process, however, has the same sort of characteristics as the eye in regard to the summation and the interpretation of energy distributions. For each color that the system can produce there is an infinite number of distributions capable of causing it to occur. Each system will produce a neutral deposit from a given energy distribution. It does not follow that the energy causing a visual neutral in the subject will appear white are gray in the reproduction nor that a pair of energy distributions that match visually will also match photographically, although many color processes meet both requirements to a surprising degree.

VISUAL ADAPTATION VERSUS FILM RESPONSE

Thus far we have dealt with the results of such a process in comparison with an eye which is assumed to have fixed characteristics. As will be apparent from a study of the eye characteristics outlined in earlier chapters, the eye is not fixed in its properties. For each condition which it encounters it takes up a different relationship of responses in such a way that it becomes in effect a null instrument indicating departures of any particular area in a scene from the average of the scene for brightness and for color. A photographic color process does not indicate such departures at all for color but does exactly this for intensity, if the exposure is calculated correctly for the scene. For color the process responds not with respect to the average for the scene but with respect to the color of a specified illuminant which is determined and set by the manufacturer.

The densities of the colors in a color photograph, therefore, are determined by the exposure that it is given. The relative concentrations of the dyes at any point are determined by the responses of the three emulsions in relation to their response to a fixed illuminant. In both cases the result is determined completely by the physics of the situation without any effect of one area on another and without regard to the nature of the whole.

This corresponds to an exact reproduction of the object as evaluated by a standard observer. If it were also true that such an observer, looking at such a reproduction, saw the same colors that he saw in the subject, no further problems would exist. Unfortunately this is not the case. To see why it is not it is necessary to review the psychology of the visual process and to consider the way in which the eye and the mind evaluate the different areas in a subject.

OBJECTS VERSUS REPRODUCTION

It was pointed out that in perception the mind tends to see the object properties and the illumination in the scene as separate entities, rather than to see the physical relationships of the energies reaching the eye. A shaded white object, for example, continues to look white although it is seen that the illumination is of lower intensity in this region. The exact physiological mechanism by which this tendency occurs is not clear and it may be that in the last analysis it must be considered a purely mental phenomenon. Expressed in terms of what actually seems to occur, however, the situation is somewhat as follows. If a white object in the scene is obviously shaded from the illuminant by another object and it is entirely apparent that this is the situation, the mind sees that the object is shaded and the perception of the whole is divided into two distinct parts. The mind *sees the object* more or less as if the illumination were completely uniform. The mind sees the object, so to speak, through the haze of the illuminant, correctly perceiving the true surface reflections to a considerable extent. The perceptions are direct and instantaneous with no conscious thought process involved, and they represent a remarkable case of the ability of the mind to adapt itself to conditions. If the intention is to see the object, it is seen if the illumination also is seen. The two are kept quite separate and distinct as long as one quite definite requirement is met, and this requirement is quite interesting in terms of any ultimate theory which may explain it. For a double perception of this sort to give the correct "answers" as far as the facts are concerned, it is necessary that it be entirely apparent what is *causing* the illumination and what is *causing* the shadows. To the extent that these causes are not apparent, a different perception may result. Suppose, for example, that a shadow is thrown into a scene by an object that is invisible to the observer and that just covers with its shadow one of the objects in the scene. Under these conditions the lower illumination will be seen—not interpreted, but *seen* as an object reflectance of lower value. This result is understandable, granted the existence of the effect in the first place, since the entire phenomenon must necessarily arise from what is visible. Absence of

303

the possibility of distinguishing between illumination and surface reflectance would lead to the belief that it was a property of the object since that is the only thing that is visible. More interesting and less easy to understand, however, is the fact that to the extent that the illumination situation is ambiguous there will be a *gradually increasing error* in the mental separation of the two. Lack of clear vision of the illumination, therefore, leads to the appearance of objects which is more and more determined by the lighting and less and less by the true reflectances of the objects. In the last analysis if there is no indication whatever of the lighting, *all* the variation that exists is *seen* (*not* interpreted) as properties of the object.

Now photography consists essentially of reproductions of small segments of scenes in which the principal objects occupy the greater part of the reproduced area and the light source or lighting conditions seldom appear directly in the picture. For this reason a photograph seldom produces in the observer a perception of the illumination approaching that which is present when he views the scene itself. Furthermore, and *to the extent* that this perception is lacking, there will be a transfer of the illumination variation to the perceived properties of the surfaces seen in the picture.

SHADOWS, BACKGROUNDS, AND GRADIENTS

The results of these facts in photography are exceedingly difficult to believe. Stated as generalizations, they run somewhat as follows. (1) Every shadow in a photograph tends to appear darker than it did in the scene and sometimes very much darker indeed. The amount of darkening depends on the clarity of the perception of the illumination as such. (2) If the illumination in a photograph is non-uniform, a considerable part of this non-uniformity will be seen as properties of the objects involved unless there is clear indication from shadows and the like just how the illumination varies. (3) If some object in the picture, such as a background, is totally unrelated to the rest of the picture, any difference in the illumination of this area is seen wholly as a property of the area and the illumination is not seen to play any part in it. This is a particularly troublesome effect in photography. A background at some distance from the main objects will appear to the eye as though it were receiving the same light as the foreground objects, but it may photograph as nearly black. An attempt to illustrate this is shown in Plate XIV. This is a purely visual effect due to the restriction of the area seen in the picture and is not otherwise directly related to photography. To obtain a convincing reproduction, however, it is necessary to light the scene so that it appears different from what is intended in order to have the part of it that is photographed come out as desired. This is a legitimate generalization that applies to all reproductions. Visual effects which are present when the scene as a whole is viewed but absent when vision is restricted to a small region must be introduced artificially into the smaller area if the *objects* are to look natural.

HUE SHIFTS

Thus far we have restricted the discussion to brightnesses and perception of surface reflectances. A very similar situation, however, exists with respect to color. To understand it, suppose we take the classical example of an orange-red vase illuminated from one side only by sunlight but by sufficient reflected white light so that the shadow side may be perceived dimly. We know from the study of vision that the hue of an orange-

PLATE XIV

The apparent visual intensity (brightness) of the background
of a scene may be quite different from its true intensity as
indicated in a photograph. In the illustration on the upper
left the illumination is such that the whole scene appeared
well illuminated to the photographer, but the background
photographs too dark. On the upper right the exposure is
increased so that the background photographs correctly, but
the foreground is over-exposed. In the illustration below an
auxiliary light on the background makes it possible to photograph the whole scene as it originally appeared visually.

PLATE XIV

The apparent visual intensity (bright
of a scene may be quite different i
indicated in a photograph. In the
left the illumination is such that th
well illuminated to the photograph
photographs too dark. On the upp
increased so that the background pho
the foreground is over-exposed. In the
auxiliary light on the background makes
graph the whole scene as it originally a

red color shifts with intensity. At high intensities it shifts toward yellow, and at low it shifts toward magenta. If we look directly at a vase illuminated in this way what we see is simply an orange-red vase with a constant surface color standing in an *illumination* which varies greatly from one side of it to the other, not in *color* but in *intensity*. Now suppose we make a hole in a gray cardboard and hold the cardboard so that only a small area of the vase may be seen through it at a time. If the cardboard is moved so that we see first the brightly lighted side and then the shadow we will see that the hue shifts from yellow-orange to red-magenta. A trained observer, having seen this demonstration or its equivalent, can see this hue shift from the object itself without such an aid, but to the naive observer the shift is not visible at all without carefully directed attention. To summarize, whereas the hue shifts caused by the illumination gradient are visible on careful inspection, to the *casual* observer they are seen as constant surface color in an illumination which varies distinctly.

One more factor must be observed, however, before we are in position to consider a photographic reproduction of such an object. The orange-red vase itself under the lighting conditions stated is seen with the illuminated side *brighter* than the front and the shaded side *darker*, that is, there is a perception of the front of the vase as the *true* color and the illuminated side as graduated *upward* from this. This perception arises from the fact that in general the brightness-adaptation level of the eye is more nearly that corresponding to the intermediate illumination of the front, and the two sides are seen with respect to the front. If for any reason the eye were adapted to a level corresponding to the *high* intensity, the high intensity side is the one which would appear orange-red, and the whole vase would

shade from this down to magenta; but the perception of strong-side illumination would be gone, the brighter side only being seen as in normal illumination.

Now if we make an exact reproduction of the chromaticities of this illuminated vase by color photography, the result when it is viewed will be quite different. On the basis of what has already been said, the reasons for this difference may be stated as follows. When a print is viewed under ordinary circumstances, the adaptation level of the eye is set, not by the print, but by its white border and its general surroundings. In general the border of the print is seen as white, and everything in the picture is darker. Since the hue shift to yellow on the more brightly lighted side was a visual effect due to its brightness being *higher* than the adaptation level and this visual effect caused the naive perception of a very high intensity, *both* these effects will be *lacking* in the reproduction. In the same manner if the environment around the photograph contains blacks that are much darker than the shaded side of the vase, the blacks also will not have as great a hue shift and will not aid in the illumination perception. The net result will be a reproduction that does not produce to the same extent as the object itself *either* the hue shifts that may be seen by a trained observer or the direct illumination perception of the naive observer. In other words it will not *look like* the object photographed, even though it may reproduce exactly the psychophysical luminances and chromaticities of the scene.

Here again, as in the case of the surface reflectances of objects, the true effect of the scene itself can be produced in the photograph only if the chromaticities are *actually* changed in the photograph to an extent capable of offsetting the loss due to the area restriction of the subject. The chromaticities can be changed by carefully controlled colored lighting provided the subject permits.

Lightness and surface hue, therefore, may appear correct in a photograph only if lighting is modified to produce the correct perception. A third factor is also present that may cause a totally incorrect perception of objects in a reproduction. Suppose a glossy object reflects a large uniform light source from its outer surface. In the scene itself movement of the head or of the object will quickly indicate the situation, and compensation will be made for the lack of saturation brought about by the reflection. In a photograph, however, no such action is possible, and such reflections are seen as the true surface colors of the objects. The remedy is simple, of course, since such reflections can usually be avoided. In the case of metallic surfaces, however, the reflection of such sources is the only possible way of making the object visible.

It will be seen, therefore, that the production of a photograph in which all objects will appear with the properties that they possess when they are examined directly becomes an artistic process requiring much skill and experience. In extreme cases combinations of objects may be found which it is essentially impossible to reproduce, even if the photographic process used is perfect in that it correctly reproduces every chromaticity and every luminance of the scene.

ILLUMINANT COLOR

In this discussion nothing has been said of the general color quality of the light which is used to illuminate the objects. It is apparent from the nature of the photographic process that only one quality of light, i.e., the one which produces the correct ratios of exposures in the three emulsions, will photograph as white or gray. If the set is illuminated by light of any other color it will photograph as such with respect to the source for which the emulsions have been designed by the manufacturer. If the light is bluer than the intended source, it will photograph as blue, etc. This effect again is not the same as the reaction of an observer to the scene. To him a light which is bluish with respect to daylight or artificial light will appear *white* after sufficient time in the scene has elapsed. On viewing the reproduction in daylight, however, the light will be seen as blue since true daylight has now become his reference point. Photographed in the light for which it was designed, of course, it would appear gray or white as in the scene itself regardless of whether the reproduction were seen in daylight or in some other normal illuminant.

Photography from the standpoint of the color expert, therefore, is somewhat different from the commonly held view that it accurately and correctly reproduces anything placed before it. To do so it is necessary that the visual situation be analyzed clearly by the photographer and that such determinants of the final perception as will be missing in the final reproduction be supplied by *distortion* of the colors and brightnesses of the scene itself. The effects involved and the corrections that must be applied are often larger than the defects of reproduction in the better of the existing processes.

It is apparent that a high degree of artistry, if the word may be applied here, is involved in the production of a satisfactory color photograph in addition to all the requirements of technical skill which may be involved in the photographic process *per se*. However, color photography is not for professionals only. Far from it. The mind soon learns to translate photographs into convincing representations of the objects, and the observer is quite satisfied with the result. The case has here been stated in the extreme only to bring out the principles that are involved when the aim is a duplication of the observer's perceptions of the scene. In the next chapter it will be seen how the artist, with his point-to-point control of the scene, may produce a more exact likeness.

It should also be noted that nothing that has been said applies only to color photographs as such. A restricted view through an aperture, an object seen by itself through a window, a reproduction in a magazine, or any of a host of other situations may produce equally large and "erroneous" effects. These effects are not confined to photography but are general properties of the visual mechanism itself.

To summarize, color photography may err if chromaticities are not accurately reproduced because its receptor system is somewhat different from the eye and its color mixture system may produce a different result. It may also present nature in the wrong guise through restriction of the scene so that the perception produced by exact psychophysical reproduction would be different even if the process were perfect. In modern commercial processes the magnitudes of the two types of errors are comparable.

BIBLIOGRAPHY

Evans, Ralph M. "Visual Processes and Color Photography." *Journal of the Optical Society of America*, **33**:579–614 (1943).

Evans, Ralph M., and Klute, Jeannette. "Brightness Constancy in Photographic Reproductions." *Journal of the Optical Society of America*, **34**: 533–540 (1944).

Mack, Julian E., and Martin, Miles J. *The Photographic Process*. New York and London: McGraw-Hill Book Co., Inc. 1939. Chapters V, VII, and XI.

Mees, C. E. Kenneth. *Photography*, 2nd ed. New York: The Macmillan Co. 1942. Chapters IV, VII, and VIII.

Mees, C. E. Kenneth. *The Theory of the Photographic Process*. New York: The Macmillan Co. 1942. Chapters IV and VI.

Merwin, H. E. "Optical Properties and Theory of Color of Pigments and Paints." *Proceedings of the American Society for Testing Materials*, **17**; Part II: 494–530 (1917).

Color in Art

CHAPTER XX

WHEN an artist starts to paint a picture in oils, water colors, or any other colored medium, he must have in mind some fairly well-defined intention as to the final result. This intention may vary in an infinite number of ways and may or may not include color as an important component of the picture. Furthermore, if color is to play an important part it may or may not bear a direct relation to the colors of any objects which may be depicted. The subject of color in art, therefore, is so diffuse that it can be discussed only by selecting certain possible intentions which are widely diversified and by assuming that all intermediate and allied possibilities exist.

MULTIPLE ROLE OF COLOR IN ART

We may start with the flat statement that exact presentation of the actual surface colors of the objects in a scene is seldom the desire of the creative artist. He is concerned with the production of a new entity called a picture which he may hope will some day be considered a work of art. This picture is a two-dimensional object more or less completely covered with paint, and the artist must concern himself with making this *paint* have the desired appearance, as well as with producing the desired impression with respect to the shapes and forms portrayed. Color always plays the two-fold role of decoration and representation. It plays many other roles, however. Color plays an important part, for example, in the composition of the picture in that some colors have far greater attention values than others and so contribute weight to the part of the picture in which they are applied. They do this, of course, not on an absolute basis but only with respect to the other colors which are present, the same color which may predominate over less strong ones being insignificant in the presence of large areas of much stronger ones, etc. Color can also be employed locally in a symbolical sense, or as an over-all color to present some aspect of the emotions, time of day, mood, or simply to segregate the areas of a picture devoted primarily to the presentation of form. In each instance color is a tool used by the artist to aid him in producing a final result which he considers desirable.

In the present chapter we shall consider color first as it is used by the artist to aid him in the presentation of three-dimensional forms and then as it is used for decoration. The more formal aspects of design and harmony will be considered in the next chapter.

OBJECT COLOR AND PERCEPTION

Every object has definite reflectances with respect to wavelength which may be determined physically and which may be considered as properties of that object. The various visual effects which have been the subject matter of previous chapters tend on the whole to make this characteristic of an object apparent to the observer under a wide variety of illumination conditions. Thus a pale blue object will be seen as pale blue both in daylight and in artificial light even though the relative energy in the red portion of the spectrum may be greater than it is in the blue in artificial light.

The visual effects of color constancy impress the naive observer with the fact that no matter what kind of light falls on an object the color of that object does not change.

The same general principle, as we have seen in the previous chapter, applies also to the relative reflectances of objects. An object that reflects a very high percentage of the incident light at all wavelengths may appear white to an observer almost without regard to the illumination conditions under which it is seen.

These are only two cases of a large number of visual phenomena in which the perception of the observer is distinctly different from what might be predicted on the basis of the purely physical energies reaching his eye, that is, the light from the various areas of the subject would be seen as quite different if viewed separately.

It was seen that in photography the difference between the object-viewing situation and that for the final photograph led to a number of necessary modifications in the lighting to produce the desired result. In painting, a somewhat similar situation exists but with the difference that the changes may be made directly in the picture rather than in the subject.

THE TONE SCALE PROBLEM

In common with photography and all other types of two-dimensional representation, paintings are intended to be viewed under uniform lighting conditions. The reflectance range of surface colors therefore determines the possible range from black to white that may be obtained. In general the scene to be portrayed will be lighted non-uniformly, since such lighting is the only condition under which good depth and modeling are seen in the subject. The normal range of surface reflectances, accordingly, is multiplied in the scene by the illumination ratio. To represent the scene, this extended range must be compressed in the painting without loss of the effects produced by the higher range. Since many effects such as hue shift with intensity, perception of lightness rather than shadow intensity, color contrast, and the like are purely visual and are produced by the lighting range of the subject, they would disappear if the painting were a perfect compression of the scene on a point-for-point basis. The artist must paint in just enough of each effect to supply the part which disappears owing to the changed viewing condition. To the extent that he obtains the effect correctly, the observer's perceptions in viewing the picture will again separate into those of illumination and of subject color as they do in the scene itself.

The painting operation, typically, is somewhat as follows, although not necessarily in this order. The greatest subject brightness range normally encountered is perhaps that of a clear sunny day. For this, therefore, the maximum possible pigment range must be reserved and since all pictures are seen with reference to white surfaces in their surroundings this full range cannot be used to represent less brightly lighted subjects except by the use of very distorted scales. Accordingly, the limitation of pigment-brightness range for the particular scene at hand is one of the first decisions that must be made. Within this range the various tone values which are to represent the different brightnesses in the scene must be assigned in such a way that they are spaced much as in the subject. This may be a purely mental operation on the part of the artist or he may actually paint the scene roughly in the proper values in order to get the required spacing of tones. He establishes the required brightness structure around which the picture is to be built.

THE COLOR PROBLEM

Perhaps the next decision which must be made is the local color of the particular objects in the scene. It is an exceedingly tricky one. The apparent surface color of an object depends on all the circumstances that can affect color. It varies to a certain extent with everything in the scene. However, it varies only over a certain range. Green grass stays green under almost all lighting conditions, for example, and its "true" color is pretty much apparent except under the most extreme conditions. However, the color that the artist must prepare to represent the local color of an object is not one that would match the object if placed beside it but one that will present the same appearance in relation to the other objects

in the *picture* as the real one does in *its* surroundings. There may, accordingly, be a rather large difference between the actual color which is prepared and that of the object. The decision does not necessarily include any consideration of the appearance of the colors when placed next to each other, but is basically an adjustment of the colors to the scale which is to be used for the reproduction. Having prepared these colors, or at least gotten them well in mind, the artist is prepared to give life to his sketch of brightnesses. This he may proceed to do in many different ways, but the result will always be that his prepared colors will come into intimate relationship with each other not only with respect to the picture as a whole but also individually with respect to their neighbors. This juxtaposition and the ensemble as a whole lead to new complications. A color seen in the new environment is not exactly what was expected. The color next to it as well as the tone scale as a whole have an effect. He must, therefore, readjust his colors for the effect desired.

This readjustment process is exceedingly complex and subtle. A cyan next to a yellow will appear bluer and darker than when on the palette. A gray in shadow may appear lighter or darker than was intended. The whole scale of the picture may be high or low, too expanded or contracted, when seen in normal surroundings. The hues of objects may not appear constant over their surfaces. All these things and many more must be readjusted. The red vase must be shaded toward yellow on the lighted side, toward magenta on the shaded one. The key of the background, perhaps, is too high, or its color too saturated and wrong because of the colors of the objects in front of it.

When he has finished, however, the artist, if he is successful, has achieved a result which, in its implications, is most extraordinary. He has succeeded in making the observer perceive things which are not present in his painting. Areas which are actually of non-uniform hue *look like* uniformly colored objects in strong illumination. Grays in the shaded areas *look like* pure white. Saturations of colors appear as high as they did in the subject although direct comparison would show them almost ridiculously different. He has accomplished all this by taking advantage of his conscious or unconscious knowledge that the observer will see the painting with eyes that are differently adjusted from their adjustment when he looked at the scene and that, therefore, the painting must be different if it is to appear the same.

In addition to these necessary compensations for the difference in the viewing conditions between the picture and the subject there are, of course, a multitude of other matters of which the painter is conscious but which will not be apparent to the observer if the work produces the intended effect. Whites in the picture, for example, will depend for their brilliance on the contrast of the picture as a whole and in particular on the brightness of the immediately surrounding areas. The early Dutch school has many examples of brilliant whites and great apparent intensities of illumination which owe their existence to the shading of the picture from large areas of black near the border to small areas of white near the center.

THE PICTURE AS DECORATION

Totally aside from all these considerations, however, is the preoccupation of the artist with the picture as a decorative two-dimensional area of canvas. While it is somewhat outside the province of this book to speak of composition and of texture of the paint and the surface, the subject cannot be neglected by the student who is anxious to learn the whole of the subject of color.

If you glance at a picture you see a decorated surface. If you look at it you see a representation of a two- or a three-dimensional subject. Unless a picture is successful in both these aspects it cannot claim to be a work of art. The subject, however, seems obscure to most people because observers as a class are not capable of distinguishing between surface and depth perception, however obvious it may be to the artist. In addition, the average observer of a painting is conscious only of the fact that it is intended to be a representation of some situation of real life. (If it is not, he is at a complete loss to understand it and complains of the tendencies of "modern" art.) Nevertheless he is greatly affected by the appearance of a picture as decoration regardless of his conscious remarks on the subject. He will reject a picture wholly if it is inconsistent with his preconceived notions of form, color, or brightness without seeing that it has merit as expression, experience of the artist, decoration, or the like.

It may be well, therefore, to review as part of the subject of color, however vague its connection may seem to the reader, the various factors that may affect the perception of a painting as two-dimensional surface and as three-dimensional depth.

DEPTH PERCEPTION IN PAINTING

The generalization mentioned before that picture contrast leads to depth has far-reaching validity. If a picture is painted purely in its local colors without regard to light and shade and the characteristic properties of shadows, it will tend to lie flat on the canvas without life or form. Its excuse for existence must be decoration pure and simple or some symbolic meaning outside the realm of pictures as here considered. For a picture lacking a deeper meaning in the forms and subject matter, a glance should suffice. It tells its whole effect in its balance of areas and colors within the frame.

Give such a picture light and shade, however, and it becomes something new and essentially creative. Glance at it and it is a forceful pattern giving a true unity within its borders. Look at it carefully and it is a carefully thought out and prepared arrangement of units, each supplying its due weight to the whole. Many are the errors which may be committed in the process, and utter failure is the reward of the artist who is insecure in his workmanship. The moment a picture has depth it has a responsibility to meet. It must be at once a picture and a segment of the world. Given only depth and realistic form it becomes simply a poor substitute for the obvious reality of concrete objects and is appraised for its true utility in this respect. Given decorative value simultaneously it invests these objects with an aura drawn partly from the picture and partly from the personality of the artist himself. The observer can say, if he needs to search his soul for explanation, "This is the way it appeared to the artist."

Art, therefore, is hardly a fit subject for unemotional discussion of the use of color. We are forced, however, to a consideration of the physical means by which the effects are produced. In cold words, they are three. The areas of a painting have color, texture, and pattern. Each may play a vital part in the artist's message. Form may be suppressed, amplified, distorted, or what you will; it speaks directly to observers trained to the belief that form is the essential substance of the universe. Texture may amplify form. Much texture leads to consciousness that the painting is a surface, and this is true even if texture takes on the nature of a bas-relief. Sculptural waves in paint merely serve to intensify the fact that the picture is a flat half-reality partaking of the nature of both surface and life. True sculpture may speak of life in frozen form, but bas-relief speaks of it as decoration or as suggested quality. As a matter of fact, the hope of the artist lies wholly in this suggestive quality. An apple, properly represented, "feels" smooth to the eye. A sculptured wave in paint "feels" wet. We are, in this discussion, far beyond the realm of pure color. Yet at the same time these considerations are the aspects of color felt by the artist that do not find their place in discussions of color measurement, color specification, color tolerance, and the like. Color is merely an implement to the production of a desired effect as long as form is present. In the total absence of form or its suppression to an extreme degree, color by itself may take the ascendancy and almost reach the importance of form. Such effects, however, are rare indeed in the art of the West.

COLOR AND FORM

So far is color subordinate to form, in fact, that accuracy of color is an unnecessary attribute of any painting worthy of consideration on a plane higher than that of reproduced reality. As Pope has repeatedly observed, the requirement of color in a painting is consistent use, not conformity to reality. Color can shade from red to yellow or to any other color in the shadow as long as all other colors shade similarly, and there will be a feeling of intended unity in the painting, as satisfying a feeling aesthetically as an accurate rendering of every shade of psychophysical response of the artist to the subject. He has produced a new entity called a "picture" as an interesting or worthwhile object. Its reference back to the subject matter which inspired its creation may be negligible or intense—it does not matter.

PLATE XV

The color balance of a picture may affect its "mood." The lower picture is more *"accurate"* than the upper, but its effectiveness as a characterization of the original scene is not so great.

It is the properties of the new whole on which it will be judged.

The reader will observe that in this discussion we have moved far from the standpoint which was taken during consideration of color in photography because the photographer necessarily relies on the actual colors of objects as they are. Such reliance, however, is not a vital part of photography. It has been indicated that in subtractive mixture of colors the result will depend to a large extent on the selective properties of the surfaces involved. The creative photographer is free to take advantage of all the possibilities inherent in these facts. A picture, whether painting or photograph, is a new entity, designed for the enjoyment or enlightenment of the spectators. Truthfulness to life or to the immediate facts of the photographer's environment is an academic artifact and not a necessity. Breadth of vision, clarity of insight, and knowledge of the medium may produce a result far beyond the merit of a point-for-point exact counterpart of the facts.

COLOR AND FEELING

In this sense color may be employed as a means of investing the picture as a whole with properties which are similar to those possessed by the original scene as perceived by the artist but which were due to the artist's attitude or feelings rather than to the objects themselves. Thus the proper use of color (and of form) may make a picture somber, bright, gay, melancholy or what you will. The artist is attempting a re-creation of experience rather than mere subject. Again his personality, his directness or indirection, his prosaic or imaginative approach, and many other phases of his character will appear as much in the way in which his colors are distributed, in his over-all tendencies toward blue or orange or magenta,

and in the forcefulness of opposition of the colors chosen for the various areas as in his choice of subject or in his delineation of the forms.

Color in art, therefore, is to be used for the purpose at hand and is not something ordinarily dictated by the properties of the objects represented.

COLOR IN DECORATION

In a sense color plays much the same sort of role in decoration. In decoration, however, we may postulate that the person who specifies the colors and their areas is concerned primarily with producing an *attractive* result. Attractiveness is not a necessary attribute of a work of art. Decoration, however, has little reason for existence if it does not add something to the situation which makes it more fitting or more enjoyable.

In the use of color in decoration, therefore, we can proceed at once to a direct consideration of color in the subject and its effect on the observer of the scene. The rules are not different from those for art *when it is intended to be decorative;* they are the same, but color in decoration has the effect on the observer almost as its only aim.

The basic principle behind the decorative use of color may be described as felt unity in the color scheme. The scene as a whole, the painting as a whole, or the decorated area, whatever its nature, must be felt to exist as a pleasing unity of colors which belong together.

Three fairly obvious factors appear to be predominant in determining the success or the failure of a color scheme.* They may

* In writing of the factors which may bring about this felt unity of colors the writer is deeply indebted to Professor Pope of Harvard who both in his lectures and in his published works has developed this

be described as the chief color or color tone of the scheme, the relationship or range of the colors involved, and the relative areas of the respective colors. It is apparent that these must be closely interrelated variables, if the whole is to produce a new unity. They may, however, be discussed separately, and their contributions to the whole determined.

PREDOMINANT COLOR

The predominant color of a color scheme needs no explanation, and its presence is apparent to the most casual observer who will take the trouble to look. A color scheme is predominantly blue, green, or red, etc. Walking into a room decorated in such a manner the observer, if he is not a student of color, at once feels a certain tendency toward unity, although he may not be sufficiently interested to try to determine the cause. In the same way he will feel that a picture with such a predominance has a certain character but if he is not conscious of color as a tool to produce such effects he may refer to the picture simply as having such and such a feeling or tone.

Thinking about such a color scheme, rather than actually seeing one, might lead the student to believe that a predominant color in a scene would necessarily be caused by a majority of the areas having that hue. In fact, however, this is not the case. A room or picture may appear to have a predominant hue even though only a small percentage of the areas, viewed directly, are actually of the hue in question. It is sufficient that all the colors in the scene are shifted toward this hue from their most probable color in everyday life. Suppose, for example, that the color scheme is to be blue

subject to a high degree. The present treatment is an adaptation for which the present writer must take full responsibility.

and the desire is to produce this impression at first glance. Regardless of the colors of the scene and their areas, if all colors are shifted toward blue, this effect will be produced. Reds, for example, will shift toward magenta, orange toward red, yellow toward green, and blues will be more intense. Expressed somewhat differently, blue will be

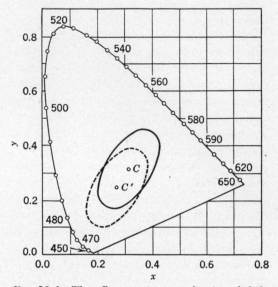

FIG. 20·1 The effect on the neutral point of shifting the color balance or predominant hue of a painting toward blue.

mixed with all the other colors. Blue is not visible in a greenish-yellow, nor in a reddish-orange and yet the completely untrained eye is capable of feeling this tendency toward blue and away from yellow. Expressed in terms of the ICI system we have a situation such as that shown in Fig. 20·1. Suppose all the colors of the scene are included in the ellipse around the illuminant point C shown by the solid line, and suppose that each of these colors is reproduced by a color which corresponds to it relative to the others but is included in the dotted ellipse which is shifted toward the bluer colors. The observer will tend to see the same sort of object colors as before but will see a tinge or strong

314

tint, as the case may be, of blue throughout all the colors. In part he will see added blue *to* the colors and in part added blue *on* the colors. This tendency is so strong in many cases, however, that even the area that is selected as the visible neutral of the picture will shift far in the blue direction, and a color which would be named blue by itself against a white background will be seen as pure white or gray.

In color photography this general over-all color tone in a print is known as color balance. If it is in the right direction it may help the picture; if wrong, it may hurt it materially. In either case it is part of the observer's reaction to the picture. In art it is almost invariably one of the means by which the artist conveys his message. Few pictures in the art gallery do not possess an over-all color of some hue or other—usually yellow—and although this may often come from varnish which has yellowed with age, it is not the least among the valuable attributes of the works of the masters. In decoration color predominance is usually equally deliberate and frequently in unpracticed hands is visible to the point of being unpleasant. A blue room which is decorated exclusively in blue, although it may represent a considerable *tour de force* on the part of the decorator (blues being what they are when placed together), may have its blueness so apparent even to the deliberately resisting observer that no "accents" of red or yellow or orange or anything else can save it from oppressive monotony. On the other hand, a room can give the feeling of being blue even if the greater percentage of its areas never reach a hue beyond a bluish-green provided yellows and all the related colors are sufficiently suppressed.

Predominance of hue and the associated suppression of colors in the range of its complementaries, therefore, is one of the characteristics that make the observer feel a cer-tain unity in a decorative scheme. It is not necessary in such a scheme to suppress contrast or control saturation; it is only necessary that hue be under control. The atmosphere may be lively or dull or what you will; the predominance of one hue will make itself felt.

Whereas color balance is perhaps the most common of the color schemes, it is far from being the only one. Suppose that instead of restricting all hues or shifting all of them in a definite direction the intention is to produce a picture, a room, or a stage set in which the atmosphere of lightness and delicacy, somberness, or quiet meditation prevails. The actual intention with respect to mood does not matter particularly here; the point is that a feeling of unity may be produced by a restriction of the brightness values of the scene, quite independently of hue. If nothing in the scene has a luminous reflectance lower than 40 percent, for example, the scene will look light and airy and much on the surface. If it contains no reflectances higher than 10 percent, except perhaps in relatively minute areas which set off the general darkness, it will appear dark and perhaps gloomy quite without regard to either the hues or the saturations of the colors.

What might be described as the average reflectance or the general value level of a scene, therefore, is one of the elements of the felt unity which is a tool to be used to fit the occasion. The net result, of course, is not independent of the hues or the saturations of the colors, or of their relative areas as we shall see in a moment. Restriction of values is *one* of the factors determining the *possibility* of unity. A dark room in saturated colors has a feeling of richness and quality, especially if it is combined with pleasing texture and well-placed areas. A light scene, done in colors of low saturation, has a feeling of light and cleanliness, especially if handled in a restricted hue range. On the other hand, a high-reflectance scene in saturated colors has spontaneity and gaiety, whereas a dark low-saturation scene tends toward depression and dullness. In any event, however, a definite single mood or feeling pervades the whole by the simple restriction of the brightness range combined with the effects of the hues and saturations involved.

Considered from the standpoint of the color solid (that is, the three-dimensional representation of all possible colors along some such axes as hue, saturation, and brightness) the results have been achieved by restriction of the colors used to some definite *region* within the solid. Expressed another way (and perhaps perversely) it is only necessary that certain regions of the possible range of colors be *omitted* for the eye to see that what is left forms some sort of unity among its colors. The omitted regions may be black or white or of high or low saturations or in any region of the hues; it is sufficient that the eye recognize that the omission has occurred. They will produce the effect of the remainder belonging together.

RELATIVE COLOR AREAS

Associated with both the restricted gamut of colors and the idea of predominant hue is the effect of relative color area in the scene. It was pointed out that it is not necessary for the greater percentage of the area to be of one hue in order to have that hue predominant although it is true that this is frequently the case. The effectiveness of the color of an area is found to be an exceedingly complex quantity when an attempt is made to judge it in comparison with others. Pope has given the term "at-

traction" to this concept of effectiveness and points out that it is a compound of the *relative* hue, saturation, and brightness of the color, heavily weighted by its area relative to the areas of other colors. This subject will be considered in more detail in the next chapter since it is of fundamental importance in the use of color in design. In a general way, however, it works out somewhat as follows. Attraction is basically a matter of contrast, and contrast is produced by differences in any of the color attributes. Brightness difference is perhaps the most striking type of contrast but saturation differences can be equally powerful. Hue differences in general are somewhat less effective and texture differences and the like are perhaps the most subtle. Brightnesses and saturations *higher* than the colors seen as background are the more powerful in their attractive force and if both are combined with a large hue difference we reach the maximum of attraction.

All these contrast relations, however, are subject to control by means of relative area. As the relative area devoted to a single color increases there is an increasing tendency to see this color first. If it is a strong color, i.e., of high brightness and saturation, its area does not need to be a high percentage of the total before it is predominant and all other colors are seen with respect to it. If it is a weak color, a much larger area may be required. At this point, however, it is necessary to distinguish between a color seen as foreground and one seen as background. If one attempts to be scientific in defining the properties of an area that make it appear as background, one becomes involved immediately in questions of psychology, since the conditions that make an area appear as background at one time may be effectively the same as those that make it appear as foreground at another. Under ordinary circumstances, however, the color seen as background is the one which *surrounds* the maximum number of smaller areas. It may or may not have the maximum attraction in the scene; in fact, it may hardly be visible at all to the casual observer. Even if this latter condition holds, however, the background is still the basic reference against which the other colors are seen. If the background is dark, the colors in front of it will tend to be seen as of higher contrast and if light, of lower.

To return to the subject of unity as produced by the color relations, the effect of area is to vary the attraction of a particular color, and unity may be produced by so assigning the relative areas that each color has about the same *degree* of attraction. Thus an exceedingly strong color may be introduced with much weaker ones if its relative area is sufficiently small. When properly balanced the strong color will fit in with the others to add to the unity rather than to detract from it. In a sense, however, this characteristic of area does not apply to any color that is seen very much as background. For the background color the area is seen in relation not so much to that of the other individual areas, as with respect to the *total* of the areas. A felt unity is still produced if there is unity in the relationships of all the foreground colors to the background, even though a similar area of the background color would seriously disrupt the scheme if it were itself seen as foreground. The background, thus, tends to stand in opposition to the other colors and may pull them together, so to speak, if it is in uniform opposition with each individually and stands in suitable area relation to the total.

All the chief factors determining the power of attraction of a color, therefore, are relative and may be stated as relative hue, relative brightness, relative saturation, and relative area. The greater the contrast in any of these attributes, the greater the difference of attraction, and any single attribute or group of attributes may be played against any of the others to produce uniformity of attraction. In this way any colors whatever may be combined to produce a color scheme in which the observer perceives some sort of unity. This unity, this feeling that the colors "go together," is perhaps the ultimate goal in decoration, whatever may be its relation to art.

BIBLIOGRAPHY

Cutler, Carl G., and Pepper, Stephen C. *Modern Color*. Cambridge, Mass.: Harvard University Press. 1923. Chapters V, VI, VII, and VIII.

Luckiesh, M. *Color and Its Applications*. New York: D. Van Nostrand Co. 1915. Chapter XIII.

Phillipps, Lisle March. *Form and Colour*. London: Duckworth. 1915.

Pope, Arthur. *An Introduction to the Language of Drawing and Painting*. Cambridge, Mass.: Harvard University Press. Vol. 1, 1929; Vol. 2, 1931.

Rood, Ogden N. *Students' Text-book of Color*. New York: D. Appleton and Co. 1916 (copyright, 1881). Chapter XVIII.

Rood, Roland. *Color and Light in Painting*. New York: Columbia University Press. 1941.

Von Bezold, Wilhelm. *The Theory of Color*, American ed. Boston: L. Prang and Co. 1876. Chapter V.

Design and Abstraction

CHAPTER XXI

THE principles of color harmony as deduced by Pope and set forth in the previous chapter are of wide general validity and apply to painting, interior decoration, and pure design. When we come to the question of likes and dislikes in single colors, however, we are in a somewhat different field even when color combinations are tested as single pairs of roughly equal area. For convenience examples of two-color design and of colors in pairs will be considered together as will colors presented singly and successively.

PLEASANTNESS OF TWO-COLOR COMBINATIONS

When only two colors are present in a given area of the field of view they are, of necessity, seen with respect to each other. Any aesthetic judgment will depend on the similarities and differences between the two as well as on the absolute characteristics of each. In addition, certain visual phenomena will come into play to an extent that is more important than when a large number of colors are present simultaneously.

SIMILARITIES IN COLOR PAIRS

Colors can be similar in any of three ways. They may approximate the same hue, the same saturation, or the same brightness. Assuming that the areas and textures are roughly the same, these are the only variables which may be compared. Since any of the three may be the same or different in a pair there are eight separate possibilities which may be treated systematically. First, however, it is worth while to consider the visual situation involved and to note the various phenomena that play a part in any favorable or unfavorable judgment of the color combination.

Suppose we have two equal areas of color placed so that the areas touch each other and, for completeness, suppose they are squares of colored paper 2 or 3 inches on a side with fairly dull surfaces which are the same on both. If these are to be viewed by an observer, he must see them placed against some sort of background since the angle which the eye includes is much larger than their areas even if it is fixed in position. Any comparison of two relatively small areas, therefore, automatically includes a third area

318

which may be called the background. The importance of the background is overlooked in much of the work done in the field. The background is usually the factor that determines the state of the eyes of the observer during the test although its action may be negative or positive. The two extremes for brightness, of course, are black and white backgrounds. These two extremes correspond to situations in which the eye condition is determined wholly by the samples themselves and to a large extent by the background alone, respectively. The importance of the relation of the eye to the background from the standpoint of an aesthetic judgment is apparent when it is realized that in the first case, i.e., with a black background, only the darker of the two samples may appear to contain gray, whereas with the white background both may appear to contain gray in large amounts. The brightness adaptation of the eye, therefore, will tend to be set by the relationship of the samples to the background and will vary from that caused by the samples to that caused by the background alone.

(If the background also possesses hue inherently this also will affect the condition of the eye and, consequently, the colors seen in the two areas. Since such a situation would really involve a three-color combination, however, this example will not be considered here beyond the effect of the illuminant. The treatment would be exactly similar to a three-color combination but the effects would be of greater magnitude.)

Since the areas and the textures of the two surfaces have been assumed alike and the areas are relatively too large for differences due to focusing of the eyes, only the three color attributes of hue, saturation, and brightness are left as variables to affect the observer's judgment of the harmony or lack of it of the two colors.

It is not known to what extent the recognition of similarity and dissimilarity affects such judgments, but it can be stated that the eye does recognize similarities in all three attributes, and this recognition must necessarily play a considerable part in the result. There are seven ways in which such a pair may be similar. All three attributes may be the same in each, in which case they match. They may be alike in each of the attributes separately, or they may have any of three pairs of attributes in which they match. If any of these seven conditions are met the colors will be seen to have something in common. If one of the latter three situations exists, i.e., if the colors of the two areas differ in only one attribute, there will be a strong feeling of unity, the strength, in part, depending on the size of the difference in the remaining attribute and on its nature. Hue differences, saturation differences, and brightness differences are not alike and cannot be compared directly. Each will have its own kind of effect on the observer, and presumably each person will react differently toward them from an aesthetic standpoint.

Unfortunately, not enough work has been done in this field so that positive statements can be made as to the relative importance of these variables in determining an observer's choice of the most pleasant combinations. There is another factor entering into the judgment, however, which must play such a large role in the decision that it may well be the deciding factor. At any rate it must be taken into account in any study of the situation. This factor is the shift in appearance of one of the areas when it is viewed directly after looking at the other. This factor will be considered in some detail both because of its possible bearing on aesthetic choice and because of its importance in understanding the visual process involved in viewing such a pair.

Suppose the two samples are placed on a very black background, and the observer is asked to decide whether or not they make a pleasing combination. In viewing the samples to make his choice the observer may follow any one or any combination of a number of different ways of viewing the pair. For example, he may look back and forth at the centers of each; he may look steadily at the dividing line between the two; he may look first at one, then at the black, and then at the other; or he may look steadily at the black and see the colors out of the corner of his eye, so to speak. The chances are good that without instructions he will do all of these in a random fashion. Watching an observer do this gives one the definite impression that the action is deliberate although oftentimes the observer is unaware of his actions. It is, of course, foolish to attempt to ascribe reasons for unconscious action because it is too easy to imagine that the cause upholds a theory. The suggestion is strong, however, that the observer does these various things because the samples actually change their appearance under each condition and he has become accustomed to this process of trying all methods when he has to make a decision. In any event it is true that the samples do change. If he looks directly at one of the colored areas for a short time and then at the other, he sees the second sample, momentarily at least, with eyes which are partially adapted to the first sample. The same thing is true if he looks at the second sample first, or if he looks at the background.

This "next-to-the-last" adaptation, so to speak, involves an adjustment for color and for brightness. Suppose the next-to-the-last area viewed is dark green. His eye tends to rise in sensitivity because the sample is dark, and the blue and the red receptors tend to rise more than the green. Sudden transfer of the gaze to the other sample will now make this one appear somewhat brighter and less green because of this condition of eye sensitivity. Suppose it is medium yellow. It should tend to appear lighter and more orange. The reverse is true on passing from the medium yellow to the green, the blue receptor becoming relatively more sensitive but the total sensitivity being somewhat reduced. Since we are assuming black for a background, looking at this first will simply raise the general eye sensitivity and either sample will look lighter if viewed second. If vision is restricted to the connecting line or if the gaze is shifted rapidly back and forth, a stable situation is produced in which the eye has tended to adapt to both colors; in any event a tendency to adapt to both colors will have been reached if the observer looks at the areas long enough. These situations have been dealt with by Judd in his article listed in the bibliography at the close of the chapter.

We can now consider briefly the nature of the differences which will be seen, remembering that all this is with reference to a black background. Still using the three-receptor hypothesis and speaking in quite general terms, we find that, if the first area viewed causes an excitation ratio in the three receptors which is quite different from that of the second, it is likely that the second sample will be seen to have a distinctly different hue from that which it would have had if the reverse order had been followed. This hue shift, in general, will also be accompanied by saturation shifts, depending on the similarity of the excitations. There are two extreme cases and all others are intermediate. If the two samples match, there will be no hue or saturation shift. If the colors are complementary, i.e., if one excites the receptors in the inverse ratios of the other, there will be only a saturation shift but no hue shift. Provided the brightnesses are the same, therefore, there will be no hue shifts or small ones if the samples are similar or complementary in hue. Between these there will be greater or lesser hue shifts, depending on the dissimilarity.

Relative brightness also plays a large part in this hue shift. If one sample is dark and the other light, even if the hues may be similar, there will tend to be a hue shift introduced by this lightness difference since exactly similar surfaces seen at different relative brightnesses are seen in general as of different hue.

It is hardly necessary to go on elaborating this scheme. It is apparent that hue, saturation, and relative brightness will vary with the order and the timing of the viewing. Therefore it is not unreasonable to imagine that it is this very *instability of apparent hue* which makes one pair of colors go poorly together and another seem harmonious. If a rule were justifiable it might be to the effect that two colors will appear to clash and seem inharmonious if on looking from one to the other the observer sees a different hue for A when the sequence is A to B from the hue that he sees when it is B to A. The reason, if the rule is true, may be that a feeling of uncertainty as to the actual colors is caused by the opposing shifts.

It is interesting to note that such a rule would lead to one of the more or less generally accepted principles of harmony, i.e., that colors closely adjacent in hue and those that are complementary form the most pleasing combinations.

Whether such hue shifts are a valid aesthetic measure it is true that the shifts do occur and can cause real uncertainty to an observer in regard to the actual nature of the color of a given area.

EFFECT OF BACKGROUND

One other factor of considerable importance must be considered in connection with samples on a dark background before we consider backgrounds of gray and of white. When samples are seen against black any adaptation that takes place must be caused by the samples themselves. The color of the illuminant used plays a different role from its role in everyday life. Under ordinary circumstances a wide variety of objects is visible and the eye tends to be in a condition which goes a long way toward making the illuminant look white. This condition also tends to subtract the illuminant color from the surfaces of the objects it illuminates. Accordingly a surface which would look yellow if separately illuminated by artificial light and seen with the daylight-adapted eye will perhaps look blue when the eye is adapted to the illuminant. Samples against black and illuminated by artificial light, therefore, may tend to be seen with much of the illuminant color included, the actual amount depending in part on the recent history of the observer's eyes. Addition of the same color to both sides may make the hues much more nearly alike and so affect the choice markedly in comparison with that which would be made in daylight.

If the samples are seen against a large gray background at some value either intermediate between the brightnesses of the two or at least of comparable value, rather complete adaptation to the color of the source will tend to be produced, and the background will be partially eliminated as a factor. Having the background of such a lightness, however, will produce another effect the exact nature of which has not been clearly established. The saturation of a color varies considerably when seen against white and against black. There seems to be some indication, however, that it reaches a maximum when the color is seen against a gray of the same brightness. It certainly is true that relatively very light and very dark areas are of lower saturation than areas that are similar to the surround even if there is no change in the physical stimulus.

Again, if the lightness of the background is intermediate between the two samples the differences in their brightnesses will tend to be exaggerated. The effect, of course, like the previous effect, is simply to introduce effectively a new pair of colors. The effect of a white background is similar. Gray is seen added to the colors, and they become, effectively, a new pair with different properties calling for a new decision as to their desirability.

This portion of the discussion, therefore, may be summarized as follows: When an aesthetic decision is made as to the attractiveness of a pair of colors there are a great variety of effects that make the exact colors seem different in one situation from what they are in another. The choice itself may be made on some such basis as instability of hue in relation to the method of looking at the samples; great care, however, must be exercised if the results of such a study are to be applied to other circumstances and to other observers. It may be this type of uncertainty as well as variations in the tastes of observers which has tended to make such studies so different from each other. Again the reader is referred to Judd's article for examples of how the samples may vary in the three attributes with the conditions.

Recognized similarities and absence of shifts that produce uncertainty as to hue may be powerful factors in the aesthetic choice. Applicability to other circumstances will depend on the extent to which the colors are seen as the same under the two circumstances.

This discussion, of course, is theoretically without reference to the observer's prefer-ence for one color over another per se. The available literature concerning experiments on the choice of single colors leads one rather definitely to the decision that such a choice is almost indeterminate. Color is a phenomenon which is inherently relative. Whether a single color can be judged alone on its aesthetic merits without at least a mental comparison with other colors is open to question. In any event no two experiments have produced results sufficiently alike so that there is a valid basis for discussion of the subject.

EFFECT OF AREA AND TEXTURE

In the previous discussion of simultaneously presented areas of two colors it was assumed first that they were of equal area and, second, that they had identical surface textures.

It is now necessary to consider these two factors briefly, although, as before, it is necessary to say that so little is known about them quantitatively that only suggestive remarks are possible. In regard to the latter factor, differences in texture, there seems to be only one statement that can be made, namely, if the textures are very different, no direct comparison can be made. Presence of a large texture difference may so change the appearance of two samples that, although they would match exactly if they had the same surfaces, only an expert can decide whether they match or not, sometimes only if he has available other samples that vary slightly from the match.

In regard to the first factor, varying relative areas, much more work has been done, and some approach seems to have been made to deduction of regularities in choices, particularly by Bradley. Here, however, we encounter the surprising fact that once relative area is allowed to vary sufficiently almost *any* two colors may appear harmonious. Relative area, therefore, may offset any rules which are devised for equal-area pairs. The indications seem to be that given adequate control of relative area any colors whatsoever may be combined to make a harmonious whole. Such results, however, seem to contain absolute visual area as a necessary ingredient, the combinations appearing harmonious only at a given distance.

It seems to be true, therefore, that there are certain fairly basic principles behind aesthetic choice in color combinations, and there seems to be at least some degree of agreement on the actual choices. Any experiment set up to deduce broad generalizations, however, must cope with a formidable list of pitfalls and deceptive truths.

ADVANCING AND RECEDING COLORS

When two or more colors are combined in a more or less formal design, or for that matter whenever two colors are adjacent to each other under any circumstances, one more, rather more optical type of, phenomenon occasionally attains great prominence. This is the phenomenon of the areas appearing to separate into different planes. It seems to be owing simply to the fact that the eye has different focal lengths for different colors, although other factors also may sometimes influence the result. The nature of the effect may be illustrated as in Figs. 21·1 and 21·2. In Fig. 21·1 objects *a* and *c* are at greater distances from the eye than *b*. If all these objects are assumed to

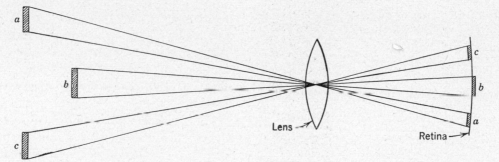

FIG. 21·1 Light from distant objects forms focused images within the eye closer to the eye lens than does light of the same color from near-by objects.

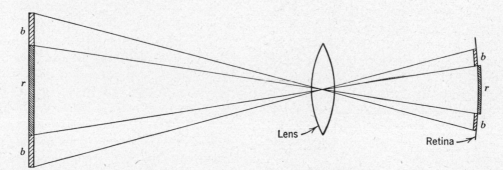

FIG. 21·2 Light from blue objects forms focused images within the eye closer to the eye lens than does light of the same color from red objects in the same plane.

323

give off the same color of monochromatic light, in the eye, the light from *a* and *c* focus closer to the eye lens than that from *b*. This difference makes possible a true interpretation of the relative position of the actual objects *a, b,* and *c*. In Fig. 21·2 three objects are shown in the same plane, but are assumed to be of different colors, *r* for red, *b* for blue. Because of chromatic aberration in the eye lens, the blue focuses nearer the lens than the red, the difference giving rise to a similar interpretation to that provided by the same relative image positions of the objects of Fig. 21·1. In this instance however, the interpretation is incorrect. If edge conditions or other such factors do not obscure the effect, blue, therefore, is seen to recede and red to advance from the estimated plane of the objects.

BIBLIOGRAPHY

Bradley, Morton C., Jr. "A Theory of Tone Attraction." *Technical Studies in the Field of the Fine Arts* (Harvard University), **2**:2–10 (1933).

Judd, Deane B. "Hue, Saturation and Lightness of Surface Colors with Chromatic Illumination." *Journal of the Optical Society of America,* **30**: 2–32 (1940).

Pope, Arthur. *An Introduction to the Language of Drawing and Painting.* Cambridge, Mass.: Harvard University Press. Vol. 1, 1929; Vol. 2, 1931.

General Bibliography

Abney, William de W. *Researches in Colour Vision and the Trichromatic Theory.* London: Longmans, Green and Co. 1913. 418 pp.

Ames, A., Jr. "Depth in Pictorial Art." *The Art Bulletin,* **8**:4–24 (1925).

Balinkin, Isay A. "Industrial Color Tolerances." *The American Journal of Psychology,* **52**:428–448 (1939).

Barnes, Norman F. "A Spectrophotometric Study of Artists' Pigments." *Technical Studies in the Field of the Fine Arts* (Harvard University), **7**:120–138 (1939).

Birren, Faber. *The Story of Color from Ancient Mysticism to Modern Science.* Westport, Conn.: The Crimson Press. 1941. 338 pp.

Boring, Edwin G. *A History of Experimental Psychology.* New York: The Century Co. 1929. 699 pp.

Boring, Edwin G. *Sensation and Perception in the History of Experimental Psychology.* New York: D. Appleton-Century Co., Inc. 1942. 644 pp.

Bradley, Morton C., Jr. "A Theory of Tone Attraction." *Technical Studies in the Field of the Fine Arts* (Harvard University), **2**:2–10 (1933).

Brunswik, Egon. "Zur Entwicklung der Albedowahrnehmung." *Zeitschrift für Psychologie,* **109**:40–115 (1929).

Burton, E. F., and Smith, May A. *The Physical Properties of Colloidal Solutions,* 3rd ed. London: Longmans, Green and Co. 1938. 235 pp.

Cady, Francis E., and Dates, Henry B. *Illuminating Engineering,* 2nd ed. New York: John Wiley and Sons, Inc. 1928. 515 pp.

Chevreul, M. E. *The Principles of Harmony and Contrast of Colours.* London: Longman, Brown, Green and Longmans. 1854. 431 pp.

Committee on Colorimetry. "Colorimetry Report." *Journal of the Optical Society of America.* "The Concept of Color," **33**:544–554 (1943); "Physical Concepts: Radiant Energy and Its Measurement," **34**:183–218 (1944); "The Psychophysics of Color," **34**:245–266 (1944); "Quantitative Data and Methods for Colorimetry," **34**:633–688 (1944); "Colorimeters and Color Standards," **35**:1–25 (1945). (This series, with additions, is to be published in book form.)

Cutler, Carl G., and Pepper, Stephen C. *Modern Color.* Cambridge, Mass.: Harvard University Press. 1923. 163 pp.

Eastman Kodak Company. *Wratten Light Filters,* 17th ed. Rochester, N. Y.: Eastman Kodak Co. 1945. 86 pp.

Edwards, Edward A., and Duntley, S. Quimby. "The Pigments and Color of Living Human Skin." *The American Journal of Anatomy,* **65**:1–33 (1939).

Evans, Ralph M. "Visual Processes and Color Photography." *Journal of the Optical Society of America,* **33**:579–614 (1943).

Evans, Ralph M., and Klute, Jeannette. "Brightness Constancy in Photographic Reproductions." *Journal of the Optical Society of America,* **34**:533–540 (1944).

Foss, Carl E., Nickerson, Dorothy, and Granville, Walter C. "Analysis of the Ostwald Color System." *Journal of the Optical Society of America,* **34**:361–381 (1944).

Gelb, Adhemar. "Die Farbenkonstanz der Sehdinge." *Handbuch der normalen und pathologischen Physiologie,* **12**:594–678 (1929).

Gettens, Rutherford J., and Stout, George L. *Painting Materials.* New York: D. Van Nostrand Co., Inc. 1942. 333 pp.

Gibson, K. S., and Tyndall, E. P. T. "Visibility of Radiant Energy." *Scientific Papers of the Bureau of Standards,* **19**:131–191 (1925).

Hardy, Arthur C., and Wurzburg, F. L., Jr. "The Theory of Three-Color Reproduction." *Journal of the Optical Society of America,* **27**:227–240 (1937).

Helmholtz's Treatise on Physiological Optics. Edited by James P. C. Southall. The Optical Society of America. Vol. 1, 1924, 482 pp.; Vol. 2, 1924, 480 pp.; Vol. 3, 1925, 736 pp.

Helson, Harry. "Fundamental Problems in Color Vision. I. The Principle Governing Changes in Hue, Saturation, and Lightness of Non-Selective

Samples in Chromatic Illumination." *Journal of Experimental Psychology*, **23**:439–476 (1938).

Helson, Harry.   "Color Tolerances as Affected by Changes in Composition and Intensity of Illumination and Reflectance of Background." *The American Journal of Psychology*, **52**:406–412 (1939).

Helson, Harry, and Jeffers, Virginia B.   "Fundamental Problems in Color Vision. II. Hue, Lightness, and Saturation of Selective Samples in Chromatic Illumination." *Journal of Experimental Psychology*, **26**:1–27 (1940).

Helson, Harry.   "Some Factors and Implications of Color Constancy." *Journal of the Optical Society of America*, **33**:555–567 (1943).

Hering, Ewald.   *Grundzüge der Lehre vom Lichtsinn*. Berlin: Julius Springer. 1920. 294 pp.

Hess, Carl, and Pretori, Hugo.   "Messende Untersuchungen über die Gesetzmässigkeit des simultanen Helligkeits-Contrastes." *Archiv für Ophthalmologie*, **40**:1–24 (1894).

International Printing Ink Corporation.   *Color as Light*, Monograph No. 2. New York: The Research Laboratories of the International Printing Ink Corp. 1935. 21 pp.

Judd, Deane B.   "A General Formula for the Computation of Colorimetric Purity." *Bureau of Standards Journal of Research*, **7**:827–841 (1931).

Judd, Deane B.   "A Maxwell Triangle Yielding Uniform Chromaticity Scales." *Journal of Research of the National Bureau of Standards*, **14**:41–57 (1935).

Judd, Deane B.   "Specification of Color Tolerances at the National Bureau of Standards." *The American Journal of Psychology*, **52**:418–427 (1939).

Judd, Deane B., and Kelly, Kenneth L.   "Method of Designating Colors." *Journal of Research of the National Bureau of Standards*, **23**:355–385 (1939).

Judd, Deane B.   "Hue, Saturation and Lightness of Surface Colors with Chromatic Illumination." *Journal of the Optical Society of America*, **30**:2–32 (1940).

Katz, David.   *The World of Colour*. London: Kegan Paul, Trench, Trubner and Co., Ltd. 1935. 300 pp.

Kelly, Kenneth L.   "Color Designations for Lights." *Journal of Research of the National Bureau of Standards*, **31**:271–278 (1943).

Köhler, Wolfgang.   *Dynamics in Psychology*. New York: Liveright Publishing Corp. 1940. 158 pp.

Köhler, Wolfgang, and Wallach, Hans.   "Figural After-Effects. An Investigation of Visual Processes." *Proceedings of the American Philosophical Society*, **88**:269–357 (1944).

Köhler, Wolfgang.   *Gestalt Psychology. An Introduction to New Concepts in Modern Psychology*. New York: Liveright Publishing Co. 1947. 369 pp.

Lovibond, Joseph W.   *Measurement of Light and Colour Sensations*. London: George Gill and Sons. n.d. 132 pp.

Luckiesh, M.   *Color and Its Applications*. New York: D. Van Nostrand Co. 1915. 357 pp.

Luckiesh, M.   *Visual Illusions, Their Causes, Characteristics and Applications*. New York: D. Van Nostrand Co. 1922. 252 pp.

Luckiesh, M.   *Lighting Fixtures and Lighting Effects*. New York: McGraw-Hill Book Co., Inc. 1925. 330 pp.

MacAdam, David L.   "Maximum Visual Efficiency of Colored Materials." *Journal of the Optical Society of America*, **25**:361–367 (1935).

MacAdam, David L.   "Subtractive Color Mixture and Color Reproduction." *Journal of the Optical Society of America*, **28**:466–480 (1938).

MacAdam, David L.   "Photographic Aspects of the Theory of Three-Colour Reproduction." *The Photographic Journal*, **81**:333–351 (1941).

MacAdam, David L.   "Visual Sensitivities to Color Differences in Daylight." *Journal of the Optical Society of America*, **32**:247–274 (1942).

Mack, Julian E., and Martin, Miles J.   *The Photographic Process*. New York and London: McGraw-Hill Book Co., Inc. 1939. 586 pp.

MacLeod, Robert B.   *An Experimental Investigation of Brightness Constancy*. Archives of Psychology, No. 135 (Columbia University). 1932. 102 pp.

Maerz, A., and Paul, M. Rea.   *A Dictionary of Color*. New York: McGraw-Hill Book Co., Inc. 1930. 207 pp.

Massachusetts Institute of Technology, the Color Measurement Laboratory.   *Handbook of Colorimetry*. Cambridge, Mass.: The Technology Press. 1936. 87 pp.

Mees, C. E. Kenneth.   *Photography*, 2nd ed. New York: The Macmillan Co. 1942. 227 pp.

Mees, C. E. Kenneth.   *The Theory of the Photographic Process*. New York: The Macmillan Co. 1942. 1124 pp.

Merwin, H. E.   "Optical Properties and Theory of Color of Pigments and Paints." *Proceedings of the American Society for Testing Materials*, **17**, Part II: 494–530 (1917).

Michelson, A. A.   *Studies in Optics*. Chicago, Ill.: The University of Chicago Press. 1927. 176 pp.

Moon, Parry.   *The Scientific Basis of Illuminating Engineering*. New York: McGraw-Hill Book Co., Inc. 1936. 608 pp.

Morgan, Clifford T.   *Physiological Psychology*. New York: McGraw-Hill Book Co., Inc. 1943. 623 pp.

Morris, Robert H.   "Metameric Formulation." *Journal of the Optical Society of America*, **37:** 669 (1947).

Munsell, A. H.   *A Color Notation*, 9th ed. Baltimore, Md.: Munsell Color Co., Inc. 1941. 74 pp.

Munsell Color Company.   *Munsell Book of Color*. Baltimore, Md.: Munsell Color Co., Inc. 1942.

Newhall, Sidney M., Nickerson, Dorothy, and Judd, Deane B.   "Final Report of the O.S.A. Subcommittee on the Spacing of the Munsell Colors." *Journal of the Optical Society of America*, **33:** 385–418 (1943).

Nickerson, Dorothy.   *Color Measurement and Its Application to the Grading of Agricultural Products*. Miscellaneous Publication 580, U. S. Department of Agriculture. 1946. 62 pp.

Ostwald, Wilhelm.   *Colour Science*. Part I, *Colour Theory and Colour Standardisation*. 1931. 141 pp. Part II, *Applied Colour Science*. 1933. 173 pp. London: Winsor and Newton, Ltd.

Parsons, Sir John Herbert.   *An Introduction to the Study of Colour Vision*, 2nd ed. Cambridge, England: The University Press. 1924. 323 pp.

Phillipps, Lisle March.   *Form and Colour*. London: Duckworth. 1915. 294 pp.

Polyak, Stephen L.   *The Retina*. Chicago, Ill.: The University of Chicago Press. 1941. 607 pp.

Pope, Arthur.   *An Introduction to the Language of Drawing and Painting*. Cambridge, Mass.: Harvard University Press. Vol. 1, 1929, 157 pp; Vol. 2, 1931, 121 pp.

Richmond, Leonard.   *The Technique of Oil Painting*. New York: Pitman Publishing Corp. 1931. 144 pp.

Rood, Ogden N.   *Students' Text-book of Color*. New York: D. Appleton and Co. 1916 (copyright, 1881). 329 pp.

Rood, Roland.   *Color and Light in Painting*. New York: Columbia University Press. 1941. 299 pp.

Schouten, Jan F.   *Visueele Meting van Adaptatie en van de wederzijdsche Beinvloeding van Netvlieselementen*. Utrecht: Drukkerij Fa. Schotanus and Jens. 1937. 95 pp.

Sears, Francis Weston.   *Principles of Physics III —Optics*, 2nd ed. Cambridge, Mass.: Addison-Wesley Press, Inc. 1946. 323 pp.

Southall, James P. C.   *Introduction to Physiological Optics*. London: Oxford University Press. 1937. 426 pp.

Thouless, Robert H.   "Phenomenal Regression to the Real Object. I." *The British Journal of Psychology*, **21:** 339–359 (1931).

Troland, Leonard T.   *The Principles of Psychophysiology*, Vol. 2. New York: D. Van Nostrand Co. 1930. 397 pp.

Vickerstaff, T.   "The Brightness of Present-Day Dyes." *The Proceedings of the Physical Society* (London) **57:** 15–31 (1945).

Von Bezold, Wilhelm.   *The Theory of Color*, American ed. Boston: L. Prang and Co. 1876. 274 pp.

Walsh, John W. T.   *Photometry*. London: Constable and Co., Ltd. 1926. 505 pp.

Weber, F. W.   *Artists' Pigments*. New York: D. Van Nostrand Co. 1923. 235 pp.

Wood, Robert W.   *Physical Optics*, 3rd ed. New York: The Macmillan Co. 1934. 846 pp.

Woodworth, Robert S.   *Experimental Psychology*. New York: Henry Holt and Co. 1938. 889 pp.

Wright, W. D.   *The Perception of Light*. New York: Chemical Publishing Co. of N. Y., Inc. 1939. 100 pp.

Wright, W. D.   *The Measurement of Colour*. London: Adam Hilger, Ltd. 1944. 223 pp.

Wright, W. D.   *Researches on Normal and Defective Colour Vision*. St. Louis, Mo.: The C. V. Mosby Co. 1947. 383 pp.

Zworykin, V. K., and Wilson, E. D.   *Photocells and Their Application*, 2nd ed. New York: John Wiley and Sons, Inc. 1932. 331 pp.

Index

Spectral-energy distribution, flash powder, 33
  Kodatron lamp, 35
  light from firefly, 36
  photoflash bulb, 34
Spectral hues, fundamental, 231
Spectral lines, 28
Spectral reflectance, 187, 188
  curves, 189
Spectrophotometer, 11, 188, 190, 191, 193, 202
Spectrophotometric curves, 11
  measurements, 202
  method of drawing, 262
Spectrophotometry, 11, 189
  abridged, 190
Spectroradiometer, 11
Spectroradiometry, 11
  visual, 204
Spectroscopes, 10
Spectrum, 11
  europium, 32
  measurements, purpose of, 15
  neon-arc, 31
Specular reflection, 192
Specular transmittance and reflection, 49
Spotlight, 49
Spreading effects, 181
Standard illuminants, 207
Standard observer, 5, 176, 205, 212
Standards, material, 200, 202, 212
Stars, 35
  colors, 24
Stimulus-directed attitude, 167
Stokes' law, 193
Subject contrast, 56
Subtractive color photography, 296
Subtractive color surface, 58
Subtractive effects, 86
Subtractive mixture, 64, 255, 267
  color, 256
Subtractive mixtures, 277
  calculating, 255
Successive contrast, 127
Sun, 22
  color, 24
  as light source, 79
Sunlight, 24, 171
  color of, 27
  range of light intensities, 93
  variations in, 79
Surface, color, dependence on angle of viewing, 63
  colored, 62, 69
  colored overcoating, 71
  colors, 183, 184
  diffusion, 62

Surface, dull, 201
  factors, affect depth perception, 145
  with high sheen, 201
  mode, 168, 201, 216
  outer, effect of, 282
  paints, 282
  reflectance, 289, 290, 309
    and illumination, 304
  reflection, 60, 80, 279
  reflections, 306
    range, 93
  with texture, 201
Surfaces, glossy, 70
  gray, 122
  considered as light sources, 54
  non-matching, 246
  non-selective, 124
  reflecting, 82, 135
Surround, 105

Teeth, colors, 90
Tempera, 278
Temperature scale, absolute or "Kelvin," 24
Textile color card, 218
Textile materials, 86
Texture, 201
  differences, 316, 322
  in paintings, 312
  in reflecting surface, 122
Thermal radiators, 22
Thermopile, 12, 16
Thouless, R. H., 161, 162
Thouless ratio, 163
Three colors, match all possible colors, 111
Three-color photography, 239, 298
Three-dimensional color solid, 215
Three-dye grid, 273
Three-dye mixture, 272
Three-receptor hypothesis, 320
Three-receptor photographic systems, 298
Time-lapse difference, 222
Tintometer, Lovibond, 215
Tolerable limits, 229
Tolerance determination, 226
Tolerance specification, 225
Tone scale, 309
Transformation of primaries, 211
Transmission, 59
Transmissions, thickness series, 257
Transmittance curve, 61
Transmittance, luminous, 273
Transmittance, in paints, 281